'This is an astonishing achievement – that very rare thing, a genuinely original book and an immediately essential guide to the failures of British politics. King and Crewe go deep, without a shred of pomposity or a phrase of false rhetoric. From now on, every political journalist, civil servant and would-be minister needs to start here.'

ANDREW MARR
presenter, *The Andrew Marr Show*

'One of the mysteries of our political system is how often it fails us, despite the best intentions of politicians and planners. *Blunders* is an enthralling analysis of how things go wrong and why. It should be every minister's bedside reading.'

DAVID DIMBLEBY
presenter, *Question Time*

'This book is not only hugely enjoyable, it is also a truly shocking cautionary tale. King and Crewe provide spectacular examples of British misgovernment, from the Suez fiasco by way of the Dangerous Dogs Act and Thatcher's poll tax to the present day. The cost of such blunders comes not only in billions of pounds wasted but in the enormous amounts of damage caused to public confidence. The lessons are clear. Don't shuffle ministers every few months. Give parliament time to make legislation effective and understandable. Above all, listen and deliberate.'

BARONESS SHIRLEY WILLIAMS
leading Liberal Democrat and former Labour cabinet minister

'Governments don't usually set out to do wrong. They just do it by mistake. This excellent guide to past cock-ups in policymaking and implementation should be required reading for every aspiring minister and civil servant to ensure that in future they at least make their own blunders instead of repeating those already made by others.'

JONATHAN POWELL
Chief of Staff to Tony Blair, 1995–2007

'Everyone makes mistakes. The question is: will we ever learn from them? This is an excellent account of blunders made by successive governments over many years. I am sometimes asked if bankers will ever repeat the mistakes they made in the years prior to 2008. The answer is undoubtedly yes – just as soon as memories fade and the institutional knowledge so vital to any organisation is lost. Most of us have made decisions which looked good at the time but two years later made us cringe with embarrassment.'

ALISTAIR DARLING
Chancellor of the Exchequer, 2007–10

'All governments appear to learn little from the mistakes of their predecessors in translating fine-sounding new initiatives into workable policies on the ground. They ignore the problems of implementation. Anthony King and Ivor Crewe apply their lengthy experience not only to highlighting common patterns in the blunders of recent governments but also, more importantly, to suggesting remedies.'

PETER RIDDELL
Director, Institute for Government

'We are all human and few can resist the index of any account of contemporary history to see how we fared. My initial disappointment at such scant recognition for nearly half a century of frontline political exposure was only modified by the memory that this book is about the great blunders of our time! I am lucky to have escaped.

This book is a valuable guide from two well-qualified observers to the pitfalls of politics. Will it help new generations to avoid them? Don't invest your money on it!'

LORD MICHAEL HESELTINE
Conservative cabinet minister, 1979–83 and 1990–97

'A timely and compelling analysis of why we have been so badly governed for the last thirty years'.

JOHN CAMPBELL
author of *The Iron Lady: Margaret Thatcher*

Contents

Introduction

Our subject in this book is the numerous blunders that have been committed by British governments of all parties in recent decades. We believe there have been far too many of them and that most, perhaps all, of them could have been avoided. In previous generations, foreign observers of British politics viewed the British political system with something like awe. Government in Britain was not only highly democratic: it was also astonishingly competent. It combined effectiveness with efficiency. British governments, unlike the governments of so many other countries, knew what they wanted to do and almost invariably succeeded in doing it. Textbooks in other countries were full of praise, and foreign political leaders often expressed regret that their own system of government could not be modelled on Britain's. Sadly, the British system is no longer held up as a model, and we suspect one reason is that today's British governments screw up so often.

They screw up more often than most people seem to realise. Our strong impression is that, while a majority of Britons know about this, that or the other cock-up, they are by no means aware of the full range of them. Most readers of this book have probably never heard of – let alone know much about – a large proportion of the cock-ups we describe in later chapters. Typically, people hear about one blunder, then another, then another, without realising that there are far too many of them to be accounted for by random one-off sets of circumstances and that they may instead have common origins. If major car crashes occur continually at the same road junction, it may be that the fault lies not primarily with the individual drivers involved in the crashes, but with the design and designers of the junction. In our view, British governments in general are blunder-prone.

Are they more blunder-prone than they used to be? Are governments in Britain more blunder-prone than the governments of other, comparable liberal democracies? Both questions are pertinent, but, alas, we are not in a position to answer either of them. It has taken us the best part of four years to complete our investigations into latter-day UK blunders, and we have not had the time or resources to compare systematically either the most recent decades with previous decades, or Britain's experience with that of other countries. We hope others will be tempted to undertake both tasks. It is certainly the case that British governments in the more distant past blundered from time to time, and we cite several postwar examples in Chapter 3. It is also the case that the governments of other countries are perfectly capable of blundering (as, for example, when Helmut Kohl's German government agreed in 1990 to exchange West German Deutschmarks on a par with hopelessly overvalued East German Ostmarks, or when a majority of European Union countries foolishly agreed to allow Greece to enter the eurozone). But, whatever Britain's past experience and whatever the experience of other countries, our central point remains the same: that modern governments in Britain blunder too often.

Our detailed investigations cover roughly the three decades from the election of the Thatcher government in 1979 to the fall of the Blair/Brown New Labour government in 2010. As for the coalition government that took office in May 2010, it is for readers to decide whether they think David Cameron and his colleagues, compared with their Conservative and Labour predecessors, turned out to be more, less or about equally blunder-prone. But we do have our own suspicions, as will emerge from a Postscript.

One thing this book is *not* about is pointing the finger of blame at individuals (though we confess to doing that from time to time, and readers can certainly engage in finger-pointing if they want to). Our reason is straightforward. If the Right Hon. Albert Adventurous was clearly the principal perpetrator of blunder X, and if he was clearly aided and abetted (or at any rate not dissuaded) by his permanent secretary, Sir Benjamin Blunderbuss, those two facts may well be of interest to psychologists, historians and gossips; but they are unlikely to be of much interest to someone concerned with the workings of British government, especially if, as is likely to be the case, both the Right Hon. Albert and his permanent secretary Sir Benjamin have long since departed the scene (possibly long before it had become apparent that the blunder in question was, indeed, a blunder). What we and other concerned citizens want to know is how it came about that either patterns of human behaviour or else the workings of the system of government were such that the Right Hon. Albert and Sir Benjamin were able to blunder as they did. If individuals on their own are solely responsible for blunders, there are no general lessons to be learned. But our interest lies precisely in any general lessons that can be drawn.

That interest underpins the structure of what follows. In Part I, we define "blunder" and set the scene. In Part II, we tell a variety of blunder-related horror stories. Our stories are worth telling in their own right. Like all good horror stories, they sometimes make one's hair stand on end. Several of them, although true, almost defy belief. But our main purpose in telling them is not to entertain (though we hope we do that) but to provide a body of evidence from which we and our readers can begin to draw general inferences. Our own conclusions are then set out in Parts III and IV.

This book is also not about party politics. It would have had to be a book with a large party-political focus if we had discovered that one or other of the two major parties appeared to be far more blunder-prone than the other when in power. But, as we shall see, that is not the case. Governments of all parties appear equally blunder-prone – a fact that in itself suggests that there are systemic defects in the British system of government, defects rooted in the culture and institutions of Whitehall and Westminster having little to do with party leaders, party members or partisan ideologies. It is not even true that there are characteristically Conservative and characteristically Labour cock-ups. Governments of both parties seem to blunder in much the same way – so much so that, if one did not already know, it would be hard to guess which party was in power when any given blunder was committed.

Although it may appear to be at times, this book is not in any way meant to be hostile to government as such. Neither of us is now a member, or ever would be, of a British outpost of the American Tea Party movement. We have no prejudice in favour of either the public or the private sector, and instead believe that decisions should be made pragmatically about where the boundaries between the two sectors should be drawn. We even have doubts about whether it is useful to think in terms of there being two separate sectors. Although we focus in these pages on government blunders, we are well aware that private-sector companies are also blunder-prone. As the record shows, such companies, far from invariably being lean, mean and competent, are frequently gross, greedy and incompetent.

Readers need no reminding of the bank failures and bail-outs that followed the collapse of Lehman Brothers in the US in 2008. They may not need to be reminded of the terrible trouble that Equitable Life had earlier got both itself and thousands of its policyholders into. But they probably have forgotten the total disappearance from the British industrial scene of the once-mighty General Electric Company (GEC). As recently as the 1980s, GEC was the largest private-sector employer in the UK. But, following the retirement of its founder, Arnold Weinstock, his successors embarked on a wildly overambitious programme of acquisitions, expansions and reorganisations. By the mid-2000s, they had effectively killed off the company. Blundering incompetence on an almost superhuman scale also led to the slow death and ultimate interment of an entire industry, one that had previously dominated the UK market: the British-owned volume car industry. Whereas Austin, Morris and Rover once led the way in Britain, foreign-owned companies – Honda, Toyota, BMW, General Motors and Ford – now do. Cumulative blunders by another British company, BP, led in 2010 to the never-to-be-forgotten Deepwater Horizon oil spill in the Gulf of Mexico – one of the most damaging escapes of crude oil into the environment in history. If governments are fallible, so undoubtedly are private companies.

We decided reluctantly at an early stage to focus almost exclusively on domestic matters. Foreign affairs and defence often raise different kinds of issues from more domestic matters, and we were not in a position to explore both. Fortunately, the two most conspicuous foreign-policy blunders of the postwar era – the Suez expedition of 1956 and the Anglo-American invasion of Iraq in 2003 (though some still maintain that the latter was not a blunder) – have been thoroughly described and analysed by historians and government commissions. And one British military undertaking that many thought was probably going to prove a blunder, the long-range expedition to recover the Falkland Islands from Argentina in 1982, in the event proved a resounding success. The islands were retaken.

Our research methods have been largely conventional. We have read the published record and learned much from parliamentary committee reports and the records of parliamentary proceedings. We have drawn heavily – but have not relied heavily – on contemporary press reports. We have read hundreds of articles and books relating to the commission of specific blunders. And we have spoken to several dozen participants in and close observers of the events that we describe, most of whose names are listed in the Acknowledgements. Apart from formal interviews, one can learn much in the course of casual conversations with politicians and officials – from, as our American colleagues say, "nosing and poking" in and around the world of politics. We have also read extensively in the academic literature dealing with both governmental successes and failures. Our voluminous bibliography can be consulted online at http://www.oneworld-publications.com/blunders. In order that the book not be festooned with footnotes like an overdecorated Christmas tree, we have confined our referencing largely to direct quotations from published sources. Where a direct quotation has not been referenced, it is drawn from the notes of one of our off-the-record interviews.

One additional point is worth making in this connection. The National Audit Office, the House of Commons Public Accounts Committee and some, though not all, other parliamentary committees are admirable bodies, and in what follows we frequently cite their reports. That said, however, their reports and the investigations that lead up to them typically suffer from two limitations, both to some extent self-imposed. One is that, partly out of a desire to operate on a non-partisan, dispassionate basis, they largely focus on the "what" questions and tend to neglect the "why" questions. They say that something went wrong, describe what went wrong and usually say what they think should be done to avoid the same kind of thing going wrong in future; but they seldom delve deeply into the causes of whatever went wrong. In particular, they seldom explore the decision making by ministers and officials that led to the committing of the blunder in question. Secondly, the various investigative bodies typically operate on a case-by-case basis. They only rarely step back and try to discern patterns of behaviour of the kind that we try to identify here. Just as much of British government is not, as they say, "joined up", so most of the research of these other bodies tends to be highly segmented, without lines being drawn between the dots. The House of Commons Public Administration Select Committee and several of the Lords committees are among the rare exceptions.

This book paints on a large canvas and undoubtedly contains some errors of fact and interpretation. We make no claim to be experts on every subject we touch on, and readers who think they have spotted substantial errors of fact or interpretation are more than welcome to get in touch with us. We will be happy to correct our errors in future editions. Fortunately, any mistakes that the book contains should not materially affect our broad-brush conclusions. If a particular airline operates aircraft that crash repeatedly, it is no use pointing out that in the case of one specific incident the plane that crashed was a Boeing 747 and not, as the authors of a book on aviation safety claimed, an Airbus 380. Random errors do not undermine a general argument. We in these pages are ultimately interested in patterns, not specific events. We believe that patterns *are* discernible in the blunders committed by British governments. Our primary concern is with reducing the overall incidence of such blunders.

A brief word about gender is required. As feminists, albeit male ones, we would like to have used gender-neutral language consistently throughout. Sadly, that would have done violence to the English language and would also have resulted in unbelievably tortuous and convoluted sentences. We hope that readers will forgive us on those grounds for writing "he" and "his" when the rendering should strictly be "he and she" and "his and hers". We have, of course, introduced gender-neutral language whenever we felicitously and grammatically could. Although a considerable number of our interviewees were women, we have, in order to protect their identity, used masculine pronouns and adjectives in referring to all of our interviewees, whether women or men.

Finally, we hope the reader will bear in mind throughout our book that, in spite of its governments' incessant blundering, the United Kingdom is in many ways a well-governed country. Our political leaders are seldom clowns or buffoons, and the vast majority of them are genuinely concerned with both the British people's welfare and the country's long-term future. To say that they are public servants is to speak the truth. They are subject to the law of the land like every other citizen. They seldom resort to crude demagoguery. They seldom seek special advantages for themselves, their families, their friends or their lovers. They seldom exploit public property for private purposes. Blatant corruption is virtually unknown in central government and rare in local government. The parliamentary expenses scandal that hit the headlines in 2009 stood out partly because it was so rare. Compared with the political élites of some countries, including some of Britain's continental neighbours, most British politicians and civil servants are models of both rectitude and public-spiritedness. If anything, these very qualities make the frequency with which they commit blunders the more surprising and disappointing.

Part I

To begin with …

1

Blunders, judgement calls and institutions

In a famous series of essays known as the *Federalist Papers* – first published in 1787 and still in print after more than two centuries – the great American statesman and political philosopher James Madison referred to "the blunders of our governments". The governments he had in mind were America's thirteen state governments, the only governments that mattered much before the ratification of the US federal constitution at the end of the 1780s. Lamenting what he believed to be the state governments' innumerable blunders, Madison suggested charitably that "these have proceeded from the heads rather than the hearts of most of the authors of them". "What indeed", he added, "are all the repealing, explaining, and amending laws, which fill and disgrace our voluminous codes, but so many monuments of deficient wisdom?"[1] Couched in suitably modern language, that question, with its dour reference to "monuments of deficient wisdom", must have occurred to millions of Britons during recent years. As we shall see in later chapters, the blunders committed by British governments in recent years have been, if not quite innumerable, then certainly exceedingly numerous. The record is a sorry one.

James Madison felt no need to say exactly what he meant when he mentioned blunders. The many examples he cited were meant to speak for themselves. But for our purposes we need to set out carefully how we intend to use the word, if only to make clear what the following chapters are – and are not – about. What exactly is a blunder, and how are blunders to be distinguished from other forms of human misfortune and folly?

A good place to start is a good dictionary. The *Concise Oxford English Dictionary* defines the noun "blunder" as "a stupid or careless mistake", and the verb "to blunder" as "to move blindly, flounder, stumble". Our use of the words is not dissimilar. We define a blunder as an episode in which a government adopts a specific course of action in order to achieve one or more objectives and, as a result largely or wholly of its own mistakes, either fails completely to achieve those objectives, or does achieve some or all of them but at a totally disproportionate cost, or else does achieve some or all of them but contrives at the same time to cause a significant amount of "collateral damage" in the form of unintended and undesired consequences. The costs and consequences of government blunders can be financial, human, political or some combination of all three.

Defining a blunder is one thing. Deciding whether a specific action on the part of a government should be condemned as having been a blunder is something else again. Although tempting, it is not good enough to say, in the manner of a postwar American trade-union leader, "If it looks like a duck, walks like a duck and quacks like a duck, then it just may be a duck."[2] The creature in question may well be a duck (it probably is) but, as the trade-union leader's words imply, it may only be another bird with webbed feet. That said, one sign that a blunder has probably been committed is if the government that first introduced the measure in question has subsequently abandoned or drastically revised it. A really serious blunder is also likely to be widely – possibly universally – acknowledged to have been such; there is usually general agreement on the point. Needless to say, ministers and ex-ministers seldom confess to having blundered, but their silence itself often speaks volumes. If the policy had succeeded, they would have boasted about it. As it failed, they typically shroud it in silence. A few of the blunders we discuss – the Thatcher government's ill-fated poll tax, for example – are well remembered; but, partly for the reason just mentioned, many of them have disappeared into a kind of historical black hole. For instance, how many people today remember the mid-2000s fiasco over individual learning accounts? The relevant memoir-writers certainly do not go out of their way to draw attention to it. It was indeed a fiasco, and we devote the whole of Chapter 9 to it.

It is also important to note that, while all blunders are mistakes, not all mistakes are blunders. Almost every day, people in government, as in all other walks of life, make what Americans often refer to as "judgement calls". People know only what they already know or can reasonably be expected to find out; and in circumstances of uncertainty and on the basis of limited evidence, they must often decide what, on balance, seems to them at the time to be the best thing to do. In making such decisions, they will sometimes be right and sometimes wrong, but the fact that they turn out to have been wrong on a particular occasion does not necessarily mean that they have blundered. It may merely mean that, like the rest of us, politicians live in an unpredictable and sometimes intractable world and have on this occasion been unlucky. In 1999 the Treasury began a programme of auctioning off a proportion of the Bank of England's gold stocks, with a view to rebalancing the country's foreign-exchange reserves. In the wake of some of the auctions, the price of gold rose, causing critics to maintain that the gold in question should not have been sold at those particular auctions or possibly not at all. But the price of gold fluctuates wildly, and those Treasury and Bank of England officials who were responsible for the programme had no way of knowing that, following those particular auctions, the price was going to go up rather than down. In our view, the officials involved did not blunder. They merely made judgement calls that, as is the way of the world, turned out badly. (Overall the programme was a success.)

The actions of governments, including their alleged blunders, also need to be judged only in the fullness of time. Government initiatives widely regarded as blunders at an early stage of their lives may look better later on. A classic instance is the building of the Sydney Opera House. Widely derided as a spectacular blunder in the course of its construction, it is now an Australian national icon. Similarly, many sceptics and doom-mongers condemned as a blunder-in-the-making the Thatcher government's privatisation of most of the UK's public utilities during the 1980s ("selling the family silver"); but privatisation is now almost universally accepted as having been a success – and the word itself has entered the language. Almost always, as in these two instances, only time will tell.

Deciding whether a policy initiated by a government is to be deemed a blunder also raises, inevitably, fundamental issues of culture and values.

What one person regards as wholly reprehensible another will regard as highly desirable, even essential. Some people still believe Britain's entry into the European Common Market was a total disaster, while others believe it was absolutely vital and long overdue. People differ over what the top rate of income tax should be, about whether university students should pay tuition fees, about immigration from abroad and about same-sex marriage. Needless to say, issues such as these raise profound and perfectly valid questions. We ourselves, however, are not in the business of taking sides on issues such as those. Instead, we focus on blunders that are generally acknowledged to have been blunders in their own terms: occasions on which ministers and officials failed to achieve their declared objectives, irrespective of whether those objectives would have been ours. We write neither as moralists nor politicians. Our approach is more detached. After all, it is perfectly possible to judge Erwin Rommel to have been a brilliant general even though he fought in a vile cause. Both Clement Attlee and Margaret Thatcher were undoubtedly first-class prime ministers, even though their styles and political objectives could hardly have differed more.

The advantages of studying blunders, as we define them, are obvious. The typical blunder, rather like the typical car crash, has a beginning and an end, and it involves a limited number of individuals and organisations. Furthermore – and more important – in the case of blunders, as in the case of car crashes, one can often derive lessons that, if acted upon, may possibly reduce the chances of similar incidents occurring in the future.

At the same time, we readily acknowledge that, just as not all mistakes made by governments should be accounted blunders, so governments may fail in ways that do not in any way involve the committing of blunders. They may just be unlucky. They may encounter obstacles that were unforeseen and unforeseeable. They may not actively blunder but may fail to address problems that ought to be addressed. The sins of governments, like the sins of private individuals, can be sins of omission as well as commission, and failures on the part of governments can be ongoing: chronic as well as acute. Successive governments during the 1960s and 1970s failed to tackle successfully the problem of exorbitant trade-union power, just as they have failed until quite recently (and, even now, only partially) to address the multiple problems posed by Britain's ageing population. We realise that our focus on blunders means that we have not even begun to address every failure on the part of modern British governments. There are many others still to be explored.

One distinction we must make is between blunders and scandals. They are not the same thing. Most political scandals in Britain have nothing to do with blunders as we define them. They typically involve sex, petty crime and low-grade financial malpractice; they seldom involve gross governmental incompetence. The notorious Profumo affair of the 1960s had everything to do with sex, very little to do with the performance of the incumbent government (even though some at the time alleged it did). Similarly, by no means all blunders morph into scandals. It would probably be a good thing if more of them did. As we shall see, most of the blunders we describe never became scandals. Occasionally they were covered up. More commonly they involved matters of such complexity and technicality that the media never reported on them at all or else gave up trying. The early-2000s public-private partnership for financing the renewal of the London Underground, which we describe in Chapter 14, utterly failed to achieve its objectives and wasted many millions of pounds of taxpayers' money; but, apart from a certain amount of specialist reporting, most newspapers took hardly any notice of it. It was too arcane and complicated. Someone we interviewed shook his head and described the episode as "one of the most appalling scandals". But in fact, although it should have become a scandal, it never did. To this day, very few people – almost no one outside London – has ever heard of it.

Blunders, needless to say, stem from a wide variety of causes. A useful distinction – one we will make use of later – is between those causes of blunders that are primarily behavioural or human in character and those that are more institutional, systemic or cultural in character. Behavioural or human factors are ones that are likely to be in play more or less any-where and at more or less any time. They and their consequences are observable all but universally. One can observe them and their effects in non-governmental as well as governmental settings – in families, neigh-bourhood meetings, social clubs, charities, workplaces, boardrooms and trade unions. Institutional, systemic or cultural factors are more specific to particular times and places. One may find them in a corporate boardroom or in a trade union but probably not in both; in an army or an air force but probably not in a wholly voluntary organisation – and so forth. Patterns of behaviour that are considered normal in one time or place, and which may be taken completely for granted in that time or place, are liable to be considered abnormal and even unconscionable somewhere else at another time. Nepotism is frowned upon in the modern UK but is considered normal, even obligatory, in modern-day Saudi Arabia.

In practice, of course, the two kinds of factors, behavioural and systemic, are usually intertwined. If one is in play in any given setting, it is usually in play along with another or others. For example, the folly of the Suez expedition of 1956 can be traced back to a large extent to the misjudgements of a small number of individuals: in this case, Sir Anthony Eden, Selwyn Lloyd and those immediately around them. Similarly, Britain's failure to devalue the pound between 1964 and 1967 can largely be traced back to the single-minded determination of Harold Wilson, the prime minister, to prevent devaluation at almost any cost. But in both cases the men in question were able to act as they did because of the absence of institutional constraints upon them. Were those two blunders human or systemic in origin? The answer is that they were both.

We shall make use of this rough-and-ready distinction between human and institutional factors in later chapters, but meanwhile we pause to remind readers that governments are not always guilty of blundering. Governments, including UK governments, are very often highly successful in their endeavours.

2

An array of successes

WHEN governments blunder, their blunders frequently make the headlines. They are blazoned across newspaper front pages and feature prominently in broadcast news bulletins. But governments often succeed, far more often than they are usually given credit for. Unfortunately for those in government, the fact that they have succeeded may well become apparent only years after they have left office. The triumphs of Winston Churchill and Margaret Thatcher are well remembered, but most prime ministers – John Major, Tony Blair or Gordon Brown – must empathise with Mark Antony's observation in *Julius Caesar* that "The evil that men do lives after them; the good is oft interred with their bones". Good news is no news. The successes of governments are apt to pass unnoticed or else be taken for granted. They should not be.

The late Sir Keith Joseph was one of Thatcher's principal mentors and a cabinet minister during her first two terms. He was a champion of free-market capitalism and a root-and-branch opponent of the big state. He once asked a Tory-supporting Englishman who had emigrated to America what he missed most about the UK. He was taken aback by the reply: "The BBC and the NHS." The BBC – a creation of government, though not its creature – is world-renowned. The National Health Service is likewise an indubitable success by any reasonable standard. It provides high-quality health care and is extraordinarily cheap to run compared with health services in other countries. Ironically, the fact that people endlessly grumble about it testifies to its success, given the fact that most of those who grumble would never dream of wanting to see it abolished.

One of the postwar Labour government's achievements has been so successful that most people now have probably never heard of it. It was the Town and Country Planning Act 1947. The minister responsible, Lewis Silkin, set out to address three problems: atmospheric pollution, especially in big cities, urban sprawl and unconstrained ribbon development. The 1947 Act required local authorities to publish detailed land-use plans for their areas. Would-be builders and developers would have to apply for planning permission, and permission would normally be denied if the proposals contained in their application did not conform to the local plan's requirements. The Act also allowed for the creation of open spaces – "green belts" – around towns and cities, and in 1955 Silkin's Conservative successor, Duncan Sandys, issued a circular actively promoting the cause of green belts. The 1947 Act, together with Sandys' initiative and much subsequent legislation, has left a beneficent legacy visible across the UK – in contrast to the unsightly sprawl surrounding many towns and cities in countries such as Greece, Italy and France.

The 1939–45 war created a serious housing shortage that persisted long after the war. Few houses were built in wartime, thousands were destroyed by German bombs, and, despite the Labour government's best efforts, postwar shortages of materials and labour meant that during the late 1940s the supply of new housing fell far short of demand. Conservative activists at the party's annual conference in 1950 committed a future Tory government to building 300,000 houses a year, and during the 1951 election campaign the party placed housing second only to national defence in its list of priorities. The minister given responsibility for achieving the party's ambitious target was Harold Macmillan. His junior minister in charge of housing, Ernest Marples, had made a fortune in the construction industry and therefore possessed "the specialised professional expertise so vital to the task in hand".[1] Through a combination of skilful management, lavish support from the Treasury, substantial deregulation of the building industry and a policy of active co-operation with local authorities (many of them Labour-controlled) Macmillan succeeded. In 1953, two years after the Conservatives took office, 327,000 "permanent dwellings" were completed. Eighty per cent were in the public sector.

Despite its declared aims, Labour's Town and Country Planning Act had done little to tackle the problem of atmospheric pollution. Britain was world-famous for its thick fogs, the notorious "pea-soupers", but in fact these so-called fogs were really smogs: noxious mixtures of natural water vapour and vast quantities of minute carbon particles belched forth by factory chimneys and hundreds of thousands of coal-burning household fires. Although the health problems created by these smogs had long been acknowledged, they had hardly been addressed. But then, in December 1952, London was blanketed by a smog so thick that it halted rail and road traffic and contributed to the deaths of some 20,000 people. Despite intense public pressure, the government of the day was slow to act. Change would be expensive and would cause enormous inconvenience. It was not until four years later that legislation reached the statute book, but it did, with all-party support. The Clean Air Act 1956 established urban zones in which only smokeless fuels could be burnt. It required factories to lower the height of their chimneys, and provided that power stations in future were to be built only at a considerable distance from towns and cities. The 1956 Act and its successor legislation have resulted not only in cleaner air (and public buildings that, once cleaned, remain clean) but in vast improvements in public health. Thanks to the legislation, on top of increases in the use of electricity, oil and gas that would have occurred anyway, Britain is now a land that, if not entirely fog-free, is nevertheless almost totally smog-free.

One of Labour prime minister Harold Wilson's more energetic ministers was his protégée Barbara Castle, whom he appointed to head the Ministry of Transport in 1965. She inherited from her predecessor and took through parliament a bill allowing the police to breath-test anyone who committed a moving traffic offence or whom they had reason to suspect of having consumed alcohol while driving. The bill also provided for an automatic twelve-month disqualification for anyone convicted of drink-driving. Opposition to these measures, embodied in the Road Safety Act 1967, was vociferous but ineffectual, and the impact of the legislation was even more dramatic than had been expected. "The official forecast of lives likely to be saved was two hundred a year. At the end of the first five months, eight hundred people were alive who statistically would have died without the breathalyser."[2] Asked by his teacher to name the patron saint of travellers, one schoolboy in Norfolk replied, "Barbara Castle."[3] The 1967 Act also required new cars to be fitted with seatbelts, and thousands of drivers began to wear them voluntarily, although wearing them became mandatory only in 1983. No estimate can be precise, but the two measures taken together have undoubtedly saved many thousands of lives over subsequent decades and prevented even more serious injuries. Castle was probably right to maintain that she – and the Ministry of Transport's officials – had launched a social revolution.

Requiring people to wear seat belts and to stop drink-driving requires them to change their behaviour. It requires them in that sense to make choices. In the case of decimalisation, people had no choice. They had to use the new decimal currency whether they liked it or not. Even so, the abrupt switch that took place in mid-February 1971 from old pounds, shillings and pence to old pounds and new pence could have descended into farce. It could have proved an administrative disaster. In the event, the transition proceeded so smoothly that some national newspapers, which certainly would have reported it if something had gone badly wrong, found it scarcely worth reporting. It was precisely the knowledge that something might go badly wrong that prevented anything from going wrong. The government announced that the country was going to go decimal as early as the spring of 1966, nearly five years in advance of the actual event. A few months later, an executive Decimal Currency Board was set up to engineer the transition. The board introduced early on two new decimal coins, which ran alongside pre-decimal coins of the same value, and it organised a massive pre-decimalisation publicity campaign, one that accelerated gradually as time went on. By February 1971 a major event had been all but transformed into a non-event. Fortunately, there was virtual consensus among politicians and commentators on the issue. Controversy was minimal. Few were prepared to defend the old currency. The only serious argument revolved around the issue of whether the new currency's basic unit should be the pound or some smaller unit, probably one with a value equivalent to ten shillings – half a pound – in the old money. But that argument was settled quickly in favour of the pound sterling and, once settled, it stayed settled. Administratively, decimalisation was a triumph.

One of the most successful governments of the entire postwar era – in the simple sense of achieving a large proportion of its (very ambitious) policy objectives – was the Conservative government of Margaret Thatcher between 1979 and 1990. Although towards the end it committed one of the most extraordinary blunders of modern times, to be described in Chapter 4, it also managed more consistently than most postwar governments to match its own means to its own ends.

The Thatcher government enjoyed one of its first major policy successes when it engineered the sale of thousands of council houses to their tenants. The Heath government had made tentative moves in that direction, and some local authorities, mostly Conservative-controlled, had already sold off a substantial number of properties. But the Thatcher government's approach was altogether more comprehensive. The Housing Act 1980 gave all council tenants the legal right to buy the property in which they lived at a substantially discounted price (the precise size of the discount depending on how long they had lived there). Michael Heseltine, the environment secretary, said of the government's bill in the House of Commons that it "lays the basis for perhaps as profound a social revolution as any in our history". "Certainly", he added, "no single piece of legislation has enabled the transfer of so much capital wealth from the State to the people."[4] The Act's effects were immediate. Council-house sales took off. In the first six years of the new policy, 643,000 council-owned houses and flats were sold to their sitting tenants. Between 1986 – when the Thatcher government made the terms of sale even more generous than they already were – and 1996, another 1,100,000 were sold. Over the next few years, another 700,000 dwellings were transferred from the public sector into the private. The policy proved not only possible but irreversible. The Labour party first opposed it, then stopped opposing it and in the end embraced it, albeit with modifications. Nearly a million council houses were sold after Labour, in the guise of New Labour, returned to power in 1997.

The Thatcher government had, and still has, a reputation for having been unwilling to involve itself in the affairs of British industry, so much so that one of its most successful ventures has been all but airbrushed out of history. It is scarcely mentioned in most of the accounts of the Thatcher years, including in Thatcher's own account of her premiership, where it is mentioned only in passing, in the context of a routine visit she made to one country while on her way to another.[5]

During the early 1980s, the Thatcher government – and officials from the Department of Trade and Industry (DTI) – made prodigious and ultimately successful efforts to persuade the Nissan Motor Company of Japan to invest in production facilities in the UK rather than in some other European country. The government subsidised the venture to the tune of £112 million. Crucial was a one-union deal brokered between Nissan and the Amalgamated Engineering Union. Initially, Nissan agreed only to the building in Sunderland of a pilot assembly plant, but over the years it expanded its Sunderland operations to the point where it was producing some 400,000 vehicles every year. Thatcher, her ministerial colleagues and the DTI officials involved sought to create jobs at a time of high unemployment, to improve the economic prospects of the North East of England, to curb trade-union power in the heavily unionised motor industry and to use Nissan as a demonstration project, showing other UK car manufacturers what could be achieved if they adopted Japanese methods and a Japanese style of management. They were successful on most counts, if not quite all.

The power of Britain's trade unions had been much on the minds of Harold Wilson in the late 1960s and Edward Heath in the early 1970s. It was also very much on Thatcher's mind. But whereas both of them had failed, as we shall see in the next chapter, she and Norman Tebbit between them succeeded. As employment secretary from 1981, Tebbit was determined to learn from his predecessors' mistakes. He was determined, as he put it, to have "enough courage to face union leaders and employers alike, however powerful they might be".[6] In the light of the Heath government's experience, he was also determined to keep trade-union leaders, however obstreperous, out of jail. "Under no circumstances", he told his officials, "will I allow any trades union activist – however hard he tries – to get himself *into* prison under my legislation."[7] Instead, he found other ways, as he put it, to skin his cats. In particular, he made the trade unions themselves, and not their leaders, activists or members, liable to be taken to court if they broke the law. Some in Thatcher's cabinet would have preferred a more confrontational approach, but with the prime minister's backing Tebbit succeeded in securing cabinet approval, and his proposals were embodied in the Employment Act 1982, subsequently reinforced by the Trade Union Act 1984. Three decades later, all the main features of Thatcher's trade-union legislation remain in force. Britain's trade unions are no longer an estate of the realm. Their power today is but a shadow of its former self.

Apart from marginalising the trade-union movement, the Thatcher government's other great achievement was the privatisation of most of the industries that had been nationalised by the postwar Labour government or, in some instances, by Conservative and Conservative-led governments before that. On this front, as on so many others, Thatcher and her people at first moved cautiously, even warily. Her government did not introduce Tebbit's trade-union reform laws until 1982, three years after it came to power, and it was not until 1984, five years after it came to power, that it undertook its first major privatisation, that of British Telecom.

The nationalised industries had long been a bone of contention between the major parties. Their very existence excited Conservative and Labour party activists and ideologues, but almost no one else. By the late 1970s, the evidence was overwhelming that most of these state-owned industries were overmanned, indifferently managed and constantly subjected to unwarranted political interference. Their performance compared badly with that of comparable private-sector companies. Yet Thatcher, despite her intense dislike of the nationalised industries, hesitated to act. Many in her own party were reluctantly content to maintain the existing balance between the public and private sectors, and it was far from clear that high-quality managers could be found to take charge of whatever industries were to be privatised just prior to, or immediately following, their privatisation. In any event, selling off such large publicly owned enterprises would be an extraordinarily complicated business both legally and technically. In the background, there was always the disturbing thought that, if the Labour party, then under the influence of the party's far left, were returned to power, it would renationalise, possibly without compensation, all the industries that had so far been privatised. That dire prospect in itself would probably render successful large-scale privatisations difficult if not impossible.

The virtual collapse of Labour's vote at the 1983 general election removed that prospect at a stroke. Labour seemed unlikely to return to power in the foreseeable future, and the practical obstacles to privatisa-tion suddenly seemed surmountable. Before the 1983 election, the sell-ing off of shares in publicly owned companies to private investors had been patchy and partial. After that election, the government embarked on a succession of mammoth and highly profitable privatisations: British

Telecom (1984), British Gas (1986), British Airways (1987), the British Airports Authority (also 1987), the regional water and sewerage companies (1989), the electricity generating companies (1990) and – after Thatcher's departure from office – the bulk of British Rail (from 1994). The receipts to the exchequer were enormous (£7.1 billion in 1988–9 alone), and the privatised companies were at least as effective – and in a majority of cases far more efficient – than their nationalised predecessors. Moreover, as in the case of council-house sales, the Conservative governments' policy was irreversible. Short of a veritable socialist revolution, no future Labour government could seriously contemplate renationalising any significant proportion of whatever had been denationalised. And subsequent Labour governments showed no signs of wishing to do any such thing. On the contrary, the process of privatisation continued under Labour, with, for example, the Blair government's part-privatisation of Britain's air traffic control system in 2000. Not the least of the Thatcher government's accomplishments was to make all but inevitable the eventual transformation of Labour from a party committed to "the common ownership of the means of production, distribution and exchange" into a party committed, as it is now, to the survival of welfare-state capitalism.

The successes of many governments are unaccompanied by either the sound of trumpets or intense partisan controversy. Asked to list the accomplishments of a government of which they themselves were a member, former ministers often overlook some of the most significant of them, especially if they were uncontentious at the time or if they emanated from a government department other than their own. For example, the Department of Health in 1988 instituted a programme of simultaneous immunisation against measles, mumps and rubella (which used to be known, quite unfairly, as "German measles" simply because it was first described by German doctors). With their parents' consent, children were henceforth to be routinely vaccinated against all three diseases by means of the so-called MMR vaccine. Previously, vaccination against measles had been widely available for babies, and vaccination against rubella had also been available for schoolgirls; but there was no provision at all for vaccination against mumps.

During the decade following the introduction of MMR, the proportion of children receiving the MMR jab before their second birthday rose from

80 per cent to 90 per cent, and the numbers of cases of measles, mumps and rubella reported to the authorities fell by between approximately 85 and 92 per cent. A spurious and later discredited claim that children who had been vaccinated with the MMR vaccine were more likely than unvaccinated children to develop autism and irritable bowel disease caused the take-up rate of the vaccine to drop in the mid-2000s, with a subsequent rise in the incidence of both mumps and measles, as in the 2013 outbreak in south Wales; but it is clear that, taking into account the whole quarter-century since its inception, the MMR vaccination programme has been a substantial success. Its critics within the medical profession, in so far as it has any, advocate its further expansion, certainly not its abolition. The author of the spurious claim that a link existed between the MMR vaccine and autism was subsequently discredited. Nowadays, however, it is the temporary hiccups in the programme, not its overall success, that tend to be remembered.

Occasionally a new line of government policy is widely regarded as risible when first introduced but turns out in the fullness of time to have been a considerable success. John Major came from a relatively modest background and detested the way in which providers of public services often treated those whom they dealt with with indifference, even disdain. "Despite many excellent public servants", he wrote, "the service offered was often patronising and arrogant."[8] His response shortly after becoming prime minister was the Citizen's Charter, a programme that, he announced, would "carry on through a decade".[9] In time, every government organisation providing a public service would publish its own charter, setting out the standards of service it expected to offer. Each charter would constitute a kind of extralegal contract between the public-service provider and its customers. When the White Paper introducing the Citizen's Charter was first debated in parliament, the Labour leader, Neil Kinnock, sniffily denounced the prime minister's project as "a mixture of the belated, the ineffectual, the banal, the vague and the damaging".[10] But by the end of the 1990s more than forty national charters covering the main public services had been published and the House of Commons Public Services Select Committee felt able to declare: "The Charter, it is plain, has to a great extent swept away the public's deference towards the providers of public services, and their readiness to accept poor services, and has taught providers to welcome the views of users as a positive assistance to good management."[11] Ironically, far from proving ineffectual, the thinking behind the Citizen's Charter lay behind the post-1997 Labour government's entire approach to reforming the public services. John Major's government, like the Thatcher government before it, had broken a spell.

One of the Blair government's enduring accomplishments was the introduction, for the first time in Britain, of an across-the-board minimum wage. New Labour ministers believed that a national minimum wage would be socially just, would raise many poor people's living standards, would reduce the burden of state benefits having to be paid to people who, although in work, were not earning enough to live on, and would have little or no cumulative impact – and certainly no negative impact – on either the level of unemployment or the country's international competitiveness. Margaret Beckett, the government's spokesperson on the issue, derided her predecessors for having turned the UK into "the sweatshop of western Europe".[12] The Conservatives, now in opposition, argued, as they had all along, that a statutory minimum wage would drive up labour costs, cause employers to lay off workers and probably result in the loss of some two million jobs.

Fortunately from the government's point of view – and from that of low-paid workers – the Conservatives were quite rapidly shown to have been wrong. The government, on the recommendation of an independent Low Pay Commission, introduced a minimum wage of £3.60 an hour in 1999, and the minimum wage has been increased periodically ever since. There appear to have been no adverse consequences, either for low-paid workers or for the economy as a whole. By the time of the 2005 general election, the then leader of the Conservative party, Michael Howard, was admitting that he had been mistaken: "I made a prediction about the consequence of the minimum wage [that it would lead to higher unemployment] which turned out to be wrong."[13] The minimum wage has achieved most of the objectives set for it by those who introduced it. Although introducing it had been controversial to begin with, there now exists an almost total consensus in its favour.

Far more visible to ordinary members of the public than most of the measures so far described were the total bans on smoking in public places imposed in Scotland in 2006 and then in England and Wales a year later. Labour's 2005 election manifesto committed the government to imposing such a ban in England and Wales, but only with respect to enclosed public spaces, workplaces and restaurants and licensed premises that served food. The Conservatives' manifesto maintained a discreet silence on the issue. But it soon emerged that both major parties, especially the Conservatives, were divided in the House of Commons. Some MPs on both sides wanted a ban that applied to all public places, including pubs, even to pubs that did not serve food. Others, on libertarian grounds, were opposed to the imposition of any ban at all. Eventually, the House, by large cross-party majorities, voted to outlaw smoking in all indoor public spaces, including in all pubs and even private members' clubs. Those in the majority insisted that the ban – embodied in the Health Act 2006 – would encourage people who wanted to give up smoking to do so and, in particular, would reduce the incidence of diseases and deaths caused by passive smoking. They acknowledged that the ban did restrict people's freedom to do whatever they liked but maintained that the new measure was nevertheless pro-portionate. The government's chief medical officer for England, Sir Liam Donaldson, said of the ban when it came into force: "It is one of the most significant health reforms in England for decades and will create the single biggest improvement in public health for a generation."[14] Although the ban has been in force for less than a decade, it has been almost universally observed, and Donaldson was probably not exaggerating the scale of its cumulative, beneficial effects.

Governments do not always manage crises well. Successive govern-ments' responses to the BSE crisis of the 1990s and the foot-and-mouth crisis of 2001 were widely, if not always fairly, criticised. But sometimes crises are so well managed that in the event they never become full-blown and are therefore quickly forgotten. In 2009 an influenza pandemic began to affect large parts of the world, especially in Asia. It was caused by the emer-gence of a new strain of the so-called swine flu virus, H1N1. Fortunately, the Department of Health in England had known for many years that an occurrence at some time of such a pandemic was all but inevitable and, in association with the other UK nations' health departments, had made elaborate preparations. It stockpiled anti-viral drugs, which could be rapidly supplemented whenever a new strain of the disease arrived in the UK. It had put in place an information campaign that could be rolled out at short notice, and it had also put itself in a position where it could quickly organise a nationwide vaccination programme covering health-care workers and others at the greatest risk. The government's chief medical officer initially warned that swine flu could cause as many as 65,000 deaths across the UK, but in the event – partly because the new strain of the virus proved less lethal than had initially been feared, but partly also because of ministers' and officials' actions – the final death toll was only 457. Had the government overreacted to the threat? Asked to investigate, a former chief medical officer for Wales, Dame Deirdre Hine, thought not. She judged that "overall, the UK response was highly satisfactory":

> The planning for a pandemic was well developed, the personnel involved were fully prepared, the scientific advice provided was expert, communication was excellent, the NHS and public health services right across the UK and their suppliers responded splendidly and the public response was calm and collaborative.[15]

Predictably, Hine's report, because it suggested that under the circumstances everything had gone rather well, received negligible coverage in the media.

The 2008 banking crisis, in terms of its scale and impact, was of a different order of magnitude. Along with the governments of other countries, the governments of the UK had undoubtedly been guilty over many years of regulating the country's banks in an excessively casual manner. However, once the full force of the banking crisis had been let loose, the British government and Britain's then prime minister, Gordon Brown, were extraordinarily successful in organising a swift and effective response.

In September 2008 the United States Treasury and Federal Reserve Bank allowed one of America's oldest and most prestigious banks, Lehman Brothers, to collapse. Officials on both sides of the Atlantic feared that that bank's collapse might precipitate the collapse of other major banking institutions, conceivably of the world's entire banking system. Hank Paulson, the American Treasury secretary, dithered. Gordon Brown acted. Even his most vociferous critics, of whom there were many, applauded his performance. He quickly decided that, if several major British banks were not to go the way of Lehman Brothers, they needed to be massively recapitalised and that the only way of achieving that end was to inject them with vast amounts of public money. Within weeks, he and his chancellor, Alistair Darling, announced that £37 billion of taxpayers' money would be pumped into the UK banks most at risk: Royal Bank of Scotland, Lloyds TSB and HBOS. The British government's bail-out ensured that those three UK banks could and probably would survive. It also galvanised the American government into action. Brown briefed Paulson and President George W. Bush in the Oval Office, finally persuading them that such a bail-out was feasible and worth the attendant risks. A *New York Times* columnist wrote a few days later: "The Brown government has shown itself willing to think clearly about the financial crisis, and act quickly on its conclusions. And this combination of clarity and decisiveness hasn't been matched by any other Western government, least of all our own."[16] The bailed-out British banks did survive. Whatever his previous role may have been in failing to forestall the banking crisis, Brown's actions in this instance were a triumphant success. They rivalled his earlier success as chancellor in keeping Britain out of the eurozone.

Individual instances of success apart – and there have been many hundreds of others, not least the 2012 London Olympic and Paralympic Games – the governance of the United Kingdom itself has been a substantial success over the past hundred years and more. Britain's governing arrangements have shown themselves to be free, democratic, legitimate, stable, non-violent, remarkably free of corruption and by and large effective. Taxes are collected and public services provided. The British political system is far from being the worst in the liberal democratic world. It is certainly not about to collapse. Nevertheless, its performance is, in our view, not good enough – and not nearly as good as it could and should be. As we shall see shortly, British governments blunder too often. To call the stories we tell in the next part of this book "horror stories" is scarcely an exaggeration.

Part II

Horror stories

3

Blunders past and present

B lunders on the part of governments are certainly nothing new. Political leaders have been committing them ever since time began. When the Philistine leadership encouraged Goliath to challenge a lone Israeli to single combat, they overestimated Goliath's strength and underestimated grossly that of the boy David, not to mention that of David's principal backer, "the Lord of hosts, the God of the armies of Israel". Both Napoleon in 1812 and Hitler in 1941 blundered when they ordered their armies to invade Russia. As it turned out, the Japanese blundered badly when they attacked the American Pacific fleet at Pearl Harbor. Economic planning in the old Soviet Union amounted to a circus of blunders, with shoe factories producing shoes only for the left foot and the dam-building department building dams that instantly submerged major trunk roads newly opened by the highways department.

British governments have blundered from time to time since at least the end of the Second World War. The postwar Labour government was broadly a success, but during its first eighteen months in power it signally failed to draw up contingency plans to deal with the possibility, foreseen by some ministers, that severe fuel shortages might combine with an unusually cold winter to cause chaos. But massive snowfalls in January and February 1947 did just that. "Factories were closed down; villages were cut off; livestock died in thousands; people froze in their homes without even the radio as a solace since that, too, was the victim of the power crisis."[1] The cabinet minister principally responsible for the crisis was called Emanuel Shinwell, and the Conservative opposition duly invited people to "shiver with Shinwell". Less devastating but perhaps even more inept was the same government's adoption of a scheme to address a serious postwar shortage of vegetable oils by planting groundnuts (peanuts) on a lavish scale in Tanganyika, one of Britain's African colonies. But ministers and their advisers chose to plant their nuts in thousands of acres that lacked both proper soil and adequate rainfall. By the time the scheme was abandoned in 1951 – with losses of £36 million (then an enormous sum) – the company responsible for the scheme on the ground had imported more nuts for use as seed than it had managed to harvest.

The postwar Conservative governments' blunders took a variety of forms. Although we focus here almost exclusively on domestic matters, we cannot resist mentioning in passing the disastrous 1956 Suez expedition, easily Britain's most egregious postwar foreign-policy blunder. The prime minister of the day, Sir Anthony Eden, horrified and rattled by Egypt's unexpected nationalisation of the Suez Canal in July 1956 and fearful that the charismatic Egyptian leader, Gamal Abdel Nasser, meant to extend his and his country's influence across the Middle East, colluded with Israel and France in a plot to invade and occupy the Suez Canal Zone. Eden's declared aims included upholding the rule of law, resisting Egyptian aggression and securing the free passage of international shipping through the canal. His undeclared aim was to remove Nasser from power or, failing that, to humiliate him and destroy his influence in the Arab world. In the event, the Egyptians sank ships in the canal, blocking it completely, Nasser became a hero throughout the Arab world, several of Eden's own ministerial colleagues resigned, the Labour opposition denounced the invasion, the United States did likewise, the General Assembly of the United Nations did the same, the pound sterling came under intense pressure, Britain's gold and dollar reserves drained away, Britain's soldiers were forced to withdraw from the canal without having secured it and Eden – humiliated, broken in health and widely (and rightly) suspected of having lied about the nature of his relationship with the French government in instigating the invasion of Egypt – resigned. Harold Macmillan, Eden's successor as prime minister, told the House of Commons: "I do not pretend that the position is satisfactory."[2] It certainly was not.

Another blunder, less serious but notorious at the time, was the Conservative government's decision to develop and build a ballistic missile system called Blue Streak. Designed in 1955 and originally intended for military use, the estimated cost of the system had sextupled by 1959 from a mere £50 million to £300 million. A year later, it was cancelled as a military project, partly because it was proving so expensive but also because it was proving impossible to devise any means of protecting it from first-strike attack. But killing off the project would have seriously embarrassed the government, so ministers decided to keep it alive. No longer, however, would Blue Streak be a weapon of war. Instead, it would be developed so that it could be used to launch civilian satellites into orbit. But that nice idea did not work either, and the project in its entirety was finally abandoned in 1972. (If anyone is interested, a few of the surviving launch vehicles are still on display in museums in Belgium, Germany, Scotland and England.)

Blue Streak was by no means alone. The governments of the 1950s and 1960s often made a poor fist of commissioning projects involving aircraft and missiles, whether military or civilian. But by far the biggest aeronautical blunder of that time was the decision to develop and build Concorde, the world's first – and last – supersonic passenger aircraft. Ministers in Harold Macmillan's government, led by the prime minister, believed that the future of civil aviation lay with planes that could fly faster than the speed of sound. They also believed that building such a plane in collaboration with the French government would ease Britain's entry into the Common Market. They were wrong on both counts. President de Gaulle of France vetoed Britain's entry into the Common Market in 1963, and Concorde was a commercial flop. No countries would allow it to fly supersonically over land, and no airlines wanted to buy it (though the two countries' state-owned airlines, Air France and British Airways, were in effect bribed into operating it). It quickly became known as "the flying white elephant". Only sixteen were ever built, and in 1979 the British government wrote off its entire, enormous investment.

Blunders usually arise out of the taking of a positive action, albeit one that is ill-advised, but occasionally they result from a decision not to act in a certain way even though the option of acting in that way is readily available. Probably the biggest single blunder committed by Harold Wilson's post-1964 Labour government was its decision not to devalue the pound, if not immediately, then at least within a year or two of taking office. Ministers were divided on the issue, but Wilson and his chancellor of the exchequer,

James Callaghan, were adamant that devaluation would damage Labour politically, tarnish Britain's international reputation and relax the economic pressures on British industry to reform and modernise itself. From late 1964 onwards, Wilson as prime minister forbade ministers from discussing even the remote possibility of devaluation. But the financial markets had other ideas. They decided that, whatever the government might think, the pound was overvalued and would have to be devalued sooner or later. Eventually, in November 1967, amidst mounting market pressures, Wilson and Callaghan did devalue it. Callaghan felt honour-bound to resign as chancellor. Wilson as prime minister clung on.

Two of the most spectacular government blunders of the postwar period – one by Harold Wilson's first Labour government, the other by Edward Heath's Conservative government – concerned industrial relations. Both were committed against a backdrop of weak industrial management, belligerent trade unions and rampant restrictive practices. The postwar decades in Britain witnessed a seemingly endless succession of "wildcat" strikes, works-to-rule, go-slows and demarcation disputes between workers belonging to rival unions – in short, by every imaginable form of industrial disruption. The Wilson and Heath governments set out, by legislative means, to tilt the balance of power in industry away from the unions towards employers and to curb the power within individual trade unions of "irresponsible" leaders and militant shop stewards. Both attempts failed miserably. It was left to Norman Tebbit more than a decade later to tread more warily.

In January 1969, the Wilson government published a White Paper entitled *In Place of Strife*. It was intended to be a preliminary to legislation and proposed to give the government and a newly created Commission on Industrial Relations powers to order a ballot of workers in the case of some industrial disputes, to impose a "cooling-off" period in the case of some wildcat strikes and *in extremis* to fine unions in the case of some disputes between rival unions. Trade unions would be required to register with the new commission under pain of a fine. The White Paper included several proposals to strengthen the unions' position, but the unions' leaders were more impressed by the sticks in the paper than the carrots. They feared what a future Tory government might do. The Trades Union Congress (TUC) came out in opposition to the document and, with the support of

Labour backbenchers and Labour ministers, forced the cabinet, including the prime minister, to back down. They withdrew the threat of legislation. Wilson and his main ally, the minister of labour, Barbara Castle, had seriously underestimated the strength of pro-union and anti-interventionist sentiment throughout the labour movement – a strange mistake for two long-serving Labour politicians to make.

Heath and the Conservatives regarded the Wilson government's climb-down over *In Place of Strife* as a pathetic display of cowardice in the face of the enemy. When they came to power, they would behave differently. They did come to power, and they did behave differently – with unfortunate consequences. Heath and his ministers sought to create a comprehensive legal framework within which both trade unions and employers would operate. Their Industrial Relations Act, which reached the statute book in August 1971, established a National Industrial Relations Court and outlawed a range of what were dubbed "unfair industrial practices". Unions registered under the Act were granted privileges and immunities that unregistered unions were not. Workers were given the right to join a trade union, but also the right not to join one. The new court could order cooling-off periods and strike ballots. The Act also sought to ban secondary picketing – picketing aimed at firms and premises not directly involved in the original dispute – and to outlaw, except in narrowly defined circumstances, the closed shop. The scope of the Act and the powers given to the new court were sweeping.

Heath and his colleagues assumed that, although the Act would initially be unpopular with the unions, they would recognise that it did have advantages from their point of view and would learn in time to live with it. They were right about the initial unpopularity, wrong about the eventual acceptance. The TUC denounced the Act. Several large unions refused straight away to register under it. Others followed suit when a court judgment led to the imprisonment of the leaders of an unofficial dockworkers' strike. The Industrial Relations Court's imposition of a cooling-off period on the main rail unions, and its subsequent insistence that the unions ballot their members, served only to postpone a national strike. "In a remarkably short length of time the Act – heralded as a cure for Britain's industrial relations troubles – had become a liability that threatened to plunge the country into yet further labour conflict."[3] Further conflict duly ensued. In

29

1970, the year before the offending Act was passed, nearly eleven million working days had been lost as a result of industrial stoppages. In 1972, the year after the Act was passed, that figure more than doubled to twenty-four million. Meanwhile, the Labour party, opposed to the Act from the outset, committed itself to repealing it as soon as it returned to power. Following the February 1974 general election, Labour did return to power – thanks in part to the Heath government's abysmal industrial-relations record – and proceeded to repeal most of it. Thus, the 1971 Industrial Relations Act achieved none of its objectives. On the contrary, it made an already bad situation worse. The Heath government's blunder was peculiarly gross by anyone's standard. A piece of legislation designed to achieve one objective – reducing the scale of industrial unrest – achieved precisely the opposite.

The Labour governments of the late 1970s, first under Harold Wilson, then under James Callaghan, were at least as blunder-prone as Heath's government had been. Their much-vaunted but now long-forgotten Community Land Act 1975 cost millions and achieved nothing. The Conservatives repealed it in 1980. A similar fate – wholly predictable and widely predicted – awaited Tony Benn's attempts to promote workers' co-operatives. A true believer in workers' co-operatives, Benn as secretary of state for industry, with the half-hearted support of his cabinet colleagues, devoted substantial sums of public money to creating and then part-funding three such schemes: Kirkby Manufacturing and Engineering Ltd, a producer of central-heating radiators, Meriden-Triumph, a motorcycle manufacturer, and (amazingly) an avowedly left-wing newspaper, the *Scottish Daily News*. The newspaper closed after six months, Kirkby Manufacturing folded in 1979 and Meriden-Triumph went into receivership in 1983. All three firms were almost certainly doomed from the start. As early as 1975–6, their financial backing from the government totalled some £10 million (at 1970s prices), and a stern report from the Public Accounts Committee later noted bleakly that the three co-operatives had probably never been viable and that "all three projects involved a high degree of risk, particularly since all three began operations in a period of general economic difficulties".[4] Benn's department admitted that it had never properly assessed the risks involved or done any serious (or even unserious) market research. Wilson quickly demoted Benn before he could conduct any more of his idiosyncratic socialist experiments.

The origins of yet another spectacularly failed venture were less ideological in character. Labour in power in the late 1970s was anxious to do whatever it could to shore up the economy of Northern Ireland, whose long-term decline had been accelerated by the violence that then afflicted the province. Accordingly, the Northern Ireland Office persuaded a reluctant Treasury and Department of Trade to invest public money in a project designed to create upwards of two thousand jobs in the province. The project, whose principal backer was an American businessman named John DeLorean, was to manufacture and market an innovative, gull-winged sports car, the DeLorean DMC-12. Newspaper photographs made it look as though the car could fly.

But it could not fly and did not, except in the *Back to the Future* movies. The production facilities were constructed as planned, but the car itself, designed almost exclusively for the American market, failed to sell in America. Some eight thousand vehicles were built, but half remained unsold when after four years the company went into receivership in 1982. It subsequently emerged that John DeLorean had all along been a big-time fraudster, embezzler, tax-evader and crook. After the car company was wound up, he was charged with cocaine smuggling in a US court and was lucky to get off. As so often on these occasions, no one has ever calculated – and probably no one could – the cost to British taxpayers of that particular doomed undertaking, but the total amount is almost certain to have been a lot more than the £77 million pumped directly into the firm by the Northern Ireland Department for Enterprise, Trade and Investment.

We shall shortly tell the stories of major blunders that have been committed more recently, since the end of the postwar era. But we must not give readers the impression that we think that the blunders we will be examining in more detail were the only ones committed by successive governments since the 1970s. There have been many more, and we would be failing in our duty if we neglected to call to mind a number of them.

As it happens, Margaret Thatcher's government committed relatively few blunders according to our definition during its first few years in office; but as time went on Thatcher and her colleagues stumbled more frequently, probably partly because Thatcher herself, having begun by being exceedingly cautious, was emboldened by success. Having previously been risk-averse, she and her colleagues started to run risks. Some of the risks they ran were not desperately important in themselves, but they did betray a degree of insouciance.

Several of the Thatcher government's latter-day blunders were events-driven and media-driven. The mid- and late 1980s witnessed a sharp increase in crowd disturbances at football matches in Britain and overseas. A riot in 1985 between Birmingham City and Leeds United fans caused the death of a teenage fan when a wall collapsed. Soon afterwards crowd violence at the Heysel Stadium in Brussels led to the death of thirty-nine spectators attending a Juventus–Liverpool match. Thatcher – and not only Thatcher – was appalled. "We have to have grounds", she said, "that are safe for our families and safe from hooligans."[5] Her government responded by introducing a Football Spectators Bill, which reached the statute book in 1989. The new legislation provided for the creation of a Football Membership Authority, which would administer a new National Football Membership Scheme. Everyone wanting to attend a professional football match in England or Wales would have to be enrolled in the scheme and be equipped with a photo-ID card, which they would have to show at the turnstiles. British football was to be hooligan-proofed.

However, doubts were at once expressed, not about the legislation's aims, which were generally agreed to be laudable, but about whether the scheme could be made to work. Critics pointed out that such a scheme, in the nature of the case, could never be wholly secure, that it would be wildly expensive to operate, that it would slash attendance at football matches and that, by causing congestion at the turnstiles, would probably cause more crowd trouble outside the grounds than it prevented inside them. The Football Association and the Football League both came out against the scheme. So did the police. In the House of Commons, Labour's Neil Kinnock quoted the Police Federation as saying, "This scheme is not going to work. When it breaks down, it will do so on match days and give rise to the threat of even worse disorder than it seeks to suppress."[6]

In the event, what looked like proving a costly blunder did not actually become one because a tragedy – one not of the government's making – unexpectedly supervened. In April 1989, with the government's bill well on its way to the statute book, ninety-six Liverpool fans were crushed to death in an incident at Sheffield's Hillsborough Stadium. Ministers must already have entertained doubts about their own proposals, because, when they commissioned Lord Taylor, a High Court judge, to enquire into the tragedy, they made it clear that he should feel free to comment on the desirability of the National Football Membership Scheme that the government's legislation provided for. He did just that. In his report, published in January 1990, Taylor noted: "It must be a rare if not unique situation for a judge, appointed to conduct an Inquiry, to have within his remit consideration for the merits and provisions of an Act of Parliament already in place."[7] His comments on the substance of the Act were scathing:

> I fully understand and respect the reasons which prompted the promotion and enactment of the Football Spectators Act 1989. However ... I have grave doubts about the feasibility of the national membership scheme and serious misgivings about its likely impact on safety. I also have grave doubts about the chances of its achieving its purposes and am very anxious about its potential impact on police commitments and control of spectators.[8]

The relevant sections of the Act remained on the statute book for a generation, but no government chose to implement them and they were repealed in 2006. Unlike the Liverpool fans at Hillsborough, the Thatcher government – and the game of football – had had a lucky escape.

Like the Football Spectators Act, the passage of the Dangerous Dogs Act 1991 was an events- and media-driven affair. During the early months of 1991, roughly a dozen Britons of all ages were attacked and severely mauled by out-of-control dogs. At least one person died. There was no reason to believe that the number of people mauled in early 1991 was significantly greater than in other recent years. Nevertheless, by the middle of May the media were demanding that something must be done, the implication being that something must be done immediately. The government, although at first doubtful about the need for new legislation, soon felt compelled to respond, and ministers' initial reluctance quickly segued into real or feigned enthusiasm. Within weeks, the then home secretary, Kenneth Baker, informed the House of Commons that the government would shortly introduce legislation banning "the breeding and ownership of pit bull terriers and other dogs bred especially for fighting".[9] However, as was quickly pointed out, most canine attacks on humans were perpetrated, not by pit bull terriers but by Alsatians, Rottweilers and seemingly innocuous breeds such as collies. The government therefore changed tack and in its emergency legislation, brought forward within weeks, focused mainly on dog owners rather than dogs, although all dogs belonging to four named breeds – the pit bull terrier, the Japanese Tosa, the Dogo Argentino and the Fila Brasileiro – were to be dealt with by a variety of means, often of some complexity.

The Dangerous Dogs Act, with the opposition parties' support, duly reached the statute book within another few weeks. It remains there still, although by now much amended. It has not, however, proved a great success. In fact, it has proved to be a blunder – not, to be sure, a gross blunder, but a blunder all the same. The courts, although given the task, have often found it difficult to decide whether an individual dog does, or does not, belong to a particular breed; and the police have spent millions of pounds locking up and sometimes destroying dogs deemed to be of "the pit bull type" (helpfully defined by the Court of Appeal as "an animal approximately amounting to, near to, having a substantial number of characteristics of the Pit Bull Terrier").[10] Despite the legal uncertainties and the substantial financial costs, the Dangerous Dogs Act might nevertheless be regarded as having, on balance, proved a success, if, by reducing the number of dangerous dogs and/or the number of careless or ill-disposed dog owners, it had led to a significant reduction in the number of serious injuries inflicted by dogs on humans. But it has not. The number of dangerous dogs in the country, including pit bull terriers, has almost certainly not been reduced since 1991; it may even have increased. Dogs still kill human beings occasionally, and the number of serious injuries inflicted by dogs on humans has not decreased since the Act's passage. The expenditure of much time, energy and money has achieved little or nothing. Bluntly, and in the eyes of history, "The Dangerous Dogs Act failed to achieve anything beyond securing a few favourable headlines to help the government during a difficult time when it was getting it in the neck."[11] It seems that adequate legislation was already in place, dating from 1871.

A few blunders (though probably not enough) are almost self-signalling in that what they propose is so complicated and the opposition to them so vehement that, however well intentioned they are, they appear from the outset to be most unlikely to endure. Housing Information Packs (HIPs) fall into that category. The Blair government provided for their introduction in the Housing Act 2004. The idea was that the housing market in England and Wales could be made to function more efficiently if, when a house was first put up for sale, the seller was required to provide would-be buyers with all the information about the house they needed, including a structural survey. These HIPs would speed up the process of buying and selling by reducing the incidence of both buyers and sellers withdrawing from informal deals struck prior to the exchange of contracts. They would, for instance, reduce the incidence of gazumping, when sellers accept offers higher than the ones they have already informally accepted. In addition, potential buyers, as they looked for a house, would not have to incur the possible expense of having to commission surveys on several houses. Ministers and officials in Whitehall were conscious of the similar arrangements that obtained in Scotland, where binding agreements between the parties were undertaken at a much earlier stage of any house-purchase transaction.

The idea seemed sensible, but it was undoubtedly going to be complicated to administer and it immediately encountered vigorous opposition. The Conservatives complained from the beginning that HIPs would be excessively costly and bureaucratic, and the National Association of Estate Agents insisted that, at a time when the housing market was already depressed, HIPs would further depress it by deterring house owners from putting their house up for sale. The government meanwhile encountered severe practical difficulties in introducing the scheme, with consequent delays and reductions in the amount of information required to be contained in the packs. In April 2010, a year after HIPs had become legally mandatory in connection with the sale of all houses, whatever their size, in England and Wales, the Conservatives' manifesto for the coming general election promised that a future Conservative government would "Abolish Labour's expensive and unnecessary Home Information Packs which increase the cost and hassle of selling homes"; and one of the first acts of the Conservative-led administration that took office in May 2010 was to suspend – in effect, to scrap – Labour's entire HIPs scheme.

The tale of the Blair government's proposed super-casinos was equally sorry if also more comic (except in the eyes of those directly involved).

Quite possibly the proposed super-casinos would have proved a great success had they gone ahead as originally planned. No one will ever know. But they were never either built or operated. The aims of the government's policy were to liberalise Britain's restrictive gambling laws and at the same time, by means of promoting super-casinos, to promote the regeneration of one or more deprived urban areas. At first, the government announced that up to forty of these large Las Vegas-style casinos would be built; but in the face of stiff opposition, some of it from within the Labour party, that ambitious figure was gradually whittled down to eight and then to just one. Ministers proceeded to create an independent body, the Casino Advisory Panel, to recommend where that one casino should be located, and twenty-seven local authorities applied to have their town chosen as the one venue. To the surprise of many, who believed that Blackpool's claim was the strongest, the panel recommended Manchester. However, the requisite enabling legislation, although it passed through the House of Commons, was narrowly defeated in the House of Lords. At this point, Gordon Brown, Blair's successor as prime minister, intervened. He began by putting a hold on Manchester's bid and then, several months later, torpedoed the whole enterprise. The reason ministers gave was the Lords' refusal to pass the government's legislation, but Brown had never felt comfortable with the idea of super-casinos, and he was also, it was claimed, anxious to appease the *Daily Mail*, which had campaigned all along against the government's proposals.

As blunders go, the super-casinos blunder – like the one relating to HIPs – was far from horrendous. No one died. There was no rioting in the streets. The incumbent government and prime minister remained in power (at least for the time being). Yet the episode was far from being trivial. Officials in Whitehall wasted days and weeks preparing legislation that, given Brown's known opposition to the whole super-casinos concept, was never likely to remain on the statute book for long or to be put into effect. A good deal of parliamentary time was wasted. Above all, the twenty-seven local authorities that submitted bids – and especially the eight authorities that were eventually short-listed – invested a great deal of time, money and effort in preparing their bids, all to no avail. Manchester alone had spent £150,000 on its bid. The whole episode smacked of a stay at Fawlty Towers.

Although both as chancellor and as prime minister Gordon Brown was implicated in the government's embarrassment over super-casinos, he did at least share responsibility for that debacle with others. By contrast, Brown was virtually the sole author of his own and the government's misfortunes over the abolition in 2007 of the 10p starting rate of income tax. As chancellor, he had introduced this low starting rate eight years earlier. "The ten-pence rate is very important", he had stated at that time, "because it's a signal about the importance we attach about getting people into work and it's of most importance to the low paid." "This is not", he added firmly, "about gimmicks."[12] However, the manner of his announcement, eight years later, that the 10p rate would be abolished was beyond doubt a gimmick. He made the announcement at the end of his annual budget speech without either warning or explanation. He simultaneously raised the threshold at which people would begin to pay income tax, clearly intending to give the impression that, as a result of this combination of changes, those on low incomes would be better off.

But he was wrong. It quickly emerged that his changes would leave some five million people – all of them poor or relatively poor – substantially worse off. Brown's predecessor as chancellor, Kenneth Clarke, denounced the measures as "cack-handed".[13] More menacingly, Frank Field, a Labour former minister, gave notice that, when Brown's proposals came before the House of Commons in the form of a Finance Bill, he would table an amendment to provide the millions of people who were disadvantaged by it with "transitional relief". The sting in Field's remarks in parliament was in the tail:

> Whatever views one has of the Chancellor, one has to be pretty deranged to say that he is not passionate about redistributing resources to the poorest. I sign up to that message. Therefore, I am puzzled that he has allowed this aspect of his Budget to go through. My feeling is that, on this one occasion, he cannot have done his sums.[14]

Field was right, dozens of Labour backbenchers agreed with him, the government faced defeat in the Commons and in May 2008 Alistair Darling, Brown's successor as chancellor (Brown by this time having become prime minister), introduced a "mini budget" rectifying – at a cost to the exchequer of £2.7 billion, no less – the fiscally regressive consequences of his predecessor's clumsy blunder. Even Brown, not someone normally given to admitting mistakes, acknowledged ruefully in a radio interview that on this occasion he had erred.

Unfortunately, it goes without saying that the blunders described in this chapter, not to mention the ones to be explored later, comprise only a small fraction of those committed by British governments in recent decades. Had we had the time and space, we would almost certainly have wished to consider discussing, for example, the Thatcher government's abolition of the Greater London Council (only for a body like it to be revived, wholly predictably, a decade later); successive governments' responses to the BSE and foot-and-mouth crises (though, arguably, no one else could have done better); the doubtful wisdom of the "care in the community" initiatives relating to mental illness (though that approach still has its defenders); the form taken by the Major government's privatisation of the railways in 1993 (with one group of companies charged with running the railways and another company taking charge, at the Treasury's behest, of the network's infrastructure); the substantial failures and/or exorbitant costs of innumerable government-initiated IT projects (a sample of which will be described in Chapter 13); the apparent necessity in recent decades of introducing and enacting, more or less annually, fresh legislation relating to crime and the criminal justice system (without that legislation having any proportionate impact on the levels of crime committed); arguably Gordon Brown's so-called raid on pension funds in 1997; the introduction in 1999 of Anti-Social Behaviour Orders in England and Wales (with insignificant, if any, effects on the incidence of anti-social behaviour in those parts); the final and failed attempt to sort out the affairs of the car manufacturer MG Rover (with five of its executives, even as the firm collapsed, departing with pay and pensions amounting to £42 million); the costly and abortive effort, opposed by many members of the cabinet, to introduce elected regional assemblies across England; the doubtfully effective legal prohibition of fox-hunting with hounds (still regretted by the then prime minister, Tony Blair); the Licensing Act 2003 (which inadvertently complicated the lives of many churches and charities and signally failed to reduce the incidence of binge drinking); the inability of one or more privately owned exam-marking outfits in England and Wales to mark thousands of school examination papers in good order and on time; and Alistair Darling's one-off supertax on bankers' bonuses in 2009 (which, although it succeeded in raising more revenue than expected, failed in its stated purpose of causing banks to rein in the awarding of large bonuses to their employees). This already long list could, of course, be further extended. More than two centuries ago, Alexander Pope in his *Essay on Man* famously declared: "For forms of government let fools contest; Whate'er is best administered is best." If Pope were still alive, he would almost certainly be expressing similar sentiments today. He would undoubtedly have expressed them a generation ago as Margaret Thatcher's government introduced and then attempted to administer a strange tax called a poll tax.

4

A tax on heads

T he Thatcher government's introduction of a poll tax in the 1980s
was a colossal blunder. We might be tempted to call it the blunder
to end all blunders – except that, far from ending all blunders, it
has been followed by numerous others. The poll tax failed to achieve its
objectives, led to rioting in the streets, wasted many millions of pounds,
occasioned much human misery and ultimately cost the prime minister
her job. Its life was short. It was collected for the first time in 1990 and the
last in 1993. Since then, no tax like it has been seriously proposed. Indeed,
more than two decades later the whole episode still evokes wonder and
astonishment. How could such a thing have been allowed to happen? It
was almost as though the gods had decreed that blind fate would drive
men, and one famous woman, to their doom. Every dire prediction made
about the poll tax was sooner or later fulfilled. Its perpetrators walked
into clearly visible traps with their eyes wide open, but they evidently saw
nothing. They blundered on, impervious to warnings. In the end, their
failure was abject and total.[1]

Prior to the introduction of the poll tax, the spending of British local
authorities was funded from three main sources: grants from central
government, charges for the use of specific services, such as municipally
owned swimming pools, and a property tax, commonly known as "the
rates", based on the assessed value of individual properties. The rates,
especially those levied on domestic properties, had three great advantages
and one great disadvantage. They were long established and well known.
They were relatively simple to administer. And they were a tax on assets

that were at once highly visible and virtually immovable (a house or flat
could not easily be made to disappear). Against that, they were manifestly
inequitable. Non-householders – for example, many tenants in rented
accommodation – paid no rates at all, and the domestic rates were levied
on houses and flats irrespective of the incomes of the people who lived
in them. In one house there lived a husband, wife and their three young
sons, all wage-earners. In an identical house next door there lived, all
by herself, a little old lady dependent on her pension. But each year the
family of five and the little old lady paid exactly the same sum to the local
council. It wasn't fair.

The Conservative party collectively was more impressed by the unfair-
ness of the rates than by their more prosaic advantages. As early as 1974, the
Conservative manifesto for the October election of that year promised that
"within the normal lifetime of a Parliament we shall abolish the domestic
rating system and replace it by taxes more broadly based and related to
people's ability to pay".[2] During the ensuing election campaign, Margaret
Thatcher, then the shadow environment secretary, whose brief included
the financing of local government, observed that "ratepayers' pockets
have been stretched to the breaking point this year", and she categorically
declared: "The next Conservative Government will release them from
this rates rack."[3] Five years later, the next Conservative government was
in power, and Thatcher herself was prime minister.

Initially, not much happened. The Conservatives' 1979 election manifesto made no mention of abolishing the rates, and during Thatcher's first
term the time of ministers, including that of the prime minister, was taken
up with other matters, notably cutting income tax, responding to riots
in Brixton and Toxteth and winning back the Falkland Islands. In 1981
Michael Heseltine, her activist secretary of state for the environment, did
publish a Green Paper on the subject of local-government finance, called
Alternatives to Domestic Rates; but it was a bland document and, despite
its title, implied that there was no real alternative to the rates, although of
course they could with advantage be reformed. In the interests of compre-
hensiveness, the Green Paper canvassed the possibility of introducing a poll
tax – a per capita tax on individuals – but it did so unenthusiastically. The
document's tone was dismissive on this point, emphasising the administrative difficulties and high costs that would accompany the introduction of

any such tax. A civil servant involved in drafting the Green Paper is said
to have remarked of a possible poll tax, "Try collecting that in Brixton."[4]
The Conservatives' manifesto for the 1983 general election, like its 1979
predecessor, made no mention of abolishing the rates and, following the
Conservatives' victory at that election, a government White Paper went
so far as to commit the government to retaining the existing rating system.

But shortly afterwards everything changed. The Thatcher government and a number of prominent local authorities were at war, and the
government's methods for curbing local-government expenditure were
in complete disarray. Matters relating to local government suddenly rose
high on the government's agenda. Having decided not to abolish the rates,
the government had instead decided to cap the rates levied by those local
authorities that it judged guilty of gross overspending. Ministers in the
Department of the Environment found themselves beset. A number of
local authorities, including several big ones, deliberately set rates in excess
of the government-imposed caps and in some cases refused to set rates at
all; a few passed budgets that were arguably illegal. The most stubbornly
disobedient of the local authorities were Labour-controlled, and many of
the Labour councillors who controlled them were on the party's far left.
Some belonged to the hyper-left Militant Tendency. The villains of the
piece – dubbed the "loony left" by the tabloid press – were men with then
familiar names such as Ken Livingstone of London, "Red Ted" Knight of
Lambeth and Derek Hatton of Liverpool.

Liverpool City Council, under Derek Hatton's influence, was especially
intransigent. It humiliated Patrick Jenkin, Heseltine's successor as environment secretary, forcing him to concede a financial settlement far in excess
of anything allowed for under the government's original plans. Taking
their cue from Liverpool, other Labour-controlled councils threatened
to face down ministers over rate caps and even to take them to court. Ken
Livingstone and the Greater London Council, which then still existed,
inflicted further pain on Jenkin by persuading the House of Lords to delay
the implementation of the government's plans to abolish it. Across a wide
range of issues, the law was in disarray. Viewing these developments, the
prime minister – and she was not alone – bundled together in her mind
the far-left Labour leaders in local government and Arthur Scargill, the
avowedly revolutionary leader of the National Union of Mineworkers,

many of whose members went on strike in the spring of 1984. "The unions were her immediate priority; but none of her ministers, least of all the beleaguered Jenkin, could mistake her views on the town hall barons."[5]

The phrase "town hall barons" spoke volumes. Quite apart from Labour's loony left, Thatcher had long since taken a dim view of local government in general. Her whole purpose in political life was to create a more market-oriented, consumer-oriented society, and in her view the majority of local authorities, even Conservative-controlled authorities, were neither market-oriented nor consumer-oriented. Instead, they were lethargic, inward-looking, self-serving and profligate. In her eyes, and the eyes of almost everyone else on the free-market wing of the Conservative party, local-government employees constituted the worst sort of producer interest, an army of workers resistant to change and more concerned with maximising their own pay, perks and time off for union meetings than with serving the public. Something must be done. Local government must be cut down to size.

The conflicts between central and local government that marked the early and mid-1980s brought to the fore an issue that had long been lurking in the background. All UK citizens were entitled to vote in local elections, but not all UK citizens paid rates. Far from it: millions paid no rates at all, either because they were non-householders, or because some other person in their household footed the whole rates bill for that household, or because they were sufficiently impecunious to be entitled to a full rates rebate. Non-ratepayers were thus in a position to elect parties and candidates who favoured extravagant local spending and swingeing local rate levels without themselves having to contribute. They thus had no incentive to hold their local council to account for overspending. They would benefit; someone else would pay. Unsurprisingly, voters in that frame of mind were to be found disproportionately in relatively poor, Labour-voting cities and towns. In the eyes of many Conservatives, there was a strong case – under the broad heading of democratic accountability – for turning the traditional slogan "No taxation without representation" on its head and making it read "No representation without taxation". Because all adult UK citizens paid national taxes in some form, even if not necessarily income tax, there was no case for depriving citizens, whoever they were, of their right to vote in national elections; but there did seem to be a strong case – especially in Conservative eyes – for requiring all voters in local elections to pay something, however modest, towards funding the services provided by their local council. In addition, many Tories remarked on the fact (or what they believed to be a fact) that a large proportion of those who depended most heavily on local services made no contribution at all towards paying for them. The little old lady living alone, if she happened to be a ratepayer, found herself willy-nilly subsidising the education of the children, possibly the many children, of her poorer – and quite possibly feckless – neighbours. For years, little old ladies living alone featured largely in Conservative rhetoric and apparently also in the thinking of Tory party activists.[6]

By the summer of 1984, in the midst of the Scargill-inspired miners' strike, the already bad relations between central and local government seemed to be spiralling downwards out of control. Unsure how to proceed and under mounting pressure from irate Conservative MPs and activists, Patrick Jenkin, with the acquiescence of Thatcher and their cabinet colleagues, announced at the Conservatives' annual conference in October that new "studies" would be undertaken of the financing of local authorities. In fact, Thatcher and other ministers' acquiescence was more than a little reluctant. They had been around the houses twice already, with the 1981 Green Paper and the 1983 White Paper, both of which suggested that, while the existing rating system might be tinkered with, no viable alternative existed to a domestic rating system in some form. Thatcher, in particular, was anxious not to raise the hopes of the Tory rank and file, only to dash them later. Her enthusiasm for radical reform grew only slowly, as she gradually became convinced that an alternative to the rates did exist. She began by being cautious. Then, she became more receptive to the idea. In the end, she embraced the alternative to the rates that she was offered, the poll tax, with all the fervour of a convert.

Jenkin personally did not undertake the so-called studies. Instead he appointed a review team comprising both ministers and civil servants, some of them junior. The idea was that the review team should be of the highest quality. According to one insider, those recruited to the team were "the brightest selection of people ever gathered" to consider local government reform.[7] Both of the two junior ministers involved, Kenneth Baker and William Waldegrave, were bright and also upwardly mobile.

They aspired to higher office and, not least for that reason, were anxious to impress the prime minister. Waldegrave, a Fellow of All Souls College, Oxford, although the more junior of the two junior ministers, quickly emerged as the team's effective leader.

Unusual in its composition, the review team was also unusual in its mode of operations. The team actually functioned as a team. Waldegrave might have been the team captain, but otherwise status and hierarchy counted for little. Ministers and officials collaborated on a basis of equality, as did senior and junior civil servants. The group appears to have developed a considerable esprit de corps. Several of its members played bridge together. Some of them occasionally partied together. There were few serious disagreements among them and no quarrels. Although there was nothing unusual in the fact that the team deliberated in private, within the confines of Whitehall there was something unusual in the degree to which its operations were self-contained. The secretary of state, Patrick Jenkin, left Waldegrave and the others to get on with it; and, although the team commissioned working papers from elsewhere in the government machine, they had relatively little contact either with other ministers or with the remainder of officialdom. Kites were never flown. Leaks to the press were very rare. There may have been none.

A few outsiders, however, were involved, if never very deeply. It was decided that it would be a good idea to involve a quartet of "assessors", who would contribute to and monitor the review team's work. Three of the four assessors – a retired academic economist, a barrister and Lord Rothschild, a distinguished scientist and government adviser with whom Waldegrave had previously worked – had no specialist knowledge of local-government finance; but the fourth, Christopher Foster, did, and a book co-authored by him had discussed the possibility, though only briefly and non-committally, of raising local revenue by means of a household tax or poll tax.[8] But, although the assessors had been recruited and were formally in place, they were in the event mostly noises off. They never met as a group, they met members of the review team only occasionally and, apart from Foster's, their intellectual input was negligible. The retired academic economist effectively withdrew as soon as it became apparent that Waldegrave and the others were taking seriously the possibility of introducing a poll tax.

In theory, the review team could have considered dispassionately any combination of four options: retaining some form of property tax (whether or not called "the rates"), recommending the introduction of a local income tax, recommending the introduction of a local sales tax or recommending the creation of a new per capita tax, a poll tax (which, if it were adopted, would be the first since 1698 and only the third since 1381, when one of William Waldegrave's ancestors had been involved). In practice, the range of options seriously discussed was considerably narrower than that. For reasons that are still not entirely clear, both a local income tax and a local sales tax were evidently regarded as being simply not on – and therefore not worth discussing. A tax of either kind would be bound to be unpopular, and introducing either of them would require a great deal of administrative effort. It was widely believed that the UK was too small a country in which to introduce taxes such as those, and a sales tax would fuel inflation. In any case, members of the review team were convinced that Thatcher and the Tory party would simply veto the introduction of either an income tax or a sales tax. Thatcher herself wanted to cut income tax, not raise it. Ruling those two taxes out of court in reality narrowed the team's choices to retaining the rates, replacing the rates with a poll tax or else identifying some means of combining the two. As by this time the whole aim of the exercise was to abolish entirely the existing grants-and-rates system, the review team really had no option but to recommend, in some form, the introduction of a per capita poll tax. Having no other option, the members of the team became poll-tax enthusiasts. They went in to bat for it. Moreover, their per capita tax would have to be a flat-rate tax, with everyone in the same local authority area paying the same amount. Otherwise it would become, in time and in effect, a local income tax, and that kind of tax was considered unacceptable.[9]

At a meeting at Chequers on Sunday 31 March 1985, a meeting etched in the memories of all who attended, the review team presented their conclusions. No formal papers were circulated in advance, and some of those present were not clear what the purpose of the meeting was. Half the cabinet turned up, along with members of the review team, Lord Rothschild and a handful of civil servants, but the chancellor of the exchequer, Nigel Lawson, stayed away, sending along a deputy instead. Baker and Waldegrave both spoke. "Colour slides, with numerous tables and pie-charts, were used for illustration, and the chairs in the Chequers drawing room were arranged theatre-style for better viewing."[10] Baker condemned root and branch the existing local government finance system, emphasising its manifold injustices and pointing out that under the existing system local residents bore only a fraction of the cost of any and all increases in spending that their local council voted. He went on to remind his distinguished and attentive audience that local voters in Britain had neither the means nor the incentive to hold their council effectively to account for the consequences of their spending decisions. Waldegrave then rose to deliver the coup de grace. The review team was recommending that domestic rates be replaced by a poll tax alongside an alternative form of property tax. A gradually increased share of local revenues would be borne by the poll tax, which in time could – and ideally should – altogether replace the remaining element of property tax. "And so Prime Minister," Waldegrave concluded with a flourish, "you will have fulfilled your promise to abolish rates."[11] Although more than a decade had passed since Thatcher had promised to abolish the rates, and although she had not renewed her promise at any time since, she undoubtedly remembered her old promise and she was a woman of her word. Waldegrave's words could not have been better chosen (they may actually have been chosen by Patrick Jenkin). A range of formalities remained to be got through, including discussion and approval by cabinet committees and the whole cabinet; but the decision to introduce a poll tax, warmly endorsed by Thatcher, was effectively taken at Chequers.

Almost all those present at the meeting welcomed the proposed changes. One member of the cabinet rejoiced: "All my political life I have been waiting for this."[12] But, in fact, among those in the know doubts about the wisdom of introducing a poll tax were already widespread, more widespread than most of those at Chequers probably realised. Four years before, during the drafting of the 1981 Green Paper, a civil servant had tried to sound the alarm.[13] The retired academic among the review team's assessors was strongly opposed to the idea; hence his decision effectively to withdraw. The team's barrister-assessor, Sir Leonard Hoffmann, although by no means claiming to be an expert on local-government finance, nevertheless took the trouble to write a paper on the subject. In the course of it, he readily acknowledged that domestic rates were not an ideal form of local taxation, but he insisted that "there is no other which is not open to more serious objections". He was utterly dismissive of the poll tax:

> The alternative to rates, in whole or in part, is a uniform *per capita* tax on all adult residents. This will require wholly new administrative machinery and will undoubtedly be more difficult to collect than rates. Its principal advantage is that it will be paid by rich and poor alike, thereby increasing accountability. On the other hand, this advantage will be bought at the cost of great administrative costs and the unpopularity bound to be caused by the introduction of an overtly regressive tax.[14]

Hoffmann could not have been more right. Somewhat surprisingly, the avuncular Lord Rothschild, although inclined to indulge members of the review team, circulated Hoffmann's critique to the team's members and also to some ministers (though not, oddly, to the initiator of the "studies", Patrick Jenkin). There is no evidence that any of those who bothered to read the paper paid any attention to it.

But the principal objector to the poll tax was not anyone directly involved in the review. Instead it was Nigel Lawson, the chancellor of the exchequer. Lawson thought the whole idea was completely batty – "folly" and "a colossal error of judgement", as he described it in his memoirs.[15] Lawson absented himself from the crucial Chequers meeting because, like many of those who did attend, he had no notion that the poll-tax idea would be taken so seriously and that the decision-making process was going to advance so far so quickly; but he did brief his junior partner, the Treasury's chief secretary, to register his firm opposition and gave him arguments to deploy. Realising a few weeks later the enormity of what had happened, Lawson circulated a "memorandum of dissent" to his fellow ministers. "It was the most strongly worded attack I launched on any policy proposal throughout my time in Government."[16] The grounds of his attack, which he set out in detail, were both substantive and political. He wrote as both chancellor of the exchequer and a Tory. He concluded emphatically: "The proposal for a poll tax would be completely unworkable and politically catastrophic."[17] But his objections were ignored then and later, and Lawson himself seems to have largely given up at some stage.

After all, he had other things on his mind. In addition, the Department of the Environment, not the Treasury, had always been the lead department on matters of local-government finance, and the relevant environment ministers – notably Baker and Waldegrave – had by this time formed what appeared to be an indestructible alliance with the prime minister. To prise Thatcher and them apart would require the expenditure of huge amounts of both energy and political capital, and the man who expended them would probably find in the end that he had spent both of them in vain. Why should he bother? If the whole thing went wrong – as he was sure it would – no one could blame him. Lawson was also conscious at a very early stage that on this particular issue he was almost wholly isolated. He had no weighty allies willing to take up the cudgels. The fact that someone who, by general consent, was one of the ablest chancellors of the twentieth century adamantly and vehemently opposed the poll tax seemed to weigh scarcely at all with other ministers. Lawson continued throughout to voice his misgivings, but he was effectively sidelined – and effectively sidelined himself.

There were other absentees from these discussions. Lawson apart, numerous other interested parties, including local-authority treasurers, applied economists, academic experts on local government and members of the general public, might have been expected to have views about – and possibly even to harbour doubts about – the wisdom and practicality of introducing a flat-rate tax. But the new policy had already been adopted before any of them were informed and consulted – and long before most of them even knew such an initiative was contemplated. As a policy, the poll tax was gestated and born wholly in-house, within one corner of the already secretive and secluded world of Whitehall.

As Waldegrave made clear at Chequers, the review team's original proposal had been that the poll tax should be phased in gradually and should for a number of years be run in tandem with some form of property tax. Initially, there was no suggestion that there should be a Big Bang, with the poll tax introduced all at once and on its own. But both politics and administrative considerations soon dictated otherwise.

The politics took a variety of forms. Thatcher promoted Baker and Waldegrave to the top two positions in the Environment Department, thus ensuring that the tax would encounter no opposition from that quarter.

When those two were later moved to other posts, all of their replace-
ments – notably Nicholas Ridley, who became environment secretary
in 1986 – were ministers deeply antipathetic towards local government,
certainly in its 1980s Labour-dominated guise. At the cabinet meeting in
January 1986 that finally approved the poll tax, Nigel Lawson remained
silent and Michael Heseltine, who had not been involved in the previous
discussions and would almost certainly have raised objections, resigned
from the cabinet on an unrelated issue before the relevant item on the
agenda was reached. Meanwhile, gatherings of the Tory faithful in the
country repeatedly and enthusiastically applauded both the idea of the poll
tax and the individual ministers responsible for bringing it forward. Among
Conservative activists, the poll tax was a hit. "Almost every key decision in
the poll tax saga was made in the immediate run up to a party conference,
by ministers anxious for something to wave from the rostrum."[18]

Particularly intense pressure to proceed with the reform came from
the Conservative party in Scotland, where a legally required revaluation
of properties in 1984–5 was partly responsible for the vast increases in the
rates paid by thousands of householders, among them large numbers of
affluent Tory supporters. Scottish Conservative activists and their leaders
were outraged. They wanted the poll tax, and they wanted it now. And
they were in luck. They got it. Even better, it was decided that north of the
border the tax was not, after all, to be phased in over a period of years. It
would replace the rating system in Scotland in its entirety as early as 1989.
The Scottish Office ministers in Thatcher's government, who had pressed
hard for the change, were ecstatic. But officials in the Scottish Office in
Edinburgh were convinced that the tax, whatever its appeal to the party
faithful, was bound to be an administrative disaster. They were appalled,
and remonstrated vigorously with ministers. Many Scots were subsequently
to claim that English ministers had wilfully chosen to inflict the poll tax on
the downtrodden people of Scotland, that the Scottish people were being
used as guinea-pigs in some nefarious English experiment. But that was
not so. The Conservative party's Scottish ministers had, of their own vol-
ition, inflicted the poll tax on their fellow countrymen and women. As the
bill relating to Scotland made its way through the House of Commons, an
English MP lauded his Scottish parliamentary colleagues as being "trail-
blazers rather than guinea-pigs".[19] Given what was to happen later, had the

Scots really been used as guinea-pigs in a genuine experiment, the poll tax might well never have been extended to other parts of the country.

On top of politics, administrative considerations also prompted minis ters to depart radically from their original intentions. In keeping with the review team's original proposals as outlined at Chequers, the government's Green Paper on the subject, called *Paying for Local Government*, made no mention of a Big Bang, suggesting only and more modestly that "Domestic rates should be phased out over a period of up to ten years and replaced by a flat rate community charge, payable by all adults".[20] Domestic rates, albeit on a diminishing scale, would continue to be collected in the interim. In the jargon of the time, there would be "dual running". As the language in the Green Paper indicated, the poll tax had ceased to be anything as vulgar as a poll tax. It had become something much more decorous, a "community charge", the idea being that the new tax should be seen not as a tax, but as a charge for the services rendered to local residents by local authorities.

The Conservatives' manifesto for the 1987 general election duly prom- ised that, if returned to power, the government would legislate during the first session of the new parliament "to abolish the unfair domestic rating system and replace rates with a fairer Community Charge"; but it made no mention of how or when the rates would be abolished and the community charge introduced, and it also made no mention of how the charge would be collected.[21] The Conservatives were returned to power in 1987, and among officials in Whitehall the process continued – it had already begun – of deciding how the government's policy objectives could best be achieved in practice. Officials, and then ministers, came gradu- ally to realise that the idea of phasing in the new tax, while a splendid idea in theory, made no sense in practice. It was a splendid idea in theory because it would give people who were eligible to pay the poll tax (that is, almost everyone in the country) time to get used to the new tax, because it would give the relevant authorities a chance to road-test various means of collecting the tax, and also because it would mean that, at least to begin with, no individuals would find themselves paying an excessive amount of tax. But in practice it made no sense at all because phasing in the tax would be a nightmare administratively, because it would bewilder the millions of people who would simultaneously have to pay two entirely different taxes, and above all, in the eyes of many Conservatives, because it would obfuscate the core purpose of the tax. That purpose was still one of establishing in voters' minds a firm link between local expenditure and local taxation, thereby substantially increasing the accountability of local councils and councillors to local voters. Gradually phasing in the tax would fail to establish that link straight away.

All of these considerations caused the acceptable period for the proposed dual running to shrink in ministers' minds from ten years (as in the Green Paper) to four or five years, then to three or four years and then, in the end, to no years at all. Under continuing pressure from keen Conservatives and to the intense relief of increasingly harassed officials in the Department of the Environment (not to mention town hall officials), the initially envisaged period of dual running, as it applied to England and Wales, was largely abandoned in late 1987 and then wholly abandoned during the following year. There was, after all, to be the biggest of all possible Big Bangs. The coming in of the poll tax was to be an enormous event.

Even so, serious doubts about both the tax and the Big Bang persisted within government. Nigel Lawson continued to shake his head in disbelief, and he also continued to refuse to cushion the poll tax's impact on local residents by increasing central-government financial support for local authorities on anything like the scale that environment ministers were demanding. Andrew Tyrie, one of Lawson's special advisers, had earlier despatched a critical minute to Patrick Jenkin and Kenneth Baker. He warned them of the serious electoral damage that the poll tax was likely to wreak, particularly among the critical group of C1 and C2 – lower-middle and skilled working-class – voters who had stuck by the Tories in the previous two elections and whose support was essential for another victory.[22]

Baker himself, by now secretary of state for education, was increasingly alarmed at the way in which a tax that he had once imagined would be a modest affair was becoming all-consuming. As a member of the cabinet, he sought unsuccessfully to block the imposition of a 20 per cent tax on students, and he then attempted, with equal lack of success, to have under-twenty-ones excluded altogether from having to pay the tax.

Outsiders to the government, once they got to know of the tax's existence, were almost uniformly astonished and dismissive. The great majority of the organisations that responded to the government's (wholly cosmetic) consultation exercise following publication of the 1986 Green Paper – including individual local authorities, the national local-government associations, the Chartered Institute of Public Finance and Accountancy and the Institute for Fiscal Studies – were critical. So was the bulk of the broadsheet press. *The Times* deplored the proposed tax and defended the rates. The *Financial Times* called for a reformed property tax, and *The Economist* was excoriating, pointing out that, when and if the tax were eventually levied, there would be losers as well as winners and that "Losers howl, while winners give little thanks".[23] Virtually nobody outside the ranks of the Conservative party seems to have supposed that the poll tax was remotely likely to prove a vote-winner for the Tories. Most informed observers thought it could prove disastrous.

But ministers, led by the prime minister, persisted. Thatcher herself publicly dubbed the poll tax the "flagship of the Tory fleet", and in December 1987 the government's Local Government Finance Bill, embodying the poll tax, was published. Although MPs had debated both the previous year's Green Paper and the bill relating to local-government finance in Scotland, this was the first sight they had had of the government's detailed proposals for England and Wales. The secluded spot in Whitehall where the policy of the poll tax had been gestated had not been home to any members of parliament beyond those who happened to be ministers. The government had acted – on its own. Parliament now had to react. In particular, Conservative MPs now had to decide whether or not to vote for the government's bill.

Ministers were already well aware that a substantial proportion of Tory backbenchers, unlike Tory activists in the country, were less than enthusiastic about what was being proposed. The more that backbench Tory MPs contemplated the possible electoral implications of introducing a poll tax south of the border, the more queasy many of them became. The chancellor of the exchequer was not alone in having doubts. Most Conservative MPs had welcomed the Green Paper *Paying for Local Government* when it was published, but even then one of them warned Baker that he ran the risk of inaugurating a "long-running period of protest beside which the Westland affair [which had provoked Michael Heseltine's resignation] will be but a brief interlude", with another noting that a poll tax "is tolerable only if it is small".[24] Later, even before publication of the actual bill, dubiety on the back benches showed signs of spreading. As Thatcher acknowledged in her memoirs, by the summer of 1987 "many of our back-benchers had got the jitters", and the whips warned her that "while over 150 were clear supporters, there were nearly 100 'doubters', with 24 outright opponents".[25] The doubters and opponents had either to be appeased or bludgeoned into submission.

In the event, both tasks proved remarkably easy. Some potential rebels were mollified by repeated – though mendacious – assurances that ministers were prepared to consider substantial amendments to the legislation. Others were browbeaten by a combination of government whips and aggressively loyal backbenchers. The whips reduced two new MPs to "tears, or pretty close to it"; and, during debates on the floor of the House, Thatcher loyalists, probably at the whips' instigation, interrupted and barracked Conservative rebels.[26] The government enjoyed comfortable majorities in both the House of Commons and the standing committee on the bill. Outside observers described the proceedings of the standing committee as "a futile marathon", "mostly a matter of posturing" and "scrutiny by slogan and soundbite".[27] When the bill was reported out of the committee and returned to the whole House, Michael Mates moved an amendment that would have substituted for the proposed flat-rate tax a poll tax banded according to income – in effect, a local income tax. But neither ministers nor a majority of Tory backbenchers were having any of that, and, although Thatcher and her colleagues were initially nervous (Thatcher was said to be "extremely concerned" about the outcome), Mates and his amendment were decisively defeated.[28] The 124 "doubters" and "outright opponents" were reduced to a rump – a substantial rump, to be sure – of 51. The Local Government Finance Bill soon passed the House of Lords unscathed. Indeed, it was a government amendment in the House of Lords that removed every element of dual running from the final Act.

One curious feature of all these proceedings was the lack of enthusiasm in the ranks of government ministers for the poll tax in the form that it finally took. Thatcher and her principal ally, Nicholas Ridley, who was by now environment secretary (in succession to Jenkin and Baker), were simultaneously isolated and unbeatable. Almost no other minister really stood by them, but no one was prepared to stand up to them either. Nigel Lawson signalled his opposition merely by refusing to put his name to the Local Government Finance Bill (a signal so faint that few apparently noticed it). Kenneth Baker, although one of the poll tax's original progenitors, was appalled by the decision that students would have to pay the tax and by the abandonment of dual running.[29] Several ministers, including one cabinet minister, actually wrote to Michael Mates privately congratulating him on his proposed amendment. It was left to Roy Jenkins in the House of Lords to draw attention to the anomalous quality of what was going on:

> I cannot discover any member of the present Cabinet, apart from the Prime Minister and the Secretary of State for the Environment himself [Ridley], who is in favour of the legislation … The total stand-off which this measure has brought forth is something which I have never previously witnessed.[30]

Jenkins by 1988 had been politically active for four decades, including seven years in the cabinet. He was well informed, and his remarks were telling. For their part, Thatcher and Ridley, although they were by now largely isolated in the cabinet, remained convinced that they had the massed ranks of the Tory party behind them – and other ministers had to admit that they had. Delegates to the Conservatives' annual conference in October 1987 voted overwhelmingly in favour of the poll tax and vigorously opposed any form of dual running. "They had the illusion", in Kenneth Baker's words, published later, "that the community charge was so perfect that the nation was just thirsting to take it down in one gulp." Baker notes that this was one of the few occasions in history "when the Tory Party Conference actually made policy".[31]

The four dozen or so Conservative MPs prepared to vote against the tax, or at least to abstain on it, objected to the tax on three grounds. The grounds were separate in logic but intimately connected in reality. The first was that the tax would be extraordinarily difficult to collect. The second was that millions of ordinary people would perceive it as being unfair (and that it would be hard to collect partly for that reason). The third was that it would damage the Conservative party (not least because it would be difficult to collect and also unfair). Michael Heseltine spoke in the second-reading debate in the House of Commons. As environment secretary in 1981, he had rejected the idea of a poll tax out of hand – he had not won the argument, he said, because there had been no argument – and he was now at pains to deny that the tax would significantly increase the accountability of local authorities to their voters. Instead, he was convinced that it would provoke huge discontent and resentment, building "upon a platform of crude regression which seeks to make equal in the eyes of the tax collector the rich and the poor, the slum dweller and the landed aristocrat, the elderly pensioners living on their limited savings and the most successful of today's entrepreneurs". As for the Conservative party, he said, "Responsibility for the rates is confused in the legacy of history. Responsibility for the poll tax will be targeted precisely and unavoidably at the Government who introduced that tax. That tax will be known as the Tory tax."[32] Heseltine and the poll tax's other critics were right on all three counts, but they might as well have saved their breath.

For the reasons given by Conservative critics of the poll tax, it should on the face of it have been a target for the Labour party as big as the side of a barn. When news that the cabinet had approved the poll tax in principle reached the Department of the Environment, one official was heard to say, "We've just won the next election for Labour."[33] But in fact most of Labour's leadership was determined to aim off. Labour's manifesto for the 1987 general election devoted only a single sentence, buried deep inside, to the poll tax, saying that a Labour government would abolish the tax in Scotland; and Labour leaders scarcely mentioned the tax during the ensuing election campaign. The Conservatives were pleased but puzzled by Labour's lack of interest in the subject. The same pattern was repeated in the new parliament, with Labour opposing the introduction of the new tax but in a way that seemed to owe more to the rituals of opposition than to any deep-seated belief that the tax was terribly wicked or that it might eventually help restore Labour to power. Until nearly the end, Labour's opposition was tepid, even slightly embarrassed.

The reason lay largely in the very circumstances that had provoked Thatcher's government into introducing the poll tax in the first place: the behaviour of some of Labour's leading figures – or at least some of its most conspicuous personalities – in local government. Labour's national leaders, Neil Kinnock and his deputy Roy Hattersley, did not want the national party to go anywhere near the likes of Hatton, Livingstone, Knight and the Militant Tendency, and they were desperately anxious lest floating voters gain the impression that a Labour government at Westminster might possibly turn out to be like the Labour-controlled councils in Liverpool and Lambeth. Their fear was of guilt by association. Their fear of being contaminated was compounded when, with the government's Local Government Bill on the statute book, eighteen Labour MPs announced publicly that they intended to break the law and not pay the tax. For months, Labour's leadership was more concerned with fighting Labour's left than with fighting the government. As Tony Benn noted in his diary at one point, "The Labour Party is more frightened of the anti-poll tax campaign than of the poll tax itself."[34] The cumulative effect was an opposition party that scarcely opposed the new tax – and certainly never opposed it effectively.

The poll tax was now on the statute book in all its glory. The blunder had been committed. It only remained to be seen how great a blunder it would prove to be. In the event, "the poll tax did not need Labour: it was its own worst enemy, and its destructive potential was soon to be manifest in the demands dropping through every letter-box in the country".[35] The size of these demands was in many cases enormous, far larger than many people expected. The long-defunct Department of the Environment review team had envisaged early on that, in conjunction with dual running, the community charge would come in at about £50 per head. By the time of the 1986 Green Paper, the equivalent figure, still on the assumption of dual running, had risen to £150. With dual running abandoned, the government suggested that a figure of £205 might be about right (though within months that figure itself had escalated to £324). Ministers still maintained, however, that, on condition that local authorities behaved themselves and limited their spending, the average poll-tax demand should still amount to only £178. By 1990, however, with the letters about to be put in the post, that relatively modest figure had risen to £278. Ministers made much of this £278 figure, mentioning it frequently in interviews and speeches as giving a clear indication of what they both wanted and expected. However, in the event, the average poll-tax bill across the country turned out to be £363 – nearly a third more than the government's target figure and more than double its previous estimate. Needless to say, the average of £363 concealed the fact that many people found themselves having to pay far more than that. In some towns and cities, the local poll-tax bills were in excess of £775.

Moreover, the number of losers in the transition from rates to poll tax far exceeded the number of winners – and many of those who lost, lost a lot. One estimate, probably reliable, reckoned that some twenty-seven million people lived in households that lost money as a result of the poll tax, compared with only eight million who had the good luck to live in households that gained. Some households found that they were more than £1500 worse off. By contrast, a minority of households in London, but only a small minority, wound up no less than £10,000 a year better off. Many of those who were hardest hit lived in modest, low-rated dwellings but who, as individuals, were sufficiently well off not to qualify for a rebate. If, say, five people lived in such a property, they could find themselves earning relatively little but at the same time paying upwards of £1800 in poll tax annually compared with the less than £1000 in rates that they had previously paid. For people in circumstances such as those, a sum of more than £800 might well amount to a substantial proportion of their combined household income. Small wonder they and others like them regarded the poll tax as unfair, especially when they read or heard about the size of the gains accruing to those lucky enough to make big gains.

Nor was it proving easy to collect the tax: in some localities, it was proving exceedingly difficult. Thousands of those who were willing and able to pay nevertheless put off paying as long as they could, especially when it was rumoured (falsely) that the government was considering abandoning the tax. Meanwhile, hundreds of thousands of those who were legally liable to pay believed they could not afford to pay and accordingly refused to. A smaller proportion, but still a very large absolute number, actually could afford to pay but still refused to, either on conscientious grounds or because they believed they could get away with not paying. During 1990–1, levels of non-payment in some inner-city areas approached 20 per cent, and local councils across the country had no option but to take thousands of non-payers, whatever their reasons for not paying, to court. Charged with the task of collecting the tax, most local councils and their employees coped well. At the same time, however, "the burden of collecting the tax precipitated a virtual collapse in the finances of some city authorities".[36] When the tax finally ceased to be collected in 1993, it emerged that some £2 billion to £2.5 billion of poll tax remained unpaid. In addition, the widespread belief that being on the electoral register or filling in a census form might make one liable to pay the poll tax led to substantial but incalculable inaccuracies in the 1991 census and to an estimated 700,000 adults disappearing from – or never appearing on – the electoral register. Short of being dynamited, houses and flats cannot simply disappear. Determined individuals can and did.

Most vocal protesters against the poll tax, of whom there were many, confined themselves to bellowing "Can't pay, won't pay". But thousands went further. Militants invaded council meetings across the country, and a march through the West End of London – attended by between 50,000 and 100,000 people, and initially peaceful and good-natured – degenerated into a riot. Fires were started, parked cars set alight, shop windows smashed, the contents of shops looted and all manner of missiles hurled at police. By the time it was over, the police had made 339 arrests, 374 police officers and at least 86 (probably more) members of the public had been injured and there were 250 reports of damage to property. News of the London riots went around the world. Foreign observers were amazed, in many cases not only by the scale of the violence in London but also by the fact that the British government had been so ill-advised as to enact a flat-rate per capita tax in the first place. No other country had gone down that road. According to one report, Paul Volcker, a Thatcher admirer and former chairman of the US Federal Reserve Board, found it "incredible" that her government should have brought in such a measure.[37]

Not only was the poll tax seen as unfair: as Michael Heseltine had predicted, it was seen almost universally as "a Tory tax". Members of the public directed their ire, not at those who invaded council meetings or London rioters, but "precisely and unavoidably", as Michael Heseltine had said they would, at the government that had brought in the tax. The Scots, who knew what was coming, ousted ten of the Conservatives' remaining twenty-one Scottish MPs at the 1987 general election (and two years later both of the Tories' last two MEPs). Opinion-poll findings demonstrated that the tax and the government were both intensely unpopular; in early April 1990, Labour's lead over the Conservatives in the Gallup Poll soared to 24.5 percentage points. During 1990, the Tories lost all three by-elections they fought, and suffered humiliating defeats in what had been two of their party's safest seats. Predictably, the Conservatives were also defeated heavily in the May 1990 local elections (though Kenneth

Baker, by then the Tory party chairman, contrived to present the rout as a veritable triumph by focusing the media's attention on two low poll-tax authorities, Westminster and Wandsworth, where the Conservatives, against the trend, did well). Scores of backbench Conservative MPs were thoroughly alarmed by now, and they pressed the government either to abandon the tax altogether or, failing that, to go to extreme lengths to make it more palatable to their constituents.

The government's response was muddled. It managed to be both rigid and gelatinously flexible at the same time. On the one hand, the prime minister – buoyed up by the Conservatives' success in Westminster and Wandsworth and enjoying the unqualified support of a newly recruited junior minister named Michael Portillo – refused to budge on the central issue: the poll tax was to replace the rates, full stop. On the other hand, other ministers tried hard, within that constraint, to mollify the public in general and in particular erstwhile Tory voters, who showed signs of deserting the party in droves. Ministers made a number of relatively minor concessions and, in addition, agreed to increase substantially the size of the central government's grants to local authorities. They also agreed to extend the life of a "transitional relief" scheme that had been announced earlier. The scheme was meant to relieve the plight of people especially hard hit by the tax.

One cabinet minister, Chris Patten, Nicholas Ridley's successor as secretary of state at the Department of the Environment, wanted to go much further. Ideally, he would have liked to call a halt to the whole poll-tax experiment; but he was new to the cabinet, preparations for collecting the tax were already well advanced and the prime minister herself, as he well knew, was adamant. He described his predicament in his memoirs:

> It did not take long for me to realize just how calamitous the new tax was likely to be. On the whole, domestic rating had weighed proportionately least heavily on middle-income families in mid-price properties in averagely prosperous areas. This is a pretty good way of describing floating voters in marginal constituencies. These were the families really clobbered by the new system, which also doubled at a stroke the number of direct taxpayers in the country. Shortly after I moved to the Environment Department ... I commissioned

a study of what would actually happen to people's bills in a selection of constituencies in the first year of the tax's operation. Predictably, the poll tax homed in like a heat-seeking missile on floating voters in marginal seats.[38]

Armed with this ammunition, Patten did something that cabinet ministers are not supposed to do. He went over the head of the chancellor, Nigel Lawson, and pleaded directly with the prime minister for additional Treasury funds to cushion the poll tax's political effects. But he achieved little. Thatcher herself could not be moved, and Lawson was furious, both at Patten's temerity in bypassing him in this unseemly manner and also at being asked to squander even more money than he had already squandered in bailing out a tax that, in his view, should never have been contemplated, let alone enacted. Patten secured only a fraction of the money he wanted. Had he got more, one of the poll tax's central purposes – increasing local authorities' accountability to local voters – would have been still further undermined. The Treasury, not local residents, would have been paying.

The tax thus remained in place for the time being. The prime minister, however, did not. Many in her party were already seriously worried about her intransigence and rigidity, not just on the poll tax but on European issues and more generally. In October 1990 the Conservatives lost the Eastbourne by-election. In November Sir Geoffrey Howe, her deputy, resigned from the government and shortly afterwards delivered a devastating resignation speech, aimed wholly at Thatcher, in the House of Commons. The next day Michael Heseltine announced that he would stand against her for the Conservative leadership, and Heseltine went on to announce that, if elected leader, he would – using a code that was easily cracked – undertake a "fundamental review" of the poll tax. A week later he won enough votes in the first ballot of the leadership election to force Thatcher from office. Within a few hours she was gone. Thatcher was part-author of the poll tax. The poll tax was part-author – in all probability the principal author – of her political destruction. Not for the first time in politics, a child had eaten its parent.

The sequel was ironic. The new prime minister, John Major, appointed Heseltine as secretary of state for the environment, believing – and certainly hoping – that Heseltine would find some means of abolishing the poll tax without hopelessly alienating Conservative grassroots opinion. Heseltine succeeded. He established a review team not unlike the one that Patrick Jenkin had established (and involving some of the same officials); but, unlike Jenkin, Baker and Waldegrave, he was publicly respectful of local government, he continually flew kites to see how the public and the party would react to his developing ideas and he worked closely with the Treasury. In March 1991, almost exactly a year after the first poll-tax demands dropped through people's letter-boxes, Heseltine announced that the community charge (he was still willing to use the term) would soon be replaced by a new system of local taxation. The new system, eventually dubbed the "council tax", embodied a banded property tax together with generous rebates for the poor and single-person discounts for people living alone. Almost exactly a year after Heseltine's announcement in March 1991, the Major government's Local Government Finance Bill reached the statute book, just in time for the 1992 general election, which the Conservatives, in the absence of both Margaret Thatcher and the poll tax, won.

Heseltine's council tax, unlike the poll tax, still exists and is still collected. The irony is that a tax very like the council tax could have been introduced at any time during the previous decade. The opportunity was always there. It was never taken. In the event, merely introducing the poll tax, seeking to implement it and then replacing it with the council tax cost the Treasury, local authorities and ultimately the British taxpayer not less than £3.5 billion (still at early-1990s prices), quite possibly a great deal more. The Thatcher government's folly was on a truly heroic scale.

In short, some of the best and the brightest in British government – none of those intimately involved was remotely a fool – nevertheless contrived to produce one of the worst and stupidest pieces of legislation in modern British history. That paradox deserves to be explained. So does the failure of individual British politicians and the British system of government as a whole to halt in good time a project that, in its speed and potential for destruction, bore a striking resemblance to a runaway train. We shall return to address these issues – as well as the sources of other blunders – in later chapters.

5

Pensions mis-sold

The Thatcher government's blunder over the poll tax was widely foreseen. Nigel Lawson knew that it would be foolish to try to introduce any such tax, and so did Michael Heseltine, Chris Patten and many others. Even so, it is probably fair to say that the full extent of the poll-tax debacle was not foreseen. Few imagined that it would lead to massive non-compliance, thousands of prosecutions, rioting in the streets and the fall of the prime minister. However, in the case of the mis-selling of personal pensions in the late 1980s and early 1990s, the full scale of the debacle was clearly foreseen by at least a few observers. But nothing was done about it. The government as a collectivity simply went ahead anyway.

The issue of pensions had been high on the political agenda long before the Thatcher government came to power in 1979. There were two principal concerns. One was that the cost to the state of retirement pensions was bound to rise in any case as the population aged – a concern intensified by the fact that payments under a new scheme called SERPS (the State Earnings Related Pension Scheme), which had only just been introduced, were bound to rise even more rapidly than the increase in the total population as the number of people entitled to pensions under the new scheme also began to rise.[1] The other concern related to so-called early leavers, those who left their existing occupational pension scheme before they retired, either because they changed jobs or were made redundant. Early leavers were almost always financially disadvantaged, and paradoxically the contributions they left behind often had the effect of subsidising those who remained in whatever scheme it was. Once upon a time, early

65

leavers had not been a serious problem because a large proportion of the country's total workforce stayed with the same employer for life, or else belonged to one of the pension schemes that covered a number of different employers, usually in the same industry. But those days were now long gone, with more and more employees changing jobs – or losing them – more and more often.

Those two concerns would have been on the minds of whichever party had won the 1979 election. The victorious Conservatives, however, were also moved by other considerations. They were concerned to free up the labour market by making it easier for workers to move from job to job knowing that they could take their full pension entitlement with them. On more philosophical grounds, they were also keen that more and more individuals should take charge of their own lives, meaning among other things that they should take responsibility for providing financially for their old age. An influential pamphlet published by the Centre for Policy Studies in 1983 recommended that "there should be a fundamental review of pension legislation to remove the penalty on changing jobs, to aid mobility and to link individuals more closely with the wealth represented by their pension fund". The authors of the pamphlet pointed out that, for most people in occupational pension schemes, their ownership of their accumulated pension pot was merely ownership at second hand. People should be encouraged to experience ownership "in the motivational sense".[2] It was this latter consideration that caused what were originally known as "portable" pensions, later to become known as "personal" pensions.

Thatcher's secretary of state for social security, Norman Fowler, took up the cause of personal pensions with enthusiasm and later in 1983 established and chaired an "Inquiry into Provision for Retirement". Although called an inquiry, Fowler intended the group to act mainly as his own policy advisers. Its members included ministers from other departments, including the Department of Trade and Industry and the Treasury, representatives of the insurance industry, an academic economist known to hold trenchant free-market views and the government actuary. It did not include representatives of employee or pensioner groups. Although the inquiry never reported except to Fowler, the ideas of some of its members fed into two documents published by the government: an informal consultative document in 1984 and a more formal Green Paper in 1985. Both envisaged the introduction of personal pensions. Both also mentioned in passing the need to provide people who were thinking of buying a personal pension with adequate consumer protection, but neither acknowledged the possibility that widespread mis-selling of pensions might just possibly emerge as an issue.

Norman Fowler initially wanted to phase out SERPS altogether, but the almost universally hostile reception he encountered to that idea, not least from the Treasury (Nigel Lawson and Fowler, by all accounts, had a furious row), caused him to back off. Even so, his Social Security Bill, when it was published towards the end of 1985, included sweeping changes to the existing state-organised pensions arrangements. The benefits accruing under SERPS were to be reduced substantially over a period of years, and they were to relate to a person's average full-career earnings, no longer to the average of his or her twenty best years; and the benefits to widows and widowers were to be cut drastically. Personal pensions, by contrast, were to be encouraged in all manner of ways. Employees could use them to aug-ment their occupational pensions while retaining the latter. Employers for their part could no longer compel new employees to join their occupational scheme, assuming they had one. On the contrary, existing employees could, if they so wished, opt out of their employer's scheme on condition that they bought a personal pension instead. In order to encourage people to buy personal pensions, the government offered employees who bought pensions a substantial rebate on their National Insurance contributions. Those enrolled in SERPS, as distinct from those enrolled in traditional occupational schemes, were offered an additional 2 per cent rebate if they withdrew from SERPS and instead bought a personal pension before April 1993. In future, banks, building societies, unit-trust companies and friendly societies, as well as insurance companies, which were the traditional pen-sion providers, were to be allowed to sell pensions.

The Labour party's opposition to the poll tax had initially been muted, but right from the beginning its opposition to Norman Fowler's personal-pensions proposals was vehement. On the day that Fowler first launched them, Labour's frontbench spokesman on the issue, Michael Meacher, ripped into them, partly because he thought they were unfair and unwork-able but partly also because he saw them as a means whereby large compan-ies and their owners could make fortunes, at least in part at the expense of poor people, who would not know what they were letting themselves in for. He was particularly scathing about the role played by the members of the small subgroup of the Fowler inquiry that had dealt with pensions:

> Is the right hon. Gentleman aware that these are potentially damaging and retrogressive proposals? Is he aware that that is perhaps not surprising as they come from such a politically loaded and unrepresentative committee which comprised five people? Unprecedentedly, it comprised two Ministers, a Right-wing economist, the chairman of the Life Offices' Association and Mr. Mark Weinberg, the managing director of Hambro Life, who has a huge vested interest in the proposals to the extent that he is expected to become a millionaire as a result of them. We deplore the partisan bias in that committee which will make a killing for some people in the City and expose thousands of people to the pitfalls of a hard sell from insurance companies, which will be strongly against their long-term best interests.

To which Norman Fowler responded in the manner of someone swatting a fly: "Even by the standards of the hon. member for Oldham, West ... that was a ridiculously hysterical response."[3]

The government's Social Security Bill was long and complicated, and on the floor of the House members made almost nothing of the potential for pensions mis-selling that Michael Meacher had claimed the proposals would create. However, later, in Standing Committee B, the subject was raised more frequently. Meacher himself returned to the charge, insisting that people who were contemplating buying a personal pension should be given adequate information on which to make an informed choice and accusing the government of providing inaccurate information.[4] Another Labour MP, Margaret Beckett, claimed that many of those buying personal pensions were already being given misleading information and predicted that the situation would become even worse when, following the enactment of the government's proposals, competition among the increased number of pension providers seriously hotted up.[5] Yet another Labour MP, Frank Haynes, a retired miner, was convinced that large numbers of people, naturally ignorant of the complexities of long-term personal finance, were about to be fleeced by ill-informed or unscrupulous salesmen. He returned to the topic repeatedly. "There are a lot of low-paid workers in the country", he said at one point, "and, when they take out personal pensions, they must have protection."[6] He suspected that many of those who took out pensions would find themselves paying exorbitant administrative charges without knowing that they were. He added on another occasion:

> I am not even convinced about the protection aspect. Despite all that has been said, I am not at all satisfied ... The Minister talks of consumer power. Who is he kidding? Consumers are said to have power in all sorts of ways, but what happens? The boys at the top get themselves together and fix things. They fix certain financial levels, and the consumer has no control.[7]

The junior ministers in day-to-day charge of the bill, when not dismissive of such criticism, tended to be emollient, insisting that no serious consumer-protection issues arose in connection with pensions and that, insofar as they did arise, they were being addressed elsewhere.

The government was deeply committed to personal pensions – on philosophical as well as economic grounds – and it went to great lengths to promote them. On the one hand, SERPS was deliberately scaled back and made to seem less attractive, and doubts were also implanted in people's minds, possibly unintentionally, about SERPS' long-term viability. On the other hand, personal pensions were made to appear an astonishingly good buy. They had a "something for nothing" air about them. There were no longer any impediments to buying one. They held out – or were made to appear to hold out – bright prospects for the future. If you bought one, you immediately paid less in National Insurance contributions (assuming you were making such contributions). If you left SERPS and instead bought a personal pension before April 1993, you paid even less in National Insurance. And, whereas previously you could buy a personal pension only from an insurance company, now you could buy one from practically anybody.

Personal pensions did not sell themselves only on their own merits. They were widely and seductively advertised. The government alone spent £1.2 million on promoting the personal-pensions cause, and the numerous financial institutions that were now vigorously competing in the newly expanded personal-pensions market spent tens of millions of pounds more on advertising. There was a lot of money to be made, and almost every financial institution in the land fought hard to secure its share of the pickings. Almost all the press advertisements gave the impression, wrongly, that buying a personal pension was a risk-free investment and that people who bought such a pension would, without doubt, be better off than if they stayed with SERPS. General Accident was one of the few firms to warn potential purchasers in the main body of its press advertising that "the value of your investment may fall as well as rise".[8] Most companies alluded to that possibility in only the tiniest of print or, quite commonly, not at all. Three years after their launch, in 1991, sales of personal pensions were given an unexpected additional fillip when it transpired that the media tycoon Robert Maxwell had systematically defrauded his own company's pension scheme, leaving thousands of his existing employees fearful for the future and thousands of those who had already drawn their pension from that scheme all but destitute. Suddenly traditional old-fashioned occupational schemes no longer looked as safe as they once had. For an anxious individual, purchasing his or her own personal pension now seemed a very tempting proposition.

The government's efforts to wean people off SERPS and to a lesser extent off occupational pension schemes and to persuade them – either instead or in addition – to buy a pension of their own were, by any standard, a spectacular success. Before personal pensions began to be sold under the new dispensation, the government actuary guessed that roughly half a million people would contract out of SERPS in favour of making alternative arrangements, although he acknowledged that there was "no basis for making a firm estimate of the likely increase".[9] In the event, the number who contracted out was more than eight times higher than the actuary imagined: it was not roughly half a million but more than 4.3 million. At the same time, the number of employees in possession of personal pensions soared from roughly 1.2 million in 1988 to 5.7 million in 1994 – little short of a fivefold increase in only six years. The total number of personal pensions sold was even higher than that because not all the purchasers of pensions were also employees. One unexpected and undesired consequence of these events was their effect on the government's revenues. Both Nigel

Lawson as chancellor in the mid-1980s and his Treasury successors had been adamant that the effect of Norman Fowler's reforms should be to save the government money or, at the very least, be revenue-neutral. Instead, the proffered National Insurance rebates alone had cost the exchequer by 1993 some £9.7 billion. The government's own forecasts had been haywire. The Treasury was not best pleased.

The vastly increased numbers of people who availed themselves of personal pensions during this period did so for a variety of reasons. Some gave careful thought to their own and their family's long-term financial prospects and concluded that buying a personal pension was the right thing to do. Some were attracted by the idea of an immediate and sharp fall in the size of their National Insurance contributions. Some were impressed by the press and television advertising. Some undoubtedly bought a pension because that was what everybody else was doing. There appears to have been a community effect, with neighbours and workmates influencing each other. But, beyond question, a very large proportion of those who bought personal pensions had not the faintest idea what they were doing. They were misled. They were deluded. In hundreds of thousands of cases, their pension had quite simply been "mis-sold".

Mis-selling is, in essence, a simple idea. An individual buys something that he or she would not otherwise have bought because the seller, either deliberately or out of ignorance, fails to inform the buyer of information that would have enabled him or her to make a more informed choice among the available options. In the case of pensions, mis-selling could refer to one or more of a wide range of situations.

It could refer to deliberate strategies to sell products to people which the firm and/or salesman knew were not suitable for them. It could refer, separately or in addition, to aggressive sales tactics: buying the names and payroll details of miners who were being made redundant; using credit cards to slip the locks in nurses homes. Alternatively, or in addition, misselling could mean failure to give advice where advice was needed: giving a person details of a [personal pension] plan, stressing its benefits, but not making a final judgement on its benefits in comparison with an [occupational pension scheme]. Finally, misselling could mean ignorant and incompetent colling· selling a product which was not suitable, unaware of the need to make comparisons with any other type of pension.[10]

Whatever the details, the essential point in the case of personal pensions was that people who bought them were frequently placed in a position in which they might suffer a financial loss – possibly a very large one – without knowing that they were running such a risk.

Andrew Marr, one of the first journalists to expose the scale of the mis-selling, reported that some 6.5 million people bought pensions at the height of the boom:

> Many will have done all right. But an unknown number ... were wrong to do so. They were too poorly paid, or too old, or in too good schemes already, to make it worth their while. These were not the people ministers met at dinner parties. They were often recruited by friends or relatives whose brief and inglorious careers as commission-only pension salesmen lasted only as long as their address book. Salesmen bought up the internal directories of companies for large sums, to push their wares. Redundant miners were given jobs selling personal pensions to their redundant colleagues.[11]

By the end, some 58,000 miners, 32,000 nurses, 27,000 teachers and 23,000 steelworkers had deserted their own occupational schemes for personal pensions that in many cases, probably the great majority, were far less advantageous from their point of view.

Not all of the government blunders described in this book became public scandals. But this one did, though fingers were pointed more commonly at the mis-sellers of pensions than at the ministers who invented them. As early as March 1990, the life-insurance industry's internal regulatory body called for a halt to misleading advertising aimed at encouraging people to contract out of SERPS. In June 1992, two industry bodies instructed their members not to advise those in occupational pension schemes to take out personal pensions. In July of the same year, Peter Lilley, one of Norman Fowler's successors as the cabinet minister responsible for pensions (there had been two others in between), convened a meeting of ministers and civil servants at Chevening to consider what remedial action the government should take. Some months later, ministers, over the heads of insurance-industry leaders, ordered the Securities and Investment Board – an arm's-length government agency – to conduct a review of the industry's selling practices. That review, launched in the autumn of 1994, resulted in nearly a decade of work devoted to identifying individuals who had been mis-sold personal pensions and endeavouring to compensate them.

The quantity of malpractice uncovered was on a horrendous scale. It emerged that more than a million people, many of them old, poor and/or ill, had been adversely affected. Many of the early advertisements had been grossly misleading. Salesmen were encouraged to engage in the hardest of hard selling, with many of them needing little encouragement. They lied or failed to divulge relevant information about the size of their own commission fees and their firms' often exorbitant administrative charges. They frequently neglected to point out to customers that their splendid new pensions were no longer effectively guaranteed, as SERPS and most occupational pensions were, but instead depended on the value of investments that might, or might not, produce a good return. Many of them failed to enquire into their prospective customers' financial circumstances. Few appear to have bothered to advise their customers to compare carefully the advantages and disadvantages of buying a personal pension as compared with relying on other sorts of investment, including, of course, staying with their existing occupational pension scheme or SERPS. Salesmen were frequently ill-trained or not trained at all. Firms that were supposed to regulate themselves internally failed to do so. The government's own regulatory bodies failed to act. In short, the government had created a situation in which it was possible, indeed easy, for the purveyors of personal pensions to inflict misery on many thousands of innocent people – people who were innocent in both senses of the word. An article in the *Observer* in early 1994, one of dozens like it, focused on the widespread mis-selling of personal pensions and other financial instruments. The headline above it read: "Anyone can sell life insurance. All you need is a smile and a shoe-shine."[12] That was not far wrong.

Inevitably, the financial fallout was massive. The firms involved grudgingly agreed to compensate those who had been wantonly mis-sold personal pensions, coming under increasing pressure to do so as time went on, first from the Major government, then from the Blair government. In November 1997 the incoming Labour government outlined a package of sanctions available to be imposed on firms that were not complying with the government's edicts or were dragging their feet. The Financial Services Authority in 2002 announced that it had taken disciplinary action against no fewer than 345 separate firms, imposing fines on them totalling more than £9.5 million. It also announced that errant firms in the financial sector had so far, under great pressure, compensated victims of mis-selling to the tune of nearly £9 billion. But of course even those enormous figures took no account of the thousands of investors who, although mis-sold a pension and out of pocket as a result, had never got round to lodging a compensation claim (possibly because they were already dead). They also took no account of those who, although they were not mis-sold a pension in any strict sense, nevertheless suffered financial losses as a result of having taken out a personal pension instead of relying on their existing arrangements.

It has to be said that the three ministers who devised the Social Security Act 1986 and piloted the enabling legislation through parliament – Norman Fowler, Tony Newton and John Major – were neither liars nor crooks. They did not foresee and certainly did not will the widespread mis-selling of pensions that subsequently occurred. As we have seen, they were warned of the dangers but failed to heed the warnings. They probably failed partly because they believed that personal pensions were an unqualifiedly good thing, partly because their reform of retirement pensions formed only part of the much larger package of welfare reforms for which they were responsible, and partly because they attributed overwhelmingly partisan motives to those who issued the warnings. The ministers in question found Michael Meacher intensely irritating and the voluble Frank Haynes even more so.

But there was probably another factor that blindsided them. The design of pension arrangements was their problem; how pensions were actually sold was someone else's. All three ministers acknowledged that fact as the legislation progressed, but they seem not to have appreciated the full significance of what they were saying. They might have responded to their critics more positively if they had.

Ministers were aware that purchasers of personal pensions would need consumer protection, as they would in connection with any other transaction of the same type. The government's informal consultative document of 1984 referred briefly to the issue, and its more formal Green Paper of 1985 devoted two paragraphs to it, the first of which began with the sentence: "There is an undoubted need for safeguards when the funds at stake are to be the basis of people's retirement income."[13] The trio of ministers in charge of the Social Security Bill made similar noises on the floor of the House of Commons and again in Standing Committee B. But from the beginning they made it clear, without in any way emphasising the point, that the ultimate – and indeed proximate – responsibility for providing these safeguards lay elsewhere, not in their department but in the Department of Trade and Industry and in that department's Financial Services Bill, which happened, by coincidence, to be passing through parliament at the same time. The formal Green Paper cited in a footnote the government's forthcoming proposals for financial-services regulation, and Fowler and his colleagues in the House of Commons referred on several occasions to the Trade and Industry Department's Financial Services Bill. In the course of a speech during the second-reading debate in the House on the Social Security Bill, Fowler focused on the desirability of people's having a choice when they made financial provision for their retirement, but he added quickly: "Hand in hand with choice must go effective investor protection. The Bill, taken with the Financial Services Bill currently before the House, will enable us to achieve a proper measure of investor protection."[14] On a later occasion John Major similarly assured fellow members of Standing Committee B that the Financial Services Bill would address their concerns, which he certainly shared, about "the unscrupulous overselling of personal pensions".[15]

Although the ministers undoubtedly gave those assurances in good faith, they were completely worthless, as the events over the next few years demonstrated. The promised safeguards scarcely existed on paper and did not exist at all in practice. The Social Security Act and the Financial Services Act came into force on the same day; but the Financial Services Act, while seeking to deal in general terms with issues of honesty and openness in the selling of financial products, made no specific mention of – and certainly made no special provisions for – the selling of personal pensions, even though the selling of pensions raised all manner of issues that the selling of other products did not, most notably the fact that personal pensions were likely to be sold to thousands of people with no previous experience of buying financial products of any kind. As a result, "one of the principal features of the mis-selling episode was regulatory blindness, on the part of firms and regulators: no-one took a strategic look at what regulation required in any one instance. No-one looked at pensions as posing particular problems because no-one knew or thought to look."[16] The government devolved responsibility for regulation to regulators. The regulators in turn devolved it to the firms that were selling pensions. The firms in turn devolved it to "compliance officers", who were meant to ensure that the firm's salesmen gave their prospective clients honest and disinterested advice, including advice about the various options open to them. But, partly because personal pensions were so new and partly because almost everyone involved was equally new to the new issues they created, every link in the chain was weak; and, of course, the firms that stood to make fortunes out of selling personal pensions had no interest in strengthening any of the links, especially as from 1988 onwards competition among the hundreds of firms now looking for business in the pensions market was intense. Firms' compliance officers were put in an impossible position, caught between, on the one hand, their duty to ensure compliance with the rules that had been laid down and, on the other, the intense pressures put upon them not to discourage sales. In some firms, the compliance department was known as the "business prevention unit". In the words of one sales director, "It's sales or compliance, you have to choose."[17] Most firms naturally chose sales.

But of course all this was a world away from what the planners and ministers in the then Department of Health and Social Security (DHSS) had in mind. They knew little or nothing of such grubby matters, and in any case assumed that – and were given every assurance that – if there were problems, the Department of Trade and Industry in its wisdom would take care of them, indeed was already taking care of them. The DHSS ministers had neither the time nor any real incentive to enquire further into these matters, let alone to organise distracting and time-consuming meetings at which they could be gone into in detail. It is far from clear that, even if such meetings had been held, the social security ministers would have known what lines of enquiry to pursue. Financial-services regulation was not part of their domain and outside their area of expertise. Norman Fowler, the secretary of state, also happened to be a relatively lowly member of the cabinet, a man anxious – like Kenneth Baker and William Waldegrave before him – to make his mark with the prime minister. He was not in a mood to pick fights. As a result, neither of the two departments took responsibility. The two of them in combination certainly did not.

In the parliamentary debates on the Social Security Bill, Michael Meacher, Margaret Beckett and Frank Haynes did their best to alert ministers to the dangers of mis-selling; but their views were taken on board, if at all, only by the three DHSS ministers centrally involved, and were probably noticed by almost no one outside the House of Commons and Standing Committee B. No relevant changes were made to the Social Security Bill. In the case of the Financial Services Bill, no mention at all was made in the Commons of the possibility of pensions mis-selling, and the subject was mentioned only once in the House of Lords, when a Labour peer, Baroness Turner of Camden, who happened to be a pensions expert, referred briefly to the fact that it was vital that people buying personal pensions should be afforded adequate protection.[18] In retrospect, it seems strange that so few MPs and peers took an interest in how personal pensions would be sold; but pensions of the kind envisaged by the government were new, they were not yet on the market and both the Social Security Bill and the Financial Services Bill, which were before parliament simultaneously, were tremendously complicated and dealt with matters of more immediate concern to members. For whatever reason, MPs were almost entirely bystanders during the formative stage of the new policy, though the mis-selling controversy was inevitably raised frequently in the Commons during the 1990s – long after it was too late.

This chapter has focused on a specific government blunder: the Thatcher government's collective failure to foresee and prevent the widespread and devastating mis-selling of personal pensions that occurred during the late 1980s and early 1990s, some of it while it was still in office, some of it years later. But of course it could be argued, and may well be the case, that, even if mis-selling on an enormous scale had not taken place, the drive for personal pensions for all would still have been a mistake, given the extent to which it rendered millions of people of all ages subject to the vagaries of volatile and unpredictable financial markets. But that possibility, however important, raises issues wider than the ones we are dealing with here.

6

Support for children – or taxpayers?

etween 1970 and the early 1990s, the proportion of children born
to unmarried mothers in the UK trebled from roughly 10 per cent
to roughly 30 per cent, and everyone who knew anything at all
about such matters expected the trend to continue upwards during the
1990s. Some unmarried mothers with children were in stable partnerships, but a majority were not; and even some of the mothers in stable
partnerships were no longer partnered by their children's father. For the
British state, these developments had huge financial implications. As the
number of unmarried mothers rose, the proportion of them receiving
maintenance payments from their children's father – or, in many cases,
fathers – fell sharply from roughly one in two at the end of the 1970s to
fewer than one in four at the end of the 1980s.

Not surprisingly, a large proportion of the mothers who received no
financial support from their children's father or fathers found themselves
dependent on the state; and the state, for its part, found itself paying out
larger and larger sums to single mothers in the form of benefits. The state
was thus increasingly paying, in effect, for child maintenance, with absent
fathers (fathers constituted the overwhelming majority of absent parents)
offloading what might reasonably have been expected to be their financial
obligations onto others, namely taxpayers. The number of individual lone
parents claiming benefits – mainly income support and family credits –
rose from 320,000 when Margaret Thatcher became prime minister in

1979 to more than a million in the early 1990s. The cost of social-security payments to lone parents rocketed correspondingly from £2.4 billion in 1979 to nearly three times that amount, £6.6 billion, in 1992.

One of the first people to draw attention to what was happening was a Labour MP, Frank Field, who had made himself an expert on child poverty. He even lobbied Thatcher on social-security issues while she remained in office. He told anyone who would listen that in his Birkenhead constituency on Merseyside responsible fatherhood had become an "optional extra". On some of the estates more than half the households were headed by a single parent. He complained that governments of both parties had made it easier and easier for fathers to move on to second and third families, leaving the state to pick up the tab. "Word had got out", he said, "that you could ditch your family and it would still receive benefits." Partly as a result of Field's efforts, and partly because the ever larger number of lone parents claiming benefits increasingly spoke for itself, the issue rose rapidly up the political agenda. Politicians of all parties agreed that the situation was out of control and that something had to be done.

At the time, responsibility for ensuring – or, rather, trying to ensure – that absent fathers made regular payments towards their children's main-tenance rested with the courts, with the various agencies that sought to mediate between separated parents and with a small Liable Relatives Unit in the Department of Social Security (DSS). To ministers and other onlook-ers, it seemed obvious that the courts, in particular, were no longer up to the job. Their procedures were too slow, different courts awarded wildly different amounts in similar-seeming cases, courts in affluent areas seemed too ready to accommodate affluent fathers and, in any case, determined fathers found it remarkably easy to evade court orders. The courts were seriously overloaded, absent fathers played the system and the interests of lone mothers were persistently neglected.

Ministers and officials in the DSS, with Number 10's full support, set about addressing the issue. They sought to put in place new arrange-ments that would achieve social and moral as well as financial objectives. The department's social aims were to lift more single mothers and their children out of poverty, to reduce their dependence on state benefits and to make it possible for more single mothers to improve their situation by going out to work. Its moral aims were to force absent fathers to honour their responsibilities towards their children and their former partners. Its financial aims were to reduce drastically the cost of child maintenance to the state and to transfer material responsibility for the welfare of children from the state to the parents of children, including absent parents.

The department published a White Paper on the issue, *Children Come First* (the title was significant), in October 1990. Introducing the paper in the House of Commons, Tony Newton, the secretary of state, emphasised its welfare objectives:

> Governments cannot, of course, ensure that all children always live with their parents, but they can and should seek to ensure that, whatever the underlying circumstances, the welfare of the children is the prime consideration. An effective system for securing their financial maintenance is an important element in achieving that objective.[1]

In his speech Newton indicated clearly that, so far as he was concerned, saving the taxpayer money was an important consideration but nevertheless a secondary one. He emphasised that it was in the interests of neither lone parents nor their children that some two-thirds of them were now wholly or partly dependent on income support. He noted only in passing that of course that scale of dependency placed "a large burden on those who pay tax, many of whom are themselves bringing up children on perhaps quite modest incomes".[2]

The White Paper was followed four months later by the publication of a government bill. The bill contained three proposals for the reform of the whole child-maintenance system (or, rather, the lack of a system). The first proposal was for a clear formula for assessing how much money absent parents, usually absent fathers, should contribute by way of maintenance. The second was to replace in their entirety the existing court-based arrangements by creating a new purpose-built Child Support Agency (CSA), charged with identifying absent parents, assessing the amount of their financial obligation and then collecting, monitoring and enforcing payment of that obligation. The third was for a set of changes to the existing welfare-benefit rules that would give single parents an incentive to cease to rely on income support and to move into paid employment, thereby achieving greater independence. Years afterwards, "We meant to do good" was one DSS official's verdict on the government's original proposals.

From the outset, the ideas contained in the White Paper enjoyed an unusually wide range of political support. Conservative activists and right-wing newspapers approved of what the government had in mind because they deplored, and were anxious to reverse, the decline of the traditional family and the rapid growth in the numbers of teenage mothers and the men they dubbed "feckless fathers". Labour politicians were sympathetic because the proposals seemed aimed at improving the lot of some of the poorest and most vulnerable of their constituents. Not least, the government's approach had the support of feminists, who were keen to make absent fathers pay what they owed in moral as well as financial terms. Almost no one took exception to the broad thrust of the proposals. Most of those who were aware of their existence applauded them.

"Doing good" was definitely what Newton and the Department of Social Security had in mind. It was not, however, what the Treasury had in mind. It had other ideas. Britain in the early 1990s was in recession, and the government's budget deficit was enormous by the standards of that time. Treasury ministers and officials therefore wanted to cut public expenditure where they could, and they wanted to cut it as quickly as they could; and Treasury officials leapt on absent partners of single mothers on benefits as being a potentially substantial source of savings. In the Treasury's view, if money could be extracted from absent fathers for mothers and children who had previously relied on benefits, the mothers' and children's benefits could be reduced by the same amount. After all, reasoned the Treasury, the mothers and children would be no worse off than before, but it would now be absent fathers rather than taxpayers who were supporting them.

With the Treasury and the DSS in fundamental disagreement, the two departments fought a series of Whitehall battles, all of which – as usual – the Treasury won. Gradually over time, and largely unbeknownst to outside observers, the whole aim of the exercise was changed radically. The proposed legislation ceased to be welfare legislation and became, in essence, fiscal legislation. Even before the 1990 White Paper was published, the Treasury won a crucial victory, though ministers played down its significance at the time. The DSS favoured a modest "disregard", so that lone mothers – and, by implication, their children – could keep at least some of the money collected from absent fathers instead of having all of it docked from their benefits. But the Treasury won that battle decisively and laid hands on the whole lot.

And the Treasury went on winning battles, including during the few months between the publication of the White Paper and the publication of the Child Support Bill. Contrary to the DSS's advice, the scope of the legislation was expanded so that the new Child Support Agency would be responsible for making claims on behalf of all lone parents – not just those on benefits – and for all the child-maintenance payments that they were owed. Moreover, the new arrangements would apply to any main-tenance payments that were in arrears, not just to future payments. On top of all that, the new arrangements would ignore completely all the private arrangements that had already been made, often perfectly amicably and satisfactorily, between parents who had separated. All separated couples with children, irrespective of their circumstances, were to be caught in the Treasury's fiscal net. If the new system worked, taxpayers would be better off. Lone parents would not.

The Treasury was also, as we have seen, in a hurry. The Child Support Bill was published in February 1991, only two months after the closing date for responses to the White Paper, and by that July it was already on the statute book. Unusually for a major piece of social legislation, the bill was introduced first in the House of Lords as "outline legislation" on the grounds that there were no disagreements among the parties about its general principles. It was left to MPs in the House of Commons to approve the detailed regulations needed to give practical effect to the bill. These too were rushed through at breakneck speed. Key elements of the govern-ment's proposals, including those relating to the CSA, were contained, not in the bill itself but in ninety-four of the detailed regulations, which were never debated. When the bill returned to the House of Lords, the government gave their lordships one day's notice and one day in which to debate 135 amendments and twelve new clauses, comprising twenty-one pages of printed text. Ministers inevitably got their way – and in any case most of the changes were largely technical.

At only one juncture did either House debate a serious matter of sub-stance. Leading for Labour as he had in connection with the introduction of personal pensions, Michael Meacher moved an amendment during the bill's second reading in the Commons opposing the bill primarily on the grounds that, in the absence of any kind of disregard, single parents on income support would be left no better off than they had been before. But the government was in no mood to listen, and the amendment was lost by 221 votes to 165. Meacher had already quipped when the White Paper had first been published that, because there was to be no disregard, the White Paper should have been called *The Treasury Comes First* instead of *Children Come First.*

Although it was another twenty-one months before the CSA was formally launched, the Treasury gave the Department of Social Security less than a year in which to appoint its chief executive and senior managers, recruit and train 5000 staff, design and install the complex IT system that would be required and to draw up its own detailed rules and regulations. At the same time it also set the fledgling agency the hugely ambitious task of collecting £530 million in maintenance payments during its first year. When the agency began operations in April 1993, its first chief executive, Ros Hepplewhite, was forthright in emphasising its importance:

> This is not an agency which is dealing with a small and irresponsible element of society: this is a major social change. Paying maintenance will become like paying income tax. It will be a feature of life for very many people, particularly given the social trend of serial relationships.[3]

It was clear right from the beginning that the number of people caught up in the new system and the amount of money involved would both be enormous. The agency itself expected to deal with a million cases during its first year and about 2.5 million as soon as it reached a steady state, at which point some five million individual parents would probably be affected. On the day of the agency's launch, Peter Lilley, Tony Newton's successor as secretary of state for social security, announced that within a year of the agency's launch he expected 800,000 single parents, double the existing number, to be receiving maintenance payments and that he expected to be making savings of some £600 million for the taxpayer.[4]

In truth, both Hepplewhite and Lilley were just spitting in the wind. The new arrangements failed spectacularly to work. Right from the beginning the CSA failed comprehensively to achieve any of its objectives. The new arrangements were supposed to make the whole system better – very much better. In practice, they made it appreciably worse. Faults inherent in the policy itself turned out to be inextricably intertwined with faults in the implementation of the policy. They formed a kind of dysfunctional double helix. Administrators who were geniuses could not possibly have made the new policy work, and the great majority of the administrators who vainly tried to make it work were anything but geniuses.

The administration, especially at the very beginning, was dreadful. The Child Support Agency soon became known as the Complete Shambles Agency. To almost all who came into contact with it – whether claimant mothers, liable fathers, welfare charity volunteers, solicitors or MPs – the CSA appeared to be, because it was, hopelessly and frustratingly incompetent. Agency staff were too few, many were undertrained or badly trained, and, to make matters worse, the newly installed IT system predictably failed to cope. There were huge delays, backlogs mounted up and about half of the initial assessments made turned out to be inaccurate. One man's story can stand for tens of thousands:

I have had dealings with the Child Support Agency (over the past year) and it has been nothing but a catalogue of errors and incompetence. Recently I have been getting threats of Deduction From Earnings Orders being served on my employers because the CSA say I am in arrears. I have always paid their demands on time and in full and I have receipts to prove that I have paid on time and in full. I have also had telephone conversations with the CSA when they have verbally agreed that no arrears exist and that no further action would be taken, only to receive another Deduction From Earnings Order a few weeks later. I have also found out that because the CSA say I am in arrears, which I am not, they have not been sending the money I have paid them for the maintenance of my son to his mother. The result is that she has had to go to the DSS and ask for emergency help.[5]

In one instance, the agency spent two years vigorously chasing a gay man who was childless, all the while insisting that he had a non-existent daughter whose name was Katie.[6]

So dreadful was the agency's reputation that the parliamentary ombudsman prepared and published a special report after only a single year. He found that the CSA's assessments were frequently based on grossly inadequate information, that requests for maintenance were often sent to the wrong individual (as in the case of the gay "father"), that wrongly addressed requests for payment, not surprisingly, inflicted strain on marriages, that maintenance payments were paid into the wrong account and could not be retrieved, that letters went unanswered for months, that breaches of confidentiality were common, that it was impossible for individuals to find out anything about the progress of their case and that CSA staff frequently misinformed both absent fathers and lone mothers about the consequences that would follow if they failed to co-operate. The ombudsman recommended that no organisation like the CSA should ever again be set up without first being piloted.[7]

Needless to say, the persistent maladministration of the new policy revealed a myriad defects in the policy itself. Many of the accusations levelled at the agency should in fairness have been levelled at whomever had devised the policy. Thousands of irate fathers were angry with the CSA as an organisation and simultaneously with the policy that the CSA was desperately trying to administer, without recognising the difference between the one and the other. Why should they? Identifying the source of the trouble would have done them no good. It was enough to know that they and/or their former partners were having a bad time.

In particular, many thousands of absent fathers were furious about the maintenance orders inflicted on them. Officials in the agency frequently calculated the assessment formula either inaccurately or on the basis of the wrong information; and, even when the assessments were legally correct, they struck thousands of absent fathers as manifestly unjust and unreasonable. The formula took no account of the father's ability to pay or of any previous agreements between former partners. The agency was not even allowed to take into account "clean-break" settlements that had been agreed upon many years before and had worked to the satisfaction of both sides ever since. So far as the law and the agency were concerned, the fact

86

that an absent father might also have financial obligations towards a new partner and her children (who might also be his) was simply irrelevant. If an absent father's income had fallen sharply, it often took the agency months, even years, to revise downwards the amount of money he owed in maintenance. Moreover, because the assessment formula had, almost certainly at the Treasury's insistence, been written into the statute itself, the agency's case officers lacked any authority to vary it. They had virtually no flexibility or discretion. And at the same time there was no formal way of appealing their decisions. Unsurprisingly, huge numbers of absent fathers simply refused to co-operate with any of this, either because they had no sense of moral responsibility towards their children, or because they were financially strapped, or because the whole thing was simply far too much hassle.

Thousands of single mothers were equally unhappy, though mostly for different reasons. Not only was the agency notoriously slow to process their claims, but case officers frequently made mistakes and often failed, despite the agency's statutory responsibilities, to enforce the payment of maintenance even after awards had been made. In any case, single mothers on benefits lacked any incentive to lodge claims with the agency because, even if their claim was accepted, they did not stand to gain anything. In the absence of any disregard, they knew their benefits would be docked, and all the money collected from the absent father(s) would go straight to the Treasury. Worse than that, many single mothers were fearful of harassment and even violence if their children's father(s) objected, as many of them did, to being reported to the agency. And, of course, a substantial proportion of them did not know where those fathers now were or, in some cases, even who they were. In addition, separated parents still in touch with one another sometimes colluded to circumvent the rules. The absent father would slip the mother cash to supplement her state benefits so long as she did not report him to the agency. If the mother in question was caught, her benefits would be cut, leaving her in an even more distressed state.

When it finally came, the political fallout from the child-maintenance debacle, although not on the same scale as with the poll tax, was massive all the same. Tens of thousands of people were affected by the new legislation, and, because the new law swept into the orbit of the social-security system every absent father in the land, regardless of his income, social status or prior personal arrangements, the most aggrieved individuals included thousands of men who were well off, well educated and capable of being extremely vocal. A fair proportion of them were also actual or potential Conservative voters. Members of parliament, as well as agency personnel, began to be inundated with phone calls and letters. Some four thousand dissatisfied CSA customers wrote to their MPs during the first year alone, and their MPs then passed on their complaints to the CSA, which received letters from MPs at the rate of nearly four hundred a week. Newspapers and broadcasters rejoiced in reporting the hardest of the hard cases, of which there were many. Some of the protests turned ugly. Angry demonstrations took place outside several of the CSA's regional offices, and members of the agency's staff found themselves on the receiving end of abusive phone calls and even hate mail. Ros Hepplewhite's successor as the agency's chief executive, Ann Chant, had to be moved to a safe house in London and assigned a driver for her personal protection. Staff resigned from the agency in droves.

Ministers and officials in the DSS – a department accustomed to giving people money as benefits rather than taking money away from them – seem to have assumed at the beginning that the CSA's problems were largely administrative in character. Fix the administration and all – well, almost all – would be well. In December 1993, after the agency had been operating for only eight months, it was agreed that 150,000 cases would be reopened and reassessed and absent parents would also be given longer to catch up with payments in arrears. During 1994 the new chief executive, Chant, was allowed to hire 700 new staff, and within a few months she and her colleagues had drastically reduced the case backlog. They did so by the simple expedient of "shelving" – in practice, forgetting about – 350,000 cases where lone mothers had been on income support since the agency had opened but where the agency had been unable to trace and therefore to assess the missing father. Some Conservative MPs were mollified by having it explained to them that the aim of the exercise really was to save taxpayers money and ease the financial burden on the state rather than to improve the lot of lone parents.

But these hard-won improvements in the administration of the scheme were far from being enough. The agency did not actually collapse, but it remained pitifully inefficient and continued to be both dreaded and despised by those who had the misfortune to come into contact with it. It was probably the most hated organ of the British state. The agency's first annual report acknowledged that child maintenance had been arranged for fewer than a third of all eligible cases compared with a target of 60 per cent. It also admitted that at least two-fifths of all assessments, and possibly as many as three-quarters, were incorrect.[8] Moreover, although the agency had distributed £312 million in maintenance payments, only £15 million of this total (less than 5 per cent) represented new money; all the rest resulted from prior agreements made between parents and from family-credit payments that would have been made anyway.[9] In reality, the amount of new money collected from absent fathers living on benefits was even smaller, a paltry £6 million.[10] These tiny amounts had, of course, to be set against the running costs of the agency, which by the end of the second year of its operations amounted to £137 million (as against an original estimate of £35 million).[11] In terms of raising revenue and improving the health of the public finances, the Treasury had shot itself in both feet – except that the Department of Social Security was left holding the gun.

After the better part – or, rather, the worse part – of two calamitous years, the DSS began to worry less about administration and more about the substance of the original policy. It promoted a new piece of legislation, which became the Child Support Act 1995 (as distinct from the Child Support Act 1991). The new Act abandoned the previous effort to collect maintenance payments retrospectively, recognised ability to pay as a factor in calculating assessments, introduced a range of permissible "departures" from the existing formula for calculating payments and instituted, not before time, a proper appeals procedure. From now on, the CSA would be allowed to take into account clean-break settlements between separated parents and the financial situation of fathers in second families with children. Either parent would henceforth be allowed to challenge an assessment on the grounds that the other parent's declared income was inconsistent with his or her (usually his) observable lifestyle. Whatever the outcome of the new assessment, no absent parent would be expected to make payments to the CSA in excess of 30 per cent of his or her net income. The new Act also embodied a small, scarcely visible departure from the Treasury's insistence that there be no disregard, that all the money collected by the CSA should be passed on to the Treasury pound-for-pound. In future, single mothers on benefits would for the first time be entitled to treat a small part of their maintenance money as a credit that would be paid to them if and when they returned to work.

There was only one problem with this new dispensation. It did address some of the manifest injustices in the old system and to some extent it succeeded – but only at the cost of rendering an administrative process that was already horrendously complicated still more complicated. In practice, allegedly better policy resulted in no better and often worse administration. The new child-maintenance assessment formula was laid out across four pages of closely typed algebra and could require up to 144 separate computations. If either parent requested a review, the initial maintenance assessment could be recalculated as often as four times a year. Needless to say, the performance of the agency, whose staff had long since become thoroughly demoralised, scarcely improved during the following years and in some ways deteriorated further. The proportion of single mothers refusing to co-operate with the agency increased steadily, reaching 70 per cent by 1998. Many of them cited fear of violence from their ex-partner as the reason because threats of violence constituted "good cause" for not having their benefits cut; but many more probably failed to engage with the agency simply because of the baffling complexity of the method of assessment – and because the great majority of them would still be no better off financially, at least in the short term.

The National Audit Office (NAO) in a scathing report in 1998 revealed that CSA officials spent 90 per cent of their time on calculating maintenance assessments and only 10 per cent on collecting the actual money. According to the NAO, the CSA after operating for five years was still taking more than six months to process close to half of all its cases. Two in five of its assessments were wrong. A backlog of 570,000 cases was still outstanding, and more than half of them had been for more than a year. Not least, £1 billion was still owed to the agency in the form of arrears, of which £750 million was reckoned to be unrecoverable. Fewer than one in seven absent fathers was regularly paying the maintenance money he owed in full, and two million children of separated parents were not receiving any maintenance money at all.[12] Despite the original White Paper, children were manifestly not coming first. Many thousands of them still seemed to be coming last. Blunder was heaped upon blunder.

But more blunders were still to come. Conservative MPs were not the only ones dismayed by the Child Support Agency's performance. Labour MPs were equally aghast. One of them, Chris Mullin, wrote in his diary:

> The surgery at Ryhope in the evening lasted three hours. Customers included a man whose wife kicked him out when she opened a letter from the Child Support Agency and learned that he was supporting a child he had fathered with another woman long before he was married. He is now living with his mother and supporting two families. Another life wrecked by the CSA.[13]

Following Labour's victory at the 1997 general election, many Labour backbenchers lobbied for the outright abolition of the CSA and the introduction of an entirely new system of child maintenance. Ministers and officials at the Department of Social Security, soon to be rechristened the Department for Work and Pensions, went away and thought about it but decided it would be both expensive and futile to start all over again. The existing scheme would be radically reformed, not done away with altogether. The emphasis would still be on making absent fathers pay.

The Labour government published a White Paper entitled *Children's Rights and Parents' Responsibilities* in 1999, and parliament during the following year passed the Child Support, Pensions and Social Security Act 2000 (the third major piece of legislation in a decade on exactly the same issue). The new legislation retained the Child Support Agency but introduced a simpler method of assessing the size of maintenance awards. These would now be based on a fixed percentage of the absent parent's net income, the percentage to vary depending on the number of dependent children involved. Awards would be reduced on the same basis if the absent parent was on a low income or was financially responsible for children in a new family. Amazingly, after the passage of ten years, there would now be a modest disregard. Lone mothers on benefits could now keep for themselves £10 a week of any maintenance money that the CSA collected.

The future looked bright. Ministers claimed that under the new regime 70 per cent of absent fathers would now be paying less than they had before and that nevertheless, because of the new disregard, 75 per cent of single mothers would be better off. Of course, there would have to be a transition period. As far as new cases were concerned, the new regime would not come into effect until late in 2001, and existing cases requiring reassessment would have to wait even longer to be dealt with. Nevertheless, the Department for Work and Pensions, as it now was, insisted that the reformed system would improve administrative efficiency, speed up processing times, increase accuracy and enable case officers to work longer and harder at securing compliance. "These reforms", the department proudly declared, "will put children at the centre of the system, making sure they get more money."[14]

Unfortunately, the reformed system fulfilled none of these promises. It performed disastrously badly from its inception and never recovered. Horror stories continued to appear in the media on much the same scale as before. In ever-growing numbers, applications for maintenance awards continued to go unprocessed or to be wrongly assessed. Awards, even when eventually made, were still allowed to go unenforced. Two more CSA chief executives came and went. A report from the House of Commons Work and Pensions Select Committee was damning:

> Whether measured by official targets or any other criteria the CSA has failed; levels of complaint continue to increase, unrecoverable debts rise, the level of staff turnover is going up, the management information to monitor progress is not available and it is clear that at present the two sectors of the public it is intended to serve treat it either with despair or contempt.[15]

Many of the problems arose from the need to install a new IT infrastructure to cope with the changes brought in by the 2000 Act. The CSA's old system had always struggled, and it could not begin to cope with the radically altered post-2000 arrangements. The agency accordingly commissioned an entirely new IT system, which would begin by handling new cases as they came in and would then, after a short settling-in period, start taking aboard the many cases that remained on the old system. But disaster followed disaster. The new system became operational only in March 2003, eighteen months behind schedule. Even then, it proved incapable of handling the volume of new cases. As late as the early months of 2006, one in four of the applications received since March 2003 were still waiting to be processed and the accumulated backlog of new cases had risen to more than a third of a million. Assessment errors were still legion. By this time, the CSA was clear that there was no way in which the thousands of old cases could possibly be transferred onto the new system, from which it followed that it would have to operate simultaneously both of the two existing inadequate systems. Five years after the passage of the 2000 Act, more than 900,000 old cases – almost two-thirds of those on the agency's books – had still not been reviewed, and 247,000 single parents whose cases had been reviewed had received either no money or only a fraction of what they were owed.

Under the circumstances, it was scarcely surprising that the agency's name continued well into the new millennium to be a byword for incompetence, inefficiency and, at least as much as in the past, gross and inexcusable injustice. It remained a widely reviled organisation. It also continued to be a wildly expensive operation to run. The failed post-2000 IT system cost upwards of half a billion pounds, and the National Audit Office calculated that, whereas in 2006 it had cost Her Majesty's Revenue and Customs 1.4p to collect each £1 of income tax, the equivalent figure for the Child Support Agency was 70p. Unsurprisingly, the NAO refused to sign off the agency's accounts in 2006 for the twelfth year in a row. The Treasury's hopes that the CSA would be a nice little money-spinner had long since been dashed, though it is doubtful whether there was anyone still in the Treasury who remembered that, way back in 1991, revenue-raising had been one of the main aims, if not the main aim, of the whole exercise.

By now the end was nigh. Under pressure from Labour backbenchers, the opposition parties and probably some of his own constituents, Tony Blair towards the end of 2005 was said to be "at his wit's end" about the CSA and announced publicly that the agency was "not properly suited" to its task.[16] A few months later he asked Sir David Henshaw, a former chief executive of Liverpool City Council and an adviser to his own Delivery Unit, to have a go at redesigning the whole child-support system. He was to report within six months. He did, and his report contained a damning critique of almost everything that had happened since 1991. Policymakers in successive governments had given the CSA "an impossible task", and as a result the agency had failed children, parents and taxpayers alike.[17] Henshaw recommended the adoption of an entirely new approach, in

which the government would step back from the regulation of child maintenance and, as far as possible, encourage separating parents to reach their
own agreements. No single agency should any longer be responsible for
superintending all separated parents' child-maintenance arrangements,
and lone parents claiming benefits should be allowed to keep their maintenance money, subject to safeguards. The Child Support Agency should
be wound up and replaced by a new organisation, responsible for child
welfare, for enforcing parental responsibilities and for chasing down
outstanding maintenance debts. The Blair government accepted all of
Henshaw's recommendations and, among other things, announced its
intention to abolish the CSA. It created a new agency, an arm's-length non-
departmental body to be called the Child Maintenance and Enforcement
Commission. That body still exists.

Members of all parties applauded the creation of the Child Support
Agency. Members of all parties condemned, over many years, the way
in which it operated. Members of all parties welcomed its demise. No
politician of any party ever paid any political price for having initiated or
perpetuated an exceedingly harmful and very expensive policy blunder.
Nor, so far as we can tell, did any senior civil servant (apart from the unfortunate heads of the CSA). The episode raised a whole host of questions
that will be addressed in Parts III and IV of this book.

7

Britain exits the ERM

I n the autumn of 1990, Margaret Thatcher's government decided to take Britain into the Exchange Rate Mechanism (ERM) of the European Community. In doing so, it took a decision that turned out to have profoundly negative consequences – in the short term for the British economy, in the longer term for the Conservative party. The decision did not affect Thatcher personally only because, when it came to be regretted two years later, she had been forced out and John Major sat in her office. In any case, it was known that she had always opposed joining the ERM and had finally agreed to the move only under extreme pressure from the Foreign Office and the Treasury. In her memoirs, Thatcher angrily dismissed Britain's entry into the ERM as a "folly [that] cost us dear".[1]

The aims of the 1990 exercise were partly political, partly economic. The Foreign Office was anxious to see Britain maintain its influence within the European Community in order to maintain its standing in the wider world. The economic aims were the Treasury's. The Treasury believed that, by providing exchange-rate stability, joining the ERM would deter the world's financial markets from launching specula-tive attacks against the pound. It also believed that being part of the ERM would help reduce Britain's high rate of inflation by forcing the Bank of England to align interest rates in Britain with those set by the notoriously tough-minded German Bundesbank. In the autumn of 1990, all three main political parties applauded the government's decision to join, as did the bulk of the business community and most of the country's trade unions. Only those adamantly hostile to any kind of further European integration were opposed. The consensus on the issue was nearly total.

In fact, however, the government in 1990 took two decisions, not just one: to join the ERM, but also to join with sterling pegged at a rate of £1 to German Deutschmark 2.95 rather than at a more modest rate. In Whitehall, strangely little thought appears to have been given to the appropriateness of that ambitious rate. Thanks to a recent increase in the value of sterling resulting from rumours that Britain was about to enter the ERM, the pound was currently trading at about that rate, and ministers and officials were clearly afraid that setting any lower rate – in other words, deliberately devaluing the pound by however modest an amount – would lead to higher import prices and therefore to higher inflation at a time when one of the main purposes of entering the ERM was precisely to bear down on inflation. They were evidently more worried about inflation than about the danger of recession even though, by the summer of 1990, a serious recession was already in the offing. Those British officials who harboured doubts about DM2.95, along with Thatcher herself, could console themselves with the thought that, if the rate proved too high, it could be adjusted downwards at a later date. That happy thought was to prove illusory.

It could be argued that hitting upon DM2.95 rather than a lower rate amounted to a judgement call more than a blunder and that, as in the case of any judgement call, there was always a risk that it would turn out to be the wrong one. But in this case the ratio of call to judgement seems to have been high. Bankers and officials in Germany and a few British officials were not alone in doubting the wisdom of DM2.95. Within days of the government's announcement of that rate, the economic commentator William Keegan condemned it in the *Observer*:

> Paradoxically, we needed a devaluation in order to give us a sporting chance of adapting within the ERM disciplines and avoiding devaluation in the future. I cannot for one moment believe that the current exchange rate will hold for more than two years and advise the Labour party and Thatcher's potential successors to be wary of making commitments that they will be unlikely to be able to honour.[2]

Keegan's doubts proved well founded.

Less than two years later, on 16 September 1992, a day soon known as Black Wednesday, Britain was forced out of the ERM. For the ministers caught up in what occurred on that day "the overwhelming emotion was of disbelieving impotence. This was a convulsive experience – the most devastating of their political careers." One of those involved said afterwards that he had been overwhelmed by a sense of failure – the greatest sense of defeat he had ever experienced.[3] John Major's Conservative government struggled on for another five years, but from the evening of Black Wednesday its fate was sealed.

Britain had joined the ERM with the pound pegged at DM2.95 but within a fairly wide adjustable band set by agreement with the other ERM countries at 6 per cent either way. At first all went well, indeed better than many expected. After a period of a few months, when it seemed that UK interest rates would have to remain high in order to prevent sterling falling towards the bottom of its permitted band, the currency – in the words of a later Treasury analysis – "moved into a virtuous circle: cuts in interest rates made ERM membership seem more successful, and the easing of market worries about pressure on the government to devalue created scope for more cuts in interest rates".[4] It was fortuitous that the Deutschmark weakened temporarily against the dollar, easing pressure on sterling. It was also fortuitous that by the late summer of 1991 the country's economy seemed to be pulling out of a recession that had dogged it since towards the end of the previous decade. Investors were no longer tempted – or were at least no longer as tempted as they had been – to move funds out of sterling into Deutschmarks. The Conservatives' victory in the April 1992 general election also had the effect of reassuring the markets that sterling would remain within its ERM bands and that the incumbent government would continue to be staunch in sterling's defence. For the time being, the markets believed that combating domestic inflation was the British government's top priority and that the government regarded ERM membership at about the existing exchange rate as being the best single means of achieving that end.

Already, however, some British ministers and officials were worried that, as had happened so often in the past, this particular silver lining brought with it a black cloud. The prime minister, John Major, feared that it might eventually prove impossible to defend the existing rate, and it was only in the autumn of 1991 he commissioned one of his closest advisers, Sarah Hogg, to write a paper addressing the possibility of Britain's realigning the pound – that is, devaluing it – within the ERM. At that stage, however, there appeared to be no great urgency, and the prime minister put Hogg's paper aside without even mentioning its existence, let alone discussing its contents, with Norman Lamont, his chancellor of the exchequer. John Major says in his memoirs that his reason for not pursuing the matter was that "Treasury forecasts suggested sterling could trade without difficulties at its existing level".[5] Other observers were not so sure. One academic economist, a man taken seriously by some in the Treasury, wondered aloud at about the same time whether it would really be possible to realign sterling while at the same time continuing to pursue a plausible anti-inflation strategy. "The worst policy of all", he added ominously, "is surely to start off with portentous declarations of how unthinkable a realignment would be and then cave in when the going gets rough."[6]

At the time that Britain joined the ERM, it was widely believed, not least by Margaret Thatcher, then still prime minister, that, if the agreed central exchange rate of DM2.95 eventually proved too ambitious, a realignment within the ERM could be negotiated relatively easily – that is, that her preferred policy of allowing the pound to float in relation to other currencies could, up to a point, be maintained. After all, "the rules of the system, a semi-fixed rather than a fixed-rate regime, allowed for periodic realignments of parities", and such realignments had been quite frequent during the mechanism's early days, with the French franc, for instance, being devalued several times in relation to the Deutschmark.[7] Throughout the lengthy discussions that culminated in the decision to join in 1990, Thatcher insisted that the band within which the pound's value would be allowed to increase or decrease in relation to other currencies must be fully 6 per cent – the same wide band as that enjoyed by the Spanish peseta – rather than anything narrower. On the very eve of Britain's entry, Thatcher was emphatic in a conversation with Kenneth Baker, a member of her cabinet sceptical of the ERM. "Kenneth", she assured him, "... when we join we will be able to adjust the value of sterling. I have been assured that we will have that flexibility."[8]

Britain did indeed have some flexibility, but not nearly as much – or as easily obtained – as Thatcher implied. The Exchange Rate Mechanism that the British joined in 1990 was not the mechanism that they thought they were joining. More precisely, British ministers and officials knew that the ERM was changing but did not fully appreciate the potential consequences of the changes that were taking place. In its inception, the ERM was a relatively rough-and-ready set of procedures for smoothing out currency fluctuations among those member states of the European Community that chose to take part. During the 1980s, it largely achieved its limited objectives, including ironing out currency fluctuations, which had previously been quite violent on occasion, and acting as a brake on inflation. However, by the end of that decade the ERM was beginning to turn into something much more ambitious: a step on the way to full economic and monetary union within the Community. In particular, Germany and, to an even greater extent, France were determined to create a common European currency under the aegis of a European central bank, and they saw the ERM as a means towards that end. They increasingly regarded the currencies aligned within the ERM as, in effect, the euro in waiting, as a fixed-rate regime, no longer a semi-fixed one. Political leaders in Germany, France and elsewhere in the EU took very seriously the business of building Europe. They were not to be deterred, and they were also not to be prised apart, a crucial fact that seems to have been lost on most of the relevant policymakers in Britain.

Not only was the ERM changing its character in the minds of Britain's most powerful economic partners, but from late 1990 onwards the economies of Britain and Germany found themselves heading in opposite directions. Sterling was pegged in the ERM to the Deutschmark, but the priorities of policymakers in Germany and Britain began to diverge radically. The German problem was inflation. The rate of inflation in Germany had risen as a consequence of two decisions taken by the federal government at the time of reunification: to trade one Deutschmark for every (hopelessly overvalued) East German Ostmark and to finance the bailing out of the (hopelessly inefficient) East German economy by means of increased borrowing instead of higher taxation. The Bundesbank, Germany's fiercely independent central bank, responded – and went on responding – by raising German interest rates. Britain's problem, by contrast, was recession and the virtual collapse of the domestic housing market (signs earlier that the country was pulling out of recession having proved illusory). What Britain needed, therefore, was not higher interest rates but lower ones. Pressure on the British government to drive down interest rates was intense, not least from among Conservative MPs. Higher interest rates in Germany had the effect of further strengthening the already strong Deutschmark. Any lowering of interest rates in Britain would almost certainly have the effect of weakening the already vulnerable pound. Investors were already gravitating to the Deutschmark. Lower interest rates in the UK would cause them to flee the pound.

Policymakers in Britain were well aware – all too well aware – of the dilemmas created by this tension between German and British monetary policies. They wanted to cut British interest rates but knew that, if they did, they would endanger the pound. They knew that the currency markets were powerful and always had been, as Harold Wilson had discovered to his cost and as Margaret Thatcher always realised. But, even so, they appear not to have taken fully on board the tremendous power of the markets, which had expanded enormously in recent years and had been substantially deregulated. By the 1990s the storm-force gales of the past were capable of morphing into hurricanes. As Philip Stephens of the *Financial Times* was to write:

> In a world of footloose capital looking for the best, short-term, return, the old assumptions no longer held. The value of sterling might still reflect over the long run the balance between the nation's exports and imports. In between times, however, investor fashions and the relative returns offered in international bond markets could drive the currency in the opposite direction. The traders hunched over their flickering screens in the world's financial centres might well attach more weight to arbitrage opportunities or to the political mood than to the status of the balance of payments.[9]

Long after the chaotic events of Black Wednesday, one of Stephens's *FT* colleagues, Sir Samuel Brittan, asked whether the UK could have remained in the ERM and then answered his own question: "I believe many mistakes were made in defence of the ERM parity ... but the one I felt most strongly about was the surprise expressed by the British authorities at the size of the speculative movement against the pound."[10] The British authorities should not have been surprised. Already by 1992, the daily turnover of the world's foreign-exchange transactions had reached $1,200 billion.

In the autumn of 1991, John Major felt able to set Sarah Hogg's paper aside, and for the next several months – to and through the April 1992 general election – the pound seemed relatively secure. But then, in the summer of 1992, the black cloud that had always hung over it began to darken. Danish voters in a referendum held in early June rejected the Maastricht Treaty, and the French government announced that a referendum on the same treaty would be held in France in late September. The Maastricht Treaty provided, among many other things, for additional steps to be taken towards European economic and monetary union, and its rejection by the Danes, and its seemingly probable rejection by the French, disturbed the markets. It suddenly seemed that the ERM itself might be liable to disruption. In Britain, the vocal contingent of Eurosceptic MPs on the Conservative backbenches in parliament, which already existed, condemned the Maastricht Treaty and Britain's membership of the ERM and blamed the two together in large part for Britain's continuing recession. Political pressure or no, it was definitely the case – and everyone knew it – that attempting to maintain sterling's parity within the ERM totally precluded any drastic cut in interest rates and therefore any drastic action to combat the recession. The markets took note of UK developments. The value of sterling against the Deutschmark fell below DM2.90 for the first time during the course of June, although still within its permitted ERM band; and during July, August and early September it fell still further – never drastically and never dramatically but increasingly ominously. The rate of decline was a fairly constant 5 pfennigs per month. As Philip Stephens later put it, "The Deutschmark rose pitilessly."[11]

Nevertheless, the mood in the Treasury and Downing Street remained relatively relaxed for several weeks. Sterling had had its downs as well as its ups ever since Britain had entered the mechanism, and there did not appear to be any great cause for immediate concern. But by early July Treasury officials were becoming seriously anxious, and the prime minister was, in his own words, "sufficiently alarmed" to begin raising the issue with continental political leaders.[12] From then on, and throughout the

disastrous three months that followed, important decisions on sterling
continued to be taken – as they had often been taken in the past – within
an almost hermetically sealed closed circle, comprising the prime minister
and his staff, the chancellor of the exchequer and his Treasury officials,
and the governor and other senior officials at the Bank of England. No
one outside the circle was centrally, or even peripherally, involved. The
Foreign Office was a notable absentee. Only on Black Wednesday itself
were other ministers in the government – Douglas Hurd, the foreign
secretary, Michael Heseltine, the deputy prime minister, Kenneth Clarke,
the home secretary, and Richard Ryder, the government chief whip –
invited to participate in what amounted to the ERM's funeral rites so far
as Britain was concerned. As Hurd reported in his memoirs, the four of
them found themselves "taking part in the high-pitched climax of a play,
at the earlier acts of which we had not been spectators, let alone actors".
The man who was then foreign secretary observed that "currency matters
were regarded as sacred mysteries entrusted only to the Prime Minister
and the Chancellor of the Exchequer".[13] Clarke later remarked that "we
were additional doctors brought in at the last moment simply to witness
the death of the patient".[14] All four ministers were there, as one of them
said, merely to dip their hands in the blood.[15]

From the moment in early July when it became clear that the position
of sterling looked like becoming precarious, those ministers and officials
who, unlike the four ministers just mentioned, were members of the
closed circle had four options available to them in principle. Until Black
Wednesday, they refused to take up either of the first two. Immediately
prior to Black Wednesday, they tried unsuccessfully to take up the third.
Throughout, except when they were trying to take up the third option,
their preferred option was the fourth. The various options, needless to say,
were not considered sequentially, one at a time. Consideration of them
came and went and was usually intertwined.

The first option, if sterling came under real pressure or seemed about
to, was unilaterally to devalue the pound while remaining, or attempting
to remain, within the ERM. The consensus in the Treasury was that that
would be a bad idea. What Britain's economy badly needed was lower interest rates, but devaluing would probably have the effect of driving rates up,
as the markets demanded higher rates as the price for continuing to hold

sterling. Moreover, devaluation would probably have the effect, later if not sooner, of fuelling domestic inflation as a consequence of its leading to increased import prices – and the whole point of being in the ERM was to curb inflation. Views differed in any case about whether Britain's partners in the ERM would actually agree to a substantial devaluation within the mechanism. The Treasury view was that they would not, though Britain's permanent representative in Brussels, a Foreign Office official, thought they might.

The second option, also rejected along with unilateral devaluation, was simply to withdraw from the ERM and allow sterling's exchange rate to float, as it had done for considerable periods in the past. The difficulty there was that sterling would probably float downwards following its departure from the ERM, thereby increasing the chances that domestic inflation would float upwards – and, again, the whole point of ERM membership was to curb inflation. Leaving the ERM would, of course, make it possible for the government to cut interest rates – which, other things being equal, it was keen to do – in order to combat the recession, but it was clear to policymakers that allowing the pound to float while at the same time cutting interest rates might only have the effect of triggering a further devaluation and further ratcheting up inflation. Leaving the ERM would almost certainly give the markets, rightly or wrongly, the impression that the government had given up the fight against inflation. Although Norman Lamont, the chancellor of the exchequer, always entertained doubts about the wisdom of British membership of the ERM, and although he claims in his memoirs that during the summer of 1992 he sought an opportunity to persuade the prime minister that Britain should withdraw, the option of straightforward, unforced, unilateral withdrawal was never considered seriously at the highest level.[16] The third option, far more attractive on the face of it than either of the other two, was to negotiate along with Britain's ERM partners a multilateral realignment of the ERM currencies. Such a realignment would, of course, have to be negotiated in secret – otherwise the markets would go berserk – and there was always a real danger that a general realignment would undermine the plausibility of the whole ERM enterprise. If it did that, the effect might be to weaken still further some of the weaker ERM currencies, including sterling at some point. If that happened, the effect in the UK would almost certainly be to force up interest rates rather than allowing them to fall. All the same, other countries in the ERM in 1992 were facing domestic economic difficulties similar to those of the UK – most of continental Europe, like Britain, was in recession – and other countries, notably Italy and Spain, were anxious to realign their own currencies in relation to the Deutschmark. At the very least, a realignment within the ERM would allow the British to retain their hard-won, post-Thatcher credentials as "good Europeans". Officials at the German Bundesbank, including its president, Helmut Schlesinger, indicated semi-publicly that, so far as they were concerned, a general realignment was not out of the question provided they were allowed to continue pursuing their own high-interest-rate policy in Germany.

From Britain's point of view, however, there were three formidable obstacles to any such general realignment, two internal, one external. One of the internal obstacles was the widespread fear among Treasury and Bank of England economists, conveyed to ministers, that a general realignment would be no more advantageous to the British economy than a unilateral devaluation: that interest rates would have to remain damagingly high if a further fall in the external value of the pound was to be avoided. The other internal obstacle was ministers' repeated public declarations that Britain was determined, come what may, to stay inside the ERM at the existing parity. A realignment, especially one initiated by the British, would represent an extremely embarrassing political climb-down. The external obstacle was France. British ministers did raise with French ministers, albeit somewhat tentatively, the possibility of a general realignment of other European currencies against the Deutschmark, a realignment that would include the French franc; but they ran into a brick wall of opposition. The French, led by President François Mitterrand, were resolutely committed to their long-standing policy of *le franc fort* and were totally uninterested in devaluation. In addition, they were equally resolutely committed to European economic and monetary union and were therefore uninterested in contemplating any course of action that might weaken the stability and credibility of one of the principal means towards that end, the ERM. In the view of both the Bank of England and Treasury officials, the French government's implacable hostility to realignment was "on its own entirely decisive".[17] General realignment thus did not provide an avenue of escape.

The French being unco-operative, ministers decided that their only alternative, short of devaluing, was to mount a frontal assault on the Germans. High German interest rates were weakening the pound and preventing the British from cutting their interest rates in order to deal with the British recession. Therefore, the Germans must be persuaded to cut their own rates or, at the very least, to stop raising them. German priorities were to be subordinated to British; a foreign country was, for some obscure reason, to be cajoled into going out of its way in order to solve the UK's problems. John Major, who was on friendly terms with the German chancellor, Helmut Kohl, constantly urged him to call a halt to the upward trend of interest rates in Germany, to which Kohl responded by saying that it was in Germany's national interest to maintain high interest rates to prevent German inflation from running out of control and that the federal government, in any case, had no power to order the independent Bundesbank to lower interest rates – or to raise them or do anything at all about them. At a meeting of European finance ministers in Bath, Norman Lamont, in the chair, attempted to browbeat Helmut Schlesinger, the Bundesbank president, into lowering German interest rates but succeeded only in annoying Schlesinger and astonishing the other ministers present by what they regarded as his display of stubborn intemperance.

Following Black Wednesday and in later years, commentators and some of those involved in the 1992 events commented on British ministers' and officials' apparent inability to grasp either how governments on the Continent actually worked or how the world as it was seen from Paris or Frankfurt might possibly differ from the world as seen from Whitehall and Westminster. At a seminar in 2007, Geoffrey Howe, by now Lord Howe and long since retired, commented that, as chancellor of the exchequer during the early 1980s and frequently in the chair at meetings of European ministers, he had "learnt a great deal about the importance of human relationships and communication with and between central bank governors and finance ministers". He also commented on the almost complete breakdown in communications during Margaret Thatcher's last years between Number 10, the Treasury and the Foreign Office ("why should the Chancellor consult the Foreign Secretary?!").[18] On the same occasion, Sir Samuel Brittan noted the long time it took before the economic and financial consequences of German reunification sank in: "A wider moral of that is [that] the world is elsewhere and not to be too fixated on what is happening in the City or Westminster."[19]

The fourth available option was to "tough it out", a phrase often used at the time: to try to persuade the markets, by whatever means, that the British government was determined to maintain, and would actually succeed in maintaining, the pound's existing position within the ERM. That was the option vigorously pursued by the prime minister and the chancellor until late on Black Wednesday itself. Choosing that particular option was to prove financially pointless and politically disastrous.

As time went on, and despite his having commissioned Sarah Hogg's paper at an earlier stage, John Major became more and more deeply committed to the cause of both the ERM and Britain's place within it. His passionate commitment was both personal and public. As chancellor of the exchequer in 1990, Major had been responsible for taking Britain into the ERM at the parity of DM2.95. He had no desire whatever to be remembered as the first Conservative prime minister to preside over a devaluation of the pound, all previous devaluations having been the work of Labour chancellors. Major was also a British patriot, and devaluation – unless disguised successfully as an orderly "realignment" – would undoubtedly represent a humiliation for the British. But, perhaps above all, Major abhorred inflation. Inflation ate inexorably into people's savings, including into the savings of some of the most vulnerable people in society. Major was a Tory, a quintessential Tory virtue was thrift, and inflation was thrift's deadliest enemy. It was ironic that Major shared his deep-seated horror of inflation in equal measure with his German nemesis, Helmut Schlesinger. By this time, Major was convinced – possibly having convinced himself – that Britain's membership of the ERM at a rigorous parity constituted the country's last, best hope of conquering inflation once and for all.

The prime minister's public statements and press briefings mirrored and, if anything, magnified his private convictions. He allowed successful membership of the ERM to become the badge and emblem of his government's success – or its failure. In mid-July 1992, with a crisis of confidence already looming, Major assured the House of Commons that his administration's commitment to sterling's place in the ERM was "100 per cent", and his press secretary briefed journalists to the effect that sterling's 2.95

rate against the Deutschmark was "non-negotiable".[20] Shortly afterwards, the prime minister could be heard telling journalists that sterling within the ERM might soon become one of the world's strongest currencies. Only a week before Black Wednesday, he was equally emphatic in an address to a Confederation of British Industry dinner in Scotland:

> All my adult life I have seen British governments driven off their virtuous pursuit of low inflation by market problems or political pressures. I was under no illusions when I took sterling into the ERM. I said at the time that membership was no soft option. The soft option, the devaluer's option, the inflationary option, would be a betrayal of our future; and that is not the government's policy ... We must bite the anti-inflation bullet or accept that we will be forever second-rate in Europe.[21]

The situation demanded, of course, that the prime minister reiterate his government's determination to maintain Britain's position in the ERM; he could not give the slightest hint that Britain might devalue the currency or quit the system. But his language and tone that evening did nothing to convince sceptical markets that sterling really was safe and did everything to ensure that, if the roof finally fell in, much of the wreckage would fall on him. Some of his fellow ministers were already crossing their fingers. "I hope it works", said one.[22]

The chancellor, Norman Lamont, felt less personally and intellectually committed to the ERM and DM2.95, but most Treasury officials were firm in their support for the existing policy, and Lamont's public pronouncements, though less florid than Major's, were just as emphatic and, coming from the chancellor, may initially have carried more weight. In a carefully worded speech delivered to the European Policy Forum in mid July, Lamont discussed in detail all the alternatives to remaining in the ERM within the existing broad band and, one by one, dismissed them all. "What they all have in common", he said, "is that each is a plea for a free lunch. As the Russians say, only mouse traps have free cheese. The result of attempting to implement any of them would be either higher interest rates, higher inflation or most likely both."[23] During the weeks that followed, Lamont never deviated from that strong line, at least publicly. Philip Stephens, in his account of the events leading up to Black Wednesday, summarises the position that had by now been reached:

> By now the policy and the rhetoric had become dangerously self-reinforcing … Once Lamont had delivered his European Policy Forum Speech … the internal discussion became circular. The die had been cast. The atmosphere in the upper echelons of the Treasury tended to stifle debate. It was an insular world, populated by clever insiders. Officials were not encouraged to think the unthinkable; instead their judgements tended to be mutually reinforcing. As one explained, "There was nothing to be gained from rocking the boat."[24]

Lamont's repeated public pronouncements also ensured that, when the roof did fall in, much of the wreckage would fall on him as well as on Major.

Reference has been made to four options that in principle were available to British policymakers. But there was also a fifth, one not mentioned in Norman Lamont's speech: namely, to raise domestic interest rates to the extent required both to maintain sterling's parity in the ERM and to damp down inflation. That option – which might be called toughing it out-plus – was raised as a possibility from time to time, including by the former chancellor Nigel Lawson, but it was never considered seriously. Given the state of the domestic economy, deep in recession, raising interest rates instead of lowering them would have struck foreign-exchange dealers as an act of desperation. The markets would have assumed that interest rates would have to go on rising. More to the point, raising interest rates in Britain during the summer of 1992 would have been politically impossible. They would not only in all probability have damaged the economy: they would have outraged Conservative backbenchers and even some Conservative ministers and would have strengthened the forces of Euroscepticism at all levels of the Conservative party and in much of the British press. The question was obvious: if being in the ERM meant higher domestic interest rates and continuing recession, why be in the ERM? The fifth option, thus, was closed. It had never really been opened.

The end, when it came, came abruptly. The British government could neither raise interest rates nor lower them. The Germans would not lower their own rates. The French vetoed any general realignment. On Sunday

13 September the Italians unilaterally devalued the lira, calling in question the parities of all the weaker ERM currencies and virtually inviting market dealers to target one or more of them; the Spanish peseta was probably highest on the list, but the pound could not be far behind. Then, on Tuesday 15 September, a leak from the German business newspaper *Handelsblatt* quoted Helmut Schlesinger of the Bundesbank as saying that "the tensions in the ERM are not over ... Further devaluations are not excluded. There may still be pressure on other currencies."[25] Schlesinger was asked to deny that he had said any such thing, but he refused. According to John Major, "After the Italian devaluation, and with sterling in the firing line, such views from one of the most influential central bankers in the world sent out only one message to the markets: 'Sell sterling.'"[26]

The next morning, foreign-exchange dealers worldwide took the hint. They bought billions of pounds – now trading freely well below the bottom of its ERM band – and at once sold them on to the Bank of England, which was obliged under the rules of the ERM to redeem all of them at the bottom of the band, the so-called intervention rate of DM2.7780. Several foreign-exchange dealers made vast fortunes; George Soros alone amassed a profit in a single day of more than $1 billion. Unsurprisingly, the British government and the Bank of England failed to cope. There was no way they could. The Bank bought sterling because it had to but also in order to try to prop up the pound's value and to restore it to some level above the bottom of its band; but Britain's foreign-exchange reserves drained rapidly away and could not be replenished.

The choice facing ministers was stark and starkly uncomfortable: either to withdraw immediately from the ERM and no longer to buy sterling at the intervention rate, or to raise interest rates to such high levels that dealers in the markets would be convinced that sterling was again worth investing in. The chancellor favoured immediate suspension of Britain's ERM membership. The prime minister, with the bemused support of the mostly pro-European ministers suddenly summoned to join the fray, favoured holding on as long as possible. The prime minister's view prevailed for a time, and Norman Lamont reluctantly agreed to raise Britain's minimum lending rate to an unprecedented 15 per cent – the day's second interest-rate rise. But even a rate as high as that was not enough to persuade the markets, and after nearly ten hours of chaotic meetings and frantic telephone calls Lamont at 7.30 that evening, speaking before massed cameras and microphones in the Treasury courtyard, announced that the increase in the minimum lending rate to 15 per cent was being rescinded and that Britain was suspending its ERM membership. "Today", he said, "has been an extremely difficult and turbulent day."[27] It was the understatement of the century.

In the event, withdrawing from the ERM did the British economy no harm and almost certainly did it good. The country emerged gradually from recession, inflation and interest rates both fell and towards the end of the decade the pound was trading, ironically, at about its original ERM parity with the Deutschmark. But the events just prior to Black Wednesday and then on the day itself cost British taxpayers at least £3.3 billion and possibly more, and the whole episode was undoubtedly a catastrophe for the prime minister, whose reputation never recovered. It was also a catastrophe for the chancellor, who was ignominiously ousted from office a few months later, and for the Conservative party, which lost its reputation for economic competence and whose chances of being returned to office for a fifth consecutive term in a few years' time all but vanished. One of the most striking features of the day is that, despite sterling's travails over many months and years beforehand, few in the higher reaches of the British government, if any, appear to have done any serious contingency thinking, let alone contingency planning. On the day, it all just happened.

8

"Cool Britannia"

S o far we have dealt with blunders all of which resulted from government initiatives intended to strengthen the public finances, improve Britain's economic prospects or improve the lot of the less well off. The New Millennium Experience – known for short at the time simply as "the Dome" – was the principal manifestation of New Labour's post-1997 "Cool Britannia" project, and it falls into a totally different category. It had little or nothing to do with the welfare of the British people. Its purposes were to entertain, impress and possibly educate those who chose to experience the Experience but also, even more, to enhance the New Labour government's standing at home and the UK's prestige abroad. It failed on almost all counts. Unlike the postwar Festival of Britain, it failed to attract anything like the expected number of visitors and it lost a great deal of money. It also embarrassed ministers and made Tony Blair's newly elected government look foolish. It was an undoubted blunder – a conspicuous flop, both financially and managerially.

The story began to unfold well before the 1997 election. As early as February 1994, the Major government established a body called the Millennium Commission to authorise grants from National Lottery funds to finance projects to mark the new millennium. The commission was a strange body. Unlike most Lottery-related bodies, it did not comprise experts in the relevant fields but instead consisted of representatives of the government and other political parties and men and women supposed to represent the UK's geographical and cultural diversity. Although it was chaired by the then national heritage secretary, its most energetic and influential member was Michael Heseltine, who became deputy prime minister in 1995. The commission quickly came to the view that a national millennium exhibition should be organised and should run from the beginning to the end of the millennium year, 2000. Some commission members were apparently lukewarm towards the idea, but the politicians, in particular Heseltine, were enthusiastic.

From the start, the commission operated on the basis of three assumptions about the proposed exhibition, assumptions that shaped its development and lay at the root of the problems that subsequently emerged.

The first was that the exhibition should be the grand centrepiece of the country's millennium celebrations, an ambitious national statement about the modern UK. It was to be reminiscent of the 1851 Great Exhibition in Hyde Park and the 1951 Festival of Britain on the South Bank. The guidelines issued by the commission to the consortia bidding to stage the exhibition suggested that they plan for an attendance of up to a hundred thousand visitors a day and said that "as a minimum it is envisaged that the exhibition will attract 15 million people" – an average of forty thousand a day for the whole of the millennium year.[1]

The commission's second assumption followed from the first, psychologically if not logically. Although the fact was never publicly acknowledged, the commission took it for granted that the exhibition must, of course, be held in London, the nation's capital. There were fifty-seven bids received to host the exhibition, but the commission apparently paid serious attention to only two of them: one proposing Birmingham as the venue, the other proposing east London. On the face of it, Birmingham would seem to have had the stronger case. The proposed Birmingham site was on land adjacent to and already owned by the National Exhibition Centre and could share some of the NEC's infrastructure. It was close to the M6 and the M42 motorways, the large NEC railway station and an international airport. It also offered ample parking capacity and was within reasonably easy reach of some thirty million people, nearly half the UK's population. By contrast, the proposed site on the Greenwich peninsula in east London was a dump, consisting of a desolate stretch of derelict land owned by British Gas, land that was heavily contaminated by toxic sludge and subject to complex planning regulations. Parking space was limited, and road and rail access were poor, although the new underground Jubilee

Line extension, with a stop at nearby North Greenwich, was scheduled to be completed in time.

But Greenwich, despite its manifest disadvantages, was the site chosen. The commission had been so impressed by the bid submitted on Birmingham's behalf by Imagination, a London-based events-management company with an impressive track record, that it invited the company to submit plans for the London as well as the Birmingham site. The commission's chief executive, Jennie Page, favoured Birmingham, whose practical advantages seemed to outweigh Greenwich's; but in February 1996 the commission announced that the exhibition would be held in Greenwich and be based on Imagination's outline ideas for Birmingham. Michael Heseltine, an enthusiast for urban regeneration, was also an enthusiast for Greenwich, believing that the Greenwich site, which bordered the Thames opposite the newly transformed Isle of Dogs, was in real need of redevelopment. Holding the exhibition there would bring thousands of jobs to an area of decay and poverty. Greenwich offered exciting opportunities. Birmingham was boring.

The commission assumed, thirdly, that private-sector organisations would effectively be responsible for the exhibition. The commission would make a substantial Lottery grant to begin with, but private companies would be responsible for the conception, financing, management, design, construction, marketing and daily operations of the exhibition and for the exhibits themselves. Members of the commission assumed that big multinational companies would be eager to sponsor both the exhibition as a whole and individual exhibits within it. Corporate sponsorship would help defray the increased costs of Greenwich as compared with Birmingham, especially if Heseltine, with his ministerial muscle and personal contacts, leaned on corporate bosses and, if need be, twisted arms.

During 1996 the project, despite difficulties, made considerable progress. The Millennium Commission set up a company, Millennium Central Ltd, to run it; a world-famous architect, Richard Rogers, was commissioned to design the main exhibition structure and, after protracted negotiations, the necessary planning permissions were obtained. The government's urban regeneration agency bought the whole of the Greenwich peninsula site from British Gas, and the government paid directly for clearing and decontaminating the site and providing new roads, cables, pipes and

landscaping. At the same time, however, the costs of the project were beginning to mount. Buying the site cost £20 million, preparing it another £200
million. Imagination's original concept of twelve time-themed pavilions
was rejected as too expensive and replaced by the idea of a single-span
dome "to keep visitors warm and dry on a windy peninsula". Millennium
Central Ltd's business plan was also rejected, its cost estimate having risen
from £500 million to £700 million. Early in 1997, before the general election of that year, the commission authorised a grant towards the project
of a further £200 million, announcing that it confidently expected to raise
£150 million from ticket sales and merchandising and another £150 million from private-sector sponsors.

Unfortunately, it turned out that private-sector sponsorship on that
scale was not readily forthcoming. The Labour party was expected to win
the coming election, and no one could be sure whether, if Labour did
win it, the new government would be committed to the project. On the
one hand, Tony Blair and one of his main allies, Peter Mandelson, were
making encouraging noises; but, on the other, Jack Cunningham, the
official opposition spokesman on national heritage matters, made it clear
that he was "not giving a blank cheque on behalf of the Labour party". In
addition, Michael Heseltine, the project's principal champion, did invite
business people to meet him at the Cabinet Office but proved relatively
unsuccessful as a fundraiser. He may have been personally persuasive,
but the people he met sensed, rightly, that he would soon be on the way
out. Why curry favour with a man who would soon have nothing to offer
in return?

Meanwhile, with the costs of the project and the levels of political
uncertainty surrounding it both steadily mounting, its managerial and
organisational structure was evolving into one of wondrous complexity,
thereby further alienating potential sponsors. The new structure made the
Tower of Babel look simple.

In early 1997 the whole millennium exhibition project still lacked private investors, and it was obvious that no single company would dream of
taking on the risk of mounting the whole exhibition, even with a substantial
infusion of National Lottery money. The government was in a quandary.
One option, at least in principle, would have been for the government,
in the form of the Department of National Heritage (shortly to morph

into the Department for Culture, Media and Sport) to take responsibility for the project and then, having done that, to commission one or more private-sector companies actually to organise the exhibition and run it. But that option was ruled out. The government, in particular the Treasury, did not want the exhibition to be a charge on the public purse, a concern shared by the Labour party, which was desperate not to seem willing to be profligate with taxpayers' money. In addition, the government was sensitive to any suspicion that Lottery funds were being used to replace, instead of to supplement, government expenditure on good works. If the government itself took over the exhibition and part-funded it with Lottery money, it would lay itself open to that suspicion. In the government's view, and also the Labour party's, it was important that Lottery projects give at least the appearance of being chosen, funded and supervised by some kind of independent, arm's-length, non-political body.

Accordingly, the Conservative government, with Labour's approval, opted for a wheeze. Instead of assuming direct responsibility for the exhibition, it nationalised Millennium Central Ltd, the private company that the Millennium Commission had set up to run the exhibition. This new publicly owned company was soon rechristened the New Millennium Exhibition Company Ltd, and it had but a single shareholder. Initially the shareholder was Roger Freeman, the Conservative chancellor of the Duchy of Lancaster. Then, following the general election, it was Peter Mandelson, wearing his new hat as millennium minister. The new publicly owned company was thus a device for enabling the government to inject substantial amounts of Lottery money into the exhibition and to play a large role in organising and running it without actually appearing to do either of those things. In that way, the fictions were maintained that both the Millennium Commission and the New Millennium Exhibition Company Ltd were traditional arm's-length bodies, free from government interference, which palpably they were not.

The result was an extraordinarily complex and overweight structure. Had there been a full-blown organisation chart, it would have looked like a Jackson Pollock painting or a smartphone app QR barcode. A National Audit Office report referred to "three distinct bodies, three accounting officers and two ministers (exercising three distinct roles)". "By any standards", the report added drily, "that is a highly complex structure."[2]

The project itself was large and complex, but it was also one whose management had to work to an unusually tight and inflexible deadline: the stroke of midnight on 31 December 1999, by now less than three years away. The New Millennium Exhibition Company itself was a hybrid, part company and part (to use the jargon) non-departmental public body. Like any other company, it had a chief executive – Jennie Page, imported from the Millennium Commission – and a board of directors charged with running the company. But, unlike most companies, it was directly accountable to the government, in the person of the single shareholder, and simultaneously to the Millennium Commission, which was responsible for awarding it Lottery funds.

The company also had to relate to the Department for Culture, Media and Sport, whose new secretary of state, Chris Smith, took over as chairman of the Millennium Commission. The company had direct executive responsibility for the exhibition. The single shareholder appointed the company's directors and controlled it by means of a financial memorandum. The commission awarded the Lottery grants and shared responsibility with the single shareholder for monitoring the company's progress. The department was responsible for issuing policy and financial directives to every Lottery body, including the Millennium Commission, and the department's permanent secretary, under the terms of a financial memorandum negotiated between the company and the single shareholder, had the power to issue the company with formal instructions. On top of all that, London Transport was supposed to complete the Jubilee Line extension on time, and those corporate sponsors that did eventually come forward effectively controlled the contents of their own exhibition zones. Jennie Page had no choice but to deal with all of the above while trying at the same time to organise the actual exhibition. Many admired her; few envied her.

Until shortly after the election in 1997, it was still not entirely clear whether there would actually be a millennium exhibition. Labour in opposition, while not against the exhibition, had never become firmly committed to it – the party's election manifesto mentioned it only in passing – and there was a great deal of opposition in other quarters. The Treasury never believed that the project was financially viable, the Department of the Environment, Transport and the Regions wanted the Greenwich site to be used for other purposes, and scores of Labour backbenchers were clearly sceptical about the project, with a majority seemingly indifferent. Apart from Michael Heseltine, still an active member of the Millennium Commission, the only heavyweight politicians committed to the project – but they were very heavyweight – were Tony Blair, the prime minister, John Prescott, his deputy and Peter Mandelson, whose grandfather had masterminded the Festival of Britain and who, if the project went ahead, hoped and expected to be in ministerial control of it. Blair and Mandelson believed the exhibition would provide them with an opportunity to project New Labour as the party of the future and the UK as a whole as young, confident, relaxed, dynamic and diverse – in short, as reflecting what some in the marketing world and some in the Labour party liked to call "Cool Britannia".[3]

The issue reached the cabinet on 19 June 1997, and a quick decision was needed: pile drivers were due to arrive on site to begin work on the Dome in less than a fortnight. Contemporary accounts differ in detail, but it seems clear that a majority at the meeting on 19 June wanted to scrap the entire Greenwich project. During a discussion lasting more than an hour, speaker after speaker lodged objections. Some objected to the cost; others feared that the dome structure that Richard Rogers by this time had designed would become a white elephant; and a considerable number complained that an overwhelmingly London-centred project would not involve people across the UK. Had a vote been taken, the project in its existing form would almost certainly have been voted down. But Tony Blair had to leave the cabinet meeting early to attend a church blessing of the new parliament, and John Prescott, his deputy, took the chair. Eventually, after much further discussion, Prescott persuaded the majority to accept, however reluctantly, the twin propositions that the decision about the project should ultimately be Blair's and that, as Blair was known to favour it, it should therefore be allowed to go ahead. Alastair Campbell, Blair's press secretary, acknowledges in his diaries that Prescott could just as easily have told the prime minister: "Sorry, Tony, there is no way we can do this."[4] But Prescott did find a way. Within a few hours, Blair and Mandelson, along with Michael Heseltine, appeared on the Greenwich site wearing hard hats to bear witness to their personal commitment to the exhibition.

At the cabinet meeting, Gordon Brown, the chancellor of the exchequer, had argued that, if the exhibition were to go ahead, it would need to pass five tests, and the five tests were duly incorporated in the government's formal announcement later the same day.[5] The exhibition must provide the UK with a lasting legacy. Its contents must entertain and inspire. It must relate to the whole nation and not just to London and the South East. There must be a new management structure to provide greater creative force than had been in evidence so far. Not least, as any chancellor of the exchequer might have been expected to stipulate, there must be no extra cost to the public purse. The Dome – both the building itself and the exhibits it would contain – was inevitably going to be judged in large measure by whether or not it passed those five tests. A formidable challenge facing everyone involved was whether those in charge could generate sufficient public interest and excitement to attract big crowds to the venue and to rack up millions upon millions of pounds in ticket sales. It was not going to be easy.

The task was not made any easier by the departure from the scene of Imagination, the company originally employed by the Millennium Commission, and also by the fact that no new management structure was forthcoming. Imagination withdrew at an early stage. It was a relatively small design house, and those in charge soon sensed that the project, as now conceived, was beyond them. They were also dismayed by the weird management structure looming above them and by the constant chopping and changing of personnel, business plans, budgets and just about everything else. They wanted out, and they got out. Their replacement was a single individual, the chief executive of the Design Museum, Stephen Bailey. After only six months, he too withdrew following a series of semi-public disputes with Peter Mandelson, whom he accused of behaving dictatorially. Another key figure to depart was the theatrical impresario Sir Cameron Mackintosh, whom the company had commissioned to create a theatrical show for the Dome. His proposals, it was claimed, were wildly extravagant, including a lavish budget that provided for the stabling of 100 horses on the site.

As for the half-promised new management structure, no serious moves appear to have been made in that direction. The activity of dismantling an already overcomplicated structure would probably in itself have proved immensely complicated, especially in the limited time available. Matters instead got worse rather than better. New members joined the board of

Jennie Page's New Millennium Exhibition Company, but they were mostly non-executive directors drawn from the boardrooms of major corporations; with the exception of Michael Grade, a prominent broadcasting executive, none had any experience of creating and managing a popular visitor attraction. In any case, the company, which was supposed to have executive responsibility for the project, enjoyed virtually no independence. As one official put it, "ministers were all over the project like a rash", with Peter Mandelson well in the lead followed by Chris Smith. And ministers were not alone in wanting to have their say, fully expecting to be listened to. Members of the still extant Millennium Commission raised their voices, as did senior civil servants and, increasingly, the new Labour ministers' special advisers. Jennie Page was expected to report to everyone in sight. Far from there being a shortage of lines of authority, there were far too many of them and none was clear. Occasionally someone outside the company would, without consulting it, take a decision that affected the company drastically. A case in point was the announcement by Lord Falconer, who succeeded Mandelson as millennium minister and the company's sole shareholder in 1998, that a million schoolchildren would be given free entry to the Dome. At a stroke, the company's owner – for that, in effect, was what Falconer was – had blithely undercut his own company's business plan, which depended heavily on large-scale sales of tickets to families. No one was in charge because everybody was – and that remained the position throughout.

All this might not have been as destructive as it was if all of those involved had been in substantial agreement; but, unsurprisingly, they were not. On the contrary, ministers and individual members of the Millennium Commission differed about almost every aspect of the exhibition except that there was to be one and that it was to be held in Greenwich. Ministers in the new government, at Gordon Brown's prompting, said vaguely that the exhibition should "entertain and inspire". But what did that mean? The previous Conservative government, to the extent that it had a considered view, assumed that the exhibition would, so to speak, teach and preach – in other words, that it would be essentially serious – and the same view was also taken by Chris Smith and probably a majority of Labour's cabinet ministers. Moreover, Imagination's original proposals had been based on that premise. But Blair and Mandelson wanted a more celebratory event, one that would entertain visitors and make them feel good about themselves, their country and, not least, New Labour. At different times, different people envisaged the exhibition as being a science showcase, a trade fair, an arts festival, a panorama of British history, a circus or possibly even an amusement park. Some in high places wanted it to be worthy; others wanted it to be fun. It was variously to promote British style, or British innovation, or Britain's tolerance and diversity. The only thing that should have been clear, but was not, was that the exhibition could not be all of those things at once. But at no time was a consensus reached, or even approximated.

The grandly named New Millennium Exhibition Company Ltd under Jennie Page had three specific tasks. The first was to build the building. The second was to persuade a range of private-sector companies to put something worthwhile inside it. The third was to fill it with people. It succeeded, quite spectacularly, in the first task. It succeeded, but only partially, in the second. And it failed miserably in the third.

Richard Rogers's dome was completed in June 1998, in plenty of time for the exhibition. Viewed from afar, it resembled a huge flying saucer that had somehow landed upside down. Strictly speaking, it was not really a dome at all but a white marquee with supporting struts. Appropriately for a building located on the Greenwich peninsula not far from the Royal Observatory, its western edge was aligned with the prime meridian and its other dimensions spoke to the hours, days, weeks and months of the year. It was, for instance, 365 metres in diameter and 52 metres in height at its highest. It was also vast, with enough floor space to accommodate 18,000 London buses. People on the whole liked it, and the media did too. The dome was quickly accepted as one of London's landmark buildings, easily recognisable from planes descending from the east towards Heathrow. Initially, the idea had been that it should be a temporary building, lasting only long enough to house the exhibition. But Peter Mandelson, possibly with his grandfather's enduring legacy on the South Bank in mind, took the decision that it should be made permanent, at the same time authorising the spending of an additional £8 million on its roof fabric in the interests of maximising its longevity.

Designing and constructing the building had proved relatively straight-forward. However, assembling its contents – the exhibition itself – proved anything but. Not only was there no one in overall charge, not only were the relevant decision-making processes complicated and fraught, not only was there no agreement about what the exhibition's principal themes were to be (apart, obviously, from celebrating the millennium), but also the companies that would, or might, sponsor individual exhibits obviously needed to be attended to. They wanted guidance about what the exhibition as a whole was supposed to be about, and they also wanted, not unnaturally, a preponderant say in the design and contents of whichever exhibit they were being asked to pay for. Recruiting potential sponsors was not made any easier by the fact that, as early as the autumn of 1997, influential newspapers were complaining, with reason, that the Dome was "a vacuum held together by rhetoric" (*Observer*) and a project "grandiose and lacking in purpose" (*Sunday Times*). The House of Commons Culture, Media and Sport Committee commented acidly: "At times the process of discovering the proposals for the content of the Dome was akin to drawing teeth. From what we know so far the Millennium Experience is not so much a journey through time ... as a journey into the unknown ... We know more about what the Experience will not be than what it will be."[6]

The relationship between Jennie Page's company and the various sponsors and potential sponsors was at least as fraught as all the other relationships associated with the project. Although the sponsors wanted to know what the exhibition was supposed to be about, the company could not tell them, partly because neither ministers nor the Millennium Commission were giving the company any guidance, and partly because the company itself could not be entirely clear until it knew what the sponsors and potential sponsors had in mind. People went round in circles. Ministers knew little or nothing about commercial sponsorship, and had wholly unrealistic expectations about the willingness of private-sector companies to act outside their own commercial interests. Also, the company, under government pressure, initially tried to charge considerably more for exhibition space than companies were willing to pay. With less than two years remaining until the opening date, full funding had been found for only four of the exhibition's fourteen zones, leaving ten underfunded or not funded at all. Negotiations between the company and potential sponsors were often protracted because many of the interested firms regarded other interested firms as competitors and suspected that they were being given favourable treatment. Although the company was ultimately responsible for the exhibition's content, it lacked any power to advise sponsoring firms about their plans, let alone to issue directions. Moreover, it had no power at all to monitor the sponsors' plans in order to ensure high quality and consistency among the various exhibits. Of strategic planning and oversight, there was none.

There was also a problem about the visitors to the exhibition – the paying customers. People normally pay in advance to attend events only if they know something about them. But people could not know anything about the millennium exhibition because there was nothing, apart from its venue, available to be known. The public and the media were in the dark because the organisers were. It was not even clear whether visitors would be able to reach the Dome because until very nearly the end of 1999 no one knew whether the Jubilee Line extension, which was running well behind schedule, would be open in time. All that was knowable and known was the price of tickets: £20 for adults and £16.50 for children. For a family of four, that came to a total of £73, even before the cost of transport, meals and the purchase of merchandise was added on. It would be an expensive day out, but what kind of day out it would be remained a total mystery. Unsurprisingly, ticket sales in the months prior to the opening were slow. Most people had decided, very sensibly, to wait and see.

That being so, and with the exhibition's finances being heavily dependent on the volume of ticket sales, it was essential that the opening night make a huge splash, with extensive publicity and favourable notices. The exhibition's organisers did their best. They invited 10,000 of the nation's great and good (or at least its famous) to celebrate the coming of the new millennium at the Dome. The guest list included all of the country's national newspaper and broadcasting editors. However, as the result of a planning error, guests did not receive their tickets on time, so it was decided that they should be collected at Stratford station at the far end of the Jubilee Line extension, which had fortunately just opened. However, the station could not begin to cope with the numbers, and long queues formed for security clearance and then onward travel to Greenwich. As a result, large numbers of London's most glittering glitterati, resplendent in their dresses and dinner jackets, were left stranded for up to four hours on a cold New Year's Eve on an East End tube platform; and, when they did finally reach the Dome long after the magic hour, many found that most of the exhibition had already closed. An unknown number felt personally humiliated. Many hundreds of them were furious.

Shortly before its opening, Tony Blair had declared that once people saw the Dome they would "flood to visit it and be part of a great British achievement". The Dome, he said, would be "a triumph of confidence over cynicism, boldness over blandness, excellence over mediocrity".[7] Unfortunately, it was not really any of those things. Most of the media had reserved judgement until after the opening, but after the disaster of opening night they turned hostile and gleefully reported everything that went wrong, of which there was a great deal. During the first few months, bizarrely, people who turned up at the Dome without tickets were unable to buy them at the door and had to leave the site to find a National Lottery outlet elsewhere that did sell them. People had to queue for up to two hours to gain entrance to the most popular zones, maps were printed upside down, escalators were often stuck, and most zones experienced equipment breakdowns of one sort or another. As for the contents of the exhibition, most reviewers complained that some of the zones lacked substantial content while others were dull or bland. Few dismissed the exhibition as a total flop, but most viewed it as anticlimactic, a real disappointment after all the advance hype, including Blair's.

The feedback from people who actually visited the Dome tended to be more positive; one survey found a satisfaction rating among visitors of fully 84 per cent.[8] But not nearly enough people did visit. The New Millennium Exhibition Company's final business plan assumed a total attendance of twelve million during 2000. But of course no one could know how many people would actually come, given all the uncertainties surrounding the project. In the course of six months, the 1851 Great Exhibition had drawn in more than six million people out of a total population of only twenty million, and the Festival of Britain, also open for only half the year, attracted 8.5 million paying visitors out of a population of roughly fifty million. The company's hoped-for total of twelve million, out of a population of nearly sixty million during the whole of 2000, was thus optimistic but not entirely fanciful, given the improvements in transport that had taken place in the interim. But, in the event, the total attendance at the Dome was

little more than half that, 6.5 million, of whom a million – Lord Falconer's
schoolchildren – were admitted free of charge.

The effect of this poor and unexpectedly low level of attendance had,
inevitably, a devastating effect on the exhibition's finances. The revenue
from sales of tickets amounted to barely more than a third of the sum
mentioned in the project's final business plan: £60 million compared
with £169 million. Although all of the Dome's zones eventually attracted
sponsors, income from sponsorship also fell short, totalling £120 million
compared with the £175 million that had been hoped for. Total receipts for
the year amounted to £189 million, little more than half of the hoped-for
receipts of £359 million. As the shortfall in visitors and income became
apparent, Jennie Page and her successor as the company's chief executive, a Frenchman named P. Y. Gerbaud recruited from the senior ranks
of Euro Disney, made strenuous efforts to cut operating costs and attract
more visitors; but, as the year-end totals indicated, they were only modestly successful. Throughout 2000, the company teetered on the brink
of insolvency and had repeatedly to be bailed out with Lottery money
from the Millennium Commission. The media had no difficulty depict-
ing the Dome, not inaccurately, as having been a monument to financial
and organisational ineptitude. When the exhibition finally closed on 31
December 2000, the total of Lottery funding had come to £628 million,
more than three times the original grant. Total spending by the government
had come to £828 million (well over £1 billion at today's prices), more
than double the government's original and apparently fixed commitment.

Nor were ministers' troubles over. It seemingly took forever to find a
buyer for the building once it was no longer needed for the exhibition;
and difficulties and delays in finding a buyer attracted widespread publicity. Proposals to convert the now redundant dome into a biotech centre,
a sports academy, a new stadium for Charlton Athletic football club or a
high-tech business centre came and went. Decommissioning the dome's
contents and trying to find a buyer for it cost the government millions, and
the media had great fun reporting the government's estimate that it cost
£1 million a month merely to keep the building in good condition while
it stood empty. Eventually in 2003 an American group called Anschutz
Entertainment bought the dome from the government and converted
it into the O_2 entertainment complex. The complex opened its doors in

2007 and the following year it overtook Madison Square Garden as the busiest popular music venue in the world. Today ticket sales at the dome are buoyant at last.

The government had set out five criteria by which the success of the Millennium Exhibition should be judged. The exhibition certainly left a permanent legacy in the form of the dome itself, but otherwise its legacy consists solely of rapidly fading memories of a monstrous cock-up. It failed by some distance to kick-start the government's ambitious plans for the regeneration of the Greenwich peninsula; fifteen years later, only a fraction of the hoped-for 10,000 new houses and apartments had been built and new investors in the development were still being sought. Against the wishes of the government (and of Gordon Brown in particular), the exhibition cost the public purse infinitely more than was ever intended. Although the exhibits undoubtedly did provide a certain amount of entertainment and possibly a modicum of inspiration, they clearly provided neither of them on anything like the scale that Blair, Mandelson and the others had originally had in mind. Furthermore, unlike the 1951 Festival of Britain, the 2000 exhibition failed utterly to relate to the whole of the UK as distinct from its South Eastern extremity. And, as we noted earlier, no new management structure was put in place – at least not until it was far too late.

But of course the New Labour government had all along a scarcely concealed sixth criterion by which it wanted the Dome to be judged: namely, its success in projecting Tony Blair and his government as a dynamic, efficient force for good in modern Britain. The Dome, if anything, had quite the opposite effect, making Blair's government look inept, depriving it of its aura of modernity and proficiency and reinforcing instead its association with hype and banality. That said, no minister was sacked or resigned (at least not over the Dome), and the fiasco appears to have had little or no effect on the outcome of the 2001 general election, which Labour under Blair won handily. It was a blunder for which the country paid a heavy financial price and a heavy price in terms of opportunities foregone, but no one in any political party ever paid a political price.

Ironically but also appropriately, whereas the very name of the Royal Festival Hall still serves in its way to commemorate the Festival of Britain, the dome's current name, the O_2, commemorates the corporate brand of a European telecoms company.

9

The great training robbery

I ndividual learning accounts – born 1996, died 2001 – lived a short life and died a sudden death. They were by no means a blunder in the grand manner; they were far from being on the scale of the poll tax or the blunders that resulted in the mis-selling of pensions. Individual learning accounts failed to achieve their principal objective, but some people did benefit. They wasted only a few hundred million pounds rather than several billion. They resulted in the defrauding of hundreds of thousands of people on low and middling incomes, but the individuals affected lost only small sums of money, some of it provided by the government, not their life savings. Hundreds of small businesses found themselves in financial difficulties, through no fault of their own, but few actually went bust. Yet, in conception, design and execution, the learning-accounts scheme was a well-nigh perfect example of a policy blunder. Some management courses in business schools still use it as a case study in failure.

Most blunders of the kind described in this book are gestated in Whitehall and occasionally in Downing Street. In this respect, individual learning accounts were different: they began their short life in opposition. The aim of the accounts was simple: to offer skills training to many of the large numbers of people who lacked any appropriate work-related qualifications. John Major's government had toyed with the idea of learning accounts, but then rejected it on the grounds that it would be administratively complex and do little more than subsidise existing training schemes. Undeterred, the Labour party in opposition took up the idea. Tony Blair and his inner circle of advisers were eager to identify new ways of tackling

Britain's most critical social and economic problems, notably social exclusion, the lack of educational opportunities and Britain's poor productivity
record compared with those of its competitor countries in the US, on the
European continent and elsewhere. Individual learning accounts appeared
to be just such a way. They would draw in large numbers of the socially
and economically excluded, and they held out the promise of raising the
levels of labour productivity in the UK. Better-trained workers would be
more productive workers.

There was clearly a serious problem to be addressed. Far too many
people, including a large proportion of school leavers, lacked qualifications
for employment of any kind. Traditional apprenticeships were in steep
decline, education for sixteen- to nineteen-year-olds (for those who were
still in education) was insufficiently vocational, and too many employers
were failing to offer their employees even minimal training. A fresh, bold
new approach was required. The idea was that the government, instead of
paying further-education colleges to run courses, or else finding ways of
encouraging employers to train their staff, should fund trainees directly, by
enabling them to open their own learning account. The prospective trainee
would put down a small initial deposit, which the government would then
generously top up. Individual account holders would then be free to spend
the money in their account in whichever way they thought most useful to
them. It was assumed that further-education colleges, commercial training
companies and other providers would respond to their demands.

For Blair and those around him, the concept of individual learning
accounts had great appeal. Improving educational standards ("education,
education, education") and tackling problems of social exclusion ranked
high in New Labour's list of priorities. So did improving the UK's economic
performance. The idea of individual learning accounts was also attractive
politically because it would help to differentiate New Labour's approach
to governing from both the Conservatives' and Old Labour's. Unlike
Conservative governments, a New Labour government, if elected, would
not expect everyone, however badly off, to fend for themselves. Instead, it
would "empower" people, by giving them the means with which to help
themselves. A New Labour government would also be unlike all previous
Labour governments. It would not allow people simply to rely on whatever
services central and local governments chose to provide. Rather, it would

encourage people to be modern citizens and to take responsibility for their own personal betterment. Individual learning accounts were in keeping with New Labour's wish to recast – and to be seen to be recasting – the traditional relationship between progressive governments and the people they served. Labour's manifesto for the 1997 general election contained a firm commitment: "We will invest public money for training in Individual Learning Accounts which individuals – for example, women returning to the labour force – can then use to gain the skills they want."[1]

Labour took office in May 1997 and the newly rechristened Department for Education and Skills (DfES) took on overall responsibility for the proposed new accounts. David Blunkett, the department's first secretary of state under Labour, was an enthusiast for the project; he was a passionate advocate of adult education and strongly committed to a scheme that formed a small but symbolically important part of a programme for transforming ordinary people's life opportunities through education. His permanent secretary, Michael Bichard, shared Blunkett's interest in expanding educational opportunities and also believed his own responsibility and that of other officials was to find creative and resourceful ways of fulfilling the government's commitments, however ambitious. "It was", as an official said, "a department where the can-do, delivery culture was very strong."

But at first nothing much happened. Blunkett and his officials had other commitments to honour. New Labour came to power with an ambitious programme for educational reform that included building new schools, expanding nursery education, improving standards, cutting class sizes in primary schools, introducing literacy and numeracy hours in primary schools, giving every school an IT infrastructure and access to the internet, establishing local education action zones in deprived communities and much else besides. All of these initiatives cost a good deal of money, attracted a significant amount of media attention and inevitably preoccupied ministers, their special advisers and their officials. The department published a consultation paper as early as July 1997 and another in February 1998, but otherwise individual learning accounts simmered quietly on the back burner and for a considerable time showed no signs of coming to the boil.

One reason for the slow progress in designing the scheme was that the department assumed that the big retail banks would be interested in attracting and managing the new accounts and accordingly made overtures to several of them. The Treasury encouraged the department to explore with banks the possibility of offering customers and potential customers a savings model similar to that offered by the recently introduced ISAs, Individual Savings Accounts. The discussions with the banks proved protracted and frustrating, however, largely because it gradually became clear that the banks regarded the prospect of managing individual learning accounts as a wholly unattractive proposition. It would involve their administering hundreds of thousands, perhaps millions, of individual accounts with only tiny deposits in them. They also doubted whether tax incentives to save for adult education – as distinct from incentives to borrow or spend money on it – would have wide appeal. They could not imagine that a savings-based individual learning account scheme would ever take off and expand into a big business in the way that ISAs had. There would be no associated loans business and no significant retail investment business. The banks, it slowly emerged, were simply not interested.

Even so, Gordon Brown, an enthusiast for the scheme, announced in his March 1999 budget, two years after New Labour took office, that every adult in Britain would soon be entitled to open his or her own individual learning account. The first million people to apply would be eligible for a £150 grant towards the cost of their course, provided they chipped in with at least £25 of their own money. Thereafter account holders would be entitled to a discount of 20 per cent, worth up to £100, on their spending on eligible courses, with larger discounts of 80 per cent, worth as much as £200, for the cost of courses in some subjects, including basic numeracy and computer literacy. A variety of tax reliefs would also be available. A month later, a number of Training and Enterprise Councils launched a modest programme of pilot schemes in various parts of the country based on the Treasury's save-to-learn concept.[2] Early in 2000 the Further Education Funding Council also ran a limited number of pilot schemes exploring the impact of fee discounts on participation in learning.

Appraisals of these pilot schemes reported mixed results, their firmest conclusion being that the save-to-learn model was not catching on and that individual learning accounts and discounts would not be enough on their own to reach the critical target groups of the unqualified and undertrained. What was needed were proactive providers and means of encouraging employers, Job Centres, welfare workers and others in a position to influence those in the greatest need of acquiring basic skills. Michael Bichard, the principal DfES official involved, alerted the Treasury to the findings from the pilots and suggested the possibility of looking again at the whole individual learning accounts idea, but the Treasury swiftly reminded him that they were a firm manifesto commitment. The department's thinking thereafter seemed to take little account of the pilots' results.

Early in 2000, after two and a half years of fruitless negotiations, the Education Department finally gave up on the banks. The scheme would have to be delivered in some other way. Simultaneously, the rapid introduction of learning accounts was gradually becoming a political imperative. Learning accounts were undoubtedly a firm manifesto commitment, and at the next election, due by now in only about eighteen months, Labour ministers would want to be able to demonstrate that they had delivered on the pledge.

Working to an increasingly tight deadline, the department proceeded to make a number of crucial decisions about the design of the scheme. Having ruled out the banks, it decided to put out to tender the task of administering the scheme. Soon the contract was awarded to Capita, a large company with extensive experience of administering big customer databases and also of working for the government. However, that was only after all five of the other bidders for the contract had withdrawn, either because they regarded the proposed timetable as impractical or because they regarded the scheme as likely to prove unprofitable, or both. But the department, while aware of the risk of dealing with only one bidder, was not unduly concerned. It had previously commissioned Capita to manage another new scheme, also one of considerable complexity, and Capita had handled that project well. Its bid also seemed to provide good value for money. The department therefore dismissed the option of standing down Capita and relying instead on its own agencies' in-house expertise.

The DfES and Capita were never meant to be partners: the department was the contractor, in charge of designing the scheme, while Capita was merely responsible for implementing it. Capita's multiple tasks were to create a national database of account holders and providers of training, to set up a system to enable prospective trainees to open, manage and monitor their accounts and to enrol in their chosen training programme and, finally, to set up a parallel system for providers to register with the scheme, publicise their courses, enrol trainees and charge their trainees' individual learning accounts for payment for the training subsequently provided. Every bit of that was to be accomplished within the space of five months, so that the scheme could be fully up and running by the autumn of 2000.

The department – in this case, ministers themselves – also decided to open up adult education and training to the market. Their civil servants presented them with the case for approving a list of accredited providers, such as further-education colleges and already established commercial training organisations; but ministers rejected any such notion. Apparently egged on by their special advisers, ministers regarded the further education and training establishment as conservative and unimaginative, especially in relation to those people most in need of training: that is, those who had left school with few or no qualifications and had since then not been in education. Ministers took the view that barriers to entering the training market should be kept as low as possible, in order to encourage new providers to enter the market, to generate competition and to provide potential trainees with the widest possible choice. It was hoped by these means to entice the hardest-to-reach groups – the unqualified, the unemployed and single mothers – into equipping themselves with employable skills. Representatives of the further-education sector warned about the risks to quality of having an unregulated market, but their warnings were dismissed as self-interested and protectionist: "They would say that, wouldn't they?" Ministers, trusting the market, wanted a demand-led, not a supply-led, scheme.

Ministers took another important decision in the same demand-led spirit. The arrangements for registering account holders and training providers, and for bringing the two sides together, should be as simple, as flexible and as fast as possible. The aim was to transform the world of adult learning by attracting into the market both hundreds of new training providers and thousands, ideally millions, of new learners. It was essential that prospective account holders were not deterred by having to fill in lengthy forms, and that prospective training companies not be put off by intrusive bureaucratic checks on their professional and financial standing and the service they were providing. Similarly, neither the department nor anyone else would screen the content of courses, their mode of delivery or the prices charged. Even if ministers or officials had wanted to do any or all of these things, there was simply not enough time.

The online registration and payment systems were therefore designed to make it as easy as possible for both potential learners and providers to sign up. Anyone aged nineteen or over who met the usual residence and nationality requirements could apply to Capita for an account. All they had to do was provide Capita with a minimum number of personal and contact details and be prepared to put at least £25 into their account. Capita would then open their account, give them a registration number and top up the account with a government grant of £150 for the purchase of eligible training (as much as £200 for some courses after the first million accounts had been opened). Those with accounts could then book any course or courses they wanted to enrol in with any registered provider. Any institution, company or individual purporting to provide training could register on the Capita database and publicise the details of the courses they were offering. All that providers had to do was register with Capita a name, address and bank account details. They did not have to produce any evidence of past experience of providing training, let alone evidence of quality or accreditation. The provider could then book the names of its eligible learners on Capita's database, confirm after seven days of the start of a course that the training was being provided and immediately claim payment (a maximum of £200 for each account holder). Every week, Capita sent a payment file to the Department for Education and Skills, and without further ado the department paid the claimed amount directly into the provider's bank account. As intended, the system was simple, flexible and fast.

It was also – surprise, surprise – wide open to fraud. It lacked any of the standard security checks. For one thing, there was no mechanism for confirming the validity of training providers' contact details. If a provider's name was removed from the register for any reason, there was nothing to stop it, him or her from re-registering under a different name and address, and there was no way of knowing whether that had happened. For another, there was also no means of checking the provider's claim that the training in question was actually being provided – or had ever been provided – until such time as a dissatisfied learner complained. During the first year of the scheme, people who claimed to be providers could even submit registration applications on behalf of individual learners; but nothing was built into the system to check the validity of the names and addresses submitted and to confirm that the individuals in question actually wanted to register. One weird feature of the system was that providers, or people claiming to be providers, were given free access to the accounts of learners who had allegedly signed on for one of their courses and could arrange for the department to pay money directly to them from the learners' accounts without the account holders' prior knowledge. These so-called learning accounts thus bore no resemblance to normal bank accounts. Unwittingly, ministers and officials had constructed a veritable adventure playground for all manner of fraudsters and crooks.

The department was well aware that the scheme carried risks with it, and during the frantic summer of 2000, with only months and then weeks to go before its launch, it did carry out a risk audit. But the audit focused solely on the number of learners, not on quality or the potential for fraud. Ministers and officials feared that the scheme would be a failure in its own terms, that it would not provide enough people with enough training, not that it might be ripped off. The department assumed that, because the cash transfers involved were for such modest amounts, significant sums of public money were not at stake. Unaccustomed to dealing with the wideboys of the wider world, officials simply failed to notice that there was scope for abuse. Capita was never asked to incorporate security and validity checks in the system, despite its substantial expertise in that area. Throughout, in the words of one official, "Fraud was simply not on the radar. It was not part of the mindset." Officials accepted, of course, that the providers of training would vary in quality and efficiency, but they assumed that market forces would quickly sort the wheat from the chaff. Satisfied learners would stay with their existing provider; dissatisfied customers would find an alternative. Simple as that. But, as a parliamentary post-mortem pointed out, that simple notion "was naïve, given that many of the people the Department was trying to encourage into learning were those least able to assess the quality of the training on offer".[3]

Individual learning accounts were launched in September 2000 and, like the personal pensions of a decade earlier, they immediately proved a roaring success. There was a surge of interest from prospective learners and providers alike. The millionth account was opened shortly before the 2001 general election, less than nine months after the launch, to the immense satisfaction of both David Blunkett and Gordon Brown. By the autumn of 2001 the number of account holders had swelled to 2.5 million. Within its first year of operation, 8910 training providers had registered with the scheme, a far larger number than anticipated given the previous size of the sector.[4] Many operators were evidently new to the industry. The government had, it seemed, achieved what it had wanted to achieve: the creation of a new, more dynamic, more inclusive system of adult education and training. "The first genuinely popular training initiative" was the excited verdict of one of David Blunkett's policy advisers.[5]

Initially, no one in the department seems to have thought that there was anything suspicious about the extraordinary growth of the adult training sector. But then, during the summer of 2001, complaints from individual account holders and local trading-standards officers began to trickle in, and disturbing stories began to appear in the press. Within a month, the trickle had become a torrent. By the end of August of that year, the department had received 4300 complaints, mainly of mis-selling, aggressive marketing, poor value for money and the blatantly low quality of some courses. *Trading Standards Today* reported that "companies have been door-knocking at residents' homes, asking them to sign up to 'free educational courses'." It added: "When the individual signs up, the 'course' organisers are able to claim their £150, but those who sign up are offered little more than cheap educational booklets and no actual support or learning opportunities."[6] The department responded by requiring learning providers to sign a learning-provider agreement as a condition of registering, by issuing good-practice guidelines to both providers and learners, by establishing a compliance unit to investigate complaints and, in late September 2001, by suspending registration of new providers. Still, the department was not unduly concerned. Officials regarded these as teething problems, inevitable under the circumstances.

But the measures taken over the summer proved totally inadequate. The torrent of allegations turned into a flood, and on 24 October 2001 Estelle Morris, who had succeeded Blunkett as education secretary, announced that the scheme would be suspended in a few weeks' time. But even a few weeks were not enough. By the end of October, only one week after Morris's announcement, it emerged that the number of filed complaints had risen to 8500, many of which alleged that money had been taken from individuals' learning accounts without their holders' knowledge. In late November it further emerged that unauthorised third parties were offering to sell providers hundreds of registration numbers of individual learning accounts. At this point, in order to protect public funds, Morris suspended the whole scheme with immediate effect. Her counterparts in the devolved administrations in Scotland, Wales and Northern Ireland followed suit.

For several weeks after the scheme ended, the department continued to underestimate the scale of the abuse and fraud that had occurred, presenting learning accounts as a victim of their own success and the suspension of the scheme as only a temporary measure. Morris herself put on a brave face, insisting on the day she announced to parliament the suspension of the scheme that learning accounts had "been a great success in bringing down the financial barriers to learning" and had "opened up access for a great many people to a wide range of learning opportunities". She added, however, that the rapid growth of the scheme had exceeded all expectations, "causing us to think again about how best to target public funds in this area and secure best value for money".[7] In response to an opposition backbencher asking for "frankness and candour" about the amount of fraud, she refused to acknowledge that it had played any part in her decision to suspend the scheme, or indeed that any substantial fraud had occurred.[8] In the course of an opposition-led debate in November 2001, she further assured MPs that fewer than 1 per cent of account holders had lodged complaints, that the number of training providers referred for investigation – about four hundred – was also small in comparison to the total number of providers, that the police were investigating only four of them and that no charges had yet been brought.[9]

Morris's assurances with regard to fraud, although undoubtedly given in good faith, were hopelessly wide of the mark. By the end of 2001 the true magnitude of the abuse and fraud to which the scheme had been subject was becoming apparent. The number of lodged complaints – and thousands of complaints must have gone unlodged – had risen to over nineteen thousand. The number of providers subject to investigation by the department had reached nearly seven hundred. What is more, in the region of 40 per cent of the complaints lodged with the department contained allegations of outright fraud. The department's field teams reported a wide range of abuses. Many of the so-called providers had neither the skills nor the facilities to provide training. One investigator reported a typical story:

> The premises where we carried out the audit had previously been a pet and garden shop (the sign was still above the door). Overall the visit atmosphere was strained. When we asked for space to work … one desk was cleared … but the provider sat on one side [of it] for the entire visit reading the newspaper. The three of us were therefore obliged to work on the one side of the desk … [The] provider had very little paperwork to support his claim. What he had was in a few folders and he brought it to the meeting in a Sainsbury's shopping basket."[10]

Another investigator said:

> One learning provider's records were stored in a garden shed. Another's records were in plastic bin bags, kept on an upstairs level of a warehouse full of cheap children's toys which had to be gingerly negotiated to access the bin bags.[11]

As though all that were not enough, it turned out – though not of course in good time – that many holders of individual learning accounts simply did not exist. They were figments of the criminal imagination. Fraudsters had found it easy to figure out how account numbers were constructed and to invent thousands upon thousands of phantom seekers after truth (or at least of a better job). In one case, 6000 learners turned out to live at the same residential address. In another, the names in which learning accounts had been opened were not proper names but Hindi swear words. Thirteen alleged providers had registered more than ten thousand learners each, making them collectively larger than 80 per cent of all the legitimate further-education colleges offering part-time courses put together.[12] The Department for Education and Skills knew nothing of these abuses, and certainly not their scale, prior to the scheme's being abandoned, because the national registration system lacked any capacity to monitor and detect them.

The most serious form of fraud, in both financial and security terms, was the siphoning off of money from unused accounts belonging to account holders who had not actually booked a course from whomever was supposed to be their provider. Some so-called providers had identified number sequences of learning accounts and developed a method of spotting unused accounts, from which they would scoop out the remaining balance without the account holders' knowledge. Others used powerful computers to generate a large volume of random numbers in the expectation that some of them would match the numbers of accounts with surplus balances. By the time the learning-accounts scheme was finally wound up, it was estimated that rogue providers had stolen from a quarter of all the accounts ever created. One of the providers investigated by the department's audit team was disarmingly frank: "We saw the ILA scheme as money lying in the street – so we went and picked it up."[13]

It took two and a half years for the DfES to assess the full magnitude of the abuse and fraud that had taken place, to identify perpetrators, to bring prosecutions and to validate claims of abuse and offer redress. The House of Commons Public Accounts Committee estimated that of the £290 million of public money spent on the whole scheme – already £90 million over budget – at least £97 million had been siphoned off by fraudsters.[14] The real sum was probably significantly greater, but the inadequate checks and controls in the department's original specification of the scheme made it impossible to know.

There were, of course, all manner of post-mortems, but none of them dug deeply. They identified in detail why the scheme had gone wrong but not why ministers and officials had contrived to devise it so that it was bound to go wrong. The relevant parliamentary committees did grill officials from the Education Department, but the ministers who had devised the scheme in the first place, and the department's permanent secretary at the time it was devised, were never asked to give evidence. All of the various verdicts were damning. The Commons Education and Skills Select Committee quoted approvingly one witness's description of the scheme as "a licence to print money", and concluded that it was "a disaster waiting to happen".[15] The National Audit Office used more measured language but its deadpan list of recommendations spoke for itself. The first of them read:

Departments wishing to implement innovative demand-led projects, for which there is very little or no relevant experience, should prepare detailed business process models and sensitivity analyses for a wide range of scenarios. They should also develop contingency plans in case the project does not proceed as expected.[16]

In other words, when government departments are trying something new, they should be alert to the probability that something will go wrong and plan accordingly. They should look before they leap.

Moreover, the findings of independent research into the scheme were clear. The scheme not only leaked money: it failed to achieve – and probably never could have achieved – its principal objective. It did succeed in bringing a large number of new and bona fide training providers to the market, largely in the private sector, and it did succeed in attracting into training some of those it was meant to help, notably women wishing to return to work. But it failed miserably to reach the vast majority of those it was meant to help: disadvantaged people lacking any sort of vocational qualifications. Perversely, its greatest success was among those who least needed it: namely, people who already had degree-level qualifications and beyond. Predictably, the better educated proved themselves far more able than the less well educated to take advantage of the opportunities – and the subsidies – offered by the new free market in training.[17] That was not at all what those who had devised the scheme had had in mind.

10

Tax credits and debits

The policy initiatives we have described so far were mostly home-grown. They were Made in Britain. Tax credits were different: to a large extent, they were imported from the United States. As shadow chancellor during the mid-1990s and then as chancellor after 1997, Gordon Brown was in the market for ideas about how to raise the incomes of Britain's poorest people. He found one such idea in the US, where a device called the Earned Income Tax Credit had been introduced in 1975 and then expanded under the administration of President Bill Clinton following his inauguration in 1993. Brown himself spent some part of most years in America, and his principal economic adviser, Ed Balls, was close to many senior figures in the Clinton administration, including Robert Reich, Clinton's first secretary of labor, and Larry Summers, later Clinton's Treasury secretary. Summers had taught Balls at Harvard.

In essence, tax credits were a simple device. They were the obverse of tax liabilities. Instead of the poor paying income tax, they would be in receipt of means-tested cash credits as a way of augmenting their incomes. Tax credits would not be universal benefits; they would be targeted at the poor. They would also, it was hoped, not discourage people from taking work; far from being a form of unemployment benefit, they would be targeted at those already in work. They might even have the effect of encouraging the unemployed to find work if they were persuaded that they would be better off in work than out of it even if the work on offer was badly paid. Indeed, in both the US and the UK, tax credits were seen as potentially forming part of a broader array of welfare-to-work policies, intended, among other things, to attack at its roots the "dependency culture" that was believed to exist on both sides of the Atlantic. They had the added advantage that they could be administered via the existing tax system; they were not in any obvious way "handouts" or a form of "welfare". If desired, tax credits could also be so arranged that they benefited, in particular, working families on low pay with dependent children. One of their key objectives could be to reduce the number of children who were living in poverty.

From Gordon Brown's point of view, tax credits as a policy option had multiple attractions. They strongly appealed to his undoubted idealism and his unfeigned abhorrence of both poverty and idleness. They appealed to him as a Labour politician and a potential Labour leader, someone who was determined to remain in the good books of his party. They also appealed to him as a Labour chancellor determined, especially in the Blair government's early years, to rein in public expenditure – or at least to rein in anything that could be made to look like public expenditure – and to convince the business community and the markets that, unlike most previous Labour chancellors, the economy and the public finances were safe in his hands. Not least, they appealed to him because, if they could be made to form an integral part of the tax system, they would automatically be under the Treasury's control and therefore under his. Whatever his mixture of motives, tax credits quickly became one of Brown's *grands projets*. He mastered the subject in its full intellectual complexity. "In this he became a member of an admired minority, because most of his colleagues found the subject of tax credits less than enthralling. Indeed, the Chancellor's obsession with tax credits became something of a joke in political and journalistic circles."[1]

Labour's manifesto for the 1997 general election was vague on the subject, saying only that a Labour government would "keep under continuous review all aspects of the tax and benefits system to ensure that they are supportive of families and children"; but Brown went further in his 1999 budget speech, the same one in which he announced individual learning accounts. He announced the introduction of a range of new tax credits and the upgrading of similar benefits that the Conservatives had already introduced, emphasising the importance of such measures for working families with children. "It is time", he said, "to reform the tax and benefit system to strengthen the family by putting children first." His long-term goal, he said, was "to bring together the different strands of our support for children" and "to create an integrated and seamless system of child financial support".[2] He made it clear that these innovations were merely works in progress, and that more would soon follow.

Like the poll tax in a previous generation, Brown's new line of policy, although imported as a concept from abroad, was otherwise developed wholly in-house – and Brown's policy house had even fewer rooms than its 1980s predecessor. It was more a tiny flat than a suburban semi. In Margaret Thatcher's time, ministers and officials in the Department of the Environment had gestated the poll tax largely on their own; but they had, within limits, sought the views of external assessors and had kept the prime minister fully on board, certainly in the aftermath of the famous 1985 Chequers meeting. Other ministers also knew what was happening. Cabinet committees and the cabinet collectively, if foolishly, endorsed the policy. By contrast, the new Labour chancellor worked almost entirely on his own, together with a small group of his own people. In Gordon Brown's view, taxation was the Treasury's business and nobody else's; and tax credits were deemed by him to be a form of taxation (albeit a very peculiar form, since they were the exact opposite of real taxes, with money being paid out rather than gathered in). Within the Treasury, Brown and his team of close advisers regarded even the most senior civil servants as high-class dogsbodies, not as genuine policymakers.

The chancellor certainly had no trouble seeing off the department that might have been expected to take the lead on financial issues relating to families and children: the Department of Social Security. He decided that tax credits were to be the core element in the government's overall anti-poverty policy without consulting DSS ministers, let alone actually doing serious business with them. His task of sidelining the DSS was made easier by the fact that its secretary of state in the early days, Harriet Harman, was one of his acolytes, someone who would not have been disposed to challenge the judgement of her political master even if she had fully understood the implications of tax credits, which, like most people, she probably did not. Potentially more troublesome was one of Harman's junior ministers, Frank Field, whom Tony Blair had installed in the social security department precisely in order to think radical, out-of-the-box thoughts. Unusually, Field did understand the implications of tax credits, and he was unpersuaded of their desirability. Partly for that reason, he did not get on well with either Harman or Brown. By the time Harman and Field's ministerial successors at the DSS appeared on the scene, the government's policy of relying very heavily on tax credits was firmly in place.

More impressive, and perhaps more surprising, was Brown's success in sidelining the prime minister. From the beginning, Tony Blair, while not objecting in principle to tax credits, doubted the wisdom and practicality of focusing on them. He acknowledged in his memoirs that he was "not a fan of tax credits".[3] He believed that tackling the problem of poverty would be better served by focusing on education and health. But the chancellor made sure that the prime minister was never allowed to stand in his way. He ensured that Blair was not kept fully informed on the issue – or sometimes not even informed at all. On one occasion, the prime minister complained to his press secretary that Brown and his people had grossly and deliberately underestimated the amounts that tax credits would cost: "They basically lied to me about it, to get it through me."[4] On another occasion, Blair sat next to the chancellor in the House of Commons as he delivered his annual budget statement. He was "astonished to hear Brown announce extra billions for his pet tax credits when he had denied money for Blair's priorities on the grounds that they couldn't be afforded" – at which point Blair turned to Alistair Darling, who was sitting on the other side of him on the front bench, and whispered: "He told me there was no money."[5] In every struggle over tax credits between the prime minister and the chancellor, the chancellor won hands down. In fact, there were very few such struggles because both sides knew beforehand who would win. Blair eventually gave up and lost whatever interest he had ever had in the subject.

With Blair's reluctant acquiescence but without his full support, Brown's work in progress continued. Two years later, in his 2001 budget statement, he announced increases in the size of the benefits already available to working families and their children and indicated that a complete overhaul of the existing system was in the offing: "Our vision of the future of the tax system for work is of one that by integrating low starting rates of tax and targeted tax credits makes work pay, brings more people into work and moves us towards our goal of full employment."[6] Towards the end of 2001, one of Brown's Treasury subordinates, a person with the apt title of paymaster-general, Dawn Primarolo, introduced in the House of Commons a Tax Credits Bill. It received its second reading in December 2001, passed uneventfully through both houses of parliament and received the royal assent a few months later as the Tax Credits Act 2002. It comprised seventy clauses (including one on polygamous marriages) and six detailed schedules. It ran to sixty-six printed pages.

This new legislation consolidated most, though not quite all, of the existing tax credits into two: a new Child Tax Credit and a new Working Tax Credit. Most of those eligible to receive the new Child Tax Credit were carers, usually mothers, responsible for looking after school-age children. The great majority of those eligible to receive the new Working Tax Credit were employees and some of the self-employed on low pay. In both cases, how much the credits were worth in practice depended largely on how much those eligible for them were earning from work and how many dependent children they had. The actual amounts of the credits were to be revised – probably upwards – from time to time. Because people's financial, family and other circumstances were likely to change frequently, and because from the outset it was acknowledged that taking into account every single one of these changes would be intolerably costly and time-consuming, the general approach was to award tax credits for a year at a time, on the basis of an individual's income over the course of the previous year. But due allowance was made for any significant changes – such as the birth of a new baby or the onset of a disability – that took place during the current year. The system was meant to be flexible, albeit within reason. It was also to be introduced in its full plenitude as quickly as possible.

The tax-credits system was thus to be far more ambitious than anything that had preceded it. At the same time, the way in which it was to be administered – and who was to be in charge of administering it – changed radically. Employers continued to be responsible for making most of the actual payments to individual employees in connection with the Working Tax Credit (as they had been in connection with the similar previous credits). Also as before, overall responsibility for that credit remained with the Inland Revenue, shortly to become Her Majesty's Revenue and Customs (HMRC), a semi-autonomous arm of the Treasury. But the arrangements for the new Child Tax Credit underwent fundamental change. Its predecessor credits had been administered and paid out, much as though they had been traditional social security benefits, by the Department for Work and Pensions, as the Department of Social Security had been rechristened. However, under the new dispensation, responsibility for the Child Tax Credit was lodged, along with responsibility for administering the Working Tax Credit, with the Inland Revenue. It seemed sensible to have the two tax credits – the recipients of which were often the same people – housed under the same administrative roof. One curious consequence of this seemingly innocuous change was that the Treasury, the traditional scourge of the so-called spending departments in Whitehall – such as the Ministry of Defence and the Department of Health – suddenly became itself a major spending department.

The massive expansion of the tax-credits system and the new arrangements for administering them were not without their critics. Treasury tax experts warned the chancellor that a heavy reliance on tax credits would be inefficient and probably ineffective. They reported that John Major, who had toyed with the idea of introducing tax credits, had been put off the idea because they would undoubtedly lead to widespread fraud. As for the imminent transfer of substantial bodies of work from the Department for Work and Pensions to the Inland Revenue, one senior Treasury official is said to have told Brown: "This requires massive reorganisation at breakneck speed."[7] As the Tax Credits Bill progressed through parliament in 2001–02, Conservative and Liberal Democrat MPs and peers were muted in their criticism, partly because many of them found the government's overall welfare-to-work concept congenial. Even so, several MPs did draw attention to the potential for fraud inherent in the scheme, and others complained of the new arrangements' sheer complexity, a degree of complexity that might lead, among other things, to fewer people taking advantage of the new credits than were legitimately entitled to. One backbench Tory MP drew attention, presciently, to a further potential defect in the scheme:

> It is a bit much to expect all claimants to be particularly adept at estimating current year income. Although we know that the Government will ask those people to make notifications of changes in their circumstances during the year, there is a severe risk that they will get that wrong and that they will continue to claim payments to which they are not entitled. They may not be acting fraudulently, but

such things may happen by accident or through their incompetence in that regard. They will then be hit with a huge bill from the Inland Revenue for the repayment of overpaid credit at the end of the year, and I can envisage that causing severe problems.[8]

But the volume of criticism, both inside and outside parliament, was limited, and in any case Gordon Brown did not take kindly to criticism and mostly ignored both his critics and whatever they had to say. Tax credits were his project, and he was determined to press on with it come what may.

In the event, an amazing amount did come the government's way, far more than most people – apart from a handful of Whitehall insiders – expected. The payment of tax credits proved to be a shambles, "a scene", as the dictionary puts it, "of disorder or devastation; a muddle, a mess". The mess that followed their introduction adversely affected hundreds of thousands of poor people, many of them exceedingly poor. It took many years to sort out – if, indeed, it ever was. The financial and other costs of attempting to sort it out were enormous. As early as 2003, the head of the Inland Revenue, Sir Nicholas Montagu, had ruefully to acknowledge to a House of Commons committee that the new scheme had gone "spectacularly wrong".[9] Eventually the prime minister himself, though hardly personally responsible for tax credits, felt obliged to apologise in parliament for the "hardship and distress" that their faulty administration had inflicted on large numbers of poor families.[10] Gordon Brown, however, appears never to have apologised, at least not in public.

The tax-credits muddle was multidimensional. To begin with, the new scheme was inordinately complicated from the point of view of thousands of claimants. The Revenue required claimants, especially those who had not previously filed income-tax returns, to provide them with a substantial volume of information pertaining to their financial and personal circumstances – and then possibly later on during any given financial year to report to the Revenue any material changes in those circumstances, which could be numerous. Even MPs complained that, when they tried to fill out the relevant forms, they frequently made mistakes. To compound that problem, the Revenue's Tax Credits Office found it impossible in the early years to deal promptly and accurately – or, in many cases, to deal at all – with the large volume of queries that customers directed at it. The Tax Credits

Office operated a Tax Credits Helpline, but initially it was hopelessly understaffed and, even when more operators were recruited or seconded to the task, they were often undertrained and unsympathetic. One claimant complained to the parliamentary ombudsman: "I have made umpteen telephone calls and each time I have to explain the situation. Every time I am told that they cannot help me further and that they merely log the call to the team who is dealing with my case. Many months later and [there is] still no solution in sight."[11] At least that person did manage to speak to an operator. In 2005 the National Audit Office estimated that during the first two and a half years of tax credits, more than a hundred million calls were made to the various regional helplines and that more than half of that huge number went unanswered.[12] Many thousands of people, frustrated at not being able to get through on the phone, wrote letters instead but never received an acknowledgement, let alone a proper reply.

Applying to be awarded a tax credit was further complicated by the fact that, whereas tax credits were usually paid weekly or monthly, the basis on which they were paid was calculated annually in arrears. At the outset, to take the extreme case, those applicants – there were several million – who had had no previous contact with the Inland Revenue and had never submitted a tax return were required to inform the Revenue of exactly how much they had earned during the financial year two years prior to their application. That task was beyond many of them and must have contributed, as several Labour and Liberal Democrat MPs had warned that it would, to the initially low take-up of tax credits. When tax credits were first introduced in April 2003, it was reckoned that, whereas some 5.7 million people were eligible for either the Child Tax Credit or the Working Tax Credit (or both), only 3.7 million had applied.[13] In time, the gap closed substantially, but the non-claiming of tax credits remained widespread.

Inevitably, the Inland Revenue had no choice but to impose deadlines, a date or dates by which claimants were supposed to have submitted their tax-credit applications to the Tax Credits Office. Millions of people met the deadlines and applied on time, but millions did not. Either way, there remained a good chance that they would receive their payments either late or not at all. The scheme as a whole was immensely complicated, people made mistakes on their applications, millions of applications had to be checked, the Inland Revenue was short-staffed for these purposes, the existing staff were not accustomed to dealing with what were, in effect, benefits rather than taxes, and they were similarly not used to dealing with frequent changes of circumstances rather than with regular PAYE and tax returns. Having been exclusively in the tax-collection business, the Inland Revenue now found itself in the benefits-dispersal business. Officials from the DSS helped as best they could, but the Treasury ensured that they played only a peripheral role, and anyway the new arrangements were almost as unfamiliar to them as they were to the Revenue.

In fact, staff shortages and inadequacies were only a part – arguably a small part – of the problem. The principal problem was that the new system was overwhelmingly IT-based and that the IT did not work properly. The Inland Revenue had long had a successful working relationship with the Texas-based IT company Electronic Data Systems (EDS); that firm had, for example, successfully engineered the switch from a system under which the Inland Revenue calculated millions of individuals' income-tax liabilities to a system – still in use – of self-assessment. EDS assured the Inland Revenue that it could design software adequate to deal with the complexity of the new tax-credits scheme, and on the basis of past experience the Inland Revenue had no reason to doubt EDS's word. In addition, the Office of Government Commerce conducted one of its regular "Gateway" reviews of a major new government procurement project and gave EDS's proposals, and the Inland Revenue's proposals for managing the project, the highest possible marks. Everything seemed set fair.

But the appearance was totally misleading. The new IT system proved not to have been adequately tested. At times it became hopelessly over-loaded. Staff were insufficiently familiar with it and often input incorrect information. Electronic scanning of applications frequently resulted in errors, some of them gross (as when claimants stroked through a box on the form relating to disability only for the computer to think that the claimant suffered a disability and calculated his or her entitlement accordingly). The system occasionally jumbled together the financial details of individuals who were unrelated but had similar names. Different elements of the system often failed to communicate with each other; and, even when they did communicate, they frequently transmitted to each other false, misleading or incomplete information (including failing to notify each other that a given tax credit had already been paid to a claimant, with the result that the same individual received the same payment twice). It took the Inland Revenue months to pick up the fact that for more than a year the system, on the occasions when it was informed that the income of one partner in a relationship had changed, automatically reduced to zero its record of the other partner's income even if that other partner's income had remained exactly the same. Needless to say, delays were endemic: delays in inputting information, delays that occurred when the system was overloaded, as it frequently was, delays in processing applications, delays in notifying claimants of the outcome of their claims and delays in the making of accurate payments. All of these system failures, and they were legion, did not result in a majority of claimants failing to receive the credits to which they were entitled: the majority – usually those whose claims were relatively straightforward – were reasonably well served, even in the early days. But the adversely affected minority was huge, running into many hundreds of thousands.

For those individuals and families adversely affected, the effects frequently bordered on the catastrophic. People who were in dire financial straits received their money late, often very late, and sometimes not at all. People who had previously been in receipt of benefits paid by the DSS found their benefits abruptly terminated without their being replaced by tax-credit payments that had not yet arrived (and which, for all they knew, might never arrive). The initial deadline for people to apply for the new tax credits was 31 January 2003. Those who applied in time and whose applications were successful were supposed to receive their payments in April of that year, but in April 2003 some three hundred thousand applications had still not been processed, and of course those individuals who had not submitted their applications by the deadline were held even longer in the enormously long queue that had developed by then. Agonised complaints flooded into MPs' surgeries and postbags, into Citizens Advice Bureaux and, sooner rather than later, into the Office of the Parliamentary Ombudsman. The ombudsman, Ann Abraham, cited in one of her highly critical reports the case of a Mrs C:

> Mrs C's April 2003 tax credits award of around £43 per week was not paid due to "technical difficulties". She made frequent calls to the Tax Credits Helpline to try and sort out the problem without

success. Eventually she was offered emergency giro payments from her nearest Revenue office, some distance away. The loss of tax credits meant that she could not afford school dinners for her six-year-old son. She suffered sleeplessness, anxiety and depression as the family's financial difficulties grew, causing arguments and conflict in her marriage. On her second visit to the local Revenue office, she was wrongly advised that tax credits had not been paid because she had failed to sign and return her award notice – which she had done. She writes: "I was so distressed, helpless and didn't know what to do next."[14]

One cabinet minister, David Blunkett, lamented to his diary: "We have had an utter fiasco with the tax credits: tens of thousands of people without any money and no sign of their getting it in the near future." He even felt moved, against his normal practice, to lend money to one of his constituents. (He was not sure whether she would pay the money back, but she did.)[15]

In the event, the Inland Revenue did succeed – by recruiting and seconding extra staff and by starting to sort out the various IT problems – in reducing the delays in paying out the credits. But then, almost at once, an entirely different problem presented itself: it emerged that the Revenue was paying out far too much money and paying it out to far too many people. Furthermore, having paid it out, it was now trying to claw much of it back. And, whereas the problem of delayed payments was sorted out tolerably quickly, the problem of overpayment proved far more intractable.

The core of the problem lay in the misfit, alluded to earlier, between the annual basis on which people's tax credits were assessed and the changes, possibly numerous, that might occur during any year in an individual's or family's circumstances. Applicants for tax credits were asked at the beginning of each year to estimate, on the basis of their previous earnings, how much they expected to earn during the coming year. If their estimate was accepted by the Revenue, they would then be paid in instalments during the course of the year the tax credit or credits to which they were – or appeared to be – entitled. Then, at the end of the year, the Revenue would compare what the recipients had actually earned during the year with what they had thought they were going to earn, and, if they had earned more than they thought they were going to, they were asked to refund some – or, in exceptional cases, all – of the money they had received. To the Revenue, with its long experience of annual demands, payments and refunds, that way of operating seemed sensible; but to hundreds of thousands of tax-credit recipients that sensible-seeming *modus operandi* rapidly turned into a nightmare, often literally.

The scale of the overpayments was vast, as people in receipt of tax credits failed to notify the Revenue of relevant changes in their financial circumstances and as the Revenue, for its part, failed to log accurately a significant proportion of the many thousands of changes that were notified. The first year, 2003–04, was the worst. There were 5,670,000 claims for tax credits. Of that total, 1,879,000 or almost exactly one-third were found at the end of the year to have been overpaid. The aggregate sum involved was a prodigious £1,931,000,000. Almost as much was overpaid during the next two years. By the middle of the decade, the situation had begun to improve, but mainly because the Revenue now disregarded a larger proportion of claimants' increases in income. Towards the end of the decade, in 2009–10, 20 per cent of all claims, affecting more than a million individuals and families, were still being overpaid, and the sum involved remained prodigious: £1,230,000,000 – that is, well over a billion pounds.[16]

The amount of human anguish caused by all this can be imagined. Of course, many thousands of claimants just took the money and either disappeared altogether or else defied the Revenue to claw it back. They took the view, in the words of one official, that tax credits were "a sweetshop". The Revenue knew who these people were (more or less) but often had no idea where they were. At the same time, however, many thousands of claimants were the innocent victims of the way in which the system operated. They had little or no idea that they were being overpaid or, if they did, by how much they were being overpaid and what they were supposed to do about it. They then received at the end of the year a demand, which could be peremptorily worded, insisting that they must repay a stated amount – an amount that was often, by the standards of poor families, enormous. It was also frequently the wrong amount. The Child Poverty Action Group complained, so did the Citizens Advice Bureaux, and the parliamentary ombudsman's reports were replete with case studies of the kinds of suffering caused. One woman realised that the income figure quoted in her initial tax-credit award notice was incorrect and immediately notified the Revenue. When she received no acknowledgement of her notification and continued to receive the tax credit, she assumed she must have made some mistake. She did not contact the Revenue again, only to be asked to repay £1449.75 – for her, an extremely large sum – at the end of the year. "It has been my sole intention", she told the ombudsman, "not to get into debt and I cannot begin to describe to you the stress and anxiety that this whole process has created."[17] Sometimes overpayments were remitted, sometimes not. Sometimes the victims of such errors were modestly compensated, sometimes not.

It can also be imagined how difficult hundreds of thousands of people, most of them poor, many of them with little education, found it to cope with the uncertainties inherent in the system. They did not know for sure what was going to happen; they could not plan ahead. The government's intention had been to provide individuals and families on low incomes with a guaranteed minimum income – a minimum, to be sure, but nevertheless one that they could count on. The CAB drew attention to the fact that people on low incomes (and probably many on not so low incomes) typically budgeted on a daily, weekly or monthly basis, not across a whole year. The poorest were often highly adept at juggling their short-term finances. But, as the CAB pointed out, the new, annualised system threw such ad hoc arrangements into confusion.[18] The ombudsman referred repeatedly to the adverse consequences of the system's "degree of inbuilt financial insecurity" and cited, among many others, the case of Mr and Mrs Q who suspected, rightly, that their tax credits were being overpaid and who alerted the Revenue to that fact on several occasions but who, thanks to a procession of Revenue errors, continued to receive for months more money than they were entitled to. Eventually the couple complained to the ombudsman about "the great worry and distress they were being caused by the uncertainty regarding their award". They were "unhappy that they could not properly manage their finances".[19] The volume of such complaints gradually diminished but never disappeared altogether.

The misfit between the system that the government was seeking to operate and what was actually happening on the ground went even wider than the discrepancy, which was already wide, between the government's insistence on "annuality" and the way in which a substantial proportion of British families managed, or tried to manage, their finances. For example, the Revenue would often inform claimants that their claim would be dealt with within twenty-eight days; but twenty-eight days, which may seem to someone who is well off to be a reasonable waiting time, may for someone who is living from hand to mouth seem an eternity. Taking full advantage of tax credits demanded from claimants the skills almost of an accountant, and, while millions of claimants did possess such skills up to a point, many hundreds of thousands did not – as a CAB report acidly noted:

> Many people suffer from a lack of basic literary and numeracy skills, yet claiming and renewing tax credits, and keeping the Revenue informed about material changes of circumstances, means people must be capable of handling complex information and maintaining full household records. We do not think this is realistic, even if the system is administered correctly [which, in the CAB's view, it was not being].[20]

This same misfit was physically embodied in the differences between local DSS benefit offices and Inland Revenue offices. The DSS offices were equipped with toilets accessible to members of the public. The Inland Revenue's were not, with the result that Revenue staff found themselves having to deal with mothers with small babies and elderly people with bladder problems. In addition, whereas the Inland Revenue's customers tended to be orderly and patient, the DSS's customers could be loud-mouthed and obstreperous. To their dismay, harassed Revenue officers found themselves for the first time confronted quite often by demanding and difficult DSS-style claimants. The officers in question did their best, but it was not easy. Some civil servants in the Department for Work and Pensions suspected that the small coterie of Treasury ministers and advisers who had concocted the new tax-credits scheme had never been anywhere near a local DSS benefits office. "They didn't know", one of them said, "what they didn't know."

Another persistent problem, though on a smaller scale, was fraud. Illegal immigrants claimed and were awarded tax credits. Individuals posing as employers and employees occasionally colluded to claim tax credits to which no one was entitled. On several occasions, criminal gangs targeted employers with large numbers of employees, stole the employees' identities and then proceeded to claim the tax credits due to those employees. One gang stole the identities of 30,000 Network Rail employees and succeeded, at least for a time, in collecting the tax credits due to 14,000 of them. Another stole the identities of 8800 men and women working for Jobcentre Plus in and around London and proceeded to lodge 2700 successful tax-credit claims. Estimates of the amounts of money lost as a result of the various frauds varied widely – no one could know for sure exactly how extensive the frauds were – but they ranged upwards towards £50 million. The head of HMRC described what was going on as "organised criminality of the vilest kind".[21]

Over time and very gradually, the tax-credits shambles was partly sorted out. It became less shambolic. Phone calls were answered. There were fewer complaints. The IT system worked better. More people were paid the right amounts of money more or less on time. The incidence of fraud diminished. But the post-2003 system never worked entirely satisfactorily, and the costs to taxpayers, as well as to thousands of individual claimants, were enormous. By the spring of 2007, HMRC had, in effect, given up on clawing back more than £2 billion it had overpaid claimants. It had also had to pay compensation to thousands of claimants whose tax-credit claims had been mishandled in one way or another. Likewise, it had failed to recoup all the money it had paid to EDS, the scheme's original IT contractor, for that firm's failure to deliver the software it had promised. The Public Accounts Committee's reports after the events were scathing. One of them noted, among other things, that in 2006–07 the parliamentary ombudsman had reviewed 393 complaints about tax credits and had fully or partially upheld 74 per cent of them. The committee added: "The proportion of complaints upheld on tax credits is higher than for any other department investigated by the Ombudsman. It is unsatisfactory that so many people have to pursue their complaint through the Ombudsman, having exhausted the Department's own complaints procedures."[22]

Gordon Brown moved from Number 11 to Number 10 Downing Street during the summer of 2007, and his successor, Alistair Darling, felt obliged during one of his first parliamentary appearances as chancellor to acknowledge that the volume of error in the tax-credits system remained unacceptably high. "We need", he said, "to get the levels of error down and ensure that the right sums are being paid to the right people."[23] Nevertheless, he defended the concept of tax credits – and the forging of a close link between the benefits system and the tax system – both in parliament and later in his account of his time as chancellor. Independent commentators also seemed to agree that the new tax credits introduced in 2002–03 had gone some distance towards reducing the incidence of poverty, especially child poverty. All the same, in the words of two of them, Gordon Brown's tax credits had been "an administrative nightmare" and ultimately no more than "a sticking plaster".[24]

Ministers in the coalition government that came to power in 2010 agreed that Labour's version of tax credits had been both of those things. Led by Iain Duncan Smith, the new secretary of state at the Department for Work and Pensions, they quickly decided to scrap Gordon Brown's scheme and to replace it with a single Universal Credit, which would retain Labour's link between the tax and benefits system, which would go further and integrate out-of-work and in-work state benefits and which would be administered solely by the Department for Work and Pensions, without any direct Treasury or HMRC involvement. From the beginning, the relevant ministers' pronouncements emphasised that they intended to make haste slowly. The decision to introduce the new system was made in 2010. The relevant legislation did not reach the statute book until 2012. No one could expect to be in receipt of a Universal Credit before 2013 at the earliest. Only very gradually would the old benefits and tax-credits arrangements be phased out. Introducing the new government's proposals to the House of Commons, Iain Duncan Smith alluded to the defects inherent in the previous government's arrangements:

> We will cut through complexity to make it easier for people to access benefits. The intention is to cut costs, reduce error and do better at tackling fraud ... A far simpler system, which operates on the basis of real-time earnings, will also reduce the scope for underpayments and overpayments. We all know from our experience as constituency MPs that that can create anxiety and disruption, and can prove very difficult to correct.[25]

156

Neither in the aftermath of Duncan Smith's initial announcement nor during the subsequent debates on the subsequent Welfare Reform Bill did anyone on the Labour benches rise to offer a robust defence – or really any defence at all – of the previous government's scheme. By the end of 2010, Gordon Brown's version of tax credits was doomed. Sometime in 2013 or 2014, it would probably be all but dead.

The former chancellor's personal commitment to tax credits had been passionate. He also managed from time to time to give the impression that he regarded them as a cure for all of the nation's ills. After Gordon Brown left the Treasury and moved to Number 10 in 2007, one of his junior ministers, David Lammy, took the opportunity of a working breakfast at Number 10 to raise with the new prime minister the issue of knife crime. Many of Lammy's Tottenham constituents were worried about it. Mothers, in particular, feared that their sons might become involved in it. "What are we doing for these women?" Lammy asked.

> Gordon looked at me quizzically while I spoke, as if I was missing something obvious. "Tax credits," he responded as soon as I had finished. "If they're single parents and they're working, they'll be entitled to them." With that there was a pat on the arm.[26]

Serious riots broke out in Tottenham in the summer of 2011. It seemed that tax credits had not done all the work they were supposed to.

11

Assets unrecovered

I n 2003 the government of the day, in a blaze of publicity, established the Assets Recovery Agency, whose wholly commendable purpose was to extract from criminals the proceeds of their criminal activities. Because that was its purpose, both parliament and the media welcomed the creation of the new agency. However, four years later, in 2007, the government announced that the agency would shortly be wound up. Almost everyone, including ministers, reckoned it had been a failure, for the simple reason that it appeared not to be doing what it was supposed to be doing. It was not recovering criminals' assets, or at any rate, it was not recovering them in sufficient quantities to justify the agency's continued existence.

Towards the end of its life, the agency's chief executive appeared before the House of Commons Public Accounts Committee; and, at the end of a gruelling session of oral evidence, the committee's chairman, Edward Leigh, summed up the position as he saw it:

[Y]ou have spent £65 million and you have recovered £23 million. You have no complete record of the cases referred to you. You have worked on over 700 cases and only managed to recover assets in a mere 52; 90 per cent of financial investigators you have trained have not completed the courses that they need to. The fact is that, despite the very effective performance you have put up today, the criminal fraternity are laughing at us, are they not?[1]

The charge sheet was damning. The Assets Recovery Agency had already been condemned.

Before taking office, Tony Blair had famously promised that any government formed by him would be "tough on crime, tough on the causes of crime". In 2000 he commissioned Number 10's Performance and Innovation Unit to recommend measures for being tough not only on crime and the causes of crime but also on the proceeds of crime. The unit's report observed that most crime was committed for profit but that Britain's criminal justice system as it stood was not equipped to recover convicted criminals' unlawful gains, whether for the community as a whole or for individual victims. Less than 1 per cent of criminal convictions resulted in a court order for the recovery of criminal assets, and the amount recovered was typically less than half the amount ordered. The problem was worsening as criminal gangs became increasingly adept at money-laundering.

The report argued that the ease with which convicted criminals were allowed to retain the proceeds of their crime was more than an affront to common justice. It was ethically repugnant, it made it harder to prevent crime and it did damage to communities. Criminal organisations invested their profits not only in enriching their leaders but in funding more criminal activities, while at the same time small-time crooks who enjoyed flaunting their ill-gotten possessions became negative role models for impressionable young men, especially in deprived neighbourhoods. Effective action to confiscate illegal profits would lower criminals' social status in addition to depriving them of cash. It would also deter crime. The report's emphasis was on the desirability of deterring crime and making communities more secure, not on any financial benefits that might accrue to taxpayers or, for that matter, victims. It called for a "joined-up strategic approach" to the confiscation of criminals' assets, an approach that would comprise new legislation, stronger powers to tax illegal income and wealth and new measures to counter money-laundering and to ensure that making confiscation orders became the norm in criminal proceedings. It also called for the creation of a cadre of well-trained specialist financial investigators and the setting up of a National Confiscation Agency under the Home Office.[2]

The Proceeds of Crime Act 2002 incorporated most of the report's recommendations. Among other things, it established the Assets Recovery

Agency and armed it with new powers of confiscation. It removed the distinction between the types of criminal profits that could, and could not, be confiscated, and it also provided that prosecutors no longer needed to prove in court that a criminal's assets were the proceeds, not only of crime in general but of specific crimes or specific types of crime. The newly established agency was to be a "non-ministerial department", one that would report directly to parliament. It was to function independently of the government of the day in the sense that ministers had no power to instruct it to target individual criminals or even specific types of crime.

The government assigned the new agency two principal tasks. One of them, somewhat tangential to the main purposes of the legislation, was to supervise and accredit the training of "financial investigators", men and women who would take part in the conduct of criminal investigations that involved either the theft of money or money-laundering (and who could in principle work for bodies other than the Assets Recovery Agency, such as the police or the Inland Revenue). The other task – on the face of it, its main one – was to disrupt organised criminal networks by recovering criminals' assets. In this latter connection, it was given various powers. It could initiate confiscation proceedings against convicted criminals, whatever the nature of the crimes they had committed. It could initiate civil proceedings in the courts that would allow it, on the balance of probabilities, to recover the proceeds of criminal activity (cash, houses, cars, jewellery and the like). It could even ask the courts to freeze or seize the assets of individuals who had been charged with a serious crime but not yet convicted. The legislation went so far as to allow the new agency's director to issue tax assessments to individuals and companies in cases where he or she had reasonable grounds for suspecting that their taxable income, gains or wealth were the product of criminal conduct even if he or she could not prove that that was the case. Reasonable cause for suspicion was all that was required, though the individual or company assessed could appeal in the usual way. The whole package was – as it was meant to be – stern stuff.

But it was also meant to be impressive stuff. Indeed, ministers behaved as though impressing the public were its principal purpose. They set about establishing the new agency at breakneck speed, allowing no more than six months between the passage of the relevant legislation and the formal launch. Ministers, including the prime minister, reckoned the launch would make a terrific news story. The Labour party had always been regarded as being soft on crime, and New Labour under Tony Blair was intent on erasing precisely that image. On the day the new agency was formally launched, David Blunkett, the home secretary, proclaimed that it would come after "the homes, yachts, mansions and luxury cars of the crime barons".[3] Number 10 was even more ambitious. Downing Street officials were keen to organise video footage on Day One of helicopters and police officers knocking down the doors of a Mister Big. They were disappointed to be told that, even if a suitable Mister Big happened to be available, the agency could hardly obtain the necessary court order before it had come into existence. Even so, the launching of the agency did make a very good news story, one carried on the main television and radio news bulletins.

The Assets Recovery Agency began work in February 2003. The Treasury was funding it, and the Treasury, as was its custom, demanded that its work be assessed on the basis of a number of key performance indicators. For reasons that are not entirely clear, it was agreed even before the agency came into being that it should aim to – would indeed be expected to – cover its costs by 2005–06 and, before that, to recover at least £60 million in criminal assets by 2004–05. However, neither the Treasury nor the Home Office, the agency's progenitor, had any basis for judging what it was reasonable to expect from its offspring. Number 10's Performance and Innovation Unit had proposed a raft of performance indicators for a confiscation agency set up along these lines, but it had attached no numbers to them and had paid no attention to practical issues of implementation. No pilot studies had been undertaken, and no one had any idea what would happen when the new agency's legal powers began to be tested in the courts.

The Home Office had also not produced any kind of business plan. Instead, the agency's first (and, as it turned out, last) director, Jane Earl, a former local-government chief executive, found herself expected to produce one within six weeks of her taking up her post. There was little to go on, because no agency like hers had ever existed before, at least in the UK. She suspected that during the first three years the pickings in terms of recovered assets would be slim, but she accepted that financial self-sufficiency within two years was a challenging but probably achievable target. However, by the time she arrived on the scene, the targets – the key performance indicators – were already in place. They would be the stand-ards by which the agency would be judged. The fact that they existed and were publicly known suited the Treasury for financial reasons, Downing Street for political reasons and the media because of their obvious news value. From the day of its launch, the agency was a high-risk operation, one that might fail to meet the exalted expectations of the Treasury and Number 10, not to mention the tabloids.

Very soon, well before the end of the agency's first year of operations, 2003, it was evident that, whatever the agency's draconian powers under the law might be, the recovery of criminals' assets was going to be hard work. It was going to be a far more protracted, complicated and expensive business than everyone in government apparently assumed. In the words of one official, "The trouble with the Home Office was that it considered success to be getting a bill onto the statute books, not how it operated in practice."

One of the many unexpected causes of delays was the referrals system created by the 2002 statute. The Assets Recovery Agency could not launch investigations on its own; it had to await cases being referred to it by other agencies, such as the police, the Inland Revenue and its successor, HMRC, and local authorities. But most of these so-called referral partners did not refer. As late as August 2006, only 129 referral partners out of a possible 696 had forwarded any cases to the agency.[4] Most of them never did get around to it. They scarcely noticed the agency's existence and were not informed about it; and they were vague about its role. Tax offices and the trading standards agencies, in particular, were in the dark. Police services tended to be more co-operative, but the law required them, if they wished to confiscate criminals' assets, to proceed in the first instance through the criminal courts rather than turning first to the civil courts or the tax system.

Moreover, even when other organisations did refer cases to the agency, the agency found it took far longer than expected to take the cases through the courts. Most actions in the civil courts take about two years to com-plete, and the agency had planned on that assumption; but, in the event, its cases tended to drag on for roughly four years. As a result, the hoped-for monies were slow to come in. The procedure for freezing criminals' assets by means of what were called "interim receiving orders" required the agency to convince the relevant court that, on the balance of probabilities, the assets in question had been unlawfully acquired. But because the law was new and there were therefore no precedents, the agency felt compelled to proceed cautiously and prepare thoroughly. Its priority was to win every case it brought, in order to establish its reputation as a responsible but also formidable litigator. It did win all the cases it brought, but such careful preparation took time.

Cases also took longer than expected because defendants and their lawyers were adept at deploying delaying tactics. Defendants simply failed to turn up to hearings or to engage with the legal process in any way, and the agency found that it had no effective sanctions for dealing with them. Defendants' lawyers sometimes asked the court to declare that their own costs be met from the assets that the agency was seeking to reclaim, and the lawyers' estimates of their costs were often implausibly high. Of course the agency challenged these estimates, but just doing that led to further delays. It did not help that, in addition, the High Court – the court with which the agency did business – sat for only thirty-four weeks a year. "The whole business progressed on a stop-start basis", one official remarked ruefully. "It was very frustrating."

The media and politicians predictably put pressure on the agency to catch really big fish in its net, but the bigger the fish the more protracted the legal proceedings. Wealthy criminals could afford to hire skilful lawyers adept at causing delays. Many of the more sophisticated criminals took care to put their assets in companies that often had complex structures of holdings. To find out what was going on, the agency and the courts required the specialist accounting skills of professional receivers; but the total amount of time spent by these receivers, and the prodigious fees that had to be paid to some of them, were effectively outside the agency's control. To be sure, the receivers in question often succeeded in identifying extensive criminal assets that would otherwise have remained hidden from the agency; but sometimes, after expending much time and effort, they discovered the opposite. The agency decided to investigate the affairs of one notorious gangster nicknamed "Doris Day". That gentleman's accumulated ill-gotten gains were widely believed to be in the order of £1 million; but, when the agency tried to seize his assets, it discovered that his net worth was actually a mere £55,000. His much-vaunted properties turned out to be rented, his jewellery fake and he had no cash. His most valuable single possession was his car. The media and the police, in particular, focused much of their attention on the big fish in the criminal fraternity; but some of them turned out to be minnows.

Pre-trial settlements or, rather, their absence was a further cause of delay. Counsel sometimes advised the agency to offer defendants a deal before a case came to trial. If, as was common in civil litigation, the defendants would offer to pay 50 per cent of what the agency said they owed, the agency would call it quits. But, on grounds it believed to be solid, the agency invariably refused. As Jane Earl told the Public Accounts Committee, "Our business is as much about ethics as it is about economics."[5] An important part of the agency's remit was to alleviate the effects of crime in communities, and to allow drug or prostitution racketeers to retain a substantial proportion of their profits would have the effect of enabling them to carry on, thereby sending quite the wrong message to their communities (and, incidentally, risking hostile stories in the press). Pre-trial settlements would have helped the agency to meet its key performance indicators but at the cost of its failing to meet the other objectives that it was supposed to be pursuing.

Similar reasoning also led the agency to pursue little fish as well as big ones. Putting out of business locally known drug dealers, loan sharks and benefit fraudsters might produce – indeed almost certainly would produce – only modest returns in terms of the agency's bottom line, but it could have a big impact on, for instance, inner-city housing estates, where petty criminals could wreak havoc. One agency official insisted: "Our business was to make bad people feel miserable" – but obviously that activity might not yield the maximum financial returns.

The agency was also not as well run as, under more propitious circumstances, it might have been. It suffered from a rapid turnover of staff, especially of trained legal staff, with the result that protracted and complex cases were seldom handled throughout by the same legal teams. Most of the agency's lawyers came on secondment from other organisations and soon left; few saw themselves as making their career in the agency. In 2005–06 alone, fully 50 per cent of its legal staff left, and 40 per cent of its training and development staff did the same.[6] The agency also failed to establish a single comprehensive database for its cases and referrals. Nor did it install a system for measuring the amount of time members of staff spent on each case. It was therefore never really in a position to monitor its own performance.

As the world goes, the agency enjoyed a long honeymoon, receiving quite a good press during its first two years, even when reporters pointed out that it was costing more to run than it was managing to retrieve. But towards the end of its third year, during 2006, the mood soured. The Conservative opposition, quoting the government's own figures, pointed out that during the first nine months of the previous financial year the agency had recovered a mere £2.7 million in cash forfeitures, a minuscule 3.4 per cent of the total of £82.6 million collected by Britain's law-enforcement agencies as a whole. The Tories branded the agency a "toothless body", lacking "the ability to hit criminals where it hurts".[7] The National Audit Office, in a highly critical report a few months later, noted that it had cost nearly twice as much to run the agency as the agency had so far succeeded in recovering from criminals. Furthermore, the proportion of referrals resulting in recoveries – 52 out of 707 – was meagre. The NAO's single most damning conclusion was that the agency had failed to meet the target set for it of becoming self-financing by 2005–06 and that, whatever the agency might say, it was unlikely to become self-financing even by 2008–09.[8]

Well before the NAO report was published, the government knew what was coming, and in January 2007 ministers announced that the Assets Recovery Agency as a free-standing entity was to be wound up and merged with the newly established Serious Organised Crime Agency (SOCA). A junior Home Office minister made the best he could of the decision, saying on the agency's last day that he was "pleased with the work of the Assets Recovery Agency, which has achieved a lot".[9] The merged agency, SOCA, perhaps performed a little better than the old one had, but not much. Reporting on its work in 2009–10, SOCA noted that the recovery of criminals' assets was just one strand of its activities but tacitly acknowledged that its assets-recovery arm was barely self-financing.[10] Given more time, the Assets Recovery Agency on its own might have been equally successful – or at least no more unsuccessful.

The government's blunder in first establishing the Assets Recovery Agency, and then in abolishing it so soon, had a number of aspects. One is that it was almost certainly a mistake to set up a small free-standing agency alongside existing agencies that were far larger and had far more experience. The new powers of investigation, freezing of assets, confiscation and taxation that the Proceeds of Crime Act created could quite easily have been assigned to existing agencies to pilot and apply. The creation of the new agency owed almost everything to political public relations, almost nothing to a consideration of the best means of recovering criminal assets. Nasty criminals were getting rich. The public was furious. Therefore, the government must be seen to be doing something. Whether that "something" could or would actually achieve anything was clearly a secondary consideration.

Another aspect of the blunder was the government's – that is, the Treasury's – insistence that the new agency's success or failure be judged, and be seen to be judged, in terms of the ratio between its running costs and the criminal assets it recovered. The agency's mission was to disrupt criminal organisations, reduce the volume of crime and protect communities. To the extent that it succeeded in doing those things, the financial benefits – let alone the other benefits – of doing them would have far outweighed the benefits that accrued in the form of recovered assets. But those potential benefits were never factored into the agency's key performance indicators, and ministers made no attempt to sell the agency's work to the public in those terms. It may also have been a mistake to wind up the agency so soon. Its performance was gradually improving, although more slowly than expected or hoped for, and merging it into SOCA caused inevitable administrative disruption.

But perhaps the most serious aspect of the blunder, a close relative of the decision to launch the new agency as a largely PR exercise, was ministers' and officials' apparently total failure to think carefully, if at all, about how the ambitious policy objectives set for the agency could be implemented in practice. All the practical problems that emerged – other agencies' failure to engage with this tiny new agency, defendants' non-co-operation, their defence lawyers' obstructive tactics, the length of time it took to process cases through the courts – should have come as no surprise. They could and should all have been foreseen. The original report from Number 10's Performance and Innovation Unit focused entirely on policy in the abstract. Its authors seemed to assume that, if the government did X with a view to achieving Y, then Y would automatically follow from X. The report said almost nothing about problems that might arise in the course of the policy's reaching its intended destination. The ministers who took the Proceeds of Crime Bill through parliament were preoccupied by the need for ensuring that it complied with human-rights legislation, scarcely at all with operational practicalities.

Only after it was known that the Assets Recovery Agency was shortly to be closed down did the ultimate source of its problems emerge with any clarity. The revelation came during the course of evidence given to the House of Commons Public Accounts Committee by Jane Earl, the agency's director. Austin Mitchell, a Labour member of the committee, questioned her about the agency's origins:

Mr Mitchell: [H]ere is something from blue skies thinking is it not?

Ms Earl: Yes.

Mr Mitchell: We want to stop that gap and get the money out of people, "What can we do", so that is the inference.

Ms Earl: Yes.

Mr Mitchell: Who then scoped it and decided whether it would work and what could be done?

Ms Earl: The original scoping was done by the Home Office as the Bill was taken through Parliament ...

Mr Mitchell: You mean the Bill was taken through first?

Ms Earl: The Bill set out the requirements for the Assets Recovery Agency and set out a very headline responsibility for us.

Mr Mitchell: Nobody thought before the Bill went in: "We can set up this Agency, here is how it will work and what it will do" ... It was the Bill first, "We can show these bastards" and then we work out how ... [T]he politicians are using easy populous [*sic*] rhetoric ...

and nobody is working out, until the Bill goes through, how that is going to be done.

Ms Earl: I think it is difficult for me to give you a categoric answer on that.

Mr Mitchell: That is likely?

Ms Earl: I am sure it is possible.[11]

In this book, we have already seen other cases where ministers and officials failed to look before they leapt. There are more to come.

12

Farmers fleeced

Sometimes the government – otherwise known as "the state" – fails to collect money that it claims citizens owe it according to the law. On other occasions, the government fails to pay citizens monies that the citizens in question have every reason to believe the government owes them. Usually actual and alleged non-payments of this kind occur on what might be called a retail basis – they affect only specific individuals or firms – but sometimes they occur on a wholesale basis, with whole classes of people adversely affected. One such case is scarcely known about, or probably not known about at all, except by those in the affected industry. It is the UK government's failure, over many years, to pay England's farmers in good order and good time monies owing to them from the European Union.

The story could be said to resemble a Keystone Kops silent movie screened in slow motion, apart from the fact that this particular performance was never comic, always serious and occasionally tragic. The story began with the decision of European Union farm ministers in June 2003 to reform and simplify the Common Agricultural Policy. Hitherto EU farmers had been subsidised on the basis of the amount they produced of a variety of different commodities: beef, wheat, maize, dairy products, rice, sugar, tobacco and so forth. From now on they would be subsidised solely on the basis of the amount of land that they maintained in good agricultural and environmental condition. The new arrangement was known as "the single-payment scheme" for the good reason that from now on farmers would receive one annual subsidy payment instead of, in many cases, a whole host of payments. The new scheme was meant, among other things, to be simpler to administer and to lighten the load on farmers. It was generally welcomed.

However, it was clear from the outset that moving from the old system to the new – "decoupling", as it was called – would not be easy. It would take time, and inevitably there would be losers as well as winners. The European Commission told individual European governments that, within reason, they could take their time, and it offered them a choice of three ways forward. One, the simplest, was to pay farmers an annual amount equal to the average of the amounts they had received under the old scheme in the course of the years 2000–02. That was, so to speak, the cheap-and-cheerful option. A second option, somewhat more complicated than the first but also more in keeping than the first with the EU's long-term objective of decoupling production from hectarage, was to pay farmers partly on the basis of what they had received during 2000–02 but partly also on the basis of the number of hectares they farmed or otherwise maintained. A third option, even more complicated than the second but also even more in keeping with the long-term objectives of the whole exercise, was to pay farmers on the same basis as in the case of the second option, but also gradually over time to taper off the 2000–02 production-based component of the payments in such a way that by the EU's target date of 2013 the payments that farmers received would be entirely hectarage-based and not at all production-based. There were bound to be administrative difficulties whichever option was chosen, and Franz Fischler, the EU agricultural commissioner, wrote to all the member states' governments warning them of the dangers of departing too far or too fast from the EU's preferred historical approach – that is, one that took the experience of the years 2000–02 largely into account. He warned them, in effect, that they should not allow the best to become the enemy of the good.

In the specific case of the UK, responsibility for agriculture had since the late 1990s been devolved to the separate national administrations in England, Scotland, Wales and Northern Ireland, and the UK government decided that, in connection with the new single-payment system, each of the four countries should be left free to go its own way. The Scottish and Welsh governments opted for the simplest approach, the cheap-and-cheerful, history-based approach. The Northern Ireland government opted for the second, somewhat more complicated history-plus-hectarage approach. The UK government, this time in its role as the government of England, opted for the third approach, the most complicated one, involving history, hectarage and, in addition, a scheme for engineering a progressive tapering off of the historic component. Although officials at the relevant government agency, the Rural Payments Agency, were already engaged in a large-scale programme of administrative change, they assured ministers – and, in particular, their boss, Margaret Beckett, the secretary of state at the Department for Environment, Food and Rural Affairs (Defra) – that it would be feasible to make single payments to English farmers on the basis of this third, more demanding approach. Beckett and her ministerial colleagues were keen on the third approach in any case. They knew it might prove hard to implement, but, precisely because it was the approach that was least based on what had happened in the past, it was deemed the most forward-looking of the three options. "Ministers considered that this model was the most suited to giving farmers in England greater freedom to respond to market demands for agricultural products, and to reward environmentally friendly farming practices."[1]

Ministers also decided to move quickly to introduce the new scheme. Two other EU countries, Germany and Finland, adopted the same so-called dynamic hybrid scheme, but they chose to postpone the introduction of the scheme's most complicated element, the tapering-off element, in the case of Germany until 2010 and in the case of Finland until 2011. By contrast, the government in London decided to introduce the whole package all at once. Beckett announced the government's decision to the House of Commons in February 2004. The new scheme would come into effect in England on 1 January 2005, with the first tranche of payments to be made on 1 December 2005 and the last on 30 June 2006. That was a very ambitious timetable. Right from the beginning, it was not adhered to. As early as January 2005, the Rural Payments Agency announced that it did not expect to make any payments to English farmers before February 2006 – that is, two months behind schedule. Worse was to come. The department and the agency had announced their own payments target. They had declared that they aimed – indeed intended – to pay 96 per cent of the monies owed to farmers for the first year of the scheme, 2005, by the end of May 2006. The EU's own legislation in any case required that more than 96 per cent be paid by the end of the month after that, June 2006.

Failure to do so would mean that the UK would be liable to a fine (or, as the EU decorously called it, "a disallowance"), possibly a substantial one.

The Rural Payments Agency spectacularly failed to meet its own target. Instead of 96 per cent of the allocated funds being dispersed by the end of May 2006, only a tiny fraction of them were: a derisory 15 per cent. This minuscule proportion compared poorly with the 90 per cent achieved in Wales, the 86 per cent achieved in Scotland and the less impressive but still respectable 70 per cent achieved in Northern Ireland (which had opted for the other, less complicated of the two hybrid systems). The scheme in England was obviously in chaos. Margaret Beckett told the National Farmers' Union annual conference that she was "bloody livid" with the whole situation, rather as though she had had nothing to do with it.[2] Towards the end of 2006, several months after payments had begun, belatedly, to be made, the National Audit Office reported that

> the agency has yet to recover £5.4 million of overpayments that were made as a result of an error introduced in the computer system. In addition, as at 15 September 2006 we had identified 34 overpayments and 79 underpayments in our sample of 363 cases which, if replicated across the whole population, are most likely to result in errors of £6.5 million and £17.4 million respectively.[3]

Those estimates were subsequently shown to be not far wrong. Meanwhile, despite the chaos in the system and although the chief executive of the Rural Payments Agency, Johnston McNeill, had been sacked, Margaret Beckett had been handsomely promoted. By now she was foreign secretary.

2006 was easily the Rural Payments Agency's worst year, but its troubles – and consequently the troubles of many hundreds of farmers – were far from over. The chaos persisted. Eventually most claims were paid, but the NAO insisted over many years that the agency was not able to administer the single-payment scheme in a cost-effective manner. One computer run in 2006 found that six farmers had been overpaid by more than £100,000 each.[4] Three years later, the NAO, increasingly irked by the agency's poor performance, reported that, whereas in Scotland the cost of administering each farmer's claim for a single payment was £285, the comparable figure south of the border was £1743 – more than six times as much. The auditors noted that the agency was heavily dependent on external IT support, "with over 100 IT contractors based permanently in its offices".[5] Twenty months after that, in July 2011, the comptroller and auditor general formally qualified Defra's annual accounts, saying:

> Penalties totalling £160 million were confirmed by the European Commission. This includes £117 million in respect of [the] Single Payment Scheme for scheme years 2005 and 2006. In my opinion the requirement to pay material disallowance penalties [i.e. fines] to the European Commission is not in accordance with Parliament's intention and is therefore irregular.[6]

In a statement to the press, he added: "There continues to be a significant loss to the taxpayer because of weaknesses in the administration of the Single Payment Scheme by the Rural Payments Agency." The chair of the House of Commons committee overseeing Defra responded by calling for the payment of bonuses to the agency's managers to be halted until the numerous outstanding problems were resolved.

The fines paid to the European Commission were not the only losses suffered by UK taxpayers. The National Audit Office complained that far too much money was being spent on IT, and by no means all the overpayments to individual farmers were ever recovered. The Public Accounts Committee for its part blamed Defra's permanent secretary "for administrative failure leading to additional costs that together risk exceeding £400 million".[7] One obvious blunder was the department's and the agency's failure to operate a strict *de minimis* policy. The relevant authorities in Germany simply ignored a farmer's claim if it totalled less than €100, but the Rural Payments Agency in England set out to meet every claim, however tiny. Had the English agency adopted the German approach, the number of claims allowed would have been reduced by some fourteen thousand, or 12 per cent. Merely administering the huge volume of small claims may well have cost taxpayers more than the amounts claimed.

Especially in the scheme's first two years, large numbers of farmers were hit hard. The forms they were sent were complicated, sometimes to the point of incomprehensibility. Telephone enquiries went unanswered or were dealt with by untrained or undertrained staff who were unable to answer them. The agency had no effective mechanism for tracking the claims of individual claimants. Hundreds of farmers, perhaps thousands, initially received no payments at all. The National Audit Office, which was on the case from the beginning, estimated as early as the autumn of 2006 that the delays in making payments had cost farmers between £18 million and £22.4 million in interest and in the fees they had to pay to arrange additional bank borrowing. "The wider knock-on effects on the farming sector are difficult to quantify, but some farmers claim to have postponed purchases, sold crops and livestock early or delayed payments to their suppliers."[8] Defra agreed to pay interest at a modest rate and did so. The bill was substantial: in October 2006 alone, Defra paid out £386,200. At one point there was even a danger that HMRC would collect income tax on payments that had not actually been made. Those farmers lucky enough to receive overpayments were not always as lucky as they may have appeared to be. An unknown number of them, not realising they had been overpaid, had already spent the money by the time the Rural Payments Agency tried to claw it back.

Many farmers suffered psychologically as well as financially. In a survey conducted during the first year during which payments were made (or were supposed to have been made), some 20 per cent of those interviewed "said that the delays had caused distress and anxiety for them and their family".[9] Hill farmers suffered disproportionately because payments from the EU via Defra constituted such a large proportion of their total income. Farmers found dealing with the Rural Payments Agency frustrating, and they were not helped by ministers' reticence in explaining what was going on. Margaret Beckett, while secretary of state, volunteered little information and mostly confined herself to making written ministerial statements. A common theme of responses to surveys conducted for the NAO was respondents' sense that Defra ministers and officials did not know what they were doing. "The whole process", one of them said, "has been developed by people who haven't been out to see what England is really like." Another commented, "Within a few minutes of speaking to the people it became evident that they had absolutely no idea about agriculture, farming, horticulture, anything."[10] At a hearing of the House of Commons Public Accounts Committee in 2006, the chairman, who happened to sit for a rural Lincolnshire constituency, reported that three Lincolnshire farmers had recently committed suicide and that one farmer, a tenant, had closed his business because, thanks to Defra's failure to make his single payment in good time, he was unable to meet his financial obligations to his landlord and the bank. He added, "Members representing rural constituencies will have many such cases." He dismissed the scheme as "a complete failure".[11] Significantly, the witness before the committee, Defra's newly appointed permanent secretary, in no way demurred.

Probably because farmers constitute such a small proportion of the English population, the Rural Payments Agency's multiple failures attracted little national media attention. The agency was, however, subjected to a steady drumbeat of often excoriating criticism from the National Audit Office and the relevant House of Commons committees. How, they wanted to know, had Defra and the agency contrived to cause so much confusion, chaos and, in some cases, hardship? How, simultaneously, had they managed to waste so much public money? One member of the Public Accounts Committee thought he knew the answer:

> The Government chose to introduce the most complex scheme on offer ... in the shortest time made available by the European Union, against the background of a departmental reorganisation which involved members of [the agency] being dismissed, with the possibility of tens of thousands of claimants who had not previously claimed agricultural support, in the absence of complete digital mapping and with a computer model using a task-based approach that had not previously been tried.

"Is that fair", he asked, "as a background statement?"[12] On this occasion, too, the witness in front of the committee did not demur.

Whatever else it was, the scheme was extraordinarily complex. That being so, the chaotic outcome was certainly predictable – and also, by some of those in the know, predicted.[13] One version of Murphy's Law holds that, if something can go wrong, it will – from which it follows logically that, if there are a large number of things that can go wrong, a large number of things will do precisely that. In the case of the single-payment scheme as introduced for English farmers by Her Majesty's Government in London, everything that could possibly go wrong did go wrong – and invariably sooner rather than later. If anything, the MP quoted above was guilty of understatement.

Quite apart from anything else, the single-payment scheme was introduced at a time when the Rural Payments Agency was already in the midst of a large-scale reorganisation – known euphemistically as a "change programme" – aimed at increased efficiency and cutting costs. The most effective way of cutting costs is almost always to cut staff, and cutting staff almost invariably means making redundant people who have worked for the organisation for a long time and therefore know a fair amount about it, about the substance of what it does and about its clientele. Introducing at speed the most complicated of the three single-payment schemes at the very moment when the Rural Payments Agency was shedding a large proportion of its most experienced staff meant that not nearly enough individual staff members were available to administer farmers' claims, and also that many of the best had already gone or were about to go. It also meant that the agency was forced to recruit all manner of new and temporary staff, people whom it did not have enough time to train properly. The results were twofold. The agency collectively made all kinds of mistakes, and the service to farmers was lamentably poor. The whole process was neither effective nor efficient.

Ministers and officials also grossly underestimated the number of farmers who would make claims. Under the old system, farmers were subsidised according to the amount they produced of specific commodities (hence the substantial overproduction for which the Common Agricultural Policy had been rightly blamed). Under the new system, farmers were, at least in part and in the fullness of time, to be subsidised, not according to how much they produced but according to how much land they maintained in good agricultural and environmental condition. In the case of England, the "fullness of time" meant immediately. Starting to make payments on the basis of hectarage instead of the production of specified commodities meant in practice that whole new classes of claimants were entitled to come forward. The land on which fruit and vegetables were grown now counted, and so did (or could) horse paddocks and land used for outdoor pig rearing. Not having taken all this into account, the Rural Payments Agency suddenly found itself confronted by 120,000 applications for single payments compared with the 80,000 it had been used to dealing with under the old system – an increase of 50 per cent. This unexpected increase resulted partly from the fact that it now paid farmers to register land that they had previously not had any incentive to register (even though they were supposed to). In previous years, the agency in a typical year had dealt with roughly nine thousand changes in land registration. In 2005 it was forced to deal with 100,000 such changes – an increase of more than 1000 per cent. It struggled to cope – and of course failed.

Yet another factor made the agency's task even harder than it was already. If the agency were to make payments to farmers on the basis of the amount of land they farmed and maintained, its staff obviously had to have means of verifying the size of individual farmers' holdings. Otherwise fraud could be, and almost certainly would be, rife. For this reason, the agency needed to have available to it accurate maps of England's farms. Moreover, the European Commission itself insisted that such maps be made available, and that they be digitised and not exist merely on paper. On top of all that, the maps needed to be three-dimensional: otherwise a hectare of land in the Cambridgeshire fens would look exactly the same size as a hectare in the Derbyshire dales. The Scottish executive had had a digitised mapping system in operation since 1997; the Welsh had one too. But their English opposite number did not and therefore had, in haste, to set about creating one. Almost inevitably, the mapping process was time-consuming and caused serious delays; and the maps produced, on being checked by farmers, were often found to contain errors, some of them gross. The agency did eventually acquire acceptable maps in a digital format, but only after a great deal of time and money had been wasted and, of course, farmers exasperated. Despite the progress eventually made, rumours persisted that the agency's most up-to-date maps still showed sheep safely grazing on the North Sea.

From early on, further confusion was caused by the agency's decision – prompted by a recommendation from PricewaterhouseCoopers – to organise its activities on the basis of tasks rather than claimants. Until the mid 2000s, regional offices of the Rural Payments Agency had dealt with every aspect of individual farmers' claims. There was, in effect, a one-on-one relationship between farmers and their regional offices. However, it was decided, with a view to improving efficiency (and saving money), that in future discrete tasks, such as mapping and customer service, would be centralised, with the result that the existing one-on-one relationship would be severed and that different aspects of individual claimants' claims would be dealt with by different people in different offices. The idea looked good – that is, cost-effective – on paper but proved clumsy and ineffective in practice, and it certainly alienated farmers, who found it impossible to track the progress of their claims. As one farmer put it, "Trying to contact the [Rural Payments Agency] and receive responses to letters is problematic and incredibly frustrating."[14] Two years after the introduction of the scheme, the Public Accounts Committee concluded that "the Agency is still not able to offer adequate advice to farmers on the progress of their claim".[15] The proportion of farmers satisfied with the agency's performance increased over time, but only very gradually.

It hardly needs to be said that everything the Rural Payments Agency did – from mapping farms, to despatching claim forms to farmers, to validating claims as they came in, to keeping farmers informed, to making actual payments, to paying out monies owed as a result of underpayments, to identifying and attempting to claw back overpayments – depended on the quality and the fitness for purpose of its IT systems. The success of the agency's task-based method of processing claims, as distinct from its former claimant-based method, depended utterly on the quality of its IT. In this connection, as in most others, every bit of the business had to know what every other bit of the business was doing. And, although the agency's IT systems were slowly improved over time, they never at any time fully met the agency's needs, and they were hideously expensive to maintain, upgrade and adapt.

The agency blamed its suppliers for working too slowly and assigning second-rate staff to work on the project. The suppliers in turn blamed the agency for endlessly changing its mind about what it wanted. The agency's managers failed to ensure that its suppliers designed software that would enable them to monitor the new scheme's progress (or lack of it). And everyone involved on both sides seemed unprepared to allow fully for the fact that there were bound, especially in the early days, to be changes in both government policy and EU regulations. The enormous gap between what England's elaborate new single-payment system demanded of the agency's IT systems and what those systems were able to supply narrowed over time but failed to close. In 2009 the NAO's report on the administration of the single-payment scheme complained that "the lack of sufficient progress in aligning the design of the scheme's systems to operational needs has … hindered efficient administration". It added:

> In the absence of reliable records we estimate that the IT costs for the scheme, which includes recovery work, maintenance costs, upgrades in response to policy and other changes, as well as over-heads, amounted to £130 million between April 2007 and March 2009. The Agency considers that the high cost reflects the complexity of the scheme in England, but when estimated earlier spending on scheme IT of £220 million is taken into account, we consider the scheme's IT to be very expensive.[16]

During the summer of 2011, more than seven years after Beckett's original statement to the House of Commons, the comptroller and auditor general noted drily in a report on the agency that concerns he had previously expressed about its performance – not least its IT performance – "remain extant".[17]

All these factors were in play simultaneously, and their dire effects were compounded many times over by other failings on the part of the agency. It failed to pilot the administrative arrangements that needed to be put in place to implement the new scheme. Its procedures for validating farmers' claims were excessively rigorous. It refused initially to make interim payments to farmers pending the full validation of their claims. It abandoned, only then to reinstate, a variety of much-needed contingency plans, and it persistently elevated the need to avoid paying fines to the European Commission above the need to pay money to England's farmers. Not least, no one, even at the highest levels, seemed to know exactly what was going on or who was supposed to be responsible for what. Neither Defra nor the Rural Payments Agency, nor individual managers within either of those organisations, effectively "owned" delivery of the scheme. Indeed, almost everyone involved agreed that no one really understood the scheme in its entirety (always assuming that it was capable of being understood). As the agency's sacked chief executive observed:

It was death by a thousand cuts. We started with something that we felt was relatively straightforward given the historical data, and moved to something that was more complex. The system developed over nearly a year, until it became so complex that we were delivering elements of it on a just-in-time basis.[18]

That is, if they were delivering them at all. The rural-payments fiasco was, to use the cliché, a perfect storm, though fortunately a storm that affected only a relatively small portion of the population.

Several of the deeper factors that led to this particular storm will be discussed in later chapters. For now, it is enough to flag up one apt remark made by the House of Commons Environment, Food and Rural Affairs Committee: "The policy reasons for the Government choosing the dynamic hybrid model are appreciated, but such decisions should not be made in isolation from practical realities."[19]

13

IT – technology and pathology

An eminent British historian has argued that one of the reasons Germany lost the Second World War was the chaotic way in which that country's armed services procured their weapons and other kit. The three armed services paid little attention to each other and seldom co-operated. Instead of seeking to make incremental improvements to existing weapons systems, they persisted in demanding the production of leading-edge, state-of-the-art weapons, despite the fact that none of those weapons had ever been tested in battle. All three services, but especially the army, habitually neglected to liaise with arms manufacturers for the purpose of ensuring that the fancy weapons they demanded were actually capable of being produced. Moreover, as the design, development and even manufacture of the various new weapons systems proceeded, the military constantly intervened, insisting that detailed modifications be made to the original specification. In short, the German military was a menace – and not just to the country's enemies. "No organisation was more guilty of limiting Germany's war potential than the military."[1]

There is a disconcerting parallel between the behaviour of the German military in procuring weapons during the Second World War and the behaviour of British governments in procuring not only military equipment but also IT systems ever since that war, especially during recent decades. We have already encountered instances of gross failures of IT systems in connection with the Child Support Agency, the administration of tax credits and the non-payment of monies owed to farmers. But there are many more examples where those came from. The amount of harm they have done to individuals and firms is literally incalculable. The amount of public money wasted could in principle be calculated but apparently never has been. It cannot have amounted to less than £50 billion and was probably a great deal more. Of course, not all British government IT schemes have been disasters, any more than all German military equipment during the Second World War proved deficient; the customers of both HMRC and the Driver and Vehicle Licensing Agency have benefited hugely from the successful exploitation of IT. But the offsetting list of expensive failures has grown so long as to be grotesque.

One of the most remarkable features of successive governments' ventures into the field of IT is that they have gone on and on making the same mistakes. They never seem to learn. Or, if they do learn, they seem unable to profit from whatever they have learned. In 2011 the Public Administration Select Committee published a report aptly entitled *Government and IT – "a recipe for rip-offs" – time for a new approach*.[2] The committee pointed to governments' over-reliance on a limited number of suppliers, to their ignorance across departments of their own IT-related activities, to the fact that "often the IT systems that government develops are already out of date before they are implemented" and to governments' lack of in-house capacity to manage suppliers and fully to understand the potential of IT to improve the quality of services.[3] The committee's members were unanimous in their views. They concluded that unless radical changes were undertaken, governments were unquestionably "doomed to repeat the mistakes of the past".[4] They gave the impression of writing more in hope than expectation.

In the space of a single chapter, we can touch on only a few of the more egregious examples of successive governments' IT blunders. We think it appropriate to leave the best – that is, the worst – of our examples to last.

A quarter of a century ago, in 1989, the Crown Prosecution Service (CPS) decided, in the interests of efficiency, to introduce a new computerised system for tracking all the prosecutions and potential prosecutions that the service was dealing with. The new system was meant to be up and running and deployed throughout the service's ninety-six branches by 1993–4. It never was. By December 1997, three years late, it had been deployed in only fifty-three branches – scarcely more than half – and was beset with problems, which arose partly out of technological advances and partly out of changes both in the relevant legislation and in how the prosecution service's branch offices operated. A critical report by the National Audit Office towards the end of 1997 led the CPS to abandon the project, at least in the sense of not extending it to the branches where it was not already installed. The cost per branch had already more than doubled. The House of Commons Public Accounts Committee welcomed the CPS's belated decision to cease implementing the project but then added: "It has been clear for some time that the case tracking system does not meet the needs of the CPS, and the decision to find a better approach could have been made much earlier."[5]

A similar fate befell an even more ambitious scheme launched by the Department of Social Security. In May 1994, the then secretary of state, Peter Lilley, told the National Federation of SubPostmasters' annual conference in Bournemouth that, in order to increase efficiency and reduce levels of fraud in the benefits-payment system, the traditional pension and child-benefit books would be replaced within a few years by modern swipe cards. Benefit claimants without a bank account would simply go to a branch post office, have their card swiped and checked against a national database and be paid the amount they were owed. The DSS permanent secretary told the Public Accounts Committee: "If it is on a computer, it can flash up, 'This person has now cashed X benefit on this, X benefit on that, on such and such a day', and it will be in our computer. It's a very, very big system."[6]

It was indeed a very, very big system, but it did not work as planned. In May 1996 the Benefits Agency and Post Office Counters Ltd awarded a contract, likely to be worth in the order of £1 billion, to a private consortium called ICL Pathway. Substantial progress towards creating a nationwide system to serve some nineteen million pensioners and other benefits claimants and to be operational in all 20,000 branch post offices was supposed to have been made by the winter of 1996–7; but, after repeated delays and protracted disputes among the Benefits Agency, Post Office Counters and Pathway, the government cancelled the entire project in May 1999. A highly critical ninety-page report published by the National Audit Office in 2000 attributed the need to cancel the project to the fact that control of it had been divided between the Benefits Agency and Post Office Counters. Not enough time had been allowed for specifying what these two different agencies required, nor had enough time been allowed for piloting the scheme. Not least, there had been inadequate risk management and openness on the part of all three parties involved. The NAO report noted: "The project was an ambitious one, and with hindsight, probably not fully deliverable within the very tight timetable originally envisaged."[7] Needless to say, the aborted project had done little, if anything, to reduce benefit fraud even though that had been the main point of introducing the swipe cards in the first place.

Altogether the 1990s were a great era for great IT disasters. Information technology was all the rage. Like many large organisations, agencies of the British government had enormous problems storing, integrating, transmitting, analysing – and then making good use of – the enormous quantities of data in their possession (or that were likely in future to come into their possession). IT – or "computerisation" as it was often called at the time – seemed a godsend. It was powerful. It was fast. It could store huge amounts of data conveniently and accessibly. It saved manpower and should save money. It was immune from random human error. For government departments, it had the additional, if somewhat perverse, advantage that ministers and top officials did not have to know a great deal about it. They could outsource almost the whole of it to suppliers and consultants – the real experts, possessors of arcane knowledge and speakers of an impenetrable but impressive-sounding language. Superman was dead. Enter Supergeek in all his glory. Unfortunately, ministers and civil servants evidently failed to notice that all manner of IT disasters had already lost private-sector companies many billions of dollars and pounds and had led to not a few of them going bust.[8]

The Home Office was one of the worst offenders. In April 1996 its Immigration and Nationality Directorate reached an agreement with a well-established IT provider, Siemens, to provide it with an integrated casework system to enable it to deal with a growing backlog of asylum, refugee and citizenship applications. The idea was that the new system would be fully operational by October 1998. It was not. It never was. After running more than a year late and missing three deadlines, the whole programme was abandoned at a cost to the exchequer – that is, taxpayers – of at least £77 million. At the time the programme was abandoned, the directorate's already huge backlog of cases had ballooned to no fewer than 76,000 asylum and 100,000 nationality cases. The Public Accounts Committee said it was "extremely concerned at the continuing existence of these backlogs, particularly the human misery for applicants and their families".[9] Both the committee and the NAO noted that Siemens' development of the IT aspects of the project and the operational requirements of the project had been allowed to get out of synch. The NAO commented that "the department should consider whether the proposed project might [have been] too ambitious to be attempted in one go".[10]

One disaster-inducing feature common to many government IT projects – even more than in the case of private-sector projects – was the knock-on consequences of changes in government policies and priorities. The law changed from time to time, and so, even more often, did departments' and agencies' operating requirements. And every such change inevitably necessitated changes, sometimes many hundreds of changes, in the specifications of pieces of software that had already been commissioned. Costs mounted. So did the probability that new errors would be introduced into existing systems that were probably error-prone already.

As we saw in Chapter 10, the payment of the government's tax credits was prone to such disruption. The Crown Prosecution Service's aborted case-tracking system suffered similarly. Yet another victim was the National Insurance Recording System (NIRS), which maintained – or was supposed to maintain – the full details of more than sixty-five million National Insurance accounts.

By the mid-1990s, the original first-generation NIRS, which had coped tolerably well, was ancient and undoubtedly needed replacement. Accordingly, in May 1995 the Contributions Agency, then housed in the Department of Social Security, awarded a contract to Andersen Consulting (subsequently rechristened Accenture) to develop NIRS's successor: dubbed, predictably, NIRS 2. This new system was meant to be considerably more than an update. In addition, it was meant to accommodate extensive changes to the National Insurance system that had been introduced by the 1995 Pensions Act. NIRS 2 was supposed to be fully operational by February 1997. However, that date soon slipped to April 1998 and then further to July of the same year. The new system did then become operational, but only partially. A great deal still remained to be done. In one of his reports, the comptroller and auditor general noted that by the end of 1998 "over 1,900 problems, of varying degrees of significance, had been raised with Andersen Consulting. Of these 1,589 were still to be resolved."[11] And multiple IT problems, many of them serious, persisted well into the new millennium, by which time the duties of the now defunct Contributions Agency had been taken over by the Inland Revenue, later by HMRC. Delays were innumerable. When delays did occur and major system errors became apparent, it often emerged that the relevant government agencies had failed to make adequate contingency plans.

The consequences of NIRS 2's failings were those that might have been predicted. Fraud and error in the operations of the whole National Insurance system were rampant and were estimated variously as having cost between £3 billion and £4 billion. The government failed to collect vast amounts of money in contributions that it should have collected, while at the same time having to pay compensation to thousands of pensioners and others who failed to receive the benefits to which they were entitled. In addition, some 280,000 purchasers of private pension schemes failed to receive the National Insurance rebates to which they were entitled and forfeited the gains in the value of their investments that would have accrued to them if the rebates had been – as they should have been – paid into their pension pots. The government not only undercollected vast sums: in the case of thousands of pensioners and other recipients of benefits, it made substantial overpayments, which were frequently hard or impossible to recover. David Davis, the Conservative chairman of the Public Accounts Committee, complained that "the failure to get this system working has plunged many thousands of people, including those recently bereaved and those moving into retirement, into uncertainty and fear: uncertainty about the level of their future income, fear that they might be running up a debt which they will have to repay, but the value of which is unknown."[12] Jeff Rooker, the Labour government's pensions minister, told MPs at the end of 2000: "I do not think it is a secret that the Department of Social Security is not proud of our information technology systems, which are rubbish."[13] Meanwhile, the tabloid press was replete with tales of woe, most of which were true.

Unlike the National Insurance fiasco, the great majority of government IT cock-ups have gone unremarked by both the media and the public. They have typically been complicated, technical, obscurely acronymic, lengthily protracted and mostly hidden from view. A few, however, have become real scandals. Although one of them did have its comic aspects, unlike NIRS 2, most of the individuals affected probably failed to see the joke.

On coming into office in 1997, the Blair government inherited from its predecessors the idea that the Passport Agency – now the Identity and Passport Service – should introduce a new IT system for processing passport applications. The newly arrived Labour ministers at the Home Office adopted the idea as their own and duly signed a contract with an IT supplier a few weeks later. Unfortunately, the supplier failed to supply the software required in good time and good order, and in the summer of 1999 there was chaos. The production of some four hundred thousand passports was lost, and thousands of anxious would-be travellers, many with expensive pre-booked holidays, were forced to queue for hours at passport offices in Liverpool (the office worst affected), Newport, Belfast, Peterborough, London and Glasgow. Some of those queuing in Glasgow equipped themselves with deck chairs, and an enterprising ice-cream vendor found he had a ready market. Emergency arrangements were quickly put in place, umbrellas were bought where necessary for people queuing (at a cost of £16,000), the home secretary apologised profusely to parliament for what had happened, and the most serious problems were eventually sorted out. All the same, a Home Office minister was heard to mutter that IT suppliers as a class were no better than "snake-oil salesmen".[14]

The mind-boggling problems associated with many of the 1990s IT projects arose in part out of the introduction by the Major government of private-finance initiatives (PFIs), under which the government of the day offered private-sector firms and groups of firms substantial financial inducements to invest in, and then to maintain and operate, public-sector infrastructure projects such as schools, hospitals and overseas embassies – and IT systems. Under PFIs, private-sector companies put in money upfront; taxpayers paid later. Sometimes PFIs worked to the benefit of taxpayers and the Treasury; sometimes they did not. Ones that manifestly did not included the Home Office's immigration-and-asylum IT fiasco, the costly collapse of the Department of Social Security's benefits-card scheme and Accenture's failure to deliver NIRS 2 in time, not to mention the Passport Agency's difficulties. This new type of financial arrangement necessitated new types of contracts and new kinds of working relationships between government agencies and private companies – and often the contracts proved unsatisfactory and the working relationships fraught. Terminations of PFI contracts were not uncommon. Nevertheless, PFIs proved, if anything, even more popular under New Labour after 1997 than they had under the Tories.

One of New Labour's early IT fiascos was called – somewhat optimistically, given that it was meant to support the work of courts dealing with alleged criminals – Libra. It should have been called Chaotica. Magistrates' courts deal with some 95 per cent of the criminal prosecutions brought in England and Wales, but the IT systems employed by the various area Magistrates' Courts Committees were initially patchy in quality and often unable to communicate either with each other or with law-enforcement agencies such as the Crown Prosecution Service and the police. Accordingly, the Lord Chancellor's Department decided to launch a PFI project designed to produce a unified and integrated IT system to serve the whole of the English and Welsh magistracy. In 1998 it awarded the contract to its preferred bidder, a firm initially known as ICL, later as Fujitsu Services. ICL/Fujitsu was supposed to begin delivering the new system in 2001 but succeeded in delivering most of it only by 2008. The comptroller and auditor general was still complaining about some of its inadequacies as late as 2011. Meanwhile, the sums intended to cover the cost of the project as a whole soared, from £146 million prior to the start date to £184 million by the time the contract was signed and to £232 million by 2002 (by which time the scope of the contract had been substantially reduced).

Not for the first time, work on the new IT system in this case got under way well before the relevant Whitehall department – the Lord Chancellor's Department, later the Department for Constitutional Affairs and after that the Ministry of Justice – and the various area magistrates' committees had been able to reach agreement (to the extent that they ever did) on exactly which tasks the new system was meant to perform. Also not for the first time, the new system, when it was finally delivered, did improve to some extent the magistrates' courts' IT capabilities, but it did so only two or three years before it emerged that it was already time to either enhance Libra significantly or else replace it by an entirely new system. In a report in the midst of this particular fiasco, the Public Accounts Committee was characteristically blunt: "This is one of the worst PFI deals that we have seen."[15]

Libra and NIRS 2 were typical of the obscure labels that officials insisted on affixing to government IT projects, but none of them was more obscure than C-NOMIS. In June 2004 the Home Office initiated something called the National Offender Management Service, with a view to dealing with offenders individually and sequentially as they passed through the post-conviction stages of the criminal justice system: prison or community service and then probation and resettlement. The stated aim was "end-to-end offender management". In part pursuit of this object-ive, HM Prison Service, then lodged in the Home Office, latterly in the Ministry of Justice, commissioned two suppliers to equip the National Offender Management Service, whose acronym was NOMS, with a new offender-management IT system, whose acronym – unhelpful to the lay person – was to be C-NOMIS. The two suppliers were a Canadian firm called Syscon Justice Systems Ltd and EDS, whose name will already be familiar to readers as a result of its association with the tax-credits fiasco.

The new computer system and the new management system were meant to complement each other across the board. It was, or sounded like, a splendid idea. Indeed, it would have been a splendid idea if it had worked. But it did not. Instead of an end-to-end IT system, the Ministry of Justice eventually got, at best, one that tracked the offender only part way through his or her time in the justice system following conviction. In June 2005 the lifetime cost of the project to 2020 was approved at £234 million. By July 2007, only two years later, the National Offender Management Service had already spent £155 million and the estimated lifetime cost of the project had nearly trebled to £690 million. At that point, the Ministry of Justice effectively scrapped the project, scaling it back drastically – "rescoping it" was the euphemism used – so that the data contained in the system, still called C-NOMIS, related only to offenders who were still incarcerated. The National Offender Management Service's board became aware of the spectacular cost overruns only in May 2007. Ministers appear to have become aware of what was going on no earlier than August of that year. In the words of one weary civil servant, new to C-NOMIS, "I knew we had problems when I asked for the budget and was told there wasn't one."[16]

The inevitable report by the National Audit Office would have sounded incredulous except that by the end of the 2000s the NAO had long since exhausted its capacity for credulity, at least in connection with government IT projects. One page of its report contained a box headed "Assessment of C-NOMIS against the eight common causes of project failure". It found the management of C-NOMIS guilty or partly guilty on no fewer than seven of its eight counts:

Lack of clear link between the project and the organisation's key strategic priorities, including agreed measures of success — In part

Lack of clear senior management and Ministerial ownership and leadership — Yes

Lack of effective engagement with stakeholders — Yes

Lack of skills and proven approach to project management and risk management — Yes

Evaluation of proposals driven by initial price rather than long-term value for money — In part...

Lack of understanding of and contact with the supply industry at senior levels of the organisation — Yes

Lack of effective project team integration between clients, the supplier team and the supply chain — Yes[17]

In other words, the organisation and management of the project might almost have been designed to ensure failure. Interviewed after the publication of the report, Edward Leigh, the chairman of the Public Accounts Committee, said that "kindergarten mistakes" had been repeated: "This Committee hears of troubled government projects all too frequently. But the litany of failings in this case are in a class of their own."[18]

A large proportion of the IT disasters discussed in this and previous chapters have affected the Home Office and its successor departments and also the Department of Social Security, now called the Department for Work and Pensions. But most government departments fouled up at one time or another, and in the mid-2000s it was the turn of the Department for Communities and Local Government. Supergeek was omnipresent. He was even managing to cast a shadow over the forthcoming 2012 London Olympic and Paralympic Games.

The Department for Communities and Local Government, formerly the Office of the Deputy Prime Minister and then the Department for Transport, Local Government and the Regions, was – and still is – the Whitehall department responsible for the Fire and Rescue Service in England. In late 2003 ministers and officials decided to improve the resilience, efficiency and technology of the service by replacing the existing forty-six local control rooms with a network of nine regional control centres. Underpinning the work of these new control centres would be a new national (or at least England-wide) computer system that would assist staff in handling 999 calls, mobilising equipment and managing incidents. In March 2007 the department signed a contract with a supplier, European Air and Defence Systems (later known as Cassidian), to design, develop and install this new IT system, which was meant to be in service by October 2009. Both the reorganisation of the overall command-and-control system and its attendant computer system were called FiReControl. However, after the by-now customary delays and cost overruns, in December 2010 the department abandoned development of the IT part of the project and cancelled its contract with the supplier. The FiReControl project as a whole, including its IT element, had originally been estimated to cost £120 million. By March 2011 over double that amount, £250 million, had already been spent. At the end, the National Audit Office calculated that, in its own words, the "minimum that will be wasted as a result of the failure to deliver the project" would be £469 million, nearly four times the original estimate.[19]

As usual, the NAO had no difficulty identifying what had gone wrong; and, as usual, it also found that many of the things that had gone wrong had also gone wrong on many previous occasions. The department in this case had grossly underestimated the complexity of the project and its probable costs. It had failed to provide the necessary oversight, leadership and management, including the management of its consultants and contractors. It had allowed development of the whole project, including its IT aspects, to run ahead of firm decisions about exactly what the project was supposed to achieve and how it was supposed to achieve it. Staff turnover within the department was inordinately high; in the course of the project's short life, there were "five different Senior Responsible Owners, four different Project Directors and five officers supervising the delivery of the technology". As in the case of the relationship between the Lord Chancellor's Department and the various area Magistrates' Courts Committees in connection with Libra, FiReControl "was flawed from the outset because it did not have the support of the majority of those essential to its success – its users".[20] Much of the time those with operational responsibility for the Fire and Rescue Service at the local level had little idea what was happening, and many remained unconvinced throughout that the proposed changes would in any way increase resilience and efficiency. The active co-operation of these local bodies was essential to the success of the project. It was seldom solicited, never elicited. Predictably under the circumstances, the department found itself constantly at odds with many of the local Fire and Rescue Authorities, with its own consultants and with European Air and Defence Systems, which it did eventually sack but not before that company had netted a fair amount of taxpayers' money (estimated by the NAO at £11.7 million).

It was rumoured that ministers' belated but in the end abrupt termination of the computer contract owed something to warnings they had received that, if they persisted with FiReControl and failed to organise something more effective in time, the fire and other emergency services might not be able to cope with serious emergencies during the Olympics. The Public Accounts Committee, in its report on the fiasco, in addition to remarking that "this is one of the worst cases of project failure that the Committee has seen in many years", noted that "Despite the scale of failure and waste, no one in the Department [for Communities and Local Government] has been held to account".[21] Fortunately, there were no serious emergencies during the 2012 Olympics.

Another case relating to the Department for Work and Pensions was far less serious than either the FiReControl fiasco or the abandonment of the earlier project to issue claimants with benefit cards. Nevertheless, it illustrates in a modest way the kinds of things that continually go wrong. As in almost all these cases, the intention behind the project was wholly benign and the idea looked good at the time. In 2002 ministers announced that, as a public service, it was developing an online "retirement planner", aimed mainly at people without ready access to professional financial advice. The idea was that the planner would enable people on low and middle incomes – indeed anyone – to work out how much retirement income they could expect to receive on the basis of existing pensions legislation together with whatever private pension arrangements they had made on their own. If it seemed they were not saving enough for their retirement, the planner would also calculate the amount by which they would need to increase their savings.

The only trouble was that the government, four years later, just before the planner was due to go live, announced that a radical overhaul of pensions policy was in the offing, as a consequence of which "delivering accurate online information about state pensions [let alone private pensions] would become increasingly difficult".[22] At the same time, pensions practitioners were pointing out that, given the multitude of uncertainties that existed at the time (and still do), the whole exercise was dodgy and that the government could find itself being investigated by its own Financial Services Authority for giving misleading financial advice. Accordingly, in 2006 ministers announced in a written statement to parliament that the entire scheme was being scrapped. Although they acted reasonably swiftly, certainly as compared with some of the other disasters, £11 million of public money nevertheless went down the drain.

That modest sum, however, was small change compared with the amount wasted on what has been – at least so far – the veritable RMS *Titanic* of IT disasters: the doomed-from-the-beginning NHS National Programme for IT (known to the cognoscenti as NPfIT). That particular fiasco deserves a book of its own, but in this book a few paragraphs will have to suffice.

Most unusually for an IT project, the prime minister of the day was centrally involved, at least at the outset. Tony Blair as prime minister had among his overriding objectives the "delivery" (the word he always used) of high-quality public services in general and reform of the National Health Service in particular. He was determined that the NHS in England should become more efficient on his watch, more effective and infinitely more user-friendly. Blair wanted to universalise the best practice that already existed in parts of the health service, and he had been one of the principal drivers of the ambitious ten-year plan for the NHS that the government had launched in 2000.

Two years later, in February 2002, following a Downing Street seminar that the prime minister chaired personally, the Department of Health announced a massive overhaul and expansion of the health service's IT infrastructure. One of its many aims was to create, within, it was hoped, about three years, a single electronic system for storing patients' records so that they could easily be accessed and shared among England's 30,000 GPs and roughly 300 hospitals. Initially, only authorised professionals would have access to the data, but it was hoped that in the fullness of time patients could access their own records. The directorate within the Health Department responsible for delivering the new system later described it, probably accurately, as "the world's biggest civil information technology programme".[23] In other words, the English NHS was being asked to play in the same league as the United States Department of Defense and NASA. Not everyone was convinced that the UK Health Department was capable of competing in such illustrious company. Even before the project was formally launched, one well-informed commentator asked: "Is the NHS up to the task?" He went on to answer his own question: "History suggests not."[24] He was right. It was not.

At the beginning, in 2002, the idea was that national standards for NHS IT would be laid down but that local NHS trusts would be left free to commission their own suppliers and choose their own software. However, Richard Granger, an IT consultant imported from Deloitte to take overall charge of the project, decided instead to nationalise it. No longer would there be a significant element of local control. Instead, the entire project would be managed from the centre, by an agency called Connecting for Health (CFH), with Granger at its head. Under this new dispensation, there would be five regional programmes, but each would have a monopoly IT supplier and each of the monopoly suppliers would be chosen by Granger and his people. In addition, all five of the regions would be linked by an England-wide IT "spine", the supplier of which would also be chosen, in practice, by Granger and Connecting for Health.

CFH was based in Harrogate. Down in London, at the Department of Health, ministers and officials were clearly much impressed by Granger. They acquiesced in the arrangements he proposed, and for the next five years they left matters almost entirely in his hands. The whole process of drawing up what were called "output-based specifications", of inviting suppliers to bid for the main contracts, of considering the bids as they came in, of choosing the firms to be awarded contracts and then of negotiating the contracts themselves – a process that usually took two or three years – in this instance was collapsed into one year. All the contracts had been signed by the end of 2003, and all the contractors were large, well-known and well-established firms such as Accenture, BT and Fujitsu.

Signs that the project was in serious trouble were slow to emerge, largely because the principal players – the Department of Health, CFH, the main IT contractors and Granger himself – were all, for obvious reasons, anxious that no signs of trouble should be allowed to emerge. Ministers were committed to the programme and frequently lauded it. Connecting for Health had deadlines to meet. The main suppliers were anxious to avoid the ignominy of failing to meet their contractual obligations. Granger, a proud man, was keen not only on succeeding but on being seen to succeed.

But during 2004 and 2005 it did finally begin to become apparent that all was not well. The British Medical Association warned GPs to exercise caution before agreeing to participate in trials of the scheme. A poll of both GPs and hospital doctors pointed to growing doubts among medical practitioners about the scheme's security. One of the main contractors, Accenture, responsible for two of the five regional networks, chose to incur a substantial loss and withdraw entirely from the scheme as soon as it became clear that there was no way in which it could meet its deadlines. Estimates of the total cost of the programme over a decade edged upwards – and sometimes bounded upwards – from £2.3 billion at one point to £6.2 billion, then to £12.4 billion, then (it was rumoured) to somewhere between £31 and £50 billion. Any cost savings that were made would not be remotely commensurate. A drumbeat of press criticism, muted at first, grew progressively louder. Both the *Daily Telegraph* and the *Guardian*, improbable allies, cast doubt on the viability and confidentiality of the scheme, and *Computer Weekly* repeatedly expressed technical and organisational doubts. Worst of all, although "delivery" was one of

the main aims of the exercise, CFH and its contractors were signally fail
ing to deliver. The system was supposed to be up and running in about
three years. While 155 administration systems for hospitals were meant
to be delivered by the spring of 2007, in the event only sixteen were. In
London, the corresponding figures were twenty-four and one. In truth,
however, the hospitals to which the systems had not been delivered, the
great majority, could count themselves lucky. Where the systems were
installed, they frequently crashed totally, malfunctioned in other ways
and/or failed to connect with other systems that they were supposed to
connect with. In September 2006 *Computer Weekly* reported 110 "major
incidents" across the English NHS during the previous four months alone.
More than twenty of them had affected multiple NHS sites, among other
things preventing medical staff from viewing x-rays on screens in wards
and operating theatres.[25]

Nevertheless, against all the accumulating evidence, most of the five
secretaries of state for health who served under Tony Blair and then
Gordon Brown during the lifetime of the project – Alan Milburn, John
Reid, Patricia Hewitt, Alan Johnson and Andy Burnham (an average of
just over two years each) – continued to insist that the programme as a
whole was worthwhile and that, if it was not already proving a success, it
soon would be – and the junior ministers in direct charge of the project
offered their own reassurances. However, political support for the project
crumbled. The House of Commons Public Accounts Committee in April
2007 published a report that was damning even by its high standards, and
by the end of that year Richard Granger had departed the scene. Alistair
Darling, Gordon Brown's successor as chancellor of the exchequer, made it
clear that he was reluctant to continue funding the project, and in August
2009 the Conservatives, who had been sceptical all along, announced that,
if returned to power, they would dismantle Labour's ambitious national –
that is, England-wide – scheme and instead encourage local NHS bodies to
make their own arrangements. Within months of coming to power in 2010,
the coalition government announced that, although some of its elements
would be retained, the grandiose programme inaugurated by Tony Blair
in 2002 would be wound down, and in September 2011 health ministers,
after yet another damning report from the Public Accounts Committee,
announced that the Labour government's centralised programme was,

in effect, being scrapped altogether. Many billions of pounds, rather than mere millions, had been wasted, though no one could say authoritatively how many. A frequently cited figure was £20 billion, more than enough to build three dozen general hospitals.

From its inception, the whole thing had been either, at best, a mess-in-waiting or, at worst, a mess already apparent. It began, more or less, at a meeting in Downing Street between a prime minister who knew next to nothing about computers and a clutch of computer enthusiasts. It was wildly overambitious. It was far from being essential. No one ever seems to have subjected it to a serious – or even a back-of-the-envelope – cost-benefit analysis. The programme's alleged benefits, even if they accrued, were going to be outweighed many times over by its exorbitant costs. No one ever thought to ask medical administrators and practitioners whether it was a high-priority project from their own point of view, or how they expected this ambitious new programme to mesh with their existing IT arrangements, or whether they would want to opt into the new system, or, come to that, whether they believed the proposed new system could actually be made to work. The timescale proposed for the project was ludicrously short. Delays were inevitable. In the early stages of the scheme, no one seems to have addressed the crucial, and predictable, issues of patient confidentiality. On top of all that, large parts of the enterprise were hopelessly mismanaged, in so far as they were managed at all. The rate of turnover of officials at the Health Department was even higher than in the case of the FiReControl fiasco; the project had no fewer than six departmental "senior responsible owners" during its first two years. Largely because the intended end-users of the scheme had been so little consulted, the various IT suppliers often had no clear idea of what they were supposed to be supplying – and in some cases merely sold the NHS whatever they happened to have on hand. One large-scale subcontractor was slow to deliver contracted-for software amidst allegations of account-ing irregularities.

As time went on, critics of the project used more and more colourful language to describe what was going on. A well-informed report in *Private Eye* attributed the shambles to "political vanity, official incompetence and vested interests".[26] But the flavour of the way in which the whole programme evolved was perhaps best captured by a witness who gave evidence to the

Public Accounts Committee, someone who had tried to warn his superiors in the Health Department about the consequences of the department's failure at the outset to consult clinicians:

> In those early days, it was like being in a juggernaut lorry going up the M1 and it did not really matter where you went as long as you arrived somewhere on time. Then, when you had arrived somewhere, you would go out and buy a product, but you were not quite sure what you wanted to buy. To be honest, I do not think the people selling it knew what we needed.[27]

But of course the people selling it usually sold it to them all the same. It was left to taxpayers to pick up the bill.

14

Down the tubes

The introduction, dismantling and replacement of the poll tax, described in Chapter 4, was one of the most expensive government blunders of modern times. It was also one of the most widely publicised. The same cannot be said of the public-private partnership (PPP) for the maintenance and upgrading of the London underground that New Labour established in 1998. That PPP was at least as much a blunder as the poll tax and may well have cost British taxpayers even more, but few people were aware of its existence at the time – certainly few people outside London – and almost no one has heard of it since. Utter the word "Metronet" – a shorthand term that the cognoscenti soon used to refer to the whole PPP – and most people simply look puzzled. The circumstances surrounding Metronet's collapse would have been a tremendous scandal if more people had been aware of it. As it was, it was merely scandalous – a scandal that should have been but never was.

Its origins were prosaic. The London underground at the end of the last millennium was in dreadful shape. The world's first underground railway was no longer a transport system Londoners could be proud of. On the contrary, millions of Londoners and incomers felt ground down by it. Rails were rickety, trains broke down, signals failed and stations were unkempt and dilapidated. There was chronic overcrowding. When things went wrong, no one bothered to tell passengers what had gone wrong or why. The story was told of a newly appointed manager who was taken on a late-night tour of the system. He spotted some charred bricks by the side of a line and asked his guide whether there had been a fire recently.

No, came the reply, the charring was left over from the days when trains on the underground were hauled by steam locomotives. The last steam-hauled train carrying passengers on the underground had run in 1905. It was that bad. And the explanation was simple: over many decades, successive governments had not spent nearly enough money on maintaining and improving the system.

By the time of the 1997 general election, both major parties acknowledged that something had to be done. The Conservatives, having privatised the mainline railways a few years earlier, promised in their manifesto to go further and to "bring forward plans to privatise London Underground". The Labour manifesto riposted that privatisation was not the answer to the underground's problems and announced instead that Labour was planning "a new public/private partnership to improve the Underground", one that would "guarantee value for money to taxpayers and passengers".[1] As the Conservatives lost the ensuing election, wholesale privatisation was off the agenda; Labour was against it, and so was John Prescott, the man appointed to head the new, grandiloquently named Department for the Environment, Transport and the Regions. However, it remained to be seen what the vague phrase "public-private partnership" would mean in practice. Apart from wholesale privatisation, it could mean almost anything.

The ministers who approached the task of creating this new partnership, most notably John Prescott and Gordon Brown, the chancellor, did so with two beliefs – some would say prejudices – firmly fixed in their minds. One was that private-sector firms could almost invariably be counted upon to outperform public-sector bodies. The private sector, they believed, was almost always more efficient and effective than the public. Private-sector firms were under continuous pressure to adapt, innovate and cut costs. Public-sector organisations were under no such pressure. On the contrary, they were always in danger of becoming costly, bureaucratic monsters. The government led by Tony Blair was pro-business through and through. Blair himself was business-friendly, Brown similarly "wanted to demonstrate that New Labour could do business with Business", and Prescott, although not a central New Labour figure, had emerged, somewhat surprisingly, during Labour's long years in opposition as a determined advocate of PFIs.[2]

Ministers' other belief, shared by many backbench Labour MPs, was that London Underground's existing managers were simply not up to the job (London Underground with a capital "U" being the organisation responsible for running the London underground with a small "u"). Its managers were, according to one London MP, "a bunch of muppets".[3] The fact that the tube as a whole was in such a mess was partly their fault. More than that, ministers and backbenchers held the management of London Underground responsible for the protracted delays and enormous cost overruns that had marked the building of the Jubilee Line extension. Originally due to open in April 1998, the line did not open until the very end of 1999. Originally estimated to cost £1.5 billion, it eventually cost some £4 billion. Many of the delays and increased costs were by no means management's fault; cost overruns are endemic to large construction projects. But the blame for some of the underground's failings could reasonably be laid at the managers' door, and in any case the truth of the matter was neither here nor there. What mattered was that the ministers who took office in 1997 brought with them the belief that London Underground's managers could not be trusted with the management of big projects.

Ministers were under an additional constraint, to some degree real, to some degree self-imposed. In 1997 the new Labour government was determined to keep overall public spending, at least for the time being, within the strict limits laid down by the outgoing Tory government. They wanted to demonstrate to both the general public and the markets that, against the run of history, a Labour government could also be a financially prudent government. That meant keeping a tight lid on what was then known as the Public Sector Borrowing Requirement, the total sum of money that the government would need to borrow in a given period. That in turn meant, according to Treasury officials and ministers, keeping the cost of any major new infrastructure project, such as one for refurbishing and upgrading the London underground, off the government's balance sheet. Treasury rules demanded, or seemed to demand, that such items could be kept off the government's balance sheet only if the financial risks involved in the project were borne by – that is, transferred to – some organisation other than the government, ideally a private-sector company.

Yet another factor introduced into an already complicated equation was the position of the UK government vis-à-vis the about-to-be-created Greater London Authority and its subsidiary body, Transport for London (TfL). The latter would soon be under the exclusive control of the mayor of London, someone who was shortly to be elected for the first time. The Treasury was determined from the outset that any financial arrangements relating to the future of the London underground should be put in place before control of the underground was handed over to the mayor and TfL. The Treasury wanted no nonsense from anybody outside its direct, or even its indirect, control. What made the Treasury even more determined, especially as time went on, was that it looked as though the first mayor of London was going to be Ken Livingstone, a particular bête noire of the Labour leadership in general and Gordon Brown in particular. Personal animosity between Brown and Livingstone may not have greatly affected what subsequently occurred, but it certainly did not help. Livingstone's well-publicised dislike of the PPP led ministers to become increasingly stubborn in its defence.

New Labour's pro-business proclivities and its collective contempt for the management of London Underground, together with the Treasury's determination to keep everything under its control and large-scale capital spending off its books, effectively determined the form that the new underground funding arrangements took. The public-private partnership was to be more private than public – and not much of a partnership. From the start, it was almost certainly doomed.

Following discussions with the Treasury and with its full agreement, John Prescott announced in the House of Commons on 20 March 1998 that the government proposed to establish a new public-private partnership with a view to creating "a showcase for a modern, integrated public transport system". A number of private contractors would pour billions of pounds over a number of decades into maintaining, refurbishing and upgrading the various London underground lines. "Our solution represents", he declared proudly, "an entirely new approach – a third way. It is not a privatisation ... nor is it an old-style, publicly funded nationalisation. It is a publicly owned, publicly accountable model to get the best from both the public and the private sector."[4] For work done, London Underground would pay the private-sector companies. Who would reimburse London Underground if there were any shortfall in its revenues was another matter.

As the scheme emerged over the next few months, it was simple in outline. London Underground would continue to manage and operate the tube; but the maintenance and renewal of the track, the rolling stock and the stations would be in the hands of privately owned companies, and each private company – given the scale and complexity of the operation – would consist of a consortium of several companies. London Underground management would be the nominal paymaster and would manage the contracts to be drawn up between it and the various consortia.

That was the outline. Filling in the details was another matter and, whereas it had been hoped to have the contracts negotiated and signed by July 2000, the whole process was not completed until April 2003. The bidding process was incredibly complicated. The number of contracts was large, and each was enormously detailed. Private law firms, as well as ministers and government officials, were involved at every stage. So were firms of private consultants. So was London Underground. So, latterly, were the mayor of London and Transport for London. The courts, too, became involved as the mayor and TfL sought (unsuccessfully) to have the whole exercise aborted.

In the end, contracts were let to two holding companies that were lumped together as Metronet and to a third company called Tube Lines. The two Metronet companies took responsibility for the Bakerloo, Central, Victoria and Waterloo & City tube lines and the Circle, District, Metropolitan, Hammersmith & City and East London sub-surface lines. Tube Lines, a much smaller operation, took responsibility for only the Jubilee, Piccadilly and Northern lines. The individual firms comprising the consortia included Amey (a railway maintenance company), Balfour Beattie (a building contractor), Bechtel (an American-owned project-management and construction company), Bombardier (a Canadian-owned train manufacturer), Jarvis (a railway infrastructure company), Seeboard (an electricity supply company, shortly to be acquired by EDF of France), Thames Water (a water and sewage company) and WS Atkins (an engineering and project-management firm).

Originally, the intention had been to award contracts for fifteen years, but in order to attract bidders that figure was soon revised upwards to thirty years, with each contract to be revisited – in the form of a review of performance and remuneration – every seven and a half years. An independent PPP Arbiter would ultimately decide whether the firms were meeting the terms of their contract and whether those terms should be revised in any way. One odd-seeming feature of the contracts was that the main umbrella organisation, Metronet, was allowed to operate – and did go on to operate – a tied-supply-chain out of arrangements under which it awarded contracts for specific pieces of work almost exclusively to its own consortium members. Metronet was clearly not keen on competitive tendering. Another odd feature of the contracts was that, by the time they were signed, the government had agreed to guarantee 95 per cent of the debt finance that the various participating companies raised. And debt finance constituted the bulk of their finance. They themselves put up almost nothing – a mere £350 million – by way of equity capital.

The London underground PPP came into operation in 2003; but the curious thing is that, from the moment it was first proposed, almost nobody thought it was a good idea. On the contrary, almost everybody who knew anything about it thought it was a very bad idea. Almost the only ones who believed in it – or said they did – were Treasury ministers, transport ministers, a few senior London Underground managers (who were prepared to go to almost any lengths to get out from under constant Treasury interference with their organisation) and those industrial companies, lawyers and consultants who reckoned, rightly, that they could make a great deal of money out of it. The critics of the partnership ranged across the political spectrum, and they included almost every individual and organisation that was well informed and at the same time disinterested. At a seminar in New York in 2000, an American transport specialist told Prescott to his face that he thought the whole idea was "insane".[5] A Conservative-inclined *Evening Standard* columnist, Simon Jenkins, wrote at about the same time: "I am an enthusiast for most forms of privatisation, but this one makes no sense. Further fragmenting ownership and investment in mass transit is stupid."[6] A railways expert in Britain, also writing in advance of the contracts being signed, said the scheme reminded him of the young John McEnroe addressing a Wimbledon umpire: "You cannot be serious."[7]

The critics of the scheme pointed out that it contained more than a dozen serious weaknesses, weaknesses that they believed would either cause it to collapse completely or would mean that, even if it failed to collapse completely, it would be grossly inefficient and fail to provide value for money. The weaknesses they identified are worth listing. There were an awful lot.

1) In its sheer scale and complexity, the PPP for the London underground was something wholly new. Nothing like it had ever been attempted before, in Britain or anywhere else. In the case of previous private-finance initiatives, the arrangements had usually been straightforward. The Department of Health, say, contracted with a private-sector firm to build and then to maintain for a period of years a new clinic or hospital. Both parties to the agreement – and there were frequently only two – were dealing with a single fixed asset or group of assets. But in the case of the arrangement for the London underground, a number of companies were to take over the day-to-day management of an extraordinarily wide range of existing assets (many of them in terrible shape) and to maintain, refurbish and modernise them – without actually operating them – over a period of several decades. Moreover, precisely because the companies' tasks were so various and because the actual operation of the assets would remain in the hands of London Underground, the business of organising the multiple points of interface between the companies and London Underground, and the related business of measuring accurately the companies' performance, were both extraordinarily complicated. The men and women who negotiated and organised the PPP were attempting a feat never before performed.

2) As a direct consequence, the detailed contracts that were eventually drawn up were also extraordinarily complicated, often to and beyond the point of absurdity. As someone wrote of the PPP in 2002, it is "something so complex that even those with an intimate knowledge of it cannot provide a detailed account of its scope and intent in less than a couple of hours".[8] In the end, the various PPP contracts comprised 135 separate documents, which ran altogether to 28,000 pages and more than two million words. Christian Wolmar in his book *Down the Tube* reports that one element that featured as a requirement in these contractual relationships was "consistency", by which was meant the regularity of Metronet's and Tube Lines' provision of services. One of the factors used in determining the required levels of consistency was the distance between train cabs at underground stations where the drivers clocked off and the toilets they used. Wolmar comments:

This is really, to put it crudely, taking the piss about taking a piss. But within the world of the PPP, it makes sense. If the distance between the cab and the toilet is a factor in determining how consistent the train service is, then it will have an effect on how much London Underground has to pay for the contract. Consequently, it has had to be factored into the formula that covers these issues. So, imagine the scene: the teams of suited consultants and lawyers, all on City rates, working out what should be the standard distance between the cab and the toilet; the speed at which drivers would walk; whether the number of stairs (are they up or down?) should be taken into account; the number of doors which have to be opened to gain access to the facilities; how to accommodate female drivers and arrive at a formula which takes into account possible changes in the percentage of women drivers; the possibility of moving the point where the trains stop; and much more. All this to ensure that an [infrastructure company] is sufficiently – but not overly – rewarded should it decide to replace a set of toilets with facilities nearer the end of the platform.[9]

Wolmar adds wryly that the calculation eventually arrived at in this connection could have been called "the bog standard" and notes in passing that drivers using the toilets would not actually be working for one of the infrastructure companies but for London Underground. Was Wolmar exaggerating? Probably a little – but not much.

Not only were the contracts extraordinarily complicated: they were often faulty and, when subsequently tested in the courts, often turned out to be technically defective. Their cross-referencing was a mess, and the lawyers who drew them up, not being economists, sometimes failed to make it clear whether specific individual prices quoted in the contracts were to be understood as having been denominated in inflation-proofed or merely nominal pounds. The contracts were also inflexible. They were meant to last for thirty years, with every "t" carefully crossed and every "i" dotted. They could not easily be adjusted in the light of changing circumstances or as new information about the underground's ghastly physical state gradually trickled in.

3) It hardly needs saying that among the major profiters (not to say profit-eers) from all this were lawyers and law firms. Well before the contracts were signed, it was estimated that the total cost of drawing them up would be at least £400 million. In the event, it was probably considerably more than that.

4) It also hardly needs to be said that firms of consultants also profited hugely from the whole exercise. At a relatively early stage – towards the end of 2000 – a junior transport minister admitted that the total consultancy bill had already reached nearly £70 million and would eventually reach at least £92 million. And whether the consultants were actually doing a good job was also questionable. Someone who watched them working on the scheme described them as "very bright people who know nothing".

5) Critics also pointed out that the consultants, like the lawyers, were con-cerned not merely to make money but to make work – and to make work in order to make money. There was a clear conflict of interest: the govern-ment's interest in saving money conflicted with the consultants' interest in making it. PricewaterhouseCoopers (PwC), for example, recommended that – short of straightforward partial privatisation, which was unacceptable to Labour ministers – the government should hive off the underground's operations from its infrastructure, with the latter to be put in the hands of one or more private companies, a recommendation that John Prescott quickly accepted. PwC also remained centrally involved in the detailed work as the PPP progressed. It had a vested interest in its continuation. As one commentator pointed out at the time, PwC promoted itself as one of the world's leading advisers to governments and firms involved in private-finance initiatives – "a role it could hardly maintain were it to conclude that the largest such transaction did not provide value for money" for the government and taxpayers.[10]

6) Even more fundamental was the issue of "risk transfer". Apart from keeping the cost of large public projects off the UK government's balance sheet, a large part of the point of private-finance initiatives, and hence of a scheme such as the London underground PPP, was to give private-sector companies additional profits in return for which they assumed most or all

of the risk of the project's going wrong. They made money, but at the same time they stood to lose it. If the clinic or hospital built and operated by a private-sector company under a private-finance initiative proved to have a leaky roof, or if the performance of its staff fell below agreed standards, that was the company's problem, not the government's. A contract – or dozens of contracts – that transferred the money but did not transfer most of the risk would be a very bad bargain from the government's point of view.[11]

Right from the beginning, those on the government side of the PPP negotiations were in a bind. On the one hand, they were desperately anxious to achieve a successful outcome to the negotiations; they desperately wanted the PPP to be got up and running and, indeed, were under strict instructions from ministers not to consider any possible alternative. On the other hand, they were well aware that those private-sector companies that might bid for PPP contracts were conscious of the high levels of risk involved; and, given that these risks could not be substantially reduced (too many uncertainties were involved and over too long a period of time), the companies would be prepared to bid for contracts only if their own financial risks were kept to a bare minimum – in other words, only if the transfer of risk on any substantial scale from the public sector to the private did not actually take place.

Confronted with this predicament, the negotiators, including ministers, did the only thing they could do: they capitulated to the potential private-sector bidders. For obvious reasons, they were initially very reluctant; but finally, in February 2002, John Prescott's successor as transport minister, Stephen Byers, published – with, of course, the Treasury's approval – what was tactfully called a "comfort letter" in which he effectively gave all the bidders the loan guarantee referred to above: that the government would underwrite fully 95 per cent of the large bank loans that the successful bidders would have to take out as a consequence of the scale of their commitments. So much for risk transfer.[12]

7) The government's loan guarantee effectively gave the private-sector companies a free ride, or at any rate a ride for which they had to pay only a minimal fare. More generally, the detail of the contracts emerged in such a way that Metronet and Tube Lines, the ultimately successful bidders, were given incentives to behave in ways that were definitely in

their own interest but were not in that of either London Underground or the travelling public. Most notable was the incentive they were offered, almost certainly inadvertently, to complete investment projects early in the life of the contracts for which they were responsible. On the face of it, that might seem a good idea: passengers would experience improved services sooner rather than later. But it was clear that, if the companies behaved in that way, London Underground would soon be in serious financial trouble, as it was forced to pay the companies hugely inflated amounts upfront. In addition, the incentive built into the contracts for the companies to undertake investments early meant that they would almost certainly begin by concentrating on those projects that could be completed quickly – such as the renovation of older stations – even if the projects in question were not the ones most conducive to improving the underground's long-term safety and efficiency. The detailed contracts overall afforded the infrastructure companies countless opportunities for "playing the system". They all but invited them to.

8) It was also pointed out beforehand that, inevitably, complex contracts and multiple participating organisations would also mean complex and multilayered management structures. All but the most routine decisions would require the involvement of managers and administrators from London Underground, from one or more of its various operating divisions, from at least one and possibly all of the infrastructure companies, quite possibly from one or more of the companies that comprised the consortia that owned the infrastructure companies and, in all probability and on occasion, one or more of the innumerable contractors to whom the infrastructure companies would be subcontracting specific pieces of work, sometimes very large pieces. Delays would be inevitable, the costs, including the transaction costs, would be enormous, and no one would ultimately know who was responsible for what. No one would "own" the whole project.

9) The Treasury had initially been keen on a PPP because it believed that such a partnership could and would be self-financing and therefore could be kept off the Treasury's books. Such a scheme would not require a public subsidy. Critics pointed out, however, that, if this were a requirement, it

 not actually going to be fulfilled – and never looked like being fulfilled. The idea was that cash contributions from London Underground and what became Transport for London – which would be largely derived from passengers' fares – would constitute the public sector's entire contribution to the cost of the PPP. Ministers gradually backed off from that position, but they continued to insist that any additional public-sector contributions – in other words, straightforward government grants – would be small. Not everyone believed them. In early 1999, years before the contracts were finally signed, a Conservative MP voiced his doubts:

> However, once the principle of supplying grants to make up the difference is conceded, obtaining them will become an annual event. Operating companies will go cap in hand to the mayoralty, to the government and to all and sundry who can be lobbied. Droves of Londoners, who will suffer bad services and high fares, will insist that the Government cough up the money.[13]

Within a few weeks, still during those very early days, Prescott's department publicly admitted that government grants might after all be needed to make up any shortfalls and to make the whole scheme viable. As predicted, such grants were soon forthcoming – on a very large scale.

10) Almost as an aside, PPP doubters wondered aloud why, if London Underground managers were so dreadful, and if no public-sector body could be trusted to manage large-scale projects properly, the government was putting those same managers in charge of managing the infrastructure companies' contracts, thus assigning them responsibility for overseeing "what is probably the biggest public procurement contract in British history outside of the defence industry".[14] Either the managers in question were not all that bad, or the government had slipped up somewhere, or it was going to have to find an entirely new lot of managers (which it showed no signs of doing). In the event, it was not clear that anyone actually succeeded in managing the contracts at all. They were the subject of constant disputes.

11) The new scheme's opponents also voiced concerns about safety on the underground, especially as the PPP was launched only a decade after

a fire at King's Cross underground station had claimed thirty-one lives. Because of that incident and because of a more recent rail crash near Paddington, which had also claimed thirty-one lives, safety issues were continually raised.

12) At least one critic of the scheme, Susan Kramer, a London politician who also happened to be a merchant banker, pointed out, in addition, that joint ventures of the kind central to the government's PPP scheme tended to be highly unstable. They were marriages of temporary convenience that, under pressure, tended to break up: "If you want to find a more unstable structure for an entity than a joint venture, I just don't think there is one. Most [joint ventures] fall apart because they discover that they came together over a long negotiating period, but their agendas are different."[15] The disparate firms that made up the consortia brought together in London underground's infrastructure companies certainly had very different agendas.

13) But, according to most of the PPP's numerous critics, the greatest single weakness of the proposed public-private partnership, one that encompassed many of the others, was that there was no need for it. It was superfluous to requirements. A much more robust alternative was readily available: namely, to finance the necessary improvements to the underground by means of an old-fashioned bonds issue backed by government guarantees. London Underground would sell the bonds; the UK government would guarantee bond-holders against any possibility that London Underground might default. Proceeding in that manner would be far cheaper than via the PPP because government-backed borrowing – at least in a financially stable country such as the UK – is always cheaper than private-sector borrowing. It would also be infinitely less cumbersome because there would be no need for the new infrastructure companies and the grotesquely complicated contracts that accompanied them. Bond finance would have the additional advantage that London Underground could negotiate contracts one at a time for specific pieces of work to be completed within specified periods of time. Some of those contracts would undoubtedly not work out satisfactorily (as some of those relating to the Jubilee Line extension had not), but the chances of all of them going wrong at once would be minimised.

London Underground's eggs would not be all in one basket – a basket, moreover, that was bound sooner or later to have big holes in it.

Bonds issues for these kinds of public-sector projects were nothing new. They had a past, and they were considered perfectly normal in comparable jurisdictions. They had been used successfully to fund the expansion and modernisation of the London underground during the 1930s. They were widely used by state-owned railways and energy companies on the Continent. A pamphlet by members of the Greater London Group at the London School of Economics pointed out that New York's Metropolitan Transportation Authority had funded $14 billion of investment since 1981 by means of bonds guaranteed by New York City and securitised on the basis of the authority's large revenue streams (overwhelmingly from passengers' fares).[16]

Ironically, the New Labour government in Britain was already moving into that territory. Prescott negotiated a deal with the Treasury that allowed airports owned by UK local authorities to borrow money without having to use private-sector companies as intermediaries. More significantly, as early as mid-1998 Prescott, with Blair's backing, persuaded the Treasury that completion of the troubled Channel Tunnel Rail Link could be part-funded by means of government-backed borrowing. Even more significantly, it was also arranged in both cases that the borrowing in question, even though government-backed, would not be counted against the Public Sector Borrowing Requirement. Unsurprisingly, opponents of the PPP scheme for the underground wondered why, if the Treasury's rules could be bent in this way for other projects, they could not be bent similarly for this one. *The Economist*, among others, was of that view. But Gordon Brown and the Treasury were having none of it. They had decided that the PPP was the way forward, and that was that.

All of these criticisms of the government's proposed PPP were cogent, but they were seldom addressed directly by the scheme's advocates, many of whom seemed to sense, perhaps unconsciously, their considerable force. In most cases, the various criticisms were simply ignored or casually waved away. Ministers pressed on, ever more doggedly. Why?

The obvious answers to that question are probably the right ones. Ministers and their official advisers had devoted much time and effort to devising the scheme. Treasury and transport ministers were publicly committed to it. The proposed scheme was fully in accord with New Labour's private-sector predilections, and by 2000–03, the government had already spent a great deal of money on it. Devising an entirely new scheme would involve having to unravel the old one and would undoubtedly consume still more time, energy and money. Not least, abandoning the PPP in 2002 or thereabouts would have been politically, and in some cases personally, humiliating. It would have constituted a major U-turn; and, even worse, Ken Livingstone, who had been elected mayor by London's voters in 2000 on a vociferously anti-PPP platform, would have emerged noisily triumphant. In fact, there were still a few people around who sincerely believed that the PPP, despite everything, could be made to work. It might be doomed, but it was not yet absolutely certain that it was. It might all come right in the end.

But it did not. The critics exaggerated the safety concerns but were soon proved right on every other count. The scheme was a disaster. Almost everything that the critics predicted ahead of time would go wrong did go wrong. No hindsight was needed: foresight could have sufficed. None of the perpetrators of the scheme could plausibly plead ignorance of the future in mitigation. Few even tried.

The infrastructure companies assumed full responsibility for the maintenance and upgrading of the underground in April 2003. Less than three years later, ominous signs that the scheme might be in serious difficulties began to emerge. In October 2005 Metronet alerted TfL that it had identified a large volume of extra costs that had not been anticipated in its original bid. By February 2006 Metronet's estimate for the total extra costs that it would incur during the first seven and a half years of the contract – that is, for the period at the end of which the various contracts would be revisited – already amounted to £1.2 billion.

Worse, Chris Bolt, the independent PPP Arbiter, later in 2006 made public his view that Metronet was poorly managed and that its management failures were probably responsible for at least £750 million of its enormous cost overruns. Over the next few months, that figure of £750 million more than doubled, with the estimated total cost of the overruns ballooning to £1.8 billion. All the while, it was becoming ever clearer that, if the independent Arbiter concluded that Metronet had not managed its contracts in an "economic and efficient manner" (the language of the relevant contracts), TfL would not be liable and there was no way in which Metronet could pay off its accumulated debts. The companies comprising the consortium that owned Metronet showed no sign of being willing to bail out their wholly owned subsidiary and showed every sign of not being willing to. After all, almost none of their own money was at stake – and their creditors also had little to lose, given the government's generous loan guarantee.

Crisis point arrived in the summer of 2007. Transport for London and Metronet finally agreed, after many delays, that they should jointly request the Arbiter to conduct an "extraordinary review" of the Metronet contract and of the way in which its terms had, or had not, been fulfilled. At issue was the extent to which the enormous cost overruns, which everyone agreed had been incurred, should be attributed to TfL, because it had demanded far more of Metronet than had been specified in the contracts, and the extent to which they should be attributed to Metronet, because of its allegedly substandard performance. Chris Bolt was in little doubt. Within weeks, he published an interim judgment in which he declared that Metronet was entitled to only £121 million – less than a quarter – of the £551 million it claimed it was owed by London Underground. The figure of £551 million actually related to only one of Metronet's two contracts with London Underground. It was generally agreed that the cost overruns on the two contracts taken together totalled some £2 billion.

Bolt's interim judgment effectively killed off Metronet. The end came on 18 July 2007 when Metronet, unable to meet its mounting financial obligations, fell into administration – in effect, went bankrupt. Transport for London, backed by the government, immediately stepped in with substantial interim finance. Later that year, in order to maintain some degree of continuity in the organisation, TfL formally took over Metronet, and a few months after that, in February 2008, the Department for Transport announced that it, rather than TfL and the Greater London Authority, would pay Metronet's outstanding debts and foot the bill for the firm's having gone into administration. Thus, what a leading article in the *Guardian* dubbed "a towering ziggurat of debt and contractual confusion" had collapsed at last.[17] Having taken the better part of five years to construct, Gordon Brown and John Prescott's much-vaunted public-private partnership had remained in being for only four years and a few months. The smaller of the infrastructure companies, Tube Lines, lasted for longer; Transport for London did not take it over until May 2010. Indeed, Tube Lines Ltd continues to this day to enjoy a separate corporate existence as a wholly owned TfL subsidiary.

A delicious irony, of course, is that a government initiative intended to achieve the part-privatisation of the London underground, an arrangement that would last for three decades, wound up within less than one decade with the whole enterprise even more securely lodged in the public sector than before. The PPP was more than a blunder: it was a blunder-plus, one of the most idiotic decisions made by a British government in modern times.

In the case of many of the blunders described in this book, there has been little in the way of follow-up; no one has apparently felt compelled to find out precisely what went wrong and why. The aborted Brown–Prescott PPP proved a partial exception. There is not much evidence of in-house soul-searching, but the House of Commons Transport Committee published a critical report in 2008, the National Audit Office another in 2009 and the House of Commons Public Accounts Committee yet a third in 2010.[18] To say that the three reports were critical is an understatement: all three were excoriating, especially the Commons Transport Committee's.

Taken together, they focused on the most conspicuous failings of the whole PPP approach, especially as the government had applied it to the underground. One was ministers' apparently uncritical assumption that the private sector would invariably outperform the public sector. In the eyes of the Commons Transport Committee, Metronet cast the gravest doubts on that assumption. Metronet had been "a spectacular failure":

> Whether or not the Metronet failure was primarily the fault of the particular companies involved, we are inclined to the view that the model itself was flawed and probably inferior to traditional public-sector management. We can be more confident in this conclusion now that the potential for inefficiency and failure in the private sector has been so clearly demonstrated ... It is worth remembering that when private companies fail to deliver on large public projects they can walk away – the taxpayer is inevitably forced to pick up the pieces.[19]

The committee was not condemning out of hand all private sector involvement in the management of public-sector projects. For one thing, it acknowledged that Tube Lines, the smaller private-sector company in the PPP, had performed better than Metronet.

Tube Lines had performed better that the other consortium partly because it put all its work out to tender and did not operate its own version of Metronet's tied-supply-chain approach – an approach permitted by the terms of the relevant contracts. The effects of the lack of competitive tendering would have been dire in any event, but they were rendered even more dire by the way in which the two Metronet companies were governed – or, rather, not governed. Susan Kramer was right. The marriage among the companies that owned Metronet was a marriage of convenience, and from the beginning the partners to the marriage appeared to want to have as little to do with each other as possible. They also wanted to have as little to do with the managers of the Metronet companies as possible. In other words, the relevant contracts treated Metronet as a single organisation with centralised leadership, whereas in reality it was at least five different organisations with scarcely any leadership at all. It was universally agreed that the managements of both Metronet companies were extremely feeble, largely because the various companies in the consortia that owned them made sure that they were.

Inevitably, the post hoc reports drew attention to the bizarre circumstance that the total amount of risk that the public sector had transferred to the private sector approximated to zero. The private-sector firms comprising the consortia were effectively guaranteed ample but almost entirely risk-free rewards: large prizes without any need to buy lottery tickets. The Commons Transport Committee was adamant:

> The return anticipated by Metronet's shareholders appears to have been out of all proportion to the level of risk associated with the contract. The parent companies were effectively able to limit their liability to the £70 million that each invested in Metronet at the outset ... In the face of this very limited liability it is difficult to lend any credence to the assertion that the Metronet PPP contracts were effective in transferring risk from the public to the private sector. In fact, the reverse is the case: Metronet's shareholders, had the

company been operated effectively, stood to make quite extravagant returns. Now that it has failed, it is the taxpayer and the Tube passengers who must meet the cost.[20]

The various bodies that examined the PPP's performance after the event looked at different aspects of it. Perhaps for that reason, they overlooked – or at least did not draw attention to – what may well have been its most damaging single pathology: its sheer complexity. For the PPP to work, every bit of it had to work, and there were far too many bits of it, and the relationships among them were far too complicated. Everything had to go right, and there were too many things that could go wrong. The timescale was too long. There were too many uncertainties and unknowns. The contracts were of mind-boggling complexity and understood by very few. Too many people were involved, and too many of those involved did not know what their individual responsibilities were supposed to be. Almost no one could see the big picture. There was no redundancy in the system, with the result that any errors that occurred, instead of being confined to a single point, had the capacity to cascade throughout the structure. A weakness at any one point, and the whole structure was in danger of collapse. A member of the Public Accounts Committee, Austin Mitchell, like the American transport expert before him, described the entire structure as "insane".[21] He was not far wrong.

The post hoc enquiries did not really try to get to the bottom of the insanity, in the sense of determining how the patient came to be insane. The National Audit Office explicitly confined itself to examining the activities of those who "sought to manage the Metronet structure as it stood", and even the Commons Transport Committee's report, though more wide-ranging, was largely confined to considering how the public-partner partnership had gone wrong rather than seeking to explain how a structure that was so liable to fall down had come to be constructed in the first place.[22] But a full explanation is probably not hard to come by.

The whole episode began with Gordon Brown and John Prescott deciding that wholesale privatisation was out but that so was old-fashioned public-sector commissioning. Those two decisions meant that some kind of private-finance initiative would have to be put in place. The proposed London underground public-private partnership was merely a private finance initiative writ large, very large – and PFIs were currently in fashion. From the outset, Gordon Brown took charge. He ensured that the Treasury called the shots. Although he was not personally involved day to day, he exerted his influence constantly via one of his closest ministerial allies, Geoffrey Robinson, and one of his closest non-ministerial advisers, Shriti Vadera (widely known as "Gordon's representative on earth"). The prime minister, Tony Blair, was scarcely involved. Although in favour of PFIs in general, he had doubts about this particular venture, on one occasion organising a secret meeting at Chequers with Transport for London's newly appointed commissioner. But his mind was mostly elsewhere, and he "kept firmly out of the controversy over the PPP, knowing it was an issue that few could understand and even fewer supported".[23] If other members of the cabinet were consulted, it was only as a formality. There was no hint of collective decision making.

A handful of ministers thus handed down from on high a tremendously ambitious strategic idea. But they did not hand down anything that remotely resembled a strategic plan. They knew roughly where they wanted to go but had little idea of how to get there, and they left others almost wholly alone to do the detailed work. Brown and his associates behaved rather in the manner of a parent throwing a small child into a swimming pool and then blithely walking away without waiting to see – and without apparently caring – whether or not the child could swim. Ministers made policy; it was up to others to implement it. Those charged with implementing it were new to working on a project on this gigantic scale, and they were under intense pressure to complete every detail and deal as quickly as possible. Under the circumstances, it is hardly surprising that they failed. The Commons Transport Committee was not exaggerating when it said at the end of the day: "A contractual arrangement which fails to incentivise efficiency in the private sector and at the same time fails to deter poor planning, lack of forethought and gold-plating in the public sector is one which is pretty much useless."[24]

The Metronet fiasco was no exception to the general rule that, when British governments blunder, it is almost always impossible to calculate accurately the purely cash cost of the blunder in question, let alone the human cost. Even the best estimates are invariably rough. Multiple government agencies, as well as private firms, will have been involved; the timescales are often long (as in the case of the poll tax, though not in the case of Britain's departure from the ERM); labour costs can be difficult to calculate. Perhaps most important of all, the costs incurred should, in an ideal world, be compared with the costs that would have been incurred if some alternative course of action had been followed (if, for example, the PPP had not existed between 2003 and 2007 and London Underground and TfL had instead contracted out the work in the usual way). Although the figures are open to dispute for these sorts of reasons, the PPP blunder certainly cost UK taxpayers not less than about £2.5 billion and probably far, far more, possibly in the region of £20–£30 billion. In the words of one of the participants in the affair, writing when some remnants of the PPP still remained, some improvements to the underground were undoubtedly achieved but at "an outrageous premium".[25]

The same writer's advice to future generations was clear: "when resources are dear and government must sort priorities, one is best advised to adopt a structure that is transparent and simple".[26] As it happens, that advice has been heeded, at least in connection with London transport, and Transport for London now operates on the basis of a long-term, government-backed business plan, one that provides for the building of an entirely new underground line, Crossrail, as well as for the maintenance and upgrading of the existing lines.

The Metronet fiasco wasted years and cost billions. Looking back, one of the people we interviewed for this book – someone who had been centrally involved – leaned back in his chair, shrugged his shoulders, laughed aloud and said: "You couldn't make it up. You simply couldn't make it up." Unfortunately, someone did make it up – and no one was there to stop him.

15

ID cards swiped

For several decades, especially during the 1990s and 2000s, successive governments seriously considered introducing individual identity cards in the UK, but in the end none of them did so. Had they done so, introducing ID cards might, or might not, have proved a blunder. Views about that differed then and still do. But, that said, governments of both major parties undoubtedly blundered in their whole approach to the subject. In the words of the dictionary, they "floundered" and "stumbled". They proceeded in fits and starts. They failed to build support for the project. Not least, they gave the impression that they had no clear idea of what identity cards, if they were ever introduced, were supposed to be for. Instead of being a possible solution to a clearly identified problem, identity cards increasingly resembled a solution desperately in search of a problem. Unable to find any one problem, the project instead found a whole slew of them.

During the Second World War, identity cards were compulsory. The law required every UK resident to possess one, and everyone had to produce his or her card on demand, either immediately or "within such time to such person and at such a place as may be prescribed".[1] At that time, identity cards were all but universally accepted; the country was at war, and everyone needed a card to obtain food and clothing rations. However, postwar governments of both parties found a variety of peacetime reasons for retaining identity cards, and the provisions of the National Registration Act 1939 were allowed to remain in force – until, that is, a stroppy Liberal parliamentary candidate named Harry Willcock decided he would make a nuisance of himself. He was stopped by policemen and asked to show his identity card. He refused, both on the spot and later at a police station. He was convicted under the terms of the National Registration Act, and, although the magistrates' court gave him an absolute discharge, he took his case to the High Court. That court held that the Act was undoubtedly still in force, but the presiding judge, the lord chief justice, Lord Goddard, clearly thought it ought not to be and said as much:

> Although the police may have powers, it does not follow that they ought to exercise them on all occasions as a matter of routine ... This Act was passed for security purposes and not for the purposes for which, apparently, it is now sought to be used. To use Acts of Parliament, passed for particular purposes during the war, in times when the war is past ... tends to turn law-abiding subjects into law-breakers, which is a most undesirable state of affairs. Further, in this country we have always prided ourselves on the good feeling that exists between the police and the public, and such action [routinely asking members of the public to show their identity documents] tends to make the people resentful of the acts of the police and inclines them to obstruct the police instead of to assist them.[2]

At the government's behest, parliament shortly afterwards repealed the offending Act.

Two decades later, acts of terrorism committed by the Irish Republican Army on the UK mainland as well as in Northern Ireland prompted newspapers and some MPs to press for the reintroduction of identity cards, and ministers did consider the possibility. But in a 1974 cabinet memorandum Roy Jenkins, the home secretary, dismissed the idea:

> I see no advantage in aiming at a full passport-type control. Nor do I see any advantage in a system of identity cards, which apart from creating difficulties for ordinary people would be extremely expensive and largely ineffective ... It goes almost without saying that we must guard against the danger of being driven to more and more extreme measures involving unwarranted infringement of personal liberty.[3]

The cabinet agreed, and the matter was not pursued further.

However, a decade and a half later, from the late 1980s onwards, a number of Conservative backbenchers began to press successive Conservative home secretaries to reintroduce cards as a means of strengthening the powers of the police. In 1988 one of them introduced a bill calling on the government to introduce a British identity card to "help in the fight against football hooligans" and "crime in general".[4] During the following year, another promoted a bill to require all those born after 1 January 1990 to be equipped with an identity card; and later that year yet another Tory MP introduced a private member's bill proposing the introduction of a national identity card to reduce the incidence of crime and football hooliganism, to assist in detecting social-security fraud and to help in the fights against drugs, truancy, underage drinking, illegal immigration and terrorism. But none of these efforts had ministers' backing, and none made any headway. Neither did a recommendation by the Home Affairs Select Committee in 1990 that the UK should introduce voluntary cards as a model for the kind of identity cards that, in the committee's view, should eventually be made available to the citizens of all European Community countries. In its response to the committee's recommendation, the government said that ministers did not consider that the limited benefits such a card might confer on the community "would be commensurate with the high cost of developing, introducing and maintaining such a system". Having said that, however, it went on to add: "Nonetheless, the Government will follow closely what further interest may be stirred by the Committee's recommendation."[5]

The Conservative party in John Major's time was deeply divided – on identity cards as it was on almost everything else. Major himself increasingly inclined towards introducing cards, and the Association of Chief Police Officers, having been doubtful, began to come round to the idea. Also, the Conservative party in the country, so far as anyone could tell, was all in favour of identity cards, mainly on law-and-order grounds. Against that, many Eurosceptics on the Conservative benches in parliament, while they might otherwise have favoured such cards, feared that a UK-specific card might morph into some kind of Euro-card, thereby promoting further European integration. Indeed, that was pretty much what the Home Affairs Committee had earlier envisaged. Many Conservatives were also dubious on civil-libertarian grounds. Given the Conservatives' divisions on the issue, given their tiny Commons majority following the 1992 general election, and given Labour's adamant opposition to identity cards (Tony Blair reckoned they would "waste hundreds of millions of pounds"), the Major government had no choice but to prevaricate – which it proceeded to do.[6] It published a non-committal Green Paper in 1995 and subsequently announced that it intended to introduce a draft bill providing for voluntary identity cards during the 1996–7 parliamentary session. It did not in the event publish its promised draft bill, but it did promise in its 1997 general election manifesto that, if returned to power, it would "introduce a voluntary identity card scheme based on the new photographic driving licence".[7] Conservative ministers clearly wished the issue would simply go away. From their point of view, it did just that: they lost the election.

By the late 1990s most of the numerous issues relating to identity cards were clearly defined, and they changed scarcely at all during the subsequent two decades. All that did change from time to time was the emphasis given to different strands of the on-again-off-again controversy.

Those in favour of introducing cards saw them as the bureaucratic equivalent of a broad-spectrum antibiotic: a single instrument that would effectively address a remarkably wide range of disparate concerns. In their view, identity cards would enable their holders to prove that they were whoever they said they were. They would be convenient to carry and could be used to provide proof of age. They could also be carried across much of Europe instead of an old-fashioned passport. They could make it easier for people entitled to a range of public services to gain access to them – and at the same time make it easier for service providers to identify people who were claiming benefits they were not entitled to. They could, in other words, be used to reduce benefit fraud. They could also be used to help private firms – banks and insurance companies, for example – to reduce private-sector fraud. If the government so decreed, identity cards could be designed to carry the bearer's medical details – details that could prove invaluable in the event of emergencies. Not least, in the eyes of almost all those advocating their introduction, identity cards would be of tremendous value to the police and other security forces in identifying criminals (and eliminating innocent people from their enquiries), in identifying and tracking illegal immigrants and in fighting "the war on terror".

The proponents of cards pointed out, correctly, that most people in Britain already carried one or more pieces of plastic in their wallet or handbag and that carrying yet another piece would not cause great inconvenience – and might even reduce the total amount of plastic people felt they had to carry. They also pointed out correctly that identity cards of one sort or another were used – and generally accepted – in almost every other European country. From the whole community's point of view, identity cards, if they were introduced, would be a substantial asset. From most individuals' point of view, they would be no big deal.

Opponents of identity cards advanced both practical and principled arguments, with the two of them often intertwined. The cards were meant to be unique identifiers, containing only accurate and up-to-date information specific to the individual bearer of the card. But people often changed their name (when marrying, for example) and might use both a family name and a professional name. They also changed their appearance over time, so that, if the card carried a photograph, it might not remain indefinitely "a true likeness". Large numbers of people also moved house frequently, so that, if the card were meant to contain its owner's address, the address might be out of date (always assuming, of course, that the owner actually had a more or less permanent place of abode). People were also apt to change their nationality. The more information the cards contained, the more frequently the information on them would have to be updated. If the cards were to contain biometric information, such as fingerprints or retina scans, people applying for a card would have to present themselves in person at an authorised office, which might be some distance from their home, rather than simply submitting documents through the post. No one on either side of the argument denied that introducing and maintaining a system of identity cards would be enormously complex administratively and would require the creation and constant updating of a huge national database. Exactly how much all this would cost – and whether it would be cost-effective – was disputed, but no one denied that introducing identity cards and then maintaining them would be exceedingly expensive.

There were also issues of accuracy, privacy and security. If cards were to be held by some forty to fifty million adults, a considerable proportion of them would be bound to contain one or more factual errors – errors that could cause substantial inconvenience and even hardship. And, of course, the more information that the cards held on them, the more likely it was that some of it would simply be wrong. Human error in administering the system was bound to be rife. In addition, criminals, including terrorists, it was alleged, would be able to steal cards, alter them fraudulently, hack into them and even forge them. One illegal immigrant was said to welcome the introduction of identity cards because then he would have to obtain only one forged document instead of a whole wodge of them. Despite the authorities' best efforts, some unscrupulous individuals might be able to obtain more than one card. Worst of all, in the eyes of many of the cards' opponents, was the near certainty that information contained in individuals' cards would from time to time, possibly quite often, be sold, leaked or traded to UK government agencies not entitled to it, to foreign governments, to private firms and even to criminals and criminal gangs. The information contained in the cards would be enormously valuable. The temptation to sell it or otherwise take advantage of it would be correspondingly enormous.

Most opponents of identity cards also raised fundamental objections on civil-libertarian grounds. As early as the mid-1990s, the legal pressure group JUSTICE maintained that cards posed a danger because "ID cards and the associated records are a natural instrument of state control and [are] easily open to misuse in the wrong hands".[8] A group of local authority associations deemed identity cards to be "detrimental to the rights of individual citizens".[9] A constitutional-reform pressure group, Charter 88, opposed identity cards on principle, citing the need for Britain to remain a free society instead of becoming a "centralised surveillance state".[10] Significantly, a pressure group acting on behalf of the West Indian community distinguished the position of the UK from that of other European countries, stating that the "principle under the British common law tradition of not being concerned with the identity of people going about their lawful business" should not be undermined.[11] Echoing Lord Goddard's remarks of a previous generation, almost all opponents of identity cards feared that such cards, if there were any hint of a requirement to produce them, would worsen relations between the police and the general public, especially members of ethnic minorities. Dislike of identity cards on civil-libertarian grounds predictably emanated more from the left of politics than the right, but a significant proportion of Conservatives also felt uneasy.

A related issue was whether, if they were introduced at all, identity cards should be voluntary or compulsory. The cards' proponents were divided. Some, initially a substantial majority, were content with their being voluntary. Others argued that, if identity cards were to be useful at all, they should be held by everyone, not least by immigrants, foreign residents of the UK and actual or potential criminals. For their part, those opposed to the introduction of cards on other grounds maintained, in addition, that the alleged voluntary/compulsory distinction was a distinction without a difference. It would quickly become normal for everyone to possess a card, and failure to possess one would in itself become grounds for suspicion. In evidence to a parliamentary committee, the Consumers' Association claimed that it was "clear from the experience of other countries ... that a voluntary scheme rapidly becomes effectively compulsory because the card is so frequently demanded by public and private sector bodies in circumstances where other forms of ID had previously been adequate".[12] Again, the effect that introducing identity cards might have on members of ethnic minorities, especially young black men, was a continuing cause for concern (including among some who otherwise favoured them).

Following Labour's election victory in 1997, the issue of identity cards remained dormant for several years, though some civil libertarians suspected that Home Office officials, ever eager to turn their department into a continental-style ministry of the interior, remained on the lookout for opportunities to press on ministers the case for reintroducing them. When a backbench MP in 1999 asked Jack Straw, New Labour's first home secretary, to make a statement on the government's policy towards the use of identity cards, Straw's response was carefully worded:

> I see no arguments to convince me in favour of compulsory identity cards whereby a failure to carry a card in a public place would become a criminal offence. Subject to that caveat, we keep under review the balance of advantages and disadvantages that national identity cards could bring.[13]

Straw failed to point out that the previous government had never proposed that possessing an identity card should be made compulsory and that no one in authority had ever proposed that failing to produce one's card on demand should be made a criminal offence. None of the main political parties in their manifestos for the 2001 general election so much as mentioned identity cards.

A few months later, however, the terrorist attacks on the World Trade Center and the Pentagon in the US suddenly reopened the whole issue of the desirability of reintroducing identity cards in the UK; but they did so in a curious, contorted manner. On the one hand, the events of 9/11 were undoubtedly crucial; prior to 9/11 almost no one in the UK was publicly advocating the reintroduction of identity cards and the issue was effectively dead. On the other hand, when British ministers proceeded soon after 9/11 to advocate the reintroduction of cards, they justified their proposals, not on the grounds that they would be effective in the fight against terrorism, but on a variety of other grounds, ones that had little or nothing to do with terrorism. It seemed that the events of 9/11 merely provided ministers with an excuse for doing what they were minded to do anyway. The dust could now be blown off plans that had long been on the shelf.

Jack Straw's successor as home secretary, David Blunkett, was certainly keen on identity cards and eager to introduce them. He made that abundantly clear in a BBC interview shortly after 9/11; but at the same time he indicated that, if identity cards were reintroduced, it would not be solely, or even primarily, on security grounds: "There are much broader issues about entitlement and citizenship and not merely security in terms of some sort of identity card which we are looking at very seriously indeed."[14] Within the government, Blunkett doggedly promoted the cause of identity cards – which he believed would have to be made compulsory if they were to be useful at all – during the three years he remained at the Home Office. The arguments he deployed were broadly those that had been used by John Major's home secretary, Michael Howard. Blunkett maintained that cards would make life more difficult for fraudsters, that they would enable claimants to prove that they were entitled to public services and benefits, that they would discourage "medical tourism", that they would make it easier to identify illegal immigrants, that they would (or might) facilitate foreign travel by Britons and that sooner or later all right-thinking, law-abiding UK citizens would think they were a wonderful idea. Blunkett and others did mention national security issues but only occasionally and never to the fore.

David Blunkett needed to be dogged in his promotion of identity cards because, from the beginning, he encountered stout resistance, not least from among his own colleagues and within his own party. Tony Blair, having pooh-poohed the introduction of cards while leader of the opposition, remained sceptical as prime minister; Gordon Brown as chancellor opposed them on cost grounds; and other ministers and Labour backbenchers opposed them on civil-libertarian grounds. Several of Blunkett's ministerial colleagues, without necessarily having strong views about the principle of identity cards, took the view that they were not worth the trouble, either financially or politically. But, in the fullness of time, and having eventually secured the prime minister's backing, Blunkett got his way. John Major's government had promised an identity-cards bill; Tony Blair's government actually produced one and then managed to get it onto the statute book. Opposition among Labour ministers was to some extent damped down by progress being made in the field of biometric technology and by the fact that the American government, following 9/11, was pressing foreign governments, including Britain's, to provide their citizens with machine-readable passports. Elaborate machine-readable technology appeared to be an idea whose time had come, and, if people were going increasingly to need machine-readable passports, why not machine-readable identity cards?

With the government's backing, the Identity Cards Act 2006 duly reached the statute book in March 2006. It mandated the secretary of state to establish and maintain a National Identity Register – that is, a nationwide database that it was hoped would sooner or later contain, in relation to every resident of the UK aged sixteen or over, his or her birth date, gender, names (present and past), addresses (present and past), nationality, entitlement to remain in the UK and "external characteristics of his that are capable of being used for identifying him".[15] In order to be placed on the register, an individual would be required to attend at an agreed or specified time and place, to allow himself to be photographed and to allow officials to take and record his fingerprints and other biometric information. Everyone on the register would be assigned a unique number. With minor exceptions, everyone on the register would also be issued with an identity card (which was, in a rare venture into legal informality, referred to in the Act simply as "an ID card"). However, with a number of minor exceptions, no one for the time being would actually be required in law to register under the terms of the Act or to possess an ID card, and no one would be required to carry his or her card at all times.

With the Act on the statute book, the government immediately took steps to implement it, beginning as early as April 2006 with the creation of the Identity and Passport Service as an executive agency of the Home Office. More than fifty private-sector firms expressed interest in bidding for contracts to supply the agency with the cards themselves and with scanning and other essential equipment – contracts that would eventually be worth several billion pounds. Soon afterwards, the Home Office announced proudly that a trial run of ID cards conducted in connection with criminal-background checks had been a success. Towards the end of 2008, ministers began the roll-out of ID cards for foreign nationals living in the UK. A few months later it was announced that from 2011 every British citizen aged sixteen or over who made a passport application would automatically be registered on the national database. Over the winter of 2009–10, ID cards were made available progressively, first to residents of Greater Manchester, then across the North West of England and finally to sixteen- to twenty-four-year-olds in London. A casual observer might have been forgiven for supposing that ID cards would soon become, as ministers hoped, a normal part of British life.

Yet, even as the government's great house of cards was being built, its foundations were crumbling. When the house finally collapsed, most of those who noticed that it had collapsed cheered loudly. Few shed tears. All along, it had been a project that had more passionate opponents than passionate supporters. Even those who, on balance, supported the project tended to be tepid in their support. Apart from some Home Office officials, David Blunkett was unusual in being an out-and-out enthusiast, a true believer.

A large and growing part of the problem was cost. Identity cards? Maybe yes, maybe no. But at what price? That question was asked more and more often as the estimated cost of the scheme escalated. At first the Home Office estimated that the cost of installing and running the scheme for a few years would fall somewhere between £1.3 billion and £3.1 billion. Where it fell within that range would depend upon, among other things, the efficiency of the private-sector firms installing and maintaining the system. But that relatively modest figure soon rose, on the government's own account, to somewhere in the region of £5.5–£5.8 billion; and, although ministers disputed the figures and the basis on which they were computed, a report by a group at the London School of Economics suggested that the total cost would eventually lie somewhere in the range of £14–£19 billion. The Labour chairman of the Commons Home Affairs Committee, John Denham, was a vocal supporter of ID cards, but even he expressed concern: "The LSE report may well be wrong, but it is the Government – my Government – who created circumstances in which anyone's guess is as good as anyone else's when it comes to the cost."[16] Moreover, the estimated costs just mentioned took no account of the financial burden that would have to be borne by those public-sector agencies – and any private-sector bodies that chose to become involved – that would be obliged to purchase and maintain scanning and other ancillary pieces of equipment if the cards were to be of use.

It was also anyone's guess just how much the cards would cost their individual owners. The Treasury all along insisted that the scheme must be self-financing. Individual UK residents would therefore have to pay for their cards themselves – less if they wanted only a card and not a passport, more if they wanted both combined. As the measure wound its way through the ranks of the government and then the two houses of parliament, the estimated fee for a combined ID card-passport – the document that a majority of UK citizens would want – increased within a few years from £77 to £93, with no guarantee that in future it would not rise still further (though ministers did propose rebates for children and the less well off). Given that in time everyone in the country would almost certainly have no option but to own an ID card, the Conservative opposition's home affairs spokesman, David Davis, was unkind, but not wrong, when he referred to ID cards in the House of Commons as "a plastic poll tax".[17] A minority of ministers and backbenchers on the Labour side reckoned he might well be right.

The proposed scheme was also expected to be costly partly because it was going to be an incredibly complex scheme to administer, more complex than even the original poll tax and the single-payment scheme for paying English farmers. The government's great house of cards was meant within a few years to be raised to a prodigious height. To begin with, there would be a huge number of such cards: a total of some sixty million, given that every adult UK resident – foreign nationals as well as UK citizens – was meant to own one. Each of the sixty million cards would contain at least six to eight pieces of information, undoubtedly more as time passed. That was the easy bit; but, in addition, every card-holder would be required by law to report to the authorities every change, for example, of his or her address. Given how frequently people in the UK change address, that in itself would place a considerable strain on the system as well as on individuals. Card-holders would frequently lose their cards or have them stolen. For elderly people or people living in the countryside, the business of registering for their card and then updating it as necessary could prove expensive, time-consuming and possibly stressful. The number of errors in the system would be prodigious. An unknown number of conscientious objectors, many of them high-profile, would undoubtedly have to be taken to court for refusing to purchase a card or for publicly destroying any card foisted on them. The cards were meant to be UK-wide, but both the Scottish parliament and the Welsh national assembly signalled that they would have nothing to do with them. All these objections to the scheme were purely practical (although those with principled objections were obviously more likely than the scheme's supporters to draw attention to them).

A series of events in the mid- and late 2000s also served to undermine support for the cause. The relevant legislation's passage through parliament followed shortly after several of the IT fiascos described in Chapter 13. David Davis in the House of Commons was far from convinced that the purely IT aspects of the project could be made to work:

> Last week, we saw that the tax credits system is in chaos because of IT problems. The Home Office itself is one of the worst-offending Departments when it comes to IT management. Remember the police national computer? One would think that that would be very accurate because it has biometric data associated with it, but an audit recently found that 65 per cent of its files contained errors. Remember the asylum seeker processing system? With a budget of £80 million, the project was scrapped after it was found to be flawed.[18]

Not only might the system not work efficiently: recent events suggested that an allegedly secure system might prove a good deal less than secure. In October 2007 Her Majesty's Revenue and Customs contrived to lose the child-benefit records of twenty-five million people, including their dates of birth, National Insurance numbers and bank and building society details. In January 2008 the Ministry of Defence lost a laptop computer containing the details of 600,000 men and women who had expressed an interest in joining one of the armed forces. During the summer of 2009 Alan Johnson – the fourth home secretary in the five years since David Blunkett, the progenitor of the ID-cards scheme, had left office – announced that, in the face of implacable trade-union opposition, the government was abandoning a scheme that would have forced airside workers at Manchester and London City airports, including pilots, to carry government-issued cards. The entire project looked as though it would probably prove accident-prone.

The general public also showed more and more signs of disenchant-ment. When Tony Blair's government first broached the idea of a nation-wide identity-card scheme in 2003–04, some 80 per cent of opinion-poll respondents said they liked the idea. But by 2008 that proportion had fallen to roughly 50 per cent, and several polls found more voters opposed to the idea than supportive of it. There were probably few votes in the issue, but ministers could no longer claim they enjoyed almost universal public backing. As early as February 2006, a YouGov survey found that, although a small majority at that time still on balance favoured the introduction of ID cards, even larger majorities believed that determined criminals and potential terrorists would always be able to find ways of forging them (80 per cent), that the scheme as a whole would cost far more than the govern-ment was claiming (75 per cent) and that the data stored on people's cards would sometimes be leaked, sold, hacked into or used improperly in other ways (71 per cent).[19] Opinion polls also showed that enormous numbers of people would object strenuously to paying anything like £93 – or even £50 – for their own card.

From the government's point of view, the issue of whether or not own-ership of an ID card should be made compulsory also remained highly problematic. The Major government, despite pressure from within the Tory party, never went beyond proposing voluntary cards, and David Blunkett, at the outset of his campaign to introduce cards, gave the impression that he would be content to see them remain voluntary, at least for the time being. However, the Blair government's line gradually hardened, and the Identity Cards Bill, as originally introduced into parliament in 2005, provided that registration on the national database and ownership of an ID card could be made compulsory even in the absence of new primary legislation. All that would be needed would be affirmative votes in both houses of parliament in favour of compulsion. But this last provision did not go nearly far enough to satisfy the scheme's critics, who also objected to the bill's provision that anyone applying for an ordinary passport would also be applying, whether they liked it or not, both to be placed on the National Identity Register and to be issued with an ID card. The bill as passed by the House of Commons met with fierce resistance in the House of Lords, which repeatedly voted in favour of requiring new primary legislation to be passed before ownership of ID cards could become compulsory and against the government's proposed linking of passport and ID-card applications. Ominously from the government's point of view, although a Liberal Democrat peer, Lord Phillips of Sudbury, led the opposition to the bill in the Lords, one of the more significant amendments adopted by their lordships had been moved by a crossbencher, Robert Armstrong (Lord Armstrong of Ilminster), a former cabinet secretary. Eventually, after the bill had repeatedly bounced back and forth between the two houses, the government capitulated on the issue. New primary legislation would, after all, be needed before owning a card could be made compulsory. The government also postponed for several years the introduction of any automatic link between passport and ID-card applications. The Act as it finally reached the statute book was not quite the one that ministers had had in mind.

As the government's difficulties in the Lords demonstrated, the political foundations underpinning the scheme were already very shaky. They soon became shakier. The Liberal Democrats from the beginning had been united in their opposition to ID cards, mainly on civil-libertarian grounds. The Labour party itself was divided. Among ministers, Tony Blair and Charles Clarke were initially dubious, and Jack Straw, Peter Hain and Patricia Hewitt were among those who voiced strenuous objections to cabinet colleagues. In a confidential letter leaked to the *Sunday Times* early on, Straw, Blunkett's immediate predecessor as home secretary, warned colleagues that "the potential for a large-scale debacle which harms the government is great". He believed the whole plan as presented by Blunkett was "fundamentally flawed".[20] Nineteen backbench MPs voted against the Identity Card Bill's second reading, twenty voted against its third and an unknown number abstained or absented themselves from both votes. An equally unknown number did vote in favour of the bill, but against their better judgement and only at the whips' behest. Sporadic backbench rebellions in the Commons undoubtedly contributed to ministers' willingness to make concessions to the Lords. One rebellious backbencher, Chris Mullin, wrote gleefully in his diary in July 2009: "Yesterday Alan Johnson announced that ID cards would not, after all, be made compulsory. Let no one say we humble backbenchers are without influence."[21] But of course not making the cards compulsory defeated much of their original purpose – or, more precisely, many of their original, numberless purposes.

However, the crucial change of policy came on the Conservative side. Like the Labour party, the Conservatives had always been divided on the issue, with what might be called the party's Home Office tendency at loggerheads with its civil-libertarian tendency. Although divided, the party had backed ID cards in some form or another during the 1990s, but during the 2000s, with Labour in power and pressing hard for cards, the Tories gradually reversed their position. David Davis on behalf of the Conservatives in the House of Commons vigorously opposed the government's bill on civil-libertarian and practicability as well as cost grounds, and he had the support of Peter Lilley, a cabinet minister under both Thatcher and Major, whose 2005 Bow Group pamphlet *Identity Crisis: The Case against ID Cards* was widely read by Conservative MPs. Lilley in parliament dismissed with contumely the Labour government's pretensions:

> One thing that is clear is that the Identity Cards Bill is not, as the Home Secretary would have us believe, a gleaming, new Labour modernising measure. I make no apology for reminding the House that it is a shop-soiled, tired old measure that had been hawked around Whitehall for many years before the Government even came to power – proposals for a compulsory, all-singing, all-dancing identity card with biometrics.[22]

Meanwhile, a little-known Conservative member of the House of Commons Home Affairs Committee was coming to the same conclusion. Giving evidence to the London School of Economics group that had concluded that the eventual cost of ID cards would far outstrip the government's estimates, David Cameron acknowledged that, as a member of a parliamentary committee that was conducting its own investigation into ID cards, he was obliged to keep an open mind on the subject; but he confessed to being "a hearty sceptic", adding, "I look forward to the rest of the investigation. I'll do my best to keep my mind open, but I fear it's closing all the time."[23] Two years later, within a few weeks of becoming his party's leader, Cameron at Prime Minister's Question Time in the House of Commons made it clear that his mind had indeed closed. "With rising deficits in the NHS", he asked, "huge costs of pension reform and tighter pressures on public spending, how can the Prime Minister claim that spending at least £600 million a year on his ID card scheme is a good use of public money?"[24] The Conservatives, having remained tactfully silent on the issue of identity cards in their 2005 election manifesto, declared categorically under David Cameron five years later that they would scrap both ID cards and the associated National Identity Register. The coalition agreement they negotiated with the Liberal Democrats in the aftermath of the 2010 general election contained the same pledge.

And that was pretty much that. Within weeks of coming to power, the incoming coalition government published its own Identity Documents Bill. The bill had obviously been drafted by officials while Gordon Brown's government was still (just) in power. Labour's opposition was desultory, and the bill became law towards the end of 2010. The Identity Documents Act 2010 demolished the whole of Labour's elaborate construction. The 15,000 ID cards already in circulation were cancelled – in other words, rendered all but useless. Their owners received nothing in the way of compensation. All the information contained on the incomplete National Identity Register, including fingerprints and photographs, was destroyed. Today, apart from those who lost money as a result of having purchased a card, neither the United Kingdom nor its individual citizens and residents appear to be markedly worse off as a result of the scheme's cancellation. Nothing seriously untoward has happened since the end of 2010, at least nothing that might have been prevented had the Labour government's ID-cards scheme still been in place.

In the opening pages of this book, we defined a blunder as "an episode in which a government adopts a specific course of action in order to achieve one or more objectives and, as a result largely or wholly of its own mistakes, either fails completely to achieve those objectives, or does achieve some or all of them but at a totally disproportionate cost, or else does achieve some or all of them but contrives at the same time to cause a significant amount of 'collateral damage' in the form of unintended and undesired consequences". On that definition, or almost any other, the Labour government's insistence on pursuing the cause of national identity cards during the 2000s was a blunder. It cost many millions of pounds (the post-2010 coalition government estimated £300 million, but that was almost certainly an underestimate). It also wasted tens of thousands of hours of people's time – the time of civil servants, ministers, MPs, peers, academics, consultants, private contractors and, in some parts of the country, ordinary citizens. Above all, it failed utterly to achieve any of its objectives. The whole thing was, as they say, a waste of space. In Parts III and IV of this book, we will explore the factors that contributed to this particular fiasco as well as to many others.

Part III

Human errors

16

Cultural disconnect

In July 2000 Tony Blair, the then prime minister, told an audience of students in Germany that he wanted Britain's police forces to have new powers to deal with drunken, noisy, loutish and anti-social behaviour. "A thug", he said, "might think twice about kicking in your gate, throwing traffic cones around your street or hurling abuse into the night sky if he thought he might get picked up by the police, taken to a cashpoint and asked to pay an on-the-spot fine of, for example, £100."[1] Nothing came of Blair's proposal. Lawyers and civil-rights groups objected to it vehemently, and the police were less than keen. But there was another problem with the proposal, one that attracted less attention. Blair assumed that the thugs he had in mind would have bank accounts, would have on them at least one valid debit card and would have as much as £100 in their bank account available to be withdrawn. But a large proportion of the thugs in question – at least one in five, almost certainly many more – would not have met, and still today would not meet, those requirements. Some of Blair's thugs and louts would undoubtedly have been well off, and a few of them might even have been rich, but many of them would have been poor and/or completely spaced out and disorganised. They would not have had either bank accounts or debit cards; nor would they have had £100 in the bank. The prime minister was clearly assuming that other people lived lives much like his own. His assumption was unfounded.

A similar episode occurred in 2012. On the eve of a threatened strike by tanker drivers, Francis Maude, the minister in charge of the Cabinet Office, advised motorists to store "a bit of extra fuel in a jerry can in the garage".[2] One of his fellow ministers pointed out that jerry cans were a lot larger than Maude thought they were, and firefighters pointed out that a full jerry can would contain more petrol than it was legal to store. Maude got into even more trouble when a woman was badly burnt a few days later pouring petrol into a container in her kitchen. But not many people seem to have noticed that there was something else wrong with Maude's advice. Maude was assuming that most motorists own or rent a garage. But millions of British motorists do not, as witness the cars parked in the streets of every city and town in the country, including in the poshest parts of London. The proportion of British households without a garage may be as high as two-thirds. Like Blair, Maude clearly assumed that almost everyone in the country lived a life that, at least in this respect, was like his own and that of his ministerial colleagues. Again, his assumption was unfounded.

Everyone projects onto others his or her lifestyles, preferences and attitudes. Some people do it all the time; most of us do it some of the time. But almost everyone does it instinctively without thinking about it. Doing it makes the world more easily comprehensible – or gives the impression that it is. Even educated professionals, such as doctors and social workers, make the same kinds of assumptions when they are not self-consciously wearing their hats as professionals. We call those kinds of assumptions "cultural disconnect". Or, more precisely, we call it that when the assumptions that politicians and civil servants make are radically wrong, when men and women in Whitehall and at Westminster unthinkingly project onto others values, attitudes and whole ways of life that are not remotely like their own.

By no means all, but a substantial proportion, of the horror stories we told in Part II had cultural disconnect as one of their principal sources. The man in Whitehall not only did not know best: he did not know that he did not know that which he badly needed to know.

Take, for instance, the poll tax. Whichever civil servant said "Try collecting that in Brixton" appears to have been virtually alone in his prescience – that is, in recognising that large swathes of urban Britain, such as Brixton in south London, had highly mobile populations including large numbers of poor people with insecure and low incomes. Partial rebates would be unlikely to entice them into paying the tax; and, if the rebates were total, they would invalidate one of the tax's main purposes, which was to ensure that everyone who benefited from local services contributed something towards paying for them. Even if the poll tax had been phased in slowly, it would have been either impossible or exceedingly expensive to collect from millions of hard-pressed and/or stroppy individuals, many of whom in any case would have gone to ground. That was one reason why no other town, city or country in modern times had sought to impose a poll tax (except in the American South, not on financial grounds but in order to exclude black people from voting).[3]

Those who designed and then attempted to implement the poll tax might almost have been recruited to maximise the chances that they would suffer from cultural disconnect in an extreme degree. They all lived settled existences. They were all comfortably off. A few of them were rich. They all paid their taxes. They knew far more about Brighton and Beaconsfield than about Bolton or Bermondsey. The prime minister had long since left her relatively humble origins behind. The four secretaries of state for the environment during the lifetime of the poll tax, between 1983 and 1990, were Patrick Jenkin (Clifton and Cambridge), Kenneth Baker (St Paul's and Oxford), Nicholas Ridley (Eton and Oxford) and Chris Patten (St Benedict's, Ealing and Oxford). William Waldegrave, the acknowledged leader of Patrick Jenkin's review team, was, like Nicholas Ridley, a product of Eton and Oxford. All five men represented affluent parliamentary constituencies; all but Patten's constituency of Bath were safely Conservative. Apart from being Conservative politicians, the five were not especially homogeneous politically – Jenkin, Baker and Patten were all Tory moderates (or "wets" in the jargon of that time) – but they were all indubitably middle class (or, in Ridley's case, upper class). No member of the review group represented any other section of British society. The only relative outsider involved in the process was Sir Terry Heiser, a senior civil servant, soon to become permanent secretary at the Environment Department; but he was more an organiser than a policymaker, and he regarded his role as executing ministers' decisions, not challenging them.

The fact that the core group of ministerial decision makers was so homogeneous and so comfortably middle class – in a context in which the behaviour of people, many of whom were not even slightly middle class, would be crucial – made it highly probable that cultural disconnect would occur; but what made it a near certainty was that the members of the core group seem never to have entertained, however remotely, the possibility that cultural disconnect could occur. They obeyed the law. They paid their taxes. Others would do the same. Simple as that. Did the members of the review team, one civil servant was asked, assume that because they paid their own taxes everybody else would pay theirs? "Yes", he replied, "that was certainly the case." He went on to add that the review team never seriously addressed the issue of compliance. Another official accepted readily the proposition "that officials and ministers probably weren't sufficiently in touch with the ordinary public and thus with its likely reaction to paying the tax".

In the case of the poll tax, the sheer intellectual power of the members of the review team was probably, paradoxically, a handicap in itself. Led by William Waldegrave, the team's members were anxious to devise a scheme that would astonish the world – and certainly the prime minister – by its simplicity, power and rigour. But those very qualities contributed to its undoing. The scheme was far simpler than a modern society shot through with complexity could possibly accommodate. One official volunteered that the poll tax's "conceptual elegance" constituted its fatal flaw. Another, himself a member of the review team, confessed: "I was seduced by the beautifully crafted, conceptually elegant papers that were produced, with their underlying philosophy of giving power back to local government and aligning voters and payers." A minister who arrived later on the scene was blunt: "It needed exceptionally clever people to produce anything so stupid."

A few years later, ministers and officials appear to have been similarly unaware of the possibility that millions of people would opt out of the State Earnings Related Pensions Scheme or their firm's occupational scheme and would instead allow themselves to be sold, in tens of thousands of cases mis-sold, personal pensions. Ministers saw the National Insurance rebate that they offered people for opting out of SERPS merely as "a nice little incentive", failing to realise that for millions of people on low incomes the incentive was definitely not little but very big. Labour politicians' warnings about mis-selling went unheeded, partly because the relevant health and social security ministers held Michael Meacher and his Labour colleagues in considerable contempt and partly because ministers and officials in the Department of Trade and Industry almost certainly never noticed that Labour's warnings had been issued. But cultural disconnect was also a factor. Offered the thought that both ministers and officials simply assumed, without thinking about it, that everybody would behave well, that the salesmen selling pensions would obey the rules and that, if the salesmen had employers, the employers would also obey the rules, a civil servant closely involved in the enterprise nodded his head and replied, "Absolutely." Someone who arrived later on the scene said he still could not decide whether the ministers in the two departments had been guilty of "woolly thinking or no thinking". Either way, he was unimpressed.

The setting up of the Child Support Agency in the early 1990s was an almost classic instance of cultural disconnect at work. The mistakes that policymakers made in establishing the agency were legion, but none did more damage than their ignorance of the lives of a large proportion of the people who would be affected by the policy they were making: fathers and mothers who had separated or never seriously been together in the first place. Ministers and officials were accustomed to a world in which couples that split up then went on to form one new family each or perhaps none. They were totally unfamiliar with a world in which fathers often had multiple children by multiple mothers, and mothers often had multiple children by multiple fathers (not all of whom they were able to identify). One senior policymaker at the Department of Social Security admitted that he had been surprised when large numbers of women began to turn up at DSS offices claiming, probably truthfully, that their children had three, four or five different fathers. "We hadn't appreciated", he added, "that very large numbers of people, both women and men, now led very complicated lives."

The scope of the disconnect went wider than that. Many absent fathers were not comfortably off businessmen, solicitors or members of parliament: as we saw in Chapter 6, they were on social security or low wages and, even if they were willing in principle to pay the sums demanded of them, they could not afford to. Thousands were supporting second families of their own. Some could see no reason why they should provide maintenance for children to whom they had been granted little or no access. Many an absent father was convinced that the mother of his children was now living with a man who earned far more than he did. The government's whole child-support policy was blighted by policymakers' false assumptions about the family life and moral reasoning of large segments of British society. Absent fathers' large-scale non-compliance with the agency's maintenance orders appears to have taken everyone at the DSS by surprise. One official actually volunteered the phrase that there had been "a total disconnect".

The disconnect in the case of individual learning accounts was equally total but of a different character. Naïve ministers and officials in the Department for Education and Skills had clearly had little experience of the cleverness and audacity of members of the criminal classes. Like those who devised the new personal pensions, they evidently assumed, without thinking about it, that both training providers and potential trainees were honest men and women who would behave properly; they would behave like the respectable people who ran further-education colleges or were students at them. Sometimes, of course, their assumption was right, but in a fatally large number of cases it was wrong. The department's routine risk assessment, focusing as it did on delivery, failed utterly to take into consideration the potential for fraud. "With hindsight", in the words of one official, "we could have considered Nigerian benefit cheats trying to defraud the system, but it never crossed our minds." Officials as well as ministers underestimated how unscrupulous people – and by no means only Nigerians – could be.

The shambolic introduction of tax credits also owed much to cultural disconnect. The Treasury ministers who designed the credits, and the Inland Revenue officials charged with administering them, in both cases knew little or nothing of those sections of the population with whom they were having to deal for the first time. As one civil servant put it, "Too little attention was paid to the behavioural profile of the people at whom the policy was aimed." In other words, a Treasury minister or official's lifestyle – and his or her way of managing the family finances – was not quite the same as that of a casually employed van driver or office cleaner. Another civil servant was contemptuous of the Brownite inner circle that invented tax credits. He doubted whether any of them had ever been near a social-security benefits office. One of the many things they did not know – and seemingly did not know that they needed to know – was that changes to people's tax credits that seemed minor and inconsequential to ministers and civil servants could have a devastating effect on the lives of tax-credit recipients, not to mention the lives of those who should have been receiving them but were not. Those in charge were likewise insensitive to the implications for poor people of having for the first time ever to attempt to organise their finances on an annual basis and of being told, for example, that they might have to wait twenty-eight days, nearly a month, for their enquiries or claims to be dealt with.

An equally strange feature of the introduction of tax credits at the particular time they were introduced, in the early 2000s, was the belief that the vast majority of the transactions under the new system should be, and could be, conducted online. But at that time, and quite possibly still, many of those eligible for tax credits, probably a majority, neither owned a computer nor had access to one. One notion was that people who did not own one ought to be encouraged to attend schools and clubs where they could become familiar with computers and at the same time organise their tax-credit arrangements. But in the first place few such schools and clubs existed. In the second place, a large proportion of those who needed help would not or could not attend the few schools and clubs that did exist. And, in the third place, the computers that were supposed to be available in such places were often nicked: "They would just walk out the door." Many of those who worked out the ways in which tax credits were to be administered appear to have been a trifle unworldly.

The best cure for the disease of cultural disconnect is, of course, for politicians and civil servants to recognise both that the disease exists and that it is potentially virulent – in other words, for those who make policy not to assume that others live lives like their own or, better still, for them to assume that, on the contrary, other people probably do *not* live lives like their own. Someone who reads *The Times* every day needs not only to know but also to recognise the implications of the fact that millions of people see only the *Sun*, the *Daily Mirror* or the *Daily Record* or, increasingly commonly, do not see a paper at all. Almost all politicians and civil servants read books, regularly take foreign holidays, frequently travel by train and closely follow the political news on radio and television. But millions of Britons do few or none of those things. They have utterly different lifestyles, tastes and preoccupations.

Once the possibility of disconnect in any given situation is acknowledged, various steps can be taken to counteract it. One is desperately obvious: try out any papers or forms that people have to fill in on members of the target population, or on newcomers to the target population, not on friends, neighbours or colleagues at work – that is, on people who spend a lot of time reading instructions and filling in forms and who know how to. As one official commented apropos the tax-credits shambles, "The people the forms had been tried out on were not the sorts of people who would find form-filling difficult." Also in connection with tax credits, the parliamentary ombudsman repeatedly drew attention to faults in the forms themselves and in the way in which they were processed. As late as 2007, several years after tax credits were introduced, she wrote in one report:

> I have continued to see a significant number of cases where failure by customers to follow to the letter the completion instructions for the application form have meant that, even though they have provided HMRC with the correct information, their [subsequent] award has been incorrect ... Examples would be where customers have struck through a box as not applicable to them (such as whether they have a qualifying disability award), but the computer has read that as saying that they have completed the box, or where they have left boxes such as "earnings" empty, but attached a letter explaining why they have done that or other evidence, such as a P60 form.[4]

In other words, if individual human beings find form-filling difficult, computers find it equally difficult to read forms if the forms in question have not been designed with the needs and capacities of the target group of form-fillers specifically in mind.

Other ways of counteracting cultural disconnect are less mundane. One is actively to seek out the views and draw on the experience of people on the other side of whichever cultural divide it is thought may exist – and also to draw on the experience of those who have had direct dealings with people on the other side of that divide. Those likely to have had such dealings include the members of organisations such as the Child Poverty Action Group, Age UK and Shelter, which undoubtedly have their own agendas but which over time have equally undoubtedly accumulated both knowledge and wisdom. "Consultation" by governments may be a charade and often is, but any process of consultation, however primitive, would have alerted the designers of the poll tax to the fact that their design, however elegant, was faulty, that their beautiful aeroplane would not fly in Brixton or probably almost anywhere else in the UK. As one of its designers subsequently acknowledged, "There should have been a consultation, but there wasn't, partly because the principle of consultation hadn't been established at that time." Similarly, in connection with the Child Support Act no one outside the Department of Social Security seems to have been asked whether they thought absent fathers could actually be made to pay up, specifically whether "feckless fathers", although feckless by definition, were nevertheless well enough off and responsible enough to make regular child-maintenance payments. Even within the department, little heed seems to have been paid to the accumulated wisdom of the ground-level civil servants who had, under the existing arrangements, spent many years trying to extract maintenance payments from absent parents. If anyone had been listening to them, they would have had many a tale to tell.

Piloting – testing schemes before introducing them more widely – is not always an option. It would have been hard, if not impossible, for example, to have piloted the introduction of personal pensions; personal pensions could hardly have been sold to people in some parts of the country but not in others, or to some sections of the population but not to others. But the proposals set out in the Child Support Act and most of the regulations issued under it could certainly have been piloted, and those who came along afterwards to find out what had gone wrong frequently lamented the absence of adequate – or any – piloting. One of them said he was amazed that the Child Support Agency had been established without, apparently, any piloting having been undertaken: there had been "no testing of the proposition". If piloting is not practicable, dummy runs and simulations often are. Dummy runs in the case of the early years of the CSA would have thrown up the fact, among others, that the proposed IT system simply could not cope.

In the case of individual learning accounts, the DfES did organise a number of pilot projects, but few of them bore any resemblance to the scheme eventually adopted. In particular, the projects mostly involved training providers who already had proven track records, and the pilot projects' administrators also took care to check the identities of both the providers and would-be trainees. In other words, the pilots could not, and did not, alert ministers and officials to the one feature of the scheme that eventually destroyed it: its vulnerability to fraud. One official confessed afterwards that he thought his public-sector colleagues tended to be too trusting. They were not used to dealing with a population that included potential fraudsters. The scale of this particular fraud came to them, he said, as "a revelation". Of course, organising pilots and conducting dummy runs takes time, and time is not always made available to either the policymakers or officials on the ground – a topic we shall come back to later.

There is another, somewhat perverse form that cultural disconnect can take: when policymakers unwittingly mistake one section of the population for another, when they imagine, wrongly, that the voices that they happen to hear are tantamount to the massed voices of the whole people. Party activists today are less numerous and influential than they used to be; the various parties' annual conferences matter less than they once did. But party leaders may still be tempted to infer the state of public opinion from the state of opinion among their most vocal followers.

Ministers in the Thatcher government certainly did make that mistake – in spades – when they promoted the poll tax. Apart from Nigel Lawson, and until the sceptical Chris Patten arrived on the scene, she and almost all her ministers seem to have imagined that a proposition that played so well with Conservative activists would play equally well, or else could be got to play as well, with the public at large. They behaved as though they imagined that the subculture in which they were embedded was somehow representative of the culture of the great majority of the whole nation. At no point do they appear to have recognised that a radical disjunction might possibly exist between what their own party activists so desperately wanted and what the rest of the country could be got to put up with.

The principal culprit in this respect was Margaret Thatcher herself, the daughter of a respectable Grantham grocer and MP for the north London suburb of Finchley. She regarded herself "as a very normal, ordinary person with all the right instinctive antennae". The authors of the classic study of the poll tax make the point that this very self-image proved her undoing:

If there was one sentiment that every home-owner in Grantham and Finchley shared, it was hatred of the rates, and resentment of the "millions" that did not pay them and sponged off those who did. Mrs Thatcher knew it; she had heard it at Tory meetings and conferences year after year; and she shared the conviction passionately. It is not difficult to see why she was so easily persuaded about the virtues of the poll tax; nor why she stuck to it even as it delved the depths of opinion-poll unpopularity and popular protest.[5]

But Thatcher was not the sole culprit. Until the very end, a majority of ministers and Conservative backbenchers shared her outlook and were convinced, just like her, that they had "all the right instinctive antennae". Nigel Lawson, Chris Patten, Michael Heseltine and the backbenchers who voted against the poll tax had far more acute antennae, but until the very end they were quite unable to prevail.

Apart from Thatcher, by far the most enthusiastic cabinet-level backer of the poll tax was Nicholas Ridley, the seriously rich son of the third Viscount Ridley, a prominent Northumberland grandee. When, during Ridley's period as Thatcher's environment secretary, someone pointed out to him that an elderly couple might find it difficult to pay their poll tax, he is said to have replied casually: "Well, they could always sell a picture." Was he joking? Apparently not.

17

Group-think

The phenomenon of cultural disconnect is far from living on its own. It has a near neighbour in the form of the more familiar phenomenon of "group-think". The two phenomena are by no means identical, but they are frequently found cohabiting. Group-think may well contribute to cultural disconnect, and cultural disconnect often has the effect of reinforcing group-think. Both phenomena, especially the two in close association, are liable to make governments even more blunder-prone than they would be otherwise.

The idea of group-think was developed during the 1960s by Irving J. Janis, an American psychology professor. Janis became intrigued by a sequence of unfortunate episodes in modern American history that seemed to him to display a number of common characteristics: the Roosevelt administration's failure in 1941 to prepare for a Japanese attack on Pearl Harbor; the Truman administration's rash decision in late 1950 to invade North Korea; the launching of President John F. Kennedy's clownish Bay of Pigs expedition in 1961; and Lyndon B. Johnson's escalation of American involvement in the Vietnam War during the mid-1960s. To that original list, he later added President Richard M. Nixon's attempt to cover up his own and his henchmen's complicity in the notorious Watergate break-in of 1972.[1]

According to Janis, whose views are now almost universally accepted, group-think is liable to occur when the members of any face-to-face group feel under pressure to maintain the group's cohesion or are anyway inclined to want to do that. It is also liable to occur when the group in question feels threatened by an outside group or comes, for whatever reason, to regard one or more outside individuals or groups as alien or hostile. Group think need not always, but often does, manifest itself in pathological ways. A majority of the group's members may become intolerant of dissenting voices within the group and find ways, subtle or overt, of silencing them. Individual group members may begin to engage in self-censorship, suppressing any doubts they harbour about courses of action that the group seems intent on adopting. Latent disagreements may thus fail to surface, one result being that the members of the group come to believe they are unanimous when in reality they may not be. Meanwhile, the group is likely to become increasingly reluctant to engage with outsiders and to seek out information that might run counter to any emerging consensus. If unwelcome information does happen to come the group's way, it is likely to be discounted or disregarded. Warning signs are ignored. The group at the same time fails to engage in rigorous reality-testing, with possible alternative courses of action not being realistically appraised. Group-think is also, in Janis's view, liable to create "an illusion of invulnerability, shared by most or all the members, which creates excessive optimism and encourages taking extreme risks".[2] Not least, those indulging in group-think are liable to persuade themselves that the majority of their opponents and critics are, if not actually wicked, then at least stupid, misguided and probably self-interested.

Not all government blunders result from group-think, and few blunders result only from group-think; but group-think makes its distinctive contribution to the committing of numerous blunders, including a number of those described in earlier chapters.

In this regard, the Thatcher government's poll tax easily – and not for the first time – takes pole position. Patrick Jenkin's "review team" was almost a parody of one of Irving Janis's face-to-face groups indulging in group-think. The team, as we noted in Chapter 4, actually did function as a team, with William Waldegrave as its captain. It showed no interest in engaging seriously with either Sir Leonard Hoffmann or Tom Wilson, the two sceptical outside assessors. Indeed, it had as little contact as possible with all outsiders, the only significant exception – but obviously the crucial one – being the prime minister. Like one of Janis's dysfunctional groups, the poll-tax review team failed to appraise realistically a range of alternative options. It never considered seriously the possibility of a banded property tax, and the team's members ruled out right from the beginning both a local sales tax and a local income tax. To be sure, they believed that both a local sales tax and a local income tax were non-starters politically, but they could have made out a case for one or the other if they had been minded to. They could also have made out a case for a banded property tax if they had not become besotted with the idea of a per capita tax. Supremely confident that a per capita tax was workable and would be acceptable to the public, they were blind to the extreme risks they were encouraging Thatcher and the rest of the government to run. Blame for the poll-tax blunder certainly does not lie wholly at the review team's door, but the team and the way in which it chose to operate undoubtedly made a substantial negative contribution.

Looking back on the review-team exercise, many of those who had been intimately involved readily confessed that the team's members, including its leaders, should have functioned differently. They should have collaborated with the Treasury instead of keeping it at arm's length, and they should also have been less secretive in their approach. They were afraid that, if word of their plans leaked out, opposition would build up; but opposition built up anyway, only far too late. In contrast, Michael Heseltine, when he came to devise the alternative council tax a few years later, was careful to work alongside the Treasury and also took care, by means of kite-flying and selective leaking, to alert outsiders to what was going on, thereby enabling himself to gauge the strength of the opposition to his emerging scheme. One member of the original review team acknowledged in hindsight that one of the problems with the Waldegrave–Baker studies had been the degree of secrecy surrounding them. Working effectively in isolation, the team's members had developed a gung-ho "Yes, we can" attitude and had failed to engage in essential joined-up thinking. They had, he said, cultivated "a seductive group-think". Indeed the language of group-think was used by several of our informants. The first edition of Janis's book had been published in 1972, more than a decade before the review team first met. Evidently, no team member had read it.

A milder form of group-think was evident towards the mid-1980s in the working up of the scheme to introduce personal pensions. The thought that the new pensions might be mis-sold on a vast scale was uncomfortable and inconvenient. Therefore, although the thought did occur to some of the government's advisers, it was never seriously addressed. Like Patrick Jenkin in the case of the poll tax, the responsible cabinet minister, Norman Fowler at the Department of Health and Social Security, established a number of advisory groups. One of them dealt with retirement pensions in general, from which a subgroup dealing specifically with personal pensions subsequently emerged. Although, unlike Jenkin's review team, the retirement-pensions group included someone from the Number 10 Policy Unit and representatives of other departments, the dominant figures were men (entirely men) from the insurance industry. The leadership role that William Waldegrave played in Jenkin's review team appears to have been played in Fowler's personal-pensions subgroup by Mark Weinberg, a prominent figure in the industry, who, as Michael Meacher maintained in the House of Commons, stood to do well out of the introduction and selling of personal pensions. Although the potential for mis-selling was raised from time to time and noted, no one seems to have had an interest in pursuing the matter and it was not pursued. If it was a problem, it was always regarded as someone else's.

The ministers, officials and advisers who invented personal pensions – the in-group – were located in the Department of Health and Social Security. But there were two out-groups, and the DHSS in-group clearly regarded both of them with considerable hostility. One of them, as we saw in Chapter 5, was the Labour opposition in the House of Commons led by Michael Meacher. The in-group "pooh-poohed" the Labour opponents of the new kind of pensions, as one participant put it, "because they were seen as a socialist group of MPs who were ideologically opposed to the very idea of personal pensions" and because Fowler could not bring himself to take Meacher seriously. The other out-group was the Department of Trade and Industry. That department was supposed to be dealing with the important issue of mis-selling, but health and social security ministers and officials preferred to keep their distance from the DTI, whose then secretary of state, Lord Young (David Young), was a formidable figure, far higher up the ministerial ladder than Norman Fowler and reckoned to be something of a bully. In that kind of us-and-them, in-group/out-group atmosphere, group-think could flourish and did.

Group pressures of the kind identified by Janis also played a part, though not a determinative part, in the circumstances of both Britain's entry into the European Exchange Rate Mechanism and its departure from it. Before the point of entry in 1990, Treasury ministers and officials were carried along by what seemed to them to be the logic of events. As one senior official remarked ruefully afterwards, "We made the classic error. When you are totally focused on doing something, you forget to ask yourself whether it is the right thing to do." A fellow official showed unintended prescience when he remarked in the summer of 1990, "Everyone agrees. So we must be wrong."[3] Two years later, Treasury officials also appear to have reckoned the die had been cast: the prime minister and the chancellor were determined to keep Britain inside the ERM come what may.

> The atmosphere in the upper echelons of the Treasury tended to stifle debate. It was an insular world, populated by clever insiders. Officials were not encouraged to think the unthinkable; instead their judgements tended to be mutually reinforcing. As one explained, "There was nothing to be gained by rocking the boat."[4]

In the end, the boat did not rock. It sank.

Group-think contributed a great deal to both the disastrous launching of tax credits and the creation of the public-private partnership for maintaining and upgrading the London underground. In those two cases, a large element of group-think was crucial. To an unusual though not unique extent, Gordon Brown as chancellor of the exchequer between 1997 and 2007 preferred to work almost exclusively through an inner group of loyal advisers. They were not people he had inherited from his predecessors. They were *his* people. He trusted them. It is probably fair to say that he trusted almost no one else. With few exceptions, he almost invariably regarded politicians and officials outside what others called his "small cell" or "inner court" as being actual or potential enemies. Brown's was a strong personality. He could be intimidating.

In a working environment of that kind, it was almost inevitable that group-think would be a prominent feature. It certainly seems to have been. The courtiers may have disagreed and argued among themselves; courtiers often do. But they seldom, perhaps never, reached out to others.

Tax credits were the product of Brown's inner court, with the Department of Social Security and the prime minister, as we saw in Chapter 10, both sidelined. One senior civil servant, who found himself having to help administer tax credits at the time, could scarcely conceal his contempt for the chancellor's inner circle:

> Gordon wanted the officials and the other ministers he dealt with to agree with him or else shut up. "The quieter, the better" was his preference. The inevitable result was that people were reluctant to say no to him. If they did, and if Brown had any control over their careers they suffered.

Another official reported that among the people around Brown there was, as he archly put it, "a certain lack of incentive to tell the truth".

In the separate case of the Metronet debacle, Brown, having secured the support of John Prescott, the transport minister, for his proposed public-private partnership, thereafter entirely dominated proceedings. The creation of the ill-fated PPP was almost entirely in the hands of the few senior Treasury officials whom he trusted and two of his devotees – Geoffrey Robinson, a junior Treasury minister, and Shriti Vadera – at the centre of his inner circle of special advisers. Everyone else who might have taken an interest, or who had an interest, was kept at bay. The man who, by a wide margin, was kept furthest at bay was, of course, Ken Livingstone, the person who would soon be responsible as mayor for the underground as well as for the rest of London transport. Livingstone was an enemy – *the* enemy. He and Brown apparently never met to discuss the best way forward.

The result was not only group-think but a seriously flawed decision-making process, one which produced an outcome, the public-private partnership, that probably doomed from the start the entire underground-upgrade enterprise and that beyond doubt cost taxpayers far more than almost any other financial arrangement would have done. Janis in *Groupthink* lists seven "Symptoms of Defective Decision-Making".[5] Largely because of the group-think prevailing within Brown's inner circle, the Metronet decision-making process presented almost all seven symptoms of malignancy. The people involved neglected to consider alternative options to what they were proposing, such as issuing bonds in the way that New York's Metropolitan Transit Authority had done. They paid scant attention, if any, to the financial risks involved. They acted on assumptions, preconceptions and prejudices instead of conducting a dispassionate information search. As things went wrong, they persisted with the PPP without conducting any form of radical reappraisal. All along, they failed to take the trouble to work out contingency plans in case things did go wrong. Janis dubs America's aborted Bay of Pigs attempt to invade Cuba in 1961 "a perfect failure". The same could be said of Metronet. "It was", in the words of one astonished observer, "pure Alice in Wonderland."

Irving Janis's own conception of group-think is tightly bounded. It refers only to situations in which members of a face-to-face group feel, consciously or subconsciously, a need to maintain the internal cohesion of the group. It is, in that sense, a purely psychological concept. But of course the notion of group-think can be extended and used more widely to refer to a variety of situations in which there exists such widespread agreement among the members of a group about the desirability of a given course of action that no threats to the groups' internal cohesion ever arise. Because there really are no dissenters in the group, no one in the group ever expresses dissent. There are no nay-sayers. Everyone is agreed. But such situations can be just as dangerous as the ones Janis describes. The decision-making processes associated with unforced agreement may be just as defective as the ones associated with suppressed dissent.

As we saw in Chapter 6, the Child Support Agency, especially in its very early years, was a disaster. Its administration was woefully inadequate. The legislation that created it was deeply flawed, and the basis on which it was sold to the public was seriously misleading. Yet the Child Support Act that created the agency had been welcomed almost universally, and the principles of the Act had passed through parliament largely unquestioned and virtually unscathed. There were few set-piece debates on the Child Support Bill, and Labour's amendment on the lack of a benefits "disregard" had been easily defeated. However, there had certainly been no group-think in the strict Janisian sense. On the contrary, the Department of Social Security and the Treasury, behind the scenes, had frequently been at loggerheads. The trouble was that everyone, in the two departments involved as well as in parliament, agreed on the agency's overarching objective (making absent parents pay); and, perhaps precisely for that reason, almost no one noticed the discrepancy between the actual substance of the legislation and the way in which it was being sold to the general public. Nor did anyone draw attention to the possibility, soon to become a reality, that the Act as it stood was unworkable.

Later, asked what had gone wrong, one senior minister was blunt: "The major defect in the whole process was that everyone involved in it was in favour of it. There was no grit in the oyster. No one saw that the whole concept was ludicrous." Left-wing feminists thought clawing back money from absent fathers was a splendid idea. Old-fashioned right-wing Tories backed it on moral grounds and because it would relieve the burden on taxpayers. The Conservative and Labour parties both backed the broad idea in parliament. Individual MPs occasionally made good points during the passage of the legislation, but they were mostly points of detail and no MP, even Michael Meacher, ever got to the heart of the matter. The senior minister just quoted said that in retrospect he rather wished the parliamentary process had actually been more adversarial. Had there been less consensus on the big idea, and had it not been so readily assumed that an agency charged with collecting child-maintenance money from absent fathers could be made to work, parliament might have looked more closely at the details – in which the devil lay.

The devil was also in the details of the Proceeds of Crime Act, which established the Assets Recovery Agency. Like the Child Support Act a decade before, the fundamental features of the bill creating the new agency passed through parliament virtually unscathed. It is said that at the committee stage in the House of Commons, the Labour minister in charge of the bill, Bob Ainsworth, and his Conservative opposite number, Damian Green, worked well together. The bill did raise human-rights concerns, and those concerns were carefully addressed, but only at the cost of complicating the business of recovering criminals' assets. "A very simple idea", we were told, "once worked through parliament, became a multi-headed monster." But the monster was born of consensus, not out of any conflict that had resulted in the reaching of a messy compromise.

Group-think similarly seems to have prevailed in the case of the non-payment of EU monies owed to English farmers. Margaret Beckett, the minister in charge, thought the most ambitious payments scheme on offer could be made to work. So did the permanent secretary, Sir Brian Bender. So, crucially, did the head of the relevant executive agency, the Rural Payments Agency. Given such a high level of unforced agreement, no effort was made to test the proposition that the scheme in question could actually be made to work. One official involved said that there probably had been "a problem of group-think" (his phrase). Another suggested that, in retrospect, it would have been a good idea "to have someone put up the case against going ahead, to argue the case on the other side". That same person added that, although some lower-level officials did harbour doubts about the scheme, anyone who had given voice to his or her doubts in the climate of that time would, sadly, have run the risk of losing credibility. In other words, group-think in the strict Janisian sense as well as in our extended sense seems to have made its contribution to the resulting fiasco.

Group-think in both the strict and extended senses is an ever-present danger in all organisations, not just in government departments. As in the case of cultural disconnect, clearly the best way of counteracting it is to begin by recognising that it is a danger and a danger that is ever-present. Once the danger is perceived, the means of addressing it all but suggest themselves.

As the wise former minister suggested, there needs always to be "grit in the oyster", at least one person present in all group discussions who has been assigned the task of arguing the case on the other side and of ferreting out potential defects in what otherwise seems an unassailable proposition. The danger, of course, is that, if the individual in question is sufficiently persuasive, the group may stall, it may not be able to reach any conclusion, or it may arrive at a compromise solution that is actually worse than sticking with the original proposal would have been. But, if that is a risk, the risks of not having grit in the oyster are greater. It was the height of folly for the review team that invented the poll tax not to have insisted that Sir Leonard Hoffmann meet the team face to face and confront them with the case against the proposed tax that he had made in his written submission. Lord Rothschild, although broadly sympathetic to the idea of a per capita tax, must also have had misgivings: otherwise he would not have taken the trouble to print and circulate Hoffmann's memo. But Rothschild, too, remained silent – and was allowed to. It was likewise the height of folly on Margaret Thatcher's part to have allowed Nigel Lawson to make his views known and then, in effect, to depart the scene. If a man as clever as Lawson thought the poll tax was a batty idea, it just possibly was.

Ways of increasing the chances that every option will be considered and every reasonable objection addressed abound. Whoever is in the chair may wish to conceal his or her preferences so that others in the room feel better able to express theirs. During the 1962 Cuban missile crisis, President Kennedy occasionally absented himself from meetings of his advisory group – the so-called Executive Committee – so that the other members of the group would feel able to express their views and not be tempted to express only the views that they imagined he held. Even if whoever is in the chair does reveal his or her preferences, the others in the room need to be made to feel relaxed about revealing theirs, even if they differ from his or hers. Someone in the group can be deliberately assigned the role of prosecuting attorney or devil's advocate and encouraged to play that role to the hilt. One retired permanent secretary – reputedly a successful one – said that when he had been in post he had sometimes organised meetings so that the same officials, sitting round a table, were required to play different roles, sometimes arguing in favour, sometimes against whatever proposal was being discussed.

An alternative approach is not to rely on the thinking or advice of any single group but to assign the same policymaking task to two or more groups, each led by a different person, on the principle that groups-think (plural) is likely to be more imaginative and various than group-think (singular). That was the approach favoured by President Franklin D. Roosevelt, who famously – and, in the eyes of his subordinates, infuriatingly – often assigned the same task to different groups of officials, sometimes without telling them that that was what he was doing. If the competing groups did know they were in competition with each other, that, too, might serve the president's purposes, on the view that it is always good for a leader and his entourage to have competing ideas to choose from. Or a single group can from time to time be split into two or more subgroups, each of them chaired by a different person and each invited to explore various options on its own.

Unless profound secrecy is required – which it almost never is – there is everything to be said for engaging with outsiders, with non-group members. Jenkin's poll-tax review team was reluctant to do that; Michael Heseltine in devising that tax's successor believed it was essential. The proponents of personal pensions talked almost exclusively to other proponents of personal pensions; they never explored with outsiders the possibility, of which they were aware, that pensions along those lines might be mis-sold. Gordon Brown, a determined policy innovator, was temperamentally averse to engaging with any outsiders who might disagree with him; he embraced allies and disdained critics and enemies (and tended to assume that critics *were* enemies). If consulted at an early stage, organisations such as the Citizens Advice Bureaux and the Child Poverty Action Group would almost certainly have advised against establishing the Child Support Agency in the form that it was and given the rules it was obliged to follow. When Margaret Beckett and her advisers opted for the most ambitious scheme for making single payments to English farmers, there is no evidence that they took steps to hold detailed discussions on the complicated practical issues involved with their less ambitious but, as it turned out, infinitely more successful colleagues in Scotland, Wales and Northern Ireland.

Irving Janis himself makes three suggestions, one seriously, one somewhat less seriously and the third (probably) not at all seriously. The perfectly serious suggestion is that "after reaching a preliminary consensus about what seems to be the best policy alternative, the policymaking group should hold a 'second-chance' meeting at which the members are expected to express as vividly as they can all their residual doubts and to rethink the entire issue before making a definitive choice".[6] The somewhat less serious suggestion is that the second-chance meeting in question should be held in a relaxed setting, at some distance removed from the corporate board room or the leader's private office. Janis's last and (probably) unserious suggestion is that any second-chance meeting should be lubricated by alcohol (as sometimes happens spontaneously anyhow):

According to a report by Herodotus dating from about 45 B.C., whenever the ancient Persians made a decision following sober deliberation, they would always reconsider the matter under the influence of wine. Tacitus claimed that during Roman times the Germans too had a custom of arriving at each decision twice, once sober, once drunk.

Janis adds, backing off somewhat:

> Some moderate, institutionalized form of allowing second thoughts to be freely expressed before the group commits itself might be remarkably effective for breaking down a false sense of unanimity and related illusions, without endangering anyone's reputation or liver.[7]

The experience of the Chequers meeting at which the poll tax was effectively adopted as government policy suggests another possible means of avoiding group-think and the too casual acceptance of propositions suddenly put before one. Everyone who attended that meeting described it afterwards in terms that pointed to its having had a positively theatrical quality. There was a largish audience. The chairs in the room were laid out in a theatre-like semicircle. Above all, Kenneth Baker and William Waldegrave, both natural thespians, laid on the most magnificent and art-fully designed slide show, replete with colourful pie-charts and dramatic histograms. "The slides", someone present said later, "were *beautiful*, like a Cartier watch." The prime minister herself agreed. According to an official, she described it over lunch afterwards as "the best presentation I've ever seen".

The visual presentation was, of course, far too good, and Baker's and Waldegrave's speeches were too good. No papers had been circulated in advance, and Thatcher and the others at the meeting – at the show, that is – seem to have been swept into making a decision at a gathering that had never been intended to be a decision-making meeting in the first place and then into adopting, all but formally, as government policy a radical idea that was wholly new to them. The ministers present were not exactly bounced, but they were definitely beguiled. The absence of papers, and the total absence of questioning or dissent, should in themselves have served as warnings. Someone in the room should have said, "Hang on a minute." But the slide show, in itself, misled the spectators into imagining that the facts, figures and projections it contained were solider and more trustworthy than they were. Precisely because it was so good, the show discouraged scepticism and the asking of awkward questions, which in any case those in the room had not been given adequate time to formulate.

Slide shows – now in the guise of PowerPoint presentations – have become, since the time of the Chequers meeting, a routine part of decision making in most large organisations, including in government departments and even in the Number 10 cabinet room. Whether that development improves the quality of collective decision making is at least doubtful. A growing body of opinion thinks not: that PowerPoint privileges the presenter in an unhealthy way and has the effect of discouraging critical discussion and analysis. It may also encourage group-think. PowerPoint is a potentially dangerous instrument of persuasion.

Group-think need not, of course, lead to the committing of blunders. A group, even if guilty of group-think, may nevertheless hit upon the best available solution to whatever problem is being addressed; and, other things being equal, cohesion and mutual loyalty are desirable properties in any human group. Nevertheless, group-think is a barrier to successful decision making more often than not. It renders blundering more probable.

18

Prejudice and pragmatism

If cultural disconnect and group-think are two ways of thinking that can sometimes get policymakers into trouble, then "intellectual prejudice" is a third. The three can easily coexist. By intellectual prejudice, we do not mean religious or racial prejudice or even a preference for some values over others – a preference for equality over liberty, say, or for forgiveness over revenge. Rather, we mean something more mundane: an unquestioned belief that some kinds of institutions and some kinds of policies can be counted upon to work better than others. To say that the beliefs that a person holds are prejudices is not to say that they are wrong. They may be right; they may be well founded in reality. It is merely to say that they are, literally, pre-judgements, beliefs to which the person who holds them is so wedded that he or she is not likely to be prepared to reappraise them in the light of new experience or evidence. They are unquestioned assumptions, important tools in his or her mental tool kit.

In the world of politics and government, prejudices of this kind are often termed "ideological". But ideology is too strong a word. It implies the existence in someone's mind of a comprehensive, integrated world view; and the thought processes of few politicians and officials in this country are ideological in that sense. Rather, intellectual prejudices are simplifying devices, presumptions, mental short-cuts, hunches even. Prejudices along these lines typically embody informal theories concerning how the world works now and how it could be made to work in the future. Theories like these are likely to be influential because they often go largely unspecified and unstated. Being unspecified and unstated, they remain unchallenged.

Intellectual prejudices are most likely to prosper if widely held because those holding them are unlikely to regard them as merely prejudices. On the contrary, those who hold them are likely to regard them as obvious truths, undeniable facts, things to be taken for granted. But what is taken for granted in one generation may seem implausible and weird to the next, possibly because the world really has changed, possibly only because intellectual fashions have changed.

During most of the three decades following the Second World War, most policymakers in Britain took it for granted that the state had a central role to play in almost every aspect of the British economy. The state would own all the major public utilities and many industrial enterprises; few senior politicians chose to exalt or privilege the private sector. Markets were regarded as suspect. Efforts to regulate them were legion. These efforts included rationing after the war, attempts during the 1950s and 1960s to engage in what was known as "indicative planning", and efforts from the early 1960s onwards to impose or negotiate a wide variety of policies for regulating either prices or incomes or both. Successive governments treated the trade unions as a respectable, if sometimes awkward, estate of the realm. The unions were to be consulted and if possible co-opted, not sidelined or beaten into submission. As a goal of policy, the desire to maintain full employment trumped the desire to damp down inflation. Keynesian economics similarly trumped monetarist economics. The major political parties differed in their emphases, of course, and more radical, contrarian wings did exist in both major parties; but the Conservatives and Labour, especially in office, travelled in broadly the same policy direction.

However, by the time Margaret Thatcher came to power in 1979, all that had started to change, and by the time Labour under Tony Blair came to power in 1997 the intellectual climate had changed utterly. State ownership of industry was out; privatisation was in. It was taken for granted that the private sector was more effective and far more efficient than the public sector. Markets were to be regulated as little as possible, ideally not at all. No one gave a moment's thought to the possibility of economic planning, whether indicative or otherwise. Prices-and-incomes policies had long since fallen off the political agenda. The trade unions had been tied down Gulliver-like by restrictive legislation, and Labour was just as determined as the Tories that they should remain so. Full employment was no longer the principal goal of public policy, which was now low inflation and stable prices. Keynesian economists still existed, but Keynesianism as a body of economic doctrine was no longer nearly as fashionable as it had once been. By the 2000s, the language of socialism was seldom spoken; private enterprise and free markets were regarded as the only engines that could power economic growth. As for government in general, there was now a strong disposition, not only among Conservatives, to regard it as part of the problem, not as part of the solution.

The result was that, whereas the postwar generation of policymakers had operated on the basis of one set of prejudices and biases, the post-1979 generation – especially after the emergence of New Labour during the 1990s – operated largely on the basis of another. Often the new set of prejudices contributed to successive governments' success in achieving their objectives. Often it probably benefited the whole nation, as with most of the original privatisations and the assault on trade-union power. But just as the old set of prejudices had led to the committing of such blunders as the Attlee government's ill-conceived groundnuts scheme and the Macmillan government's determination to build Concorde, so the new set of prejudices also contributed to the committing of egregious blunders.

Curiously, although Margaret Thatcher's intense dislike of trade unions, socialism and socialists contributed significantly to the poll-tax blunder, a different kind of intellectual prejudice – an older and less obviously Thatcherite prejudice – played, if anything, an even bigger part. The members of Patrick Jenkin's review team and the first two secretaries of state who succeeded him – Kenneth Baker and Nicholas Ridley – shared an *idée fixe*: that those who benefited from local services (and everyone benefited to some extent) should make at least some contribution towards paying for them. It was their moral duty to pay; and also, if they had to pay, they would be less likely to vote for spendthrift parties. This line of thinking was certainly not absurd. It could easily be justified. It suffered, however, from the disadvantage of never having been tested – even, apparently, in policymakers' own minds – against reality. Many people could not afford to pay a per capita tax, and some would refuse to pay. If the tax was large, the number who could not or would not pay would also be large (as in the event it was); but, if it was small, possibly only a token amount, the general principle that the policymakers had in mind would be upheld, but the cost of collecting the tax would be out of all proportion to the amounts raised. And phasing in the tax gradually never made any sense administratively. In the case of the poll tax, the triumph of prejudice over reason was complete.

Other elements of intellectual prejudice were also in play. Members of Jenkin's review team never seriously considered, probably because they believed they were not allowed to consider, replacing the old rates with either a local income tax or a local sales tax. The pressure on the team's members to ignore those two options was partly political; either kind of tax would be likely to be extremely unpopular. But it also stemmed partly from prejudice. For instance, it was held that a local income tax would be hard and expensive to collect; but such a tax could quite easily be collected on local authorities' behalf by the Inland Revenue. Similarly, it was held that a local sales tax would make no sense in a small country such as Britain because shoppers would simply take their custom away from the shops in high-tax local authorities and transfer it to shops in towns where the tax was lower; but of course, precisely for that reason, all local authorities would be under intense pressure to keep their local sales tax low, thus giving local authorities every reason to control their spending. In that way, a regime of local sales taxes might well have served the Thatcher administration's purposes. But prejudice combined with politics to foreclose both options.

Intellectual prejudice also played a part in the invention of personal pensions and, more to the point, in their mis-selling. As with the poll tax, it was always easy to make out a good case for personal pensions. They increased individuals' personal responsibility for their well-being in old age; they were portable, as people moved from job to job and in and out of employment; and they reduced the financial burdens on the state. But only an unthinking belief in the innate superiority of free markets – and in the moral integrity of the individuals and firms that would operate in this new market – can have led ministers and officials to overlook the need to impose strict regulations on the new market and to go on to ensure that those regulations were properly enforced. Despite being warned to the contrary by their Labour opposite numbers, ministers simply assumed that the personal-pensions market would work in the same way that the traditional markets in private pensions and life insurance had worked. But, as we saw in Chapter 5, it did not. It was too time-consuming and difficult for purchasers of the new pensions to obtain all the information they required; a large proportion of the sellers were ignorant and/or dishonest; intense competition tended to drive down quality and standards rather than drive them up; and the government, far from imposing tight regulations, more or less bribed members of the public to invest in pensions about which they knew little or nothing and that were riskier than they were led to believe. In short, ministers' theories about the way the world would work were hopelessly flawed. Across the Atlantic, President Ronald Reagan's first director of the Bureau of the Budget, David Stockman, had recently made a similar discovery: "The world was less manageable than he had imagined; this machine had too many crazy moving parts to incorporate in a single lucid theory."[1] The government and the insurance industry in Britain also had "too many crazy moving parts".

It is one of the oddities of late twentieth-century British history that the New Labour government elected in 1997 was almost as committed to the new intellectual dispensation as its Conservative predecessors had been. Its priorities differed from its predecessors'; it was more concerned than the Conservatives had been to address problems of poverty and even, albeit stealthily, in a modest way to redistribute income. But most of its prejudices and predilections remained the same. It gave the fight against inflation pride of place in its macroeconomic strategy, it regulated the banking sector with only the lightest of light touches, it kept the trade unions in their place, it showed a willingness to sell off state-owned assets, it introduced market mechanisms and private capital into the National Health Service, its rhetoric lauded the private sector – and so forth.

The Blair government's faith in private enterprise and market forces enjoyed successes – for example, in commissioning private health-care providers to open clinics specialising in cataract operations, thereby shortening waiting times for patients. However, in the case of individual learning accounts New Labour's faith proved magnificently unfounded. The accounts undoubtedly encouraged private enterprise, but not quite the kind of private enterprise that ministers had in mind.

In this case, ministers' prejudice seems to have bordered on dogmatism. Ministers believed, not entirely without reason, that the existing training sector, dominated by further-education colleges, was not up to the job of recruiting and training large numbers of new entrants into training, many of whom would be youngsters who had found their previous experience of formal education unsatisfactory and could only with great difficulty be enticed back into it. Accordingly, ministers rejected officials' recommendations that the bulk of training should remain in the hands of existing providers or that some system for the formal accreditation of would-be providers should be put in place. In other words, ministers rejected the notion that the market in training provision, whatever its exact form, should continue to be regulated and to some extent closed. Then, having rejected what they regarded as a cautious, fuddy-duddy approach, ministers plunged straight away into a fantasy world of their own making. They believed implicitly in free markets and on that basis fantasised that a free market in training provision would supply all the goodies that the traditional system had failed to supply. They also took the same view on the demand side. The market should rule. Potential trainees should be treated exactly like customers in a supermarket and left free to spend the money in their learning account on any product they liked. They should not be put off by bureaucracy and form-filling. So convinced were the top people in the Department for Education and Skills of the correctness of their approach that, as we saw in Chapter 9, they were delighted instead of dismayed when the numbers of providers and trainees totted up far faster than they had expected. What they ought to have heard as alarm bells they heard instead as church bells. Because of the resulting fraud, the whole scheme collapsed in under a year. No factor was more instrumental in causing the scheme's collapse than the prejudice of the kind we are discussing in this chapter.

Prejudices – plural in this case – played an equally large but more complicated part in the case of the grotesque scheme for financing the London underground's renewal. In this case, four distinct prejudices were involved, and their interaction was lethal (though, as usual, not to the careers of those who had devised the scheme).

One prejudice was that of John Prescott, the minister responsible for transport and someone who, as deputy prime minister and a loyal lieutenant to Tony Blair, was a political big-hitter. Prescott was dead set against wholesale privatisation of the tube, partly because he was a Labour man through and through and Labour had always been opposed to privatisation, partly because he had not long before been on the Labour party's left wing and had actually stood against Blair for the party leadership in 1994, and partly because, as a staunch trade unionist and member of one of the big transport unions, he doubted whether a privatised London Underground would honour its workers' terms and conditions of service. Certainly some of the privatised mainline and suburban railway companies had failed to do just that.

The second prejudice, rampant in the New Labour leadership during the 1990s and shared by both Prescott and Gordon Brown, was the conviction that private-sector companies would under almost all circumstances outperform public-sector bodies. In Whitehall at the time people even joked that, given half a chance, New Labour would have privatised the army. New Labour not only wanted to give the impression that it was pro-business: it *was* pro-business, and being pro-business meant taking a favourable view of both the private sector's performance and its personnel. Blair was particularly outspoken in his praise of private business people. "You are the front-line troops of Britain's new economy", he told a conference of venture capitalists in 1999, adding that he personally bore scars on his back from two years spent trying to introduce reforms in the public sector: "People in the public sector are more rooted in the concept that 'If it's always done this way, it must always be done this way' than any [other] group of people I've come across."[2] Brown would never have been so blunt – partly because he wanted to retain his credentials as a man of the left – but his sympathies tended strongly in the same direction.

The third prejudice was related to the second but had a life of its own; and it was only partly a prejudice: it also drew on recent experience. As we also noted in Chapter 14, Brown, Prescott and those immediately around them had it in for London Underground's management – that "bunch of muppets".[3] The tube's managers were blamed, and not just by Labour politicians, for the fire that had taken thirty-one lives at King's Cross station in 1987, for the generally dilapidated condition of the underground's stations and rolling stock and for its seemingly interminable shut-downs, delays and cancellations. On top of all that had come the cost overruns on the Jubilee Line extension and the protracted delays before it opened. Based as much on gossip as on a balanced assessment of the evidence, ministers' negative judgement of London Underground's management may not have been entirely fair, but neither Brown nor Prescott was in a forgiving mood.

The fourth prejudice, shared by both Brown and Prescott, was more personal. Neither man could stand Ken Livingstone, the probable and then actual mayor of London, whom they regarded as untrustworthy, self-serving and a traitor to the Labour party. When Livingstone was eventually readmitted to the party in 2004, Prescott, according to Livingstone, asked him: "Given you lied to us about not running as an independent [which he had done for the mayoralty in 2000], how can we ever believe anything you say?"[4] The ill will endured.

The simultaneous presence of these four prejudices had the effect of blocking off a wide range of policy options. They were not even seriously considered, let alone adopted. Prescott's adamant refusal to consider wholesale privatisation – a cause advocated by at least one senior Treasury official – ruled out that option, which would probably have been hard to sell to the Labour party anyway. Brown's equally strongly held belief in the innate superiority of the private over the public sector meant that whatever policy was adopted would have to include a substantial element of private-sector participation. The belief held by both men that London Underground's management was useless meant that that particular organisation could not possibly be allowed to lead any renewal operation. Indeed, London Underground seems to have been such a toxic brand that serious consideration was never given to the idea of simply installing new management. In addition, Brown and Prescott's intense dislike of Livingstone served to reinforce their view that a new financial regime for the underground, organised by the Treasury, needed to be put in place as quickly as possible. Organising the new regime should definitely not be left in the hands of the new Greater London Authority. The first London mayoral election was about to be held, and it looked as though Livingstone might win it. Brown and Prescott's refusal to contemplate the issuing of government-backed bonds also owed something to their personal dislike of Livingstone, though it owed more to Brown's and the Treasury's insistence that the large sums of money that would be needed to upgrade the tube should not be allowed to come anywhere near the government's balance sheet. Brown seems never to have considered an arrangement like the ones negotiated for municipally owned airports and the Channel

Tunnel Rail Link, arrangements that enabled the affected organisations to raise private capital without the sums they borrowed having to figure in the then Public Sector Borrowing Requirement.

The public-private partnership for the London underground was thus not a policy chosen from among a range of options: given ministers' prejudices, it or something very like it was the only policy on the table. But, as we saw earlier, it was a very bad policy – a gross, even grotesque blunder. One commentator, a man not unsympathetic towards Brown, records that as chancellor he made "several calamitous errors", adding:

> The biggest was the introduction of a Public Private Partnership for the decaying, increasingly unreliable London Underground. The policy revealed Brown's lack of any clear sense as to when the private sector worked well in the delivery of essential services and when it did not, a tendency to assume that any private deal would be better value, and a small-minded determination never to concede to political enemies, in this case Ken Livingstone ... who wanted to raise the much needed investment by other more sensible means.[5]

Issues of how Brown and Prescott were permitted to get away with it – how they were enabled to commit such a calamitous blunder – will arise in later chapters.

As most readers have probably already noticed, one activity that the presence of strong prejudices seems to preclude is pragmatism – that is, a careful, dispassionate approach to problem solving, one that evaluates beliefs or theories in terms of the probable success of their practical application.[6] On the face of it, it would seem sensible for policymakers to proceed in their own minds and also collectively in an orderly manner, identifying objectives, prioritising them, weighing them in the balance against other objectives, identifying a variety of possible means of achieving them, addressing the advantages and disadvantages of each of them and only then deciding on a course of action. That often happens – the Thatcher government's cautious, step-by-step approach to both privatisation and trade-union reform exemplifies successful decision making of that type – but it by no means happens uniformly, even allowing for the inevitable exigencies of practical politics, personal rivalries and what Harold Macmillan once described as "events, dear boy, events".

In the strange case of on-again, off-again ID cards, no clear objectives seem ever to have been identified. Or, rather, far too many objectives were. The prejudice, which certainly existed, was in favour of a policy for its own sake, with the objectives to be decided later. Much the same could be said of the Dome. It was almost impossible to decide how best to achieve the objectives of the New Millennium Experience because no one had decided beforehand what its objectives were. In the case of the poll tax, orderly policymaking did take place after a fashion – the review team did its homework and the tax went through all the proper procedures – except that the range of options available to the policymakers was effectively narrowed to one. In the case of the marketing and sale of personal pensions, nothing that could reasonably be described as policymaking occurred at all. The issue of possible mis-selling – and there certainly was an issue, as Meacher and others pointed out – simply floated off into a void. A decade later, Brown and Prescott's decision to go for a public-private financial arrangement for the London underground resembled the Thatcher government's decision to go for a poll tax. In both cases, so many options were ruled out in advance that only one remained – except that that option was not really an option because it was the only one left.

One probable consequence of intellectual prejudice, especially if it is conjoined with either cultural disconnect or group-think (or both), is that policymakers never get around to doing any contingency planning. There are no Plans B. Those who make policy, if they are seriously prejudiced, or who know nothing of the people at whom their policy is aimed, or who are the victims of group-think, typically feel no need to figure out what they will do if their plans go wrong: they convince themselves that there is no way in which their plans could go wrong. They ignore Robert Burns's warning that "the best laid schemes o' mice an' men gang aft a-gley".

Our catalogue of Plans A unsupported by Plans B is a long one. Our horror stories in Part II were horrible not least because almost all those directly involved in almost every instance seem to have been taken unawares by the failure of their policy and, having assumed that their policy would work, to have given no thought to what they would do in the event that it failed to. Putting the same point another way, they neglected, in most cases utterly, to contemplate worst-case scenarios and to be clear in their own minds what they would do if one of their putative worst-case scenarios turned out to be what actually happened. If they bothered to assess the risks to their policy at all, they failed to follow up their risk assessment by devising, even if only on a just-in-case basis, one or more Plans B.

The Plan B for the poll tax, a banded property tax, appears to have existed only in Michael Heseltine's head. When Norman Fowler's personal pensions were mis-sold on a lavish scale, it was left to the various regulatory bodies to figure out what to do next, and it took them years to do so. The legislation setting up the Child Support Agency contained nothing in the way of fail-safe mechanisms. Neither did the legislation that established the Assets Recovery Agency. The same was true of the ill-fated individual learning accounts, which were abandoned almost overnight. Nothing was available on the shelf to replace them. It took years to sort out – and even then not completely – the arrangements for paying tax credits. Metronet, like individual learning accounts, simply collapsed in a heap, leaving the London underground precisely where Gordon Brown and John Prescott had been so anxious that it should not be: in full public ownership. In the case of Britain's exit from the ERM, undertaking contingency planning would, of course, have been exceedingly difficult. If word had leaked out that such planning was under way, that in itself would almost certainly have brought about Britain's abrupt departure. Nevertheless, the events of 16 September 1992 give the impression that not only had there been no contingency planning in either the Treasury or the Bank of England: there seems to have been little, if any, contingency thinking either. Exiting the ERM proved to be John Major's Plan B – but without its ever having been a plan.

There is yet another factor militating against contingency planning. It is what in the next chapter we call "operational disconnect". That phenomenon has been at the heart of numerous government blunders.

19

Operational disconnect

I t is an old maxim that anyone planning a military operation should ideally be put in charge of it – and should know in advance that he is going to be put in charge of it. Joining together planning and operations in that way means that the individual in charge is playing for high stakes. He owns the operation. If it succeeds, he stands to be decorated and promoted. If it fails, he alone is to blame. A person put in that position has every incentive to plan the forthcoming operation with tremendous care, to ensure that he has sufficient troops at his disposal, that they are properly trained and equipped and that he has a good appreciation of the obstacles that may stand between him and success. In the course of planning the operation, he will want to familiarise himself with the main details of the plan as well as its broad outline. He will also want to familiarise himself with the principal tasks that others will have to perform and with the qualities and capacities of the junior officers and other ranks who will have to perform them. Commanding officers in the Second World War are said to have been more successful than their 1914–18 predecessors because they were closer to the front line. The age of "château generalship" was over.

No feature of the blunders we have studied stands out more prominently – or more frequently – than the divorce between policymaking and implementation and, in human terms, between those who made policies and those charged with implementing them. Sometimes the divorce was partial. Sometimes it was virtually complete. The general officers, in the form of ministers and permanent secretaries, remained safely ensconced in their Whitehall offices. It was left to the poor bloody infantry, in the form of civil servants and other government employees at all levels, to try to achieve ministers' objectives for them.

Here, in rough paraphrase, are some of the things that the people we interviewed – some of them former ministers, some of them retired civil servants – had to say. In most cases, they volunteered remarks like these. They seldom needed to be prompted.

Ministers simply aren't interested in operations.

The original legislation meant that officials had to deal simultaneously with extreme complexity and extreme volatility. No wonder they couldn't cope. The original policymakers had painted everything in simple black and white. No shades of grey were allowed for.

One lesson? Always talk to the people who are going to have to implement a policy.

My department [said a former minister who had inherited his predecessors' policy] had a small outfit that had some experience of dealing with these things, but the outfit was small and nobody in the department seemed to know much about it or take much interest in it. It doesn't seem to have been involved in developing policy.

The idea was to decide on the principle and then let others work out how the principle was to be worked out in practice. It was ridiculous.

The policymaking process, all too often, is a million miles away from knowing how to run things. There's a pervasive view in Whitehall that those who do are below the salt, while those who think are above the salt.

One former minister who had been centrally involved in developing a policy that had gone badly wrong admitted ruefully afterwards: "Having devised it, we should have been left to administer it."

The divorce between policymakers and implementers in the case of the poll tax was all but total. Jenkin's review team spoke. Thatcher listened. Only after the theatrical meeting at Chequers did officials in the Department of the Environment begin to try to work out who exactly should pay the tax and how it should be collected. The department had never before been in the business of collecting taxes – that was the Treasury's and the Inland Revenue's business – and before long dozens of officials, who knew perfectly well what the problems were, "were tearing their hair out". One of them was clearly unhappy but accepted the rules of the official–ministerial game: "We had a lot of anxiety about the workability of a per capita tax, but ministers were very determined on the direction of policy and, at the end of the day, it was civil servants' duty to deliver whatever ministers wanted."

The fact that the poll tax or "community charge" would prove impossible to administer could easily have been foreseen but never was. Civil servants were left to cope. They tried hard but failed. No one could have succeeded.

Nor could anyone have implemented successfully the Child Support Act in its 1991 incarnation. The flaws in the legislation were deep-seated, partly, as we saw in Chapter 6, as a result of the Treasury's never-ending victories in its battles with the Department of Social Security. Ministers as well as officials in the DSS found themselves saddled with the task of implementing, or trying to implement, via the agency, a policy markedly different from the policy they had originally devised. The ministers and officials in the Treasury who, along with the prime minister, insisted on the principal features of the new policy, with its heavy emphasis on revenue-raising rather than child welfare, were devoid of any relevant experience or expertise. For all their Whitehall clout, they were innocents in practical terms; they had no idea what they were doing. In any case, because the Treasury's policy would be administered by ministers and officials in another government department, no Treasury minister or official would ever bear any responsibility if things eventually went wrong. Officials in the Child Support Agency were thus landed with a complicated set of rules to administer, almost zero discretion in administering them and tens of thousands of exceedingly angry customers. Those involved at the top of the DSS were conscious that the policy they had devised would have been difficult to implement in my case, but the policy with which they were saddled simply could not be implemented. And it was not.

The expensive failure of the London underground PPP exhibited many of the same characteristics. Outright privatisation might have made sense; Ken Livingstone is said to have remarked afterwards, "They should have just privatised it." Issuing bonds might also have made sense. "But", as one official put it, "we finished up with the worst of both worlds." On this occasion, as with the poll tax, a large part of the trouble stemmed from the fact that Gordon Brown and John Prescott took a mega-policy decision and then just walked away from it. Policy was for them. Delivering the policy was for others. Evidently the ministers who devised the policy did not feel they had a personal duty, or that it was in their personal interest, to make sure that the policy they had devised could be made to work. To increase the probability that the policy would fail, Brown in particular, who distrusted most of his own officials as well as the management of London Underground, outsourced most of the practical work of implementation to (very expensive) lawyers and consultants, most of whom knew no more about the matters at hand than he did. According to one observer, "There were endless large meetings – some fifty or sixty – involving Shriti Vadera [Brown's personal aide], officials, lawyers and consultants." Brown himself is said never to have met, and to have refused to meet, the man eventually appointed to run the underground, Bob Kiley.

Operational disconnect manifested itself similarly in connection with the tax-credits shambles. In designing the new policy, the chancellor side-lined not only the Department of Social Security, the prime minister and most Treasury officials: neither he nor other members of his inner circle appear to have engaged seriously with the Inland Revenue, which would have to administer the newly expanded programme. In designing the new scheme without benefiting from the on-the-ground experience either of DSS officials or people from the Revenue, Brown and his associates all but guaranteed that in its early years the new system would not work because it could not be made to. One official with wide experience told us that his greatest personal regret was that he had not been more assertive in pointing out beforehand what the administrative problems were almost certain to be. "I didn't fight hard enough", he said. One problem, he added, was that

Gordon Brown wanted officials and the other ministers he dealt with to agree with him or else shut up. It seems they mostly shut up.

As we shall see in a later chapter, prime ministers surprisingly seldom initiate policy. They can strongly support the policies of others, and often (though not in the case of tax credits) they can veto them; but they only rarely launch major domestic initiatives on their own. One of those rare exceptions, as we saw in Chapter 13, was the launch in early 2002 of the NHS National Programme for IT. The launch followed a gathering at Number 10 chaired by the prime minister, Tony Blair, and attended almost exclusively by IT enthusiasts – with titles such as "e-champion" and "e-envoy" – from the Department of Health, from the NHS itself and from the prime minister's newly established Delivery Unit. No nay-sayer seems to have been present, nor any asker of awkward questions. Group-think was able to take charge – and did.

But operational disconnect was clearly also at work. Blair himself freely admitted that he knew nothing of either computers or IT, and it was probably largely for that reason that he was an unqualified admirer of both. Computers and information technology appeared to him to have almost magical properties, with Bill Gates, whom he had recently met, cast by him in the role of magician-in-chief. He described him as "the computer maestro transforming our times".[1] The early-2002 meeting at Number 10 appears to have been just as definitive in deciding that this new IT project should go forward as the 1985 Chequers meeting had been in deciding that introducing a poll tax would become government policy. In both cases, none of those who would actually have to make the policy work were centrally – or even, so far as one can tell, peripherally – involved. Had they been, group-think would almost certainly not have been able to take hold.

Among those who would have to work hard to make Blair's new IT scheme a success were clinicians and administrators in the English NHS. But no one seems to have thought to ask either group whether they actually wanted this marvel of technology, whether they would use it if they were offered it, what specific design features they thought should be built into it or what technical and ethical problems they believed the NHS as a whole – and their particular organisations – might run into if and when it was introduced. One element of the situation that both the Number 10 enthusiasts and Richard Granger and his team at Connecting for Health seem entirely to have overlooked is that, for their purposes, there was no such thing as *the* NHS, even in England. Instead there existed a myriad GP practices, hospitals, hospital trusts and other NHS bodies, each with its own preferences, priorities, methods of working and databases. Even a cursory attempt to consult a range of potential users of the projected IT system would have revealed how diverse the potential users were. Once again, the divorce between policymakers and those who would have to implement the policy on the ground was virtually total. Partly for that reason, huge sums of money that could have been spent on other NHS projects – including more modest NHS IT projects – were totally wasted. It seems the age of château generalship was not over after all.

One academic writer on organisations and management captures the central point well. His language is idiosyncratic, but his meaning is clear:

> It appears that the relationship between "higher" and "lower" clusters of activities is, indeed, not symmetrical: whereas you can do your job adequately in a lower order of comprehension without taking into account considerations that belong in a higher order, the reverse is not true: you cannot do your job adequately in a higher order of comprehension without taking some account of considerations that belong in a lower order.[2]

In other words, the frontline worker does not need to know a great deal about the organisation in which he or she works, but the top manager needs to have at least some grasp of what actually happens on or close to the front line. There is mild irony in the fact that in his memoirs Tony Blair, referring to the war in Afghanistan, cites Jesus' parable in the Gospel according to Luke: "For which of you, intending to build a tower, sitteth not down first and counteth the cost, whether he have sufficient to finish it?"[3] But Blair himself certainly did not sit down and count the cost of his grandiose NHS IT project (of which he makes no mention in his book). He had no grasp of what needed to be done on the front line.

One consequence of operational disconnect of the kind we are describing is that probably no one individual, or even a small group of individuals, will own the whole project in the sense of feeling a responsibility to see it through from start to finish. Nor, if personnel move on and circumstances change, is ownership of the whole project passed in an orderly way from one group or individual to another. Successive heads of the Child Support Agency owned that project for as long as they were in charge, but they had played no part in drafting the relevant legislation and knew in most cases that they would have long since left the scene by the time any changes that they initiated had either borne fruit or failed to. No one ever owned the Metronet–Tube Lines project. Whether it lived or died, succeeded or failed, would never be any one individual's, or any one organisation's, responsibility. All each individual had to do was his or her job in one of the "lower orders of comprehension" – and sometimes it was not even clear what that particular job was.

One participant-observer in the costly poll-tax saga commented on how everyone who was involved assumed that someone else was calculating the political risks involved and addressing the practical issues of implementation. The members of Patrick Jenkin's review team, all of them relatively junior, assumed that ministers a long way above them in the hierarchy, including the prime minister herself, would be taking into account the political risks. They also assumed that officials elsewhere in the Department of the Environment would be dealing with the practical details. If they received no negative feedback from either of those quarters, then all must be well. Meanwhile, Margaret Thatcher and most other members of the cabinet simply assumed – until it was far too late – that, if neither the members of the review team nor the frontline civil servants were sounding alarm bells, then the tax must, indeed, be collectable. But neither the members of the review team nor the environment officials thought that it was their job to sound alarm bells. In any case, the members of the review team were not interested in delivery and therefore probably did not begin to know what alarm bells to ring. The frontline environment officials, in contrast, were interested in delivery, but they reckoned they had been instructed by ministers to deliver, so they had better just get on with it. They, like the members of the review team, assumed that their political masters, and in particular their political mistress, "knew the tax would be hard to collect and were prepared to live with the consequences and to take the political hit if there was one". Everyone operated on the basis of false assumptions about the thinking of others without realising that that was what they were doing. The general staff and the frontline infantry never communicated properly – until, of course, it was too late and the enemy was at the gates.

The military analogy is worth pursuing further. The failure to involve those who will have to implement a policy in the development of that policy almost invariably leads to a failure to "map backwards". In many of the world's armies, it is standard operating procedure not simply to consider the steps required to move, say, a tank regiment or infantry battalion from point A to point Z, but to imagine instead that the unit in question has already arrived at point Z and to consider what needs to have gone right – and what might possibly have gone wrong – in the course of its move from A to Z. Are there any maps between the two points? If there are, where are they? Who has them? From whom do we find out whether the roads between A and Z are passable in all weathers? Who will make sure that the tanks do not arrive in the vicinity of point Z parked so close together and exposed that they make an easy target for enemy aircraft? And so forth.

Experience in business as well as in armies suggests that mapping backwards, instead of relying solely on mapping forwards, concentrates the mind. It alerts planners to potential pitfalls (as well as, possibly, to previously undetected opportunities). More particularly, it forces them to think through operations from the beginning to the very end. The procedure does not allow them to plan an operation from point A only as far as point M and then to down tools, whether because they are tired, or have run out of time, or have lost interest, or because they have naïvely assumed that, if their soldiers were able to reach point M, they would – surely? – be able to proceed further to point Z. In imagination, one can start at A and work forwards only as far as M, but there is no way in which one can start at Z without remembering that all along one's starting point was A.

It happens that during the 1970s, two academics in the United States were given a rare opportunity to write for an incoming cabinet-level secretary a detailed post-mortem report on a blunder that had been committed by officials in the outgoing administration. The incoming cabinet officer did not want to use the report for partisan purposes, to castigate the outgoing administration. He wanted to know what had gone wrong so that he could avoid making similar mistakes of his own. The authors of the report were clear that one of the things that had gone wrong in this case was the failure of those who decided on the policy to take into account issues of implementation. "Implementation", they noted, "is not only something to be done after decision, it is as much or more a thing to think about before decision, right along with substance." They went on to quote one of the decision makers who realised, in retrospect, that there had been something wrong with the whole decision-making process:

> Hell, the thing that was needed in planning the program was a day around the table brainstorming Murphy's Law: "If anything can go wrong, it will"; and all the permutations one could think of. That would have done it. It certainly would have caught a lot of the things that went wrong – they weren't so hard to think of, after all.[4]

The authors also make the point that, while planning forwards via each stage of implementing a policy towards its ultimate goal is obviously desirable, it is at least as desirable, perhaps more so, to plan backwards carefully from the ultimate goal via each implementation stage to the initial jumping-off point.

No brainstorming of the kind alluded to or any systematic backwards-mapping seems to have preceded the initiation of any of the blunders described in this book. The policymaking in every case was top-down and, in so far as it was planned at all, was planned solely in a forwards direction. One core aim of the poll tax was to rein in the lavish spending of mostly Labour-controlled local authorities by requiring the people who voted for them to feel personally, in their pockets and purses, the consequences of what they were doing. Most such people lived in big cities and often in the most deprived areas of those cities. Those were the places where it was most important that the tax should be made to bite. It might therefore have been thought prudent to try to figure out in advance how hard or easy it would be to collect the tax in precisely such places.

But no such effort was made. Imagine what would probably have happened to the poll tax if at some early stage the Department of the Environment had sent scouting parties into a variety of deprived inner-city areas – for example, if they had commissioned survey research in the London Borough of Lambeth, where Brixton is located – and had also taken the trouble to interview local council officers there. Any such exercise would, at the very least, have given policymakers pause. It might well have caused the entire project to be aborted. A generation later, it still remains baffling that ministers at all levels and officials in Whitehall paid so little attention to the issue of exactly who at the local level was going to have to do exactly what if the new tax was to be paid in an orderly way by virtually every adult in the country. They simply assumed that, if they started from point of decision *A*, their safe arrival at point of action *Z* would follow automatically. It was a bizarre assumption.

Similarly – but, in some ways, even more remarkably – the Treasury ministers and officials responsible for the principal elements of the original Child Support Act evidently failed entirely to draw on the experience of those officials in the Department of Social Security who in the recent past had sought, sometimes with considerable success, to extract child maintenance payments from absent fathers. Officials in the Liable Relatives Unit were uniquely well placed to inform policymakers of the obstacles they were likely to encounter if they really expected absent fathers, and indeed single mothers, to co-operate with a scheme that in no way advantaged the mothers and often hassled impecunious fathers. Treasury ministers and officials seem not to have noticed the significance of the fact that they and their junior officials were utterly devoid of relevant experience. Of course, the DSS was not housed in the same building as the Treasury and, unlike the Treasury, was far from being one of the top dogs in Whitehall; but those facts in themselves might have alerted Treasury officials to potential dangers ahead. Instead, they remained – apparently quite happily – ignorant of their ignorance.

An absence of backwards-mapping also marked many other of our blunders: the non-payment and overpayment of tax credits, the failure to pay English farmers the EU monies they were owed, almost all the IT disasters described in Chapter 13, and successive governments' failure to think through exactly how a system of ID cards would work in practice, not in the rarefied world of policymakers but in the workaday world of police officers, postal clerks and civil servants in benefits offices. Paradoxically, detailed backwards-mapping had of necessity to take place in connection with the negotiation of the innumerable Metronet and Tube Lines contracts. The negotiators did have to calculate exactly how long it would take the drivers of tube trains to go to the loo. In that case, the sheer number of points *B*, *C*, *D* and so forth, and the difficulty of arriving at many of them, should have alerted those in authority to the impossibility, or at least the wild improbability, of arriving safely at point *Z*. But of course those in authority were not remotely interested in such mundane matters.

In the UK, the possibility of serious operational disconnect occurring may actually have been institutionalised by the creation, beginning in the late 1980s, of executive agencies, what are sometimes called Next Steps agencies.[5] The idea was, and still is, to retain policymaking in the hands of senior Whitehall civil servants but to delegate responsibility for the implementation of whatever policy has been decided upon to these semi-autonomous agencies. The heads of the agencies in question are supposed to be told in broad terms by their ministerial and official masters what to do and then to be left largely free to get on with doing it. Professionalism, flexibility and efficiency are supposed to be maximised. Often they are, but the obvious risk is that thinking and doing may become detached, with policymakers relying on assurances given by agency heads and failing themselves to address practical issues of doability. That undoubtedly happened in the case of the English farmers fiasco, with Defra ministers and civil servants simply, but misguidedly, accepting the head of the Rural Payments Agency's assurances that he and his staff could deliver the most complicated payments scheme on offer. It also happened in the case of the 1999 passports fiasco, as Jack Straw, who bore the brunt of the public's wrath, ruefully recounts:

> At first sight, transferring passport administration to [the Passport Agency] made perfect sense. There was no politics, no inherent controversy. The business of issuing passports accurately, promptly and efficiently could safely be left to those who knew the business best.
>
> That though was the problem. It was out of sight, out of mind for the Home Office ... Virtually no one in the Home Office had any idea what the agency was actually up to, still less was there any routine supervision of their work. They did not feature at all on my radar – until disaster struck, and I discovered a catalogue of elementary management errors that still bring me out in a sweat ...
>
> We were in for a perfect storm; and we got it.[6]

Like the Rural Payments Agency, the Passports Agency was biting off more than it could chew – and ministers and senior department officials seemingly knew nothing about it.

The author of a classic American study argues that the essence of good decision making involves more than merely making decisions: it involves incorporating into the decision-making process, right from the beginning, considerations of doability. "It is not", the author says, "that we have too many good analytic solutions to problems. It is, rather, that we have more good solutions than we have appropriate actions."

> If one is primarily interested in what the government actually does, the unavoidable question is: What percentage of the work of achieving a desired governmental action is done when the preferred analytic alternative has been identified? My guess is about 10 percent in the normal case, ranging as high as 50 percent for some problems.[7]

In other words, the easy bit, though it may not seem easy at the time, is deciding what ought to be done: the hard bit is the doing of it, and the hard bit is likely to be very hard. As must be evident, most of the policymakers responsible for the blunders we have been describing – whether in Defra, the Home Office or anywhere else – assumed that they had done the hard bit when they had decided what government policy should be. Clearly they were wrong. They had done only a small percentage of what needed to be done.

One final point needs to be made. The analysis in this chapter has been based on a single unstated major premise: that policymakers in British government, like the military commanders mentioned at the start, actually do want to get from A to Z and that they care very much about whether or not they get there. But, one may ask, is that true? Do ministers and senior officials care enough about arriving at point Z to make them want to think long and hard about how they are going to get there? Those are bottom-line questions that deserve to be asked. We ask them in Chapter 24.

20

Panic, symbols and spin

Frequently the cry goes up, "Something must be done!" Newspapers, especially the tabloids, typically take the lead and cry the loudest, but they are often followed closely by other media; and opinion polls frequently suggest that the cause that the press is currently advocating, whatever it happens to be, actually does have broad public support. Ministers then need to decide whether they should do something and, if so, what that something should be. They are often under intense pressure to act quickly; and of course, if they do act quickly, they are liable to blunder. They may also wish to give the impression that they are taking prompt and decisive action when in reality they are doing no such thing. In addition, the party or parties in power almost invariably want to put the best face they can on all of their major undertakings and, in order to do that, they often apply thick layers of cosmetics. Policies as well as pensions can be mis-sold.

The original Dangerous Dogs Act was certainly such a policy. It was panic-driven, almost wholly symbolic in character and spun to maximum ministerial advantage. Initially ministers, as we noted in Chapter 3, were reluctant to introduce new legislation, believing that, in a dog-owning culture such as Britain's, attacks by dogs on humans were inevitable from time to time and that the existing statutes, if enforced, offered members of the public as much protection as the state and the law could reasonably be expected to provide. But in the spring of 1991, once a few especially savage assaults by dogs had been reported, newspapers and broadcasters began to report a whole spate of them. Within a few weeks, the media were projecting a series of isolated incidents as a veritable epidemic. The cases were often sad, the details gruesome. Under the headline "Devil dog chews up wife's arm", the *Daily Express* reported the case of a family pet – a Rottweiler, as it happened – that had bitten its owner, a Bristol housewife, seventeen times and had broken her arm in several places.[1] Within days, the *Bradford Telegraph and Argus* reported what had happened to a little girl in Bradford called Rukhsana Khan:

> Rukhsana was tossed about like a rag doll by the ferocious dog for 15 minutes while onlookers struggled to free her from its vice-like grip. The six-year-old from Springfield Street, Manningham, Bradford, suffered 23 dog bites to her back and three deep bites to the left hand side of her chest where the dog gripped on for dear life. She has five other bites to her chest and lost two teeth in the attack.[2]

The dog in this case was a pit bull terrier. The savage attack on Rukhsana was publicised nationwide.

By now, media pressure on the government to act was intense, and the tabloids' vehement language in editorials was matched by that of the broadsheets. The normally restrained *Times*, alluding to incidents like the attack on Rukhsana, declared that "such incidents or worse will be repeated endlessly until the government acts". It added: "Every single case will be because of the government's delay."[3] The *Independent* insisted that "it cannot be beyond the wit of politicians to design some adequate scheme of dog registration, which would require that the animals should be kept under control and that certain breeds such as pit bull terriers and Rottweilers should not be privately owned at all".[4] A leading article in the *Guardian*, under the heading "The dogs of war", agreed: "No British government easily confronts the dog lobby here: even so, it is still a mystery why the Home Secretary has done so little in the past decade to staunch the flow of the killer breeds."[5] A poll published in the *Sunday Express* suggested that 61 per cent of voters would support the banning of dangerous breeds such as Rottweilers. A majority also favoured stiffer penalties for the owners of dangerous dogs, including possible imprisonment.[6]

Only a brave or foolhardy government could have resisted such an onslaught, especially if, as was the case in the spring of 1991, the next

general election was due in under a year's time. Ministers in any government would have had to be seen to be doing something even if they
doubted whether a great deal could actually be done to prevent dangerous
dogs – not to mention dogs that did not appear to be dangerous – from
attacking people. In the case of John Major's government in 1991, it was
also under intense pressure from the Labour party, as well as the media,
to introduce draconian legislation. Labour wanted the government to
require the registration of all dogs, whatever their breed.

The government undoubtedly had to be seen to be doing something.
But what it actually did – introducing under intense pressure at great speed
the specific piece of legislation that it did – was bound to fail, in policy
terms if not in party-political terms (the Conservatives won the 1992
election). The legislation, with its loose drafting and its primary focus
on dangerous dogs and dogs bred specifically for fighting, could never
have significantly reduced either the population of potentially dangerous
dogs in the UK or the incidence of serious attacks by dogs of all breeds on
individual humans. Enacting the measure was overwhelmingly a symbolic
act, intended to symbolise the government's determination to deal with
an issue, not really to achieve anything in particular. The measure was, in
addition, oversold, which is probably one of the reasons it has had such a
bad reputation ever since. Winding up the second-reading debate on the
proposed legislation in the House of Commons, Kenneth Baker, the home
secretary, made claims on its behalf that were, to say the least, ambitious:

> The provisions contained in this public protection Bill are tough and
> specific. Their aim is to deal quickly and effectively with a serious
> danger. I believe that an overwhelming majority of the public want
> this preventive measure, which is intended to avoid a repetition of
> the attacks that we have witnessed recently, to pass quickly into law.[7]

The majority of the public probably did want the bill passed into law, but
that was almost certainly largely because of the positive spin the government had put on it. The measure had been, among other things, mis-sold
or at least grossly oversold. Its effects have been negligible.

Symbolism also appears to have been to the fore in connection
with two pieces of legislation not so far mentioned: the soberly named

Firearms (Amendment) Act 1997 and its soon-enacted sequel, the Firearms (Amendment) (No. 2) Act 1997. Both Acts were responses to the Dunblane massacre of the previous year, when a lone gunman, equipped with four high-calibre handguns, all of them legally owned, had shot dead sixteen Scottish schoolchildren and their teacher. Both Acts largely failed in their principal stated purpose of reducing the possession and use of handguns. No outsider can know for sure what was in the minds of the two home secretaries, Michael Howard and Jack Straw, who between them introduced a ban on the legal ownership of high-calibre handguns and then a ban on the legal ownership of low-calibre handguns. However, the official report of their speeches in the House of Commons makes it clear that both men were well aware that, unlike in the case of Dunblane, a large proportion of the handguns used by criminals in the course of committing crimes were not held legally but illegally and that they might therefore be affected little, if at all, by the new legislation. Both men nevertheless maintained in parliament that they believed that their proposed bans would reduce the levels of handgun-related crime; Straw, for example, told MPs that "there is no doubt that if the availability of handguns is restricted, the prospect of their being used in crime is much less".[8] But the record of the parliamentary debates conveys the distinct impression that everyone in favour of a ban on handguns – on both sides of the House – were motivated more by the horrors of Dunblane and the evidence of overwhelming public support for such a ban than by any real belief that a ban would reduce the incidence of gun-related crime. Those who supported a ban appear to have done so more in hope – a somewhat forlorn hope – than in expectation. In other words, they were largely engaged in symbolic politics, the politics of the appropriate public gesture. The ban was not perhaps a blunder. It was certainly not a major one. But it was a clear instance of politicians raising expectations that were unlikely to be fulfilled.

The New Millennium Experience – a.k.a. the Dome – was, needless to say, overwhelmingly an essay in symbolism. Conservative and Labour politicians alike hoped it would symbolise the vibrancy of the new United Kingdom. Labour politicians after 1997 hoped it would symbolise New Labour's governing capacity, drive and imagination. Michael Heseltine was one of the few senior politicians involved who saw it as principally an essay in job creation, housing and urban regeneration. The fact that the Dome was almost universally regarded as a failure owed a great deal to the overwrought expectations engendered by its enthusiastic Labour backers. Peter Mandelson, writing in the *Evening Standard*, waxed lyrical about the Dome within months of Labour's return to power:

> It will make a powerful statement to the rest of the world about Britain's new-found pride and self-confidence ... We must create more than simply a fine building and a great popular Experience. The nation's Millennium celebration must have a deeper, underlying purpose which unites and inspires the country and offers a bold new British identity to the rest of the world. The National Programme being developed as part of the Millennium Experience is all about inspiring and helping people to think about where we are, and it will make a difference on the big issues we all face.[9]

Visiting the Dome on the eve of the exhibition's opening, Tony Blair lambasted its critics as insecure cynics who "despise anything modern and are made uneasy by success".[10] But the Dome never made anyone uneasy because of its success. It did not succeed. Blair himself in his memoirs conceded that he had erred in going ahead with it: "It wasn't dreadful. It just wasn't brilliant." The whole thing, he said, "never quite struck a note sufficiently attuned to the millennium".[11] Had the UK's millennium celebrations been conceived in less symbolic and more concrete terms – if they had taken the form of, say, the building and opening of new hospitals or schools – they would probably have been more successful. Prestige projects that fail to yield prestige are doubly damned.

Tony Blair in his memoirs neglects to mention the setting up and subsequent abolition of the Assets Recovery Agency, and in his published diaries David Blunkett, the responsible cabinet minister, mentions the launching of the agency only in passing; but its failure, like the failure of the Dome, owed a good deal to hyperbole and spin. The hype and spin created expectations that could not be met.

Most of the claims made by ministers in the House of Commons on behalf of the new agency were actually quite modest. Nevertheless, during the second-reading debate on the Proceeds of Crime Bill, John Denham, the Home Office minister in charge of the bill, announced that the aim of the exercise was to take the profit out of crime. He assured the House that the new agency's director would "play a leading role in the development and implementation of the [government's] asset recovery strategy" and that the agency itself would be "a champion for and raise the profile of asset recovery".[12] Then, when the agency was finally launched in February 2003, the publicity machines of both the Home Office and 10 Downing Street went into overdrive and encouraged Jane Earl, the agency's director, to do the same. Not only, as we noted in Chapter 11, did the Number 10 press office set out to organise dramatic video footage of police officers knocking down the doors of a Mister Big, but an article entitled "Why I'll make the criminal pay ... not the crime" appeared in the *Sunday Express* under the byline of no less than the prime minister. The article's real author, whoever he or she was, informed readers that the government, as well as stepping up its drive to bring more criminals to justice, was "going to hit them hard where it hurts most – in their pockets. We are going to seize their yachts, their cars, their homes and their cash wherever and whenever we find their ill-gotten gains."[13]

And the word quickly went out across the country, appearing in local newspapers as well as on radio and television:

"Hitting criminals where it hurts" (*Bath Chronicle*)

"Time called on wealthy 'Mr Bigs'" (*Western Mail*)

"Gangsters to lose profits of crime" (*Mirror*)

"Action on criminals who enjoy high life" (*The Sentinel*, Stoke-on-Trent)

"Crooks to lose loot: government agency plans to seize the assets of criminals" (*South Wales Echo*)

Jane Earl herself, interviewed by the *Observer*, was more circumspect. She welcomed the fact that the Assets Recovery Agency could demand that someone with enormous and suspicious-looking assets demonstrate to a court that they had been acquired legally: "If you have a large house and five places in the Caribbean, with no visible means of support, no rich aunties who have recently died leaving the odd five million and no successful lottery tickets, it won't do to say that someone gave you the money." But she recognised that it would be a challenge for her agency to reach its annual confiscation target, and she emphasised that one of the agency's principal purposes, in addition to recovering assets, was to make communities and local businesses feel safer.[14] Unfortunately, as we saw earlier, the agency came to be judged almost exclusively in terms of how much money it retrieved and how quickly it retrieved it. The spin and exaggeration that accompanied its launch did not kill off the agency on their own, but they certainly made its ultimate demise more probable. Although in the end ID cards were never introduced, the fact that they remained on the political agenda for so long owed a great deal to pressure from tabloid newspapers and many politicians' belief – based initially on supportive opinion-poll findings – that identity cards would play well with the electorate.

Legislation that is purely symbolic is quite common in other democracies, with foreign parliaments putting on their nations' statute books enactments that amount to little more than statements of good intentions, often prefaced by extravagant expressions of the highest-flown sentiments. Such legislation has been rare in Britain. The Parliament Act 1911 was certainly more than purely symbolic – it abolished at a stroke the House of Lords' absolute veto over legislation passed by the House of Commons – but it did open with a statement that *was* purely symbolic. The Act's preamble declared that the government of the day "intended to substitute for the House of Lords as it presently exists a Second Chamber constituted on a popular instead of hereditary basis". But that robust declaration, despite its embodiment in a statute, was no more than a gesture, lacking any legal or political force. More than a century later, no second chamber constituted on a popular basis has been created (or, at the time of writing, looks like being created). But explicit symbolism of that kind has been unusual in the government of this country. Most of the symbolism in British Acts of Parliament – and in the acts of British governments generally – has been implicit, with ministers claiming that they could achieve more than they possibly could.

However, there is, or was, a rare exception, dating from as recently as February 2010. The Fiscal Responsibility Act 2010, which received the royal assent in that month, began by solemnly declaring that it was "an Act to make provision for and in connection with the imposition of duties for securing sound public finances"; and it went on to lay solemn duties upon the Treasury, one of them being, for example, that "The Treasury must ensure that, for the financial year ending in 2014, public sector net borrowing expressed as a percentage of gross domestic product is no more than half of what it was for the financial year ending in 2010".[15] But of course those portentous-sounding words were never of any practical value. They were no more than symbolic. Under the British system, no parliament can bind its successors in the way that the Act implied, and the Act itself provided no effective – or, for that matter, any ineffective – means for its own enforcement. In the event, it and its symbolism remained on the statute book for little more than a year. The Cameron government repealed it in March 2011.

The Fiscal Responsibility Act's purely symbolic character was recognised from the outset. When the chancellor of the exchequer, Alistair Darling, introduced the bill that preceded it in the House of Commons in January 2010, a Liberal Democrat backbencher intervened to ask him what could prevent either him or some future chancellor of another party from introducing amendments to alter the targets contained in the bill: "This", the backbencher said, "is a policy statement rather than a binding objective."[16] On the same occasion, the shadow chancellor, George Osborne, moved an amendment pointing out that "the duties imposed by the Bill are not accompanied by any corresponding sanctions", and he dismissed the whole bill as "vacuous and irrelevant", "fundamentally dishonest" and "the biggest load of nonsense that this Government have had the audacity to present to Parliament in this Session".[17] He was, he said, pretty sure that the whole idea had been cooked up, not by Darling, who was present in the Commons, but by Gordon Brown, the prime minister. And, in saying that, Osborne was quite right. Darling's advocacy of the bill in the House was no more than tepid, and in his memoirs he explains how it came to be introduced in the first place. It was a sop he had thrown to Brown in advance of a round of fraught negotiations between the two of them:

In the early autumn [of 2009] Gordon told me he accepted that we had to show we were mindful of the deficit. He therefore proposed a Fiscal Responsibility Act which would commit us to reducing the deficit by half over a five-year period. In my opinion, such a move was wide open to the argument that you didn't need a law to ensure that you acted as you should. In the circumstances, though, I seized on it because it did at least provide me with the equivalent of a fiscal rule … The Act was eventually introduced in early 2010, to almost universal derision. Legislation is no substitute for sound judgement.[18]

Nor does legislation make the exercise of sound judgement any more probable.

All governments spin in some degree. All of them engage from time to time in symbolic politics, whether pure or otherwise. But symbolism and spin are always dangerous, including to the symbolists and the spinners. They can contribute to flawed legislation, as in the case of the Dangerous Dogs Act. They can undercut the purposes even of sensible legislation, as in the case of the Assets Recovery Agency. They can make leading politicians look foolish, as in the case of the Dome. They can make them look shallow and dishonest, as in the case of the Fiscal Responsibility Act. Not least, they can make a major contribution towards reducing ordinary citizens' confidence in both the processes of government and the integrity of the entire political class. It is still debatable whether or not Britain's participation in the American-led invasion of Iraq in 2003 was a blunder, but episodes such as the "dodgy dossier", which grossly exaggerated the scale of the threat posed by the Iraqi regime to the outside world, seriously damaged the public standing of politicians in general, not just the reputations of Tony Blair and the Labour party.

All of the phenomena described in the last five chapters – cultural disconnect, group-think, intellectual prejudice, operational disconnect and symbolism and spin – can be found everywhere and in all walks of life. They are confined neither to governments in general nor to British governments in particular. They affect, and frequently infect, large corporations, small businesses, schools, universities, trade unions, charities and all forms of human organisation, including families. But all of them are more pervasive in British government than is often realised. It is also the case that the British system of government as a whole suffers from specific institutional flaws that make British governments more blunder-prone than they need to be or ought to be. It is to these UK-specific flaws that we now turn.

Part IV

System failures

21

The centre cannot hold

A study of the blunders committed by British governments in recent decades draws attention to two crucial features of the British system. One of the two is quite well known, though better known to government insiders than to outsiders. The other seems to be less well known. The two are intimately related.

The better-known of the two is the extent to which departments and agencies within British government – as within most countries' governments – resemble sovereign states, with each department and agency having its own history, outlook and interests, sometimes co-operating with other departments, sometimes competing with them and much of the time carrying on independently of them, as though their bureaucratic neighbours did not exist. Government in Whitehall – as in most capitals – resembles a conglomerate organisation such as the United Nations more than it resembles a tightly knit body that deserves to be called *the* government (singular) of the UK. British government is not a single, unified entity. The closer one looks at it, the more disparate it seems.

The other feature of the British system, less well known, is the limited extent to which any prime minister can command and control everything that goes on inside his or her administration. At least since the time of Clement Attlee, the prime minister has seemed to embody in his person the government of the country. He travels the world. He makes speeches and holds press conferences. He answers questions in parliament every week. Clips from his numerous public appearances are aired on radio and television. Newspaper articles, though seldom actually written by him, appear under his byline. He can be heard expressing his views on just about every conceivable subject. Latterly, some British prime ministers – notably Margaret Thatcher and Tony Blair – have come to resemble movie stars, able after their retirement to command enormous lecture fees. Today's media even take an interest in premiers' spouses. Long gone are the days when Violet Attlee could drive her husband (dangerously) around the country, almost unnoticed, in the modest family saloon. Naturally, people have inferred from all that that the prime minister of the day is The Great Mover and Shaker within the British system. Everything that happens on his watch is down to him.

But, pomp and power being far from the same thing, the truth is more complicated. Some prime ministers, especially those with forceful personalities and those who have recently won general elections, can undoubtedly move and shake; but all prime ministers, even the most forceful and determined of them, are institutionally weak as well as strong. On the one hand, they have the sole prerogative of appointing, reshuffling and dismissing ministers. Unusually among the world's heads of government, they can invent and uninvent government departments and agencies at will. They enjoy the authority inherent in their high office. They can throw their weight behind projects they favour and are usually able to veto projects of which they strongly disapprove. Occasionally they can even take policy initiatives of their own. In the age of summitry, they are bound to a large extent to be their own foreign secretary.

But, against all that, any occupant of 10 Downing Street is only one individual, someone who very often has powerful political colleagues and always has numerous parliamentary and other political duties to perform. He is frequently somewhere abroad. His knowledge and grasp of specific issues will almost invariably be limited, and there are only so many hours in the day, with time devoted to one issue meaning time not devoted to a myriad others. By international standards, the British prime minister also has strictly limited staff resources. There are not many people, and certainly not many policy experts and administrators, who are *his* people, not anybody else's, and who work closely with him. The British prime minister, of course, is not entirely alone on the front line, but by international standards he or she very nearly is.

Almost all the blunders we studied in detail exhibited some combination of, on the one hand, the fragmented departmentalism just described and, on the other, a Number 10 whose interventions were almost invariably sporadic and occasionally completely ineffectual. Over a range of domestic matters, even Margaret Thatcher was not as imperious or as effectual as she often appeared.

The poll tax is yet again a classic instance of both phenomena. It was gestated entirely within the Department of the Environment. The Treasury, the department normally responsible for every aspect of taxation, played no part in devising the tax, and Nigel Lawson, the chancellor, did not bother to turn up to the crucial Chequers meeting that endorsed it and then went on to fight a low-intensity guerrilla campaign against it. At first, his opposition took the form of critical mutterings and memoranda. Later, and more devastatingly, it took the form of refusing to countenance increased central-government funding of local authorities in order to keep the rate of the tax within politically acceptable bounds. No one other than the chancellor knew whether he deliberately set out to scupper the tax, but he certainly never befriended it and took as few steps as he could to save it when it was obviously in peril. He and Chris Patten, the environment secretary, had a furious row when Patten attempted to talk the prime minister into leaning on Lawson to be more helpful. Lawson in his memoirs captures the flavour of his involvement in the aborted negotiations:

> I was in no doubt that the tax was so fundamentally flawed that no amount of tinkering could make it acceptable; and it was tiresome to have to spend so much time on this complex and futile patching up exercise on the very morning that the Bundesbank had just raised German interest rates, immediately ahead of the 1989 Party Conference.[1]

It was only after Lawson had left Number 11, and Thatcher had left Number 10, that relations between the Treasury and the Environment Department improved to the point where the Treasury under Norman Lamont was prepared to mitigate the immediate effects of the poll tax and to ease the introduction of the new council tax.

The prime minister's interventions in the poll-tax episode were decisive, occasional and of course ultimately self-destructive. At first she was unconvinced of the merits of a per capita tax. Then at Chequers she became a convert. Then, for a long time, she focused her attention on developments elsewhere and let events run their course, doing little beyond giving the tax her public support and appointing to ministerial posts in the Environment Department men known to be either sympathetic towards the tax or enthusiastically in favour of it. She made no attempt to stop one of her favourite ministers, Nicholas Ridley, from accelerating the introduction of the tax. Then, at the last moment, when the tax in some form might conceivably have been saved, she rebuffed Chris Patten's desperate efforts to try to save it.

Throughout, she was simultaneously active and passive: active in promoting the tax and insisting that it go forward, passive and inactive in not carefully monitoring its progress and assessing continually its administrative viability and possible political consequences. She neither performed the twin tasks of monitoring and assessing herself nor had anyone else in place to perform those tasks on her behalf. There were jobs that needed to be done. No one did them. In the late 1980s her principal preoccupations were the sterling exchange rate, especially vis-à-vis the Deutschmark, Britain's entry into the European Exchange Rate Mechanism and Britain's relations with Europe generally. Issues relating to the poll tax were a mere distraction – and the lady was not to be distracted.

The case of personal pensions and their mis-selling was different in some ways but eerily similar in others. Two departments were again involved, the Department of Social Security and the Department of Trade and Industry, but, whereas in the case of the poll tax the Treasury and the Environment Department came into direct conflict (at least when Nigel Lawson was personally engaged), the two departments involved in personal pensions appear to have run along parallel lines that never met. Neither department focused on the potential for pensions mis-selling, and neither department noticed that the other was not focusing on it. Both suffered from tunnel vision, and it did not help that the two secretaries of state who between them should have addressed the issue, Norman Fowler and Lord Young, did not hold each other in high regard. As for the prime minister, she applauded the cause of personal pensions and gave Fowler her full backing in introducing them, but otherwise Number 10 played almost no part in the whole episode.

Because it is the department responsible for controlling, or trying to control, public expenditure, the Treasury is continually at odds with all the big spending departments and sometimes with other departments as well. Accounts of face-to-face meetings between Treasury ministers and officials and their equivalents from other departments suggest that they range from the affable but guarded ("Everyone is polite and restrained. The tone is agreeable. They are sharing information. But there is an undercurrent") to the positively testy and aggressive ("Daggers drawn, it's a thoroughly unpleasant exercise, bullying, there was no meeting of minds at all").[2] One of our interviewees, after a long and wide-ranging discussion, said there was one important issue we had not raised. "What was that?" we asked. "The Treasury", he replied. He blamed the Treasury for almost all of Britain's ills dating back over many decades and wondered aloud why an organisation that had presided for so long over such poor economic performance was still held in such high esteem. The short answer may be that, at least within Whitehall, it is less esteemed than feared.

The Treasury did not succeed entirely on its own in destroying the poll tax, though it certainly did its best; but its multiple victories in its battles with the Department of Social Security over the early-1990s arrangements for child maintenance almost certainly doomed what was going in any case to be an extraordinarily difficult enterprise. The Treasury not only succeeded in turning a welfare measure into a fiscal measure – from *Children Come First* into *The Treasury Comes First* – but in close association with the Inland Revenue succeeded in insisting that the money collected from absent parents should be collected, not by the Revenue but by the Social Security Department, which as time went on became an increasingly disinterested party. Its executive agency, the Child Support Agency, was not actually collecting money on behalf of the department, which could then pass it on, at least in part, to lone parents. It was collecting it on behalf of the Treasury. That was a task it was never properly equipped to perform. Beyond the prime minister's approving in general terms the idea that feckless fathers should be made to pay, Number 10 seems scarcely to have been present.

The wondrous-to-behold fiasco of individual learning accounts exhibits several of the same characteristics, with another added on. It was only one of a large number of educational initiatives being pursued by the Blair government, and Tony Blair's attention was mostly focused on the others. Individual learning accounts were, or appeared to be, desirable but also relatively straightforward and therefore a matter that could safely be left to line departments. The Treasury's interest was more intense, partly because learning accounts involved spending government money and partly because Gordon Brown, the chancellor, wanted to be seen to be actively promoting back-to-work and poverty-reduction policies. It was Gordon Brown, not David Blunkett, the education minister, who initially announced the imminent introduction of individual learning accounts, and it was the Treasury that initially encouraged the Department for Education and Skills to try to persuade the clearing banks to promote and manage the accounts. Only when those negotiations failed did the Treasury dump responsibility for organising and managing the accounts wholly onto the DfES. The differences of opinion between the Treasury and the Education Department did not amount to much, and Number 10 could not be expected to focus, and did not focus, on the matter. Instead, what forced the issue up the political agenda – and, in the course of doing that, greatly speeded up the whole process and substantially increased the chances of the government's blundering – was the single sentence (out of many hundreds) in Labour's 1997 election manifesto committing a Labour government to introducing learning accounts. It is not entirely clear why ministers allowed that single sentence – which, in itself, had never featured prominently in political debate – to drive policy to the extent that it did.

Jockeying for position in Whitehall has seldom been more intense and more multilateral than in the case of the introduction of tax credits. In this case, as we saw in Chapter 10, there was one clear winner and two clear losers. The winner was the Treasury under the leadership of Gordon Brown. He wanted tax credits. He did not want anyone else to have them. He got them. His victory was not wholly predictable because his principal opponent was his putative boss, the prime minister. Blair did not actually hate tax credits, but he had serious doubts about them and certainly would not, on his own, have accorded them high priority. But, confronted by an adamant chancellor, he had no choice but either to acquiesce and agree to them or else to sack his chancellor or otherwise force him out of office. He was not prepared to do that for good political reasons – reasons of which the chancellor was well aware. In a classic game of chicken, the chancellor drove on; it was the prime minister who swerved to avoid a collision that was potentially fatal for both. The other loser was, predictably, the Department of Social Security. That department and its ministers, lacking strong support from Downing Street or any sign of such support, never stood a chance against the hard-driving Brown, a man well known to be capable of road rage. The blunder duly ensued.

A similar triangle of unequal forces contributed to the Metronet fiasco. Gordon Brown, seconded by John Prescott, was determined that some kind of private-finance initiative should be developed to finance improvements to the London underground. The department that might have been expected to be centrally involved, the Department for Transport, happened at that point not to exist. It had been subsumed – temporarily, as it turned out – into Prescott's mega Office of the Deputy Prime Minister. There was, however, a minister nominally in charge of transport; indeed, four individuals served as ministers of transport during New Labour's first four years. But none of them and few of their senior officials played a significant role in the development of the ill-fated public-private partnership. After all, transport was clearly too serious a matter to be left in the hands of people who knew anything about transport. Money – and politics – was all that mattered. Tony Blair, the prime minister, was mostly an onlooker, though one who occasionally tried to patch things up, especially when the PPP looked as though it might prove politically damaging. On one occasion, he arranged a private meeting at Chequers with Bob Kiley, the newly appointed London transport commissioner. According to Kiley, there were just the two of them at that meeting:

> He had the contracts strewn all over his worktable, which covers two walls of his study, which is a big study. The Northern Line PFI contract was there as well as the PPP and he [Blair] remarked: "The language in this Northern Line contract is a lot better than the language in this PPP contract." I agreed.[3]

311

Blair, a lawyer, clearly suspected something was wrong, but nevertheless he continued to give the PPP the go-ahead. When Stephen Byers replaced John Prescott as the cabinet-level minister in charge of transport in 2001, he was clear that his instructions from Number 10 precluded altogether his scrapping the PPP. Instead, the so-called partnership was left to scrap itself – but only after a lot more money had gone down the drain.

Commentators on British government frequently describe Whitehall departments as living their lives within "silos". One can see what they mean: British government departments do typically have their own cultures and their own causes, which they seek to promote. Yet at the same time the silos metaphor is an odd one. It implies that government departments are not only tall but also free-standing and independent of each other, having, like farm silos, little or no connection with one another. But, of course, in practice Whitehall departments are intimately and continuously connected with each other, all of them with the Treasury, many of them with one or more other line departments. Government is a lattice, not a set of uprights.

That said, blunders may sometimes occur because departments are left entirely on their own to make major policy decisions without having to – or feeling any need to – consult other departments or even Number 10. On such occasions, the departments in question really do operate in metaphorical silos. With regard to the decision of the Department for Environment, Food and Rural Affairs in 2003 to opt for the most complicated possible way of making payments to English farmers, the silos metaphor is wholly apt. For once, the money to be dispersed came directly from Brussels, so there was no need for Defra to haggle with the Treasury; and, as only farmers and landowners were involved, there was also no need for it to do business with other government departments. Defra's unilateral decision may well have been cleared in some formal sense with Number 10, but there is no reason to think Downing Street was involved in any significant way. It was left to middle-ranking and junior officials in Defra and the Rural Payments Agency – those towards the bottom of the silo – to express their doubts about the workability of the proposed scheme; but, if any of them did harbour doubts, which some of them are thought to have done, they never actually got round to expressing them. Perhaps, as has been suggested, they feared losing credibility and damaging their careers. Perhaps they simply did not think it was their job to second-guess their superiors.

For all their high-profile visibility, British prime ministers only occasionally take policy initiatives. Most of the time they are otherwise occupied, not least with crisis management. Also, as we noted earlier, they mostly lack staff who could take charge of their initiatives, develop them and follow them through. It is also the case that prime ministers are the ministers furthest removed from any need to address problems of implementation. If heads of line departments are capable of presiding over what we call operational disconnect, prime ministers are even more so. It was all very well for Margaret Thatcher to give the poll tax her blessing at the famous Chequers gathering; but she might not have blessed it so readily if she or her people (of whom there were so few) had paused to consider the tax's practical – and therefore its political – implications.

Only one of the blunders discussed in Part II stemmed directly from a prime-ministerial initiative, unchecked by anyone else; but in its way it was pretty spectacular. That was the costly and ultimately aborted NHS National Programme for Information Technology. Tony Blair readily admitted that he was a total IT innocent, and the informal seminar at which he effectively launched the disastrous programme appears to have been a somewhat casual affair, one whose membership almost guaranteed that the prime minister would be isolated from reality. Only one of the participants was in any sense (and that in a very loose sense) a member of Blair's staff, and that one person was a so-called e-envoy, an individual who was new to the job and who was not in any position to make sound judgements about either the workability of the proposed scheme or Blair's personal reputational stakes in launching it. The Department of Health was represented only by a junior House of Lords minister and the department's in-house "e-champion".[4] Had a wider range of Health Department officials been involved, they could have warned the prime minister that the ambitious project's chances of succeeding were poor. Blair subsequently took little interest in the project, and the same was true of his successor, Gordon Brown. In effect, the project was a prime-ministerial bauble – a toy that could be, and was, discarded.

All of these episodes raise obvious questions about the curious mix that exists in the British system between departmentalism – inevitable in any large bureaucratic organisation – and a "centre" that is, in fact, only sporadically centripetal. For all the fashionable talk of "prime-ministerial power" and "presidentialism", the truth is that, looked at close up, British government turns out to be more chaotic than dictatorial. Neither the prime minister nor any other powerful institution at or very near the centre of government is capable in practice of checking and balancing, let alone controlling and directing, much of what goes on elsewhere.

In practice, the centre is weak, under-organised and understaffed, a fact that helps account for many of our blunders. Thatcher, given all her other responsibilities and preoccupations, had at her disposal no institutional means for assessing coolly the original poll-tax proposition and then of keeping an eye on what was going on when it began to be implemented. Similarly, no one at the centre seems to have spotted that the Department of Social Security and the Department of Trade and Industry were between them letting the possibility of pensions mis-selling fall between the cracks. Likewise, no one anywhere near Downing Street seems to have spotted early on that the Child Support Act was a mis-sold mess or that individual learning accounts needed to have probing questions asked about them. In the cases of both tax credits and the London underground PPP, Tony Blair was left almost alone to deal not only with the implacable character of his chancellor of the exchequer but with the substance of two extraordinarily complex practical issues. Gordon Brown, being unsackable, would probably have won in any case; but, properly briefed, Blair might at least have been able to ask awkward questions (and to make it known to others that he had asked such questions). In many ways, Blair was a strong and forceful prime minister. There is therefore something pathetic about his having to festoon his own study at Chequers with copies of the PFI and PPP contracts and to see Bob Kiley on his own. With regard to the wisdom and practicality of Blair's hyper-ambitious NHS IT project, he himself should have been asked tough questions by people who were close to him. It looks from the outside as though he just winged it.

Prime ministers have long recognised their aloneness, their lack of institutional capacity. They are reasonably well equipped in the fields of foreign policy and defence but less so in domestic matters. As long ago as the time of Harold Macmillan, his personal factotum, Lord Egremont, noted that his boss (who was also his friend) relied almost entirely for all purposes on his own phone and his Number 10 Private Office, which comprised only a few junior civil servants, all of whom were exceedingly able but could only do so much.

> The point is that the Prime Minister had only four young men on whom to depend. Other Ministers presided over great Departments with all the apparatus which they command. If you are an ambitious Minister, it is important for you to be a Minister with a great Department behind you. The resounding titles like Lord President of the Council and Lord Privy Seal are as sounding brass or a tinkling cymbal because they are without large Departments. The Prime Minister is in a like position except for the fact that he has the hiring and the firing of his ministerial colleagues, which does make a difference. Nevertheless he may very well ache to collar a Department for himself and thus expand the horizon of his office beyond his four young men.[5]

Harold Wilson and Edward Heath certainly ached for more personal back-up just as Macmillan had. In their time, the Cabinet Office served and serviced the whole cabinet, though the cabinet secretary did work directly to both of them in their cabinet chairmanship role. The customary Wednesday-morning meeting of departmental permanent secretaries, although useful in its way, served the permanent secretaries' purposes, not the prime minister's. Apart from locating a few Labour-friendly economists in the Cabinet Office, Wilson largely put up with the status quo during his first term as prime minister, but Heath created a body called the Central Policy Review Staff (CPRS) – which, in his view, "provided a valuable reinforcement of the government's capacity for the analysis of policy at the centre" – and Wilson during his second term kept the CPRS and added a small, seven-person Policy Unit to provide him personally with advice on both the substance of policy and the political implications of whatever policies were being proposed.[6] James Callaghan retained both the CPRS and the Policy Unit, the latter being, in his words, "one of Harold Wilson's effective creations which I was happy to inherit".[7] Number 10 was gradually expanding. There were now more, although not many more, than four young men.

Even Margaret Thatcher, although content to rely on her own instincts and resources for most purposes, was conscious of needing help, not least though not only because she distrusted the civil service. She abolished the Central Policy Review Staff, which, she thought, "had become a freelance 'Ministry of Bright Ideas', some of which were sound, some not, many remote from the Government's philosophy"; but she retained her version of the Wilson–Callaghan Policy Unit, which she much enlarged and used extensively in cross-questioning ministers about the performance of their departments and in the preparation of the Conservative party's election manifestos, which in turn she used as a means of forcing forward thinking among her ministers.[8] She also established an Efficiency Unit formally lodged in the Cabinet Office but reporting directly to her. John Major, a self-consciously traditionalist prime minister more in the mould of Harold Macmillan than either Wilson or Thatcher, retained the Policy Unit but otherwise made no effort to expand Number 10's institutional capacity either to command or control.

His successor, Tony Blair, was cut from different cloth. He wanted both to move and shake. He shared Thatcher's distrust of the civil service, and he felt duty bound to lead the first successful Labour administration since the time of Clement Attlee just as he had led the Labour party to victory after eighteen years in the political wilderness. He was sure he was up to the job. He was not sure that many of his ministers were. His responses included importing into 10 Downing Street – into the building itself and its numerous outposts – the largest-ever number of politically appointed special advisers (more than eighty at times) and inaugurating what somebody soon dubbed "government by unit". The Number 10 Policy Unit by now was well established. It remained and was joined by the Strategic Communications Unit, the Research and Information Unit, the Social Exclusion Unit, the Performance and Innovation Unit and, in the fullness of time, following the 2001 general election, the Strategy Unit and the Delivery Unit. Blair made himself lord of the most extensive prime-ministerial manor in British history. His vast estate comprised many farms and tenants.

Yet our survey of government blunders suggests that, even under a would-be dominant prime minister like Tony Blair, Downing Street and Whitehall were far from being a blunder-free zone. On the contrary, the

Blair government and its successor under Gordon Brown were at least as blunder-prone as their immediate predecessors, possibly more so. Number 10 under Blair and Brown and their various units undoubtedly did much good work. Blair himself is proud of the work done by both the Strategy Unit and the Delivery Unit. But neither they nor the prime minister himself, whatever their other accomplishments, succeeded in avoiding the car crashes described in detail in Chapters 4–15 and numerous other accidents that we have not had room to describe. Obviously, no quick or even slow institutional fix can eliminate blunders altogether. Human beings and organisations being what they are, there will always be blunders. But a certain amount of institutional tinkering might possibly contribute to reducing their number.

On the face of it, there are two possibilities. One, favoured by traditionalists, is to restore cabinet government, by which is usually meant the taking of important decisions – in fact as well as in form – by the cabinet as a whole and by cabinet committees. Cabinet government to some extent still survives. Cabinet committees still sort out many cross-departmental issues, and the full cabinet often discusses important issues, even if they have normally been pre-decided by smaller groups of ministers, usually including the prime minister. As they reach their own decisions, these smaller groups almost invariably bear the possibility of cabinet dissent in mind. Thatcher was punctilious in adhering to the forms of cabinet government, and the poll tax was vetted, if not initiated, by all the relevant committees and the cabinet itself. Blair was less formal and punctilious, but even in his time most of the routine business of government was conducted in the traditional way. At the very least, the cabinet was used as a political sounding board. For his part, Major practised cabinet government as well as preaching it. Perhaps that was because during most of his time in office he was too weak politically to do anything else.

But cabinet government has inherent limitations. It emerged at a time when ministers found it relatively easy to be generalists, capable of having reasonably well-informed views across a wide range of issues. But that time has largely passed. The agendas of all governments, including paradoxically the agendas of governments that are allegedly intent on downsizing government, are huge. Many of the issues that ministers have to deal with are technical and complex. Cabinet-level ministers are also exceedingly busy men and women. Media pressure on many of them is intense. So, sometimes, is parliamentary pressure. Many of them, including the prime minister, spend large swathes of time in firefighting and crisis management. Some ministers, especially those in charge of departments whose responsibilities overlap with those of EU institutions, spend substantial amounts of time in Brussels and elsewhere. It follows that most ministers are simply not in a position, even if they are so minded, to keep abreast of the work of other departments and the government as a whole. Unless they have a departmental or personal stake in the matter at hand, they are liable to turn up to ministerial meetings without having read their papers carefully or possibly at all. Most ministers who were asked individually about the poll tax during the mid-1980s thought it was probably all right; the ministers in charge of it claimed it was all right, so it probably was. Any minister could, of course, have a saloon-bar view about the Millennium Dome, and many ministers did have views, some of them well informed, about the practicality of ID cards; but tax credits could hardly have been a more arcane topic, and the financing of the London underground fell well outside the purview of most ministers. The danger inherent in the routines of cabinet government is that matters will appear to have been thoroughly discussed and thrashed out when in fact they have not been. Proper form will conceal defective practice.

In any case, given the pressures on ministers and the fact that most ministers cannot possibly have anything useful to contribute to the discussion of complex issues that lie well outside their own spheres of experience and responsibility, both decision making and policy development have inevitably been devolved outwards, downwards and sideways to smaller, often ad hoc clusters of people. These clusters sometimes include the prime minister himself. They always include other ministers and frequently include senior Whitehall officials, senior figures in the military, officials from executive agencies, scientific advisers and so forth. They comprise, in short, individuals whom the prime minister or other senior ministers believe do actually have something to contribute. The precise quantum of devolution along these lines varies from prime minister to prime minister, but it is almost certainly desirable as well as inevitable. "Decisions are well made if the right people are in the room and they have all the available facts before them, on paper or orally, if those in the room feel free to challenge propositions and argue, and if the decisions are properly recorded and dis-seminated."[9] Cabinet committees that are focused on particular issues may well have the right people in the room, but full cabinet meetings are most unlikely to: too many of the right people are not in the room; too many extraneous people are. The cabinet's collective functions are, and ought to be, essentially political rather than policy-oriented: briefing ministers on contentious issues, allowing their voices to be heard and, if possible, maintaining some degree of political cohesion at the top.

The other possible way of reducing the incidence of egregious blunders, if old-style cabinet government is not to be restored, and it should not be, is to strengthen the position of the centre, not by creating new units at both a physical and a political distance from the prime minister, but by expanding and adding to the functions of the long-established Policy Unit both physically and politically close to the premier. A striking feature of the policymaking processes that culminated in the blunders described in this book is that "the right people" were often *not* in the room and that neither the prime minister nor anyone else at the centre possessed both the knowledge and the clout "to challenge propositions and argue". Nigel Lawson challenged the poll-tax proposition but was seldom in the room, and no one in Margaret Thatcher's entourage felt it was his or her respon-sibility to argue the anti case, if only to act as devil's advocate. Gordon Brown was a law unto himself, and, quite apart from the delicate balance of political power between the two, Blair was seldom sufficiently well briefed to be able to challenge Brown's numerous policy propositions on purely intellectual and substantive grounds. It appears that in the case of the ill-fated NHS IT initiative many of the right people were never, ever in the room together.

The prime minister's Policy Unit, as it has existed in recent years, has been very small – still with only seven or eight members – and has been overwhelmingly occupied with day-to-day matters and policy issues of immediate concern to the prime minister. It has been organised on a pol-icy-area by policy-area basis, and its individual members have frequently, though not always, been civil servants seconded from departments. Its membership and preoccupations have meant that it has had neither the time nor the remit to act effectively, or at all, as an early-warning system, alerting the boss to potential blunders lying in wait and capable of briefing him, or of organising others to brief him, on what might be done to avoid them. At the very least, members of a modestly expanded Policy Unit could draw the prime minister's attention to occasions on which important decisions were about to be taken without the right people being in the room and without the right questions being asked. The members of the small Policy Unit that presently exists spend much of their time trouble-shooting but apparently less time looking for trouble – that is, sniffing around for blunders in the making. Their number might usefully be augmented by the importation of one or two sniffer-dogs, ideally not puppies but individuals with rich experience of Whitehall's numerous kennels.

Certainly the size of the British prime minister's staff – those individuals with significant political clout who work directly to and with him or her – is minuscule by international standards. The governments of all other Westminster-model countries have what amount to prime ministers' departments. Canada has its Privy Council Office, Australia its Department of the Prime Minister and Cabinet, New Zealand its department with the same name (but with the emphasis in both cases on the Prime Minister rather than the Cabinet). The heads of government of almost all European countries have more robust staff support than prime ministers in the UK. Over-mighty and over-large prime ministers' departments, such as Germany's *Bundeskanzleramt*, are undoubtedly liable to become ossified, slow and overly bureaucratic; Number 10 in its current form certainly enjoys the advantages that someone who recently worked there identified as "small size, nimbleness and personal contact".[10] All the same, our study of blunders suggests that, far from the UK prime minister being too strong and presidential, he or she may in reality often be too weak to be able to ride herd, as the Americans say, on the activities of warring departments and impetuous ministers. The centre in the British system ought to be able to hold, but often it does not because it cannot.

22

Musical chairs

Most British ministers spend a lot of time doing the job they are currently doing, but typically they do not spend very long doing that particular job. They move from post to post at a remarkably rapid rate, from which it follows that government departments and specific lines of policy seldom remain in the same hands for any sustained period of time. The Treasury is unusual in having been headed by one individual, Gordon Brown, for an entire decade. Chancellors in general tend to stay in post longer than other ministers. Foreign secretaries also tend to stay in post for several years. Elsewhere in Whitehall, the picture is different. During the three decades covered by our study, there were thirteen home secretaries, with an average tenure of little more than two years, thirteen cabinet ministers responsible for education, also with an average tenure of little more than two years, and fourteen cabinet ministers responsible for pensions, yet again with an average tenure of little more than two years.

The UK is an outlier in this regard. In Britain, holders of important portfolios come and go; in most other countries, they come and stay, at least for a while. Cross-national comparisons consistently show that ministers in other countries remain in office – and, more particularly, remain in the same office – for considerably longer periods than their opposite numbers in Britain. Among the few countries with higher rates of turnover are France and Italy.[1] The contrast between Britain and Germany, in particular, is stark. Reshuffles in Britain occur more or less annually. In Germany there have been only about half a dozen large-scale cabinet reshuffles in the entire history of the Federal Republic. Since the Federal Republic was established in 1949, there have been fifteen ministers of economics: that is, ministers with oversight of business and industry as distinct from the public finances. The equivalent figure for Britain during the same period has been more than double that: thirty-five.[2] There may just possibly be some connection between those numbers and the comparative performance of the British and German economies since the Second World War. At the very least, one is entitled to ask whether the rapid rate of ministerial turnover in Britain renders British governments more blunder-prone than they would otherwise be.

A rapid turnover of ministers is certainly taken for granted in this country. During almost every late spring and early summer, speculation is rife at Westminster and in the media about the impending cabinet reshuffle. The speculation is invariably about who will be brought in or promoted, who will be sacked and who will be moved from one department to another. It is seldom about whether a reshuffle will actually take place, and almost never about whether government reshuffles as such make for good government.

Two views exist about the desirability or otherwise of Britain's ministerial musical chairs. Those who think that moving ministers around a lot is a good idea maintain that ministers who remain in the same post for more than a few years are liable to become the captive of their department's officials and to function increasingly as no more than that department's spokesman. Long-serving ministers may also in time acquire a personal interest in defending their own and their department's failed policies. A situation may arise in which only someone new is capable of taking a new look. An experienced minister, Enoch Powell, deemed it "a popular fallacy ... that a minister should have either a deep knowledge of the subject matter of his department or at least remain there long enough to acquire it". In Powell's view, ministers should retain a certain detachment from their department, and the more immersed a minister becomes in the detail of his department's business, the greater the danger that he will lose that detachment:

> When a minister begins to think like his officials and understands before they explain, his work in that office is done: he is losing the

power to see the issues in a political light from the outside which alone is what he is there for.[3]

Reasonably rapid movement also means that in practice a large proportion of departmental ministers will have had experience of working in other departments, with the result that they are probably in a better position to question the wisdom of the policies now being advocated by those other departments. Rapid movement, it is claimed, promotes the taking of government-wide views.

Those who doubt the desirability of moving ministers around so often disagree. They insist that the alleged advantages of rapid turnover are far outweighed by the numerous disadvantages. Rapid turnover inevitably means that a substantial proportion of ministers at any given moment will be new or relatively new in post. Ministers who remain in post for only a few years may never take effective charge of their current department; they may never have time in which to master the detail in which the devil so often resides. In addition, ministers who are new or relatively new to their department may well, far from being detached from their officials, be overly reliant on them. Ministers who are highly mobile rarely find themselves forced to see difficult tasks through to completion. Worse, ministers who know in advance that they are very likely to be moved quickly from their present department to some other department have no real incentive to engage in serious long-term planning (whether forwards, backwards or in any other direction). On the contrary, they have every incentive to focus on the short term, on making themselves look good in the eyes of headline-writers, their party and the prime minister. In such ministers' minds, making an immediate impact is almost certain to trump promoting lines of policy that have a good chance of becoming permanently bedded down. Rapid turnover is also a gourmet recipe for operational disconnect, with new-in-post ministers having little or no idea what is required if their wonderfully bright ideas are to be given practical effect.

Our view is that, of these two schools of thought, the critics of rapid turnover easily have the better of the argument. Few ministers are outstandingly able and capable of quickly mastering a complex brief. Even fewer are prepared to sacrifice the short term to the long. By no means all our blunders, but a considerable proportion of them, were committed by ministers who were new in post and/or had high hopes of moving onwards and upwards from whichever post they currently held. Several of the ministers in question were new brooms; some were very new. But instead of sweeping clean they raised dust clouds.

Although one might suppose otherwise, rapid turnover probably played very little part in the case of the mis-selling of personal pensions. When personal pensions were first launched in 1983, one of their principal progenitors, Norman Fowler, had been in post for only two years, but he appears to have mastered the subject, and, although he was ambitious, he was also dogged and determined that personal pensions should remain a permanent feature of the retirement landscape. Lord Young at the Department of Trade and Industry *was* new to his job, arriving on the scene only in the middle of 1987, by which time the details of both the personal-pensions scheme and the establishment of the new Financial Services Authority were already on their way to being worked out. But the pensions mis-selling horrors that followed probably owed little to either man's being new to the job or thinking only of his immediate advantage. It had far more to do with cultural disconnect and rampant departmentalism.

The same, however, was emphatically not true in the case of the Dome. Tony Blair, John Prescott and Peter Mandelson were all new to government and keen to make a splash. No doubt, greater governmental experience would probably not have caused them to jettison altogether the idea of organising a lavish millennium celebration, but it might well have caused them to reconsider the idea of staging a single celebration at a single venue and, moreover, a celebration that had neither a settled purpose nor proper oversight. In the case of the introduction of individual learning accounts, the calamity probably also owed something to the fact that, when they were first announced, neither of their two principal authors, Gordon Brown at the Treasury and David Blunkett at the Department for Education and Skills, had been in post for as much as two years. Similarly, the announcement that the Assets Recovery Agency would shortly be set up – in itself a public-relations exercise as much as anything else – came when the minister responsible, David Blunkett, the new home secretary, had been in post for only a few months. Gordon Brown and John Prescott had actually been in office for only a few weeks when it became clear that they were determined to press ahead with some kind of mammoth public-private partnership for the London underground. In all these instances, the new kids on the block were determined to make their presence felt. They did – but not in quite the way they intended.

Along with the mis-selling of pensions, the fiasco of the Rural Payments Agency's failure to make the correct payments – or any payments at all – to English farmers is probably one of the few fiascos that owed little, if anything, to a new minister's unfamiliarity with new territory. The minister responsible for English agriculture, Margaret Beckett, had been in post for the better part of three years before she made the fatal mistake (though not for her) of opting for the most complicated scheme available for making the payments in question, and it still seems odd that she did so. But she certainly cannot be accused of short-termism: she opted for the ambitious scheme that she did precisely because it appeared to be the right one for the long term.

For its part, the prolonged poll-tax saga was accompanied by a remarkably rapid turnover of ministers. During the roughly six years between the tax's initial conception in 1984 and the first poll-tax bills dropping through people's letter-boxes in 1989–90, the department in charge of the tax, the Department of the Environment, was presided over by four different cabinet ministers (Patrick Jenkin, Kenneth Baker, Nicholas Ridley and Chris Patten), and during the same period a total of no fewer than seven junior ministers in the same department were briefly in charge of local-government affairs (Kenneth Baker, William Waldegrave, Sir Rhodes Boyson, Michael Howard, John Gummer, David Hunt and Michael Portillo). Both Baker and Waldegrave, the two ministerial members of the review team that invented the tax, were neophytes. Baker had previously served as a minister in the Department of Trade and Industry and Waldegrave had served as a junior minister in the Education Department, but both were entirely new to the subject of local-government finance. It is worth noting that, by the time Baker and Waldegrave arrived in the department, every one of the department's ministers who only three years before, in 1981, had categorically rejected any form of per capita tax had long since moved on. At the ministerial level, the department suffered from collective amnesia.

Even so, historians have expressed two views about whether this demonstrably high rate of turnover made any significant difference to the final, disastrous outcome. The authors of the classic account of the whole episode, David Butler, Andrew Adonis and Tony Travers, rather doubt it. They point out that Nicholas Ridley, the one environment secretary who was adamant that the poll tax should be introduced all at once instead of being phased in gradually, had already been at the helm of the department for more than three years when he persuaded his colleagues to go down that road, and they maintain that most of the key mistakes were made under Ridley, "save that of having dreamt up the tax in the first place".[4] In contrast, Simon Jenkins, without being absolutely categorical, inclines towards the opposite view: that the rapid rate of ministerial turnover had unfortunate consequences. Each new environment secretary, he says, "was more eager [than the last] to conjure up a reform and more terrified of turning back".[5]

The crucial words above, however, are "save that of having dreamt up the tax in the first place". Once the tax had been dreamt up, and once Margaret Thatcher had dreamt the dream, there was probably not a lot that successive secretaries of state could do about it beyond trying to wake her up. That said, it is possible that Patrick Jenkin and Kenneth Baker, had they been forced to live longer with attempting to introduce the tax, might have realised that there was no way in which they possibly could and that the government, if only on narrowly political grounds, had somehow to find a way out. Chris Patten's own instinct was to do just that; but, when his turn in the office came in 1989, he had only just been promoted, he was new to the cabinet, and he was understandably reluctant to risk his newly acquired position by picking a fight, one he would almost certainly lose, with one of the most dominant and domineering prime ministers of all time. Had Baker still been in the same post at the end of the 1980s, he *might* have had the departmental experience and the political clout to find some means of escape. Indeed, as one of the original authors of the misbegotten tax, he might also have been in the best position to be the author of its destruction.

That said, Butler, Adonis and Travers are right to identify the original dreaming up of the tax, and its adoption by ministers including the prime minister at Chequers, as the real moment when things began to go wrong. That original blunder, however, despite what those authors say, almost certainly owes a great deal, though not everything, to rapid ministerial turnover, to the fact that the two responsible ministers – indeed, all three of them if Patrick Jenkin is included – were almost entirely new to both local government and local-government finance. In the case of Baker, two and a bit years in another department as minister for trade and information technology were perhaps not wholly adequate preparation for revolutionising the funding of local government. William Waldegrave brought to the same demanding task a formidable intellect and an interest in the subject but, as already mentioned, only two years' practical experience as a junior minister in another department.

There was, of course, a twist to the end of the poll-tax tale. If ministerial turnover contributed to the birth of the tax, it also contributed to its death. In 1990 Chris Patten, after only a year and a half in the job, was moved out of the Environment Department, making way for Michael Heseltine, who was appointed specifically in order to see the poll tax replaced with something more politically acceptable (and administratively practicable). Heseltine triumphantly succeeded. But one of the reasons he was able to do that was because he had been environment secretary before and on that occasion, knowing all the arguments, had comprehensively rejected the idea of introducing any such tax. That kind of thing – a senior minister returning to the same department to clear up a mess made by his successors – is a rare event.

Needless to say, ministerial turnover does not invariably produce dire consequences. There are occasions when a minister new to a job is able to succeed where his predecessors have failed, when fresh thinking is brought to bear and a new broom does sweep clean. Harold Macmillan had not been long at the Treasury when he invented premium bonds. But for the determination of Barbara Castle, new to the Ministry of Transport, the introduction of seat belts in cars might have been delayed for years. It almost certainly required the substitution of Norman Tebbit for James Prior at the Department of Employment to bring about the Thatcher administration's radical reforms of trade-union law. Politicians and officials had talked for years of making the Bank of England responsible for setting interest rates, but it took a new chancellor, Gordon Brown, only hours to translate the talk into action.

On balance, however, it is hard to disagree with John Major's judgement that "moving ministers around too quickly is not conducive to good government", or the conclusion of an Institute for Government report that "a real constraint on ministerial effectiveness is that many ministers

do not stay in their posts long enough, as a result of over-frequent reshuffles".[6] Ministers, former ministers and officials are all but unanimous in
deploring rapid turnover:

> Rotating ministers really quickly is ridiculous. (Minister)

> A reasonable amount of time in post is hugely important – 18
> months at a minimum, and two and a half years [is] good. (Senior
> civil servant)

> Unless you leave ministers there for some time, actual ministerial
> power is hugely constrained. (Minister)

> [Ministers are] assumed to have made their mark within a year or
> two … they are going to want to do something quickly. The last
> thing they are going to want to do is to focus on maintaining a
> programme that is going to take 10 years to produce results when
> they will not be there to get the benefit of the praise. That, I think,
> is an insidious culture. (Minister)[7]

Giving evidence to the House of Commons Public Administration Select
Committee, a former Labour minister, Nick Raynsford, was emphatic: "I
do think … we can do a lot more to ensure that ministerial office is treated
more in terms of outcomes and less in terms of the success of the individual
minister in climbing the greasy pole." Giving evidence on the same occasion, a vastly experienced Conservative minister, Kenneth Clarke, chimed
in: "I agree with Nick very strongly on the reshuffling point; it is farcical."[8]
Another ex-minister, Jack Straw, felt so strongly about the undesirability of
what he called "the constant churn" of ministers, especially of junior ministers, that he devoted a substantial passage to that topic in his memoirs.[9]

Furthermore, ministers are not the only ones who move around. No
one seems to know how often senior civil servants, apart from permanent
secretaries, move from one department to another or between unrelated
or only loosely related posts within the same department; but, if it is
"ridiculous" to rotate ministers "really quickly", as the anonymous minister
claimed, then the same must be true of rotating officials rapidly, especially

as ministers inevitably rely heavily on those same officials. If both ministers and officials are rapidly rotating at the same time and in relation to one another, the results are almost certain to be suboptimal. When it was put to one cabinet minister that he must know less about the work of his department than the civil servants who worked under him, he replied vehemently that the opposite was true: he had not been in the department long and might not know much, but his civil servants endlessly came and went and knew even less than he did. Another minister complained, in connection with a specific project, that he had had six officials working on it under him in the course of two years and that only one of them had hung around long enough to be able to master the details of it; and, he added soulfully, as soon as that one official had succeeded in mastering the relevant details, he had sought and won promotion to a post in another department. Our researches do not allow us to say exactly how much any rapid turnover of civil servants, as distinct from the undoubtedly rapid turnover of ministers, contributed to the blunders described here, but it must have been considerable. Among other things, officials new to a job, especially junior officials, are most unlikely to question the wisdom of their superiors even when they think that perhaps they should.

As for the notion that rapid ministerial turnover, whatever its other consequences may be, has the benign effect of affording ministers broad experience of other departments, thus enabling them to contribute usefully to debates in cabinet and cabinet committees, precious few signs emerged that such contributions had been made in connection with the blunders we investigated.

Several of the blunders were committed early in the life of a government, when there were no ministers with relevant experience around. Even after a government has been in power for some time, and despite rapid turnover, there are unlikely to be many ministers still in the government with experience relevant to the matter in hand. The cabinet that endorsed the Child Support Bill in 1991 contained one former chancellor of the exchequer but no one with previous cabinet-level experience of the Department of Social Security. Similarly, the cabinet that endorsed the Proceeds of Crime Bill 2001 did contain a former home secretary, Jack Straw, but Straw was foreign secretary by this time and almost certainly did not take the time and trouble to engage with what must have seemed to him a relatively minor matter. The full cabinet may possibly have endorsed Margaret Beckett's decision in late 2003 or early 2004 to make payments to English farmers in the way she proposed, but, if it did, there was no one at the cabinet table with previous experience of agriculture in a position to query her judgement. And so on. Ironically, Michael Heseltine, a former environment secretary, was still a minister in 1986 on the day that the poll tax first came before the full cabinet, but, as we saw in Chapter 4, he walked out of that day's meeting before the relevant item on the agenda was reached. No one will ever know, probably not even he, what would have had happened if he had remained in the room.

The notion that ministerial turnover promotes collective cabinet discussion – and therefore, presumably, blunder avoidance – suffers from further defects. Ministers are reluctant to interfere, and seldom do interfere, in the affairs of departments other than their own; if they stray onto others' turf, others may stray onto theirs. Moreover, few ministers have the time or energy to read detailed papers and engage in prolonged discussions of matters that, in strict ministerial terms, have nothing to do with them: they have better, more pressing things to do. It is also the case that the world moves on; knowledge of one set of issues gained at one point in time is unlikely to be relevant to other issues that emerge at some other point in time, perhaps many years later, even if the issues in question do happen to arise in a department in which the minister has served before. Even if someone who had served in Defra had still been around when Margaret Beckett made her fateful decision, he or she would almost certainly have known little or nothing about the reformed Common Agricultural Policy and nothing at all about the alternative arrangements on offer for paying English farmers. Jack Straw was unusual in that, when his successor as home secretary revisited the possibility of introducing ID cards, he still did know a lot about their pros and cons, and also because the issues relating to the cards had remained much the same ever since he had left the Home Office. Still a member of the cabinet, he could and did weigh in, though to no immediate effect.

If ministerial turnover in Britain is too high and increases the chances that British governments will blunder, what might be done about it? At a minimum, British prime ministers could decide to exercise greater restraint. They could move ministers around only when absolutely necessary, when an incumbent minister has died, voluntarily resigned or proved him or herself to be manifestly incompetent. At the risk of frustrating the ambitions of backbenchers and junior ministers, prime ministers could also keep the consequential changes to a minimum even when someone has died, resigned or turned out to be a dud. James Callaghan caused something of a stir in 1977 when, following the sudden death of the foreign secretary, Anthony Crosland, he simply appointed as Crosland's successor a middle-ranking Foreign Office minister, David Owen, instead of shuffling a whole host of other ministers. Callaghan's example might be worth following.

A more ambitious answer to the question would be to enlarge the pool from which the great majority of ministers are drawn: namely, the majority party or parties in the House of Commons. Either more peers than at present could be appointed to ministerial posts (and possibly granted peerages for that purpose) or the requirement that British government ministers must also be parliamentarians could be relaxed or abolished entirely. (Britain and its former colony Ireland are the only countries in the European Union that require their ministers also to be parliamentarians. Several countries require that they *not* be parliamentarians.) Substantially enlarging the pool of persons eligible to be ministers might well be desirable on other grounds, but it would also mean that prime ministers could from time to time replace dead or unsatisfactory colleagues by introducing outsiders into their administration instead of simply moving existing ministers around.

As we shall see in the next chapter, ministers in the UK not only move around a lot: they tend to be restless in whatever post they currently occupy, with arguably unfortunate consequences for the quality of British government.

23

Ministers as activists

The story is still told in Whitehall of the newly appointed cabinet minister in Harold Macmillan's time who arrived at his new department at 10 a.m. on his first day, spent two or three hours meeting officials and reading papers and then blithely announced that he was taking his granddaughter out to lunch and afterwards to the pictures. He would be out of the office for the rest of the day. He would be back in the morning. Even by the standards of the early 1960s, that chap's leisurely approach to high ministerial office was thought a trifle strange. Half a century later it would be unthinkable. Ministers today are expected not merely to *be* but to *do*. Moreover, they are expected to do a great deal. Along with party workers, bloggers and political campaigners, they are meant to be activists. Some of them are clearly hyperactive.

It is by no means a caricature to suggest that until roughly the 1980s British government was effectively a duopoly. Senior civil servants more or less ran the country, while for their part ministers gave officials political direction, bore responsibility in public for their officials' actions and initiated policies of their own only on special occasions and under special circumstances. As active participants in policymaking, the special advisers of today – the "spads" – did not exist. A shrewd American observer of British government wrote in 1965: "The politicians *lean* on their officials. They *expect* to be advised. Most importantly, they very often do what they are told, and follow the advice that they receive." The essence of government at the highest levels in Britain, he believed, was "the relations between ministers and civil servants in the making of a government decision":

The senior civil servants neither stall nor buck decisions of the government once taken in due form by their political masters. "Due form" means consultation, among other things, but having been consulted these officials act without public complaint or private evasion, even though they may have fought what they are doing up to the last moment of decision.[1]

In such a world, a minister like the fellow described at the beginning of this chapter could feel at ease.

He would not feel at ease today, nor would he come anywhere near achieving cabinet rank and being made responsible for a large department. The world has changed.

Margaret Thatcher came to power in 1979 with two principal convictions. She desperately wanted to change Britain, its values, its entire culture and the way its economy worked; and she believed that the traditional civil service, with all its power and influence, was self-satisfied, drearily pessimistic and one of the main obstacles in the way of change. She therefore recast the role of ministers. From now on, they were no longer to lean on officials, let alone sheepishly to accept their advice. They were to be initiators and leaders, the dynamos of change – and the sheer quantity of change she sought to achieve was enormous. The ministers she most admired, and most promoted, were therefore men of action, ministers who brought forward radical new ideas, promoted them actively and overrode recalcitrant civil servants, indeed who won plaudits for imposing their will on them. She famously said of Lord Young, "Others bring me problems, David brings me solutions."[2]

In recasting the role of ministers, Thatcher simultaneously recast the role of civil servants. They were no longer to be more or less equal partners in the delivery of good government. Henceforth they were to be, as their name implied, civil *servants*, charged, not with "fighting proposals until the last moment of decision" but with enthusiastically developing, promoting and implementing whatever policy ideas strong-minded ministers had in mind. That was the role ministers wanted them to play, and it was a role that most civil servants accepted that they ought to play. Ministers, after all, were their legitimate, democratically elected bosses. Obedience, not recalcitrance, was the proper frame of mind in which officials should approach their duties. They could ask questions, of course, but they were discouraged from raising objections. Those officials who did raise objections, a diminishing minority, frequently found their careers blighted. "Can do" was Thatcher's watchword, seldom "Hang on a moment".

The approach of the New Labour government that came to power in 1997 was all but identical. Tony Blair, like Thatcher, was ambitious; he wanted to achieve great things. New Labour was to mean a New Britain. He, like Thatcher, wanted activist, energetic ministers serving under him. Also like Thatcher, he and most of those around him deeply distrusted the civil service. Labour had been out of power for eighteen years, and during that time officialdom had predictably become imbued – or so Labour ministers believed – with Thatcherite ideas and ideals. It was also true that the civil service had been downsized under the Conservatives and that, partly as a result, it was – or so Labour ministers believed – no longer the high-quality outfit it had once been. Moreover, whereas many of Thatcher's ministers, at least in the early days, had served in previous Conservative administrations, almost all of Blair's ministers were new to government and were inclined in some cases to be nervous and peremptory as a result. As under Thatcher, yea-sayers were much preferred to nay-sayers in the ranks of ministers and officials alike. Delivery was what mattered.

Whatever the advantages of this new dispensation, it has had – and probably still has – one serious disadvantage. Our study of blunders suggests that officials, at least in many government departments and in many policy areas, have become remarkably reluctant to speak truth to power. They do not want to speak largely because they believe power does not want to listen. Objection is construed as obstruction. Again and again in our interviews, former ministers as well as retired civil servants commented on the fact that, even when officials had harboured serious reservations about ministers' latest bright ideas, they had failed openly to express their reservations. They had either kept them to themselves or else shared them only in private and with trusted colleagues. Several of the blunders we describe undoubtedly resulted, at least in part, from this formidable combination of ministerial activism and official reticence.

In the case of the poll tax, we repeatedly asked our interviewees how on earth this piece of arrant folly had come to be perpetrated. What had ministers thought they were doing? Why had officials in the Environment

Department many of whom, unlike their political masters, know a great deal about the complexities of local-government finance – apparently not warned ministers about the perils first of trying to sell politically, and then of trying to collect, any kind of per capita tax?

Their answers are instructive. They obviously did not attribute the fiasco of the tax entirely to ministerial activism and officials' reticence, but they made frequent reference to both. One minister, a career politician like all those involved, described himself as "an ambitious young minister", someone "willing to put his head above the parapet". He clearly implied that he wanted to make his mark with the prime minister. The same was undoubtedly true of most of the other ministers involved in the early stages. Butler, Adonis and Travers in their book about the affair note that the two ministerial leaders of the Jenkin review team, Kenneth Baker and William Waldegrave, "both had spurs to earn to become 'One of Us'" – that is, one of Thatcher's favourites – and they knew it".[3] One of the officials working with the two men similarly observed that the two of them "would have known that Mrs T disliked caution". Another volunteered that "Thatcher's role was crucial. People were intimidated by her. They had their own careers to make." In a different context, one former Conservative cabinet minister observed that ministers these days arrive in their departments under intense pressure to innovate, not just to administer existing policies. "You get brownie points for the former, none for the latter."

Several officials, questioned years afterwards, said they regretted not having raised objections to the poll tax. Some of them arrived on the scene too late, by which time the tax had acquired unstoppable political momentum, but one of those who had been involved early on said that one of the lessons he drew from the experience of the tax was that officials should have been more assertive. They should, he felt, have "fed the idea of a council tax to ministers straight away". He believed that ministers, including the prime minister, would have accepted the idea of a banded property tax. In his view, the Environment Department should simply have presented the prime minister and the cabinet with a banded property tax as a fait accompli, not as an option. All the department really needed to do was promote a banded property tax as an alternative to the rates – which, up to a point, it would have been. But nothing like that happened. One of the ministers involved early on believed that the civil servants working under him simply took it for granted that their constitutional duty was to advise ministers and implement their decisions; it was not their job to make trouble for ministers by suggesting, let alone arguing strongly, that their policy initiatives were unlikely to work.

The themes of ministerial activism combined with officials' reticence recurred again and again as we interviewed former ministers and civil servants during our enquiries. In connection with the malformed Child Support Agency, one minister who arrived late on the scene regretted in retrospect that the option of doing nothing had clearly never been on the table. He also regretted that his predecessors in office never seem to have considered – or been allowed to consider – building incrementally on the experience and personnel of the already existing Liable Relatives Unit in the Social Security Department. He deplored activist ministers' determination to get everything right – all of it – the first time round. Ministers and officials alike, he said, were always under pressure, including from Number 10, "to go for the final solution, the Big Bang".

In connection with individual learning accounts, one centrally involved official commented that David Blunkett as education secretary had been "a doer", someone keen to get on with as many things as possible. He reckoned that Blunkett's department was trying to do so much that, as a result, "quality was very poor", at least at the margins. In the "can-do delivery culture" of the time, officials, whatever their doubts, were left with no option but to remain silent and to try to deliver. Sometimes they could deliver, and did. Sometimes – as in the case of individual learning accounts – they failed. As for the Dome, one of our interviewees, refer- ring to officialdom, said forcefully that amidst the mounting chaos of the preparations for the millennium, "No one had the balls to say, 'Look, let's stand back and reassess.'" Whatever else they did, civil servants had failed to perform their historic function.

Impatient and activist ministers often complain that the wheels of Whitehall grind too slowly, that officials prioritise procedures over out- comes, that they insist on touching all possible bases before reaching decisions, that they are rule-bound rather than action-oriented, that their critical faculties are more fully developed than their creative ones, that they are risk-averse and desperate to cover their backs, that their response to new ideas is typically hostile and that, at worst, asked by ministers to do something they do not want to do, they simply drag their feet or claim that they are indeed doing whatever they were asked to do when in fact they are not. Almost every minister has tales to tell of asking urgently for a paper to be produced on X or Y and then noticing a day, a week or even a month later that the paper has never appeared. In short, almost every minister is an instinctive fan – and probably a real fan – of Yes, Minister.

Jonathan Powell, a former Foreign Office official who served as Tony Blair's chief of staff throughout Blair's time in office, regards "the deeply ingrained fatalism" of senior civil servants as a problem for all governments.

> Having been a civil servant myself, it is easy to understand how it develops. When you have been wrestling with a problem for decades and you are familiar with how difficult it is to resolve, when you know there are no easy answers and are reconciled to failing again and again, it is difficult not to be cynical about the fresh-eyed, bushy-tailed aspirations of a new minister who knows next to nothing about the problem and whose "new" policies are not new at all.[4]

That civil servants can on occasion be lethargic to the point of being obstructive is beyond question, and on those occasions ministers are entitled to complain and even to sack the worst offenders.

Of course, motorists driving slowly on busy highways can be exceedingly irritating; but speed kills, and our study of blunders suggests that today's activist ministers often drive not too slowly but far too fast. Our study suggests that officials probably ought to be readier than they now are to put it politely to their minister that, instead of speeding up, he or she should perhaps press down less firmly on the accelerator. Even members of Winston Churchill's staff sometimes – rightly – ignored the great man's more impetuous "Action this day" demands. Jonathan Powell himself adds in the passage quoted above that, despite his evident frustration at many civil servants' lethargy and fatalism, he nevertheless regards it as part of their job "to warn their ministers of the elephant traps into which they are about to walk ... and they know where the traps are, unlike their minister".[5] And it goes without saying that speeding ministers are more likely to fall into elephant traps than ones who take their time.

The tendency of activist ministers to be speedsters – always to insist on cracking on – has a variety of sources. Some are temperamental. Activist ministers want to act in the way that sprinters want to sprint and novelists want to write novels. Some ministers find themselves in politics as a result of happenstance or family tradition, but a large proportion have gone into politics because they want to change the world. They have causes to promote, and promoting them is their life's mission. Jonathan Powell used to tease Tony Blair about his "Messiah complex", but a large proportion of today's ministers clearly aspire to be mini-Messiahs. During the three decades of our studies, Blair in his messianic role passionately wanted to bring peace to Northern Ireland, Norman Fowler passionately believed in the desirability of personal pensions, Peter Mandelson was desperate to make a success of the millennium celebrations, Gordon Brown's personal commitment to reducing poverty was never in doubt, David Blunkett was an enthusiast for further education and training, and any number of people were enthusiasts for IT. In some ways unfortunately, enthusiasts are very often people in a great hurry – men and women, so to speak, on speed.

Competition may also come into it, not the familiar competition between the political parties but among ministers themselves. Occasionally the competition is personal, as it was between Gordon Brown and Tony Blair (at least on Brown's side). More often it is competition for funds from the Treasury, for slots in the parliamentary timetable, for opportunities to appear on *Question Time* and, above all, for promotion onwards and upwards in the ministerial hierarchy, from parliamentary secretary to minister of state, from minister of state to secretary of state and perhaps one day – who knows? – from secretary of state to prime minister. Ministers also compete to promote their own cherished causes, to be noticed by the prime minister and to shine in the House of Commons, on radio, on television and at the annual party conference. Competition is the stuff of politics, and competitors, like all activists, are often in a hurry.

A considerable proportion of our blunders were committed at speed, whether because of competition among ministers, the determination and ambition of individual ministers, pressure from grassroots party activists, the felt need to fulfil a manifesto commitment made at one general election in time for the next election or, in the bizarre case of the London underground PPP disaster, Treasury ministers' insistence that they alone should decide how the underground upgrade should be financed and that on no account should the decision be allowed to fall into the hands of the first mayor of London, shortly to be elected. Harold Macmillan as prime minister famously had pinned to the cabinet door the message "Quiet calm deliberation disentangles every knot". That statement may not be strictly true, but failure to take enough time to deliberate can certainly have the effect of further entangling knots that are already tied. (Macmillan, whose grandchildren often played at Number 10, also caused a notice to be posted reading "No roller-skating on Cabinet days".)

At one level, the poll tax was not at all rushed; it passed in a stately fashion through all the relevant cabinet committees and the cabinet itself, and five years elapsed between Patrick Jenkin's announcement at a Conservative party conference that he would be undertaking "studies" of local-government finance and the poll tax's introduction. But, at another level, there were two moments when the whole process was drastically speeded up. The first came right at the beginning, almost as soon as Jenkin had announced that the studies would take place. The existing arrangements for local-government finance appeared to be falling apart, with Labour local authorities running rings around ministers while at the same time preparing their next year's high-spending budgets. Tory activists across the country were in uproar. The result was that Sir Terry Heiser, the Department of the Environment's permanent secretary, gave the review team that he appointed under Patrick Jenkin's aegis a mere six months in which to come up with some means of addressing these woes. "The team moved at breakneck speed. This was no old-style committee or commission where the great and the good pored over widely collected evidence for months or years."[6] At breakneck speed, the team came up with the poll tax.

The second moment came some two years after the Chequers meeting and was, arguably, even more critical in ramming the poll tax into position, thereby sealing Thatcher's fate. Scottish Conservatives were hot for the poll tax, having been appalled by the negative political fallout from a re-rating that had recently taken place in their part of the world. Needless to say, the re-rating had pushed most Scottish householders' rates upwards, often a long way upwards. Scottish Tories wanted the poll tax introduced straight away, and ministers, including the incumbent

Scottish Office ministers, agreed not only that Scots could have it before anyone else but that – lucky people that they were – they could have it all at once. Nicholas Ridley, the environment minister, a true believer in the tax, wanted England and Wales to follow the splendid example being set by the Scots, but at first he encountered stiff opposition from cabinet colleagues. At the end of July 1987 the government, against his wishes, announced that, despite what was happening in Scotland, the tax would still be phased in in England and Wales. But Ridley persisted, and in the end Ridley got his way. Representatives at the Conservatives' annual conference in October 1987 applauded ecstatically a speech by a former Scottish MP calling for the immediate introduction of the poll tax, minus any transition period, south of the border as well as north of it. The proceedings of the party conference were decisive. They had the effect of suddenly converting Thatcher to the Big Bang cause, and she and Ridley between them overbore those of their colleagues who still doubted the wisdom of proceeding so precipitously. Fewer than fourteen weeks elapsed between ministers' decision to continue with dual running in England and Wales and their decision totally to abandon it. The Big Bang that resulted was very big.

There is a pendant to this part of the poll-tax story. As we noted earlier, the civil servants advising the ministers responsible for local-government finance in England and Wales never tried to persuade their ministerial bosses of the folly of any such tax and the folly of trying to introduce it all at once rather than incrementally. To that extent, officials south of the border were complicit in what happened: they failed to operate on the basis of Jonathan Powell's assumption that the job of civil servants is to warn ministers of elephant traps into which they may be about to walk. In contrast, the top officials north of the border, in what was then the Scottish Office, did warn ministers – and were apparently surprised to discover that their colleagues south of the border were not doing the same (and were also unwilling to lend their Scottish colleagues their active support). The Scottish Office officials did warn their ministerial superiors not only of the practical problems but that, if the tax were introduced, the number of losers would far outweigh the number of gainers. But the senior ministers in the Scottish Office, as was their right, either ignored their officials' warnings altogether or else discounted them. The relevant

341

non-Scottish ministers, including Ridley, may not even have known about them. Despite having been warned, or perhaps because they had not known of the warnings, all the ministers in question proceeded to fall headlong into the waiting trap.

In connection with the remit of the Child Support Agency, the party that was on speed was the Treasury. It wanted to lay its hands on absent parents' and feckless fathers' money (not that many of the latter had much), and it wanted do that as quickly as possible; but, as we saw in earlier chapters, neither the Department of Social Security nor the agency itself could deliver – or could reasonably have been expected to deliver – in the time allowed. Neither could cope. The same insistence on pressing ahead was present in the case of individual learning accounts, where an absolute determination to deliver the scheme before the 2001 general election trumped any attempt to think carefully through its feasibility. The main cause of the scheme's collapse was undoubtedly cultural disconnect – the naïvety of Education Department officials who had no idea how many crooks were lying in wait for them – but it did not help that the department's IT supplier, Capita, was given only months in which to design software that proved, not to be overengineered and overly ambitious but, as a result of the remit the firm had been given, not nearly ambitious enough. One civil servant observed after the event, with some irritation: "Blair's memoirs lament having wasted his first years in office, but it didn't feel like that at the time. It's not surprising that some of the wheels came off the coaches. We tried to do too much at once. The system couldn't cope."

Another official in the same department added that there was a pervasive feeling that civil servants had to do everything they could to prove that they could be trusted by New Labour ministers: "We wanted to avoid a Sir Humphrey image. We became afraid to say 'No, Minister.'"

Our enquiries also convince us that the chaotic delivery of tax credits owed much to the determination of Gordon Brown and Ed Balls to press ahead with them at all possible speed and to civil servants' reluctance to cross either of them. Asked about that particular fiasco, one official, who had clearly thought long and hard about the matter, volunteered as a large part of the answer "the over-aggressive timescale". Brown and Balls were simply in too much of a hurry. He added that, of course, Brown himself was part of the problem. Among the people around him, there was – how should he put it? – "a certain lack of incentive to tell the truth". He observed that one of Brown's colleagues was clearly afraid of him. When things began to go wrong, as they soon did, the colleague in question would often say, "Gosh, I've got to tell Gordon", making it clear that he was not looking forward to the experience. Another official, said to be one of the brightest and ablest in the business, volunteered that people in the Treasury were extremely reluctant to say no to Brown. If they did, and if Brown had any control over their careers, they suffered.

Ironically, the delivery culture inculcated at the centre by Margaret Thatcher and then Tony Blair seems sometimes to have had a perverse effect. It caused ministers and officials, indeed, to deliver – but the wrong commodities. It is evident that officials who said "Yes, Minister" and who really meant it were sometimes doing their minister – and the prime minister – no favours. Blair himself might well have been grateful if Treasury officials had been successful in saying no to his nemesis, Gordon Brown, more frequently.

Comparing the blunders committed in haste by activist ministers with the government successes listed in Chapter 2 is instructive. Many of the most enduring successes achieved by postwar governments had quite long gestation periods. The legislation authorising the creation of green belts was enacted in 1947, but green belts began to be created on a large scale only in the mid-1950s. The Clean Air Act lagged several years behind London's killer smog of 1953. Both the breathalyser and the compulsory wearing of seat belts arrived only slowly on the scene. It took more than a decade for the policy of selling council houses to their tenants to be fully bedded down. The ban on smoking in public places was also slow in coming.

Intriguingly – and contrary to received wisdom – Margaret Thatcher, although undoubtedly an activist, was never, until towards the very end, a woman in a hurry. On the contrary, she was content to take her time in connection with almost every important domestic matter. Although she took office in 1979, her ministers did not initiate a comprehensive overhaul of trade-union law until 1982. Privatisation, although something she always favoured in principle, did not become a central or even peripheral element of her government's policy until she was well into her second term. Similarly, when she was first confronted with the prospect of a miners' strike, she quickly backed off; but she then took steps to

ensure that the next time the miners threatened to strike she would be
in a position to stand firm. Even in connection with the poll tax, she was
not easily persuaded either that the tax was a good idea or that it should
be introduced all in one go. She was uncharacteristically rash at Chequers
in 1985 to agree to the idea of the tax in the first place, and even rasher
in 1987 to agree – on the flimsy basis of applause at a Conservative party
conference – that it should be introduced all at once. By 1987 prolonged
success had evidently bred in her the idea that failure, for her at least, was
inconceivable. Daniel Kahneman, the Nobel prize-winning economist, was
thinking of a notional businesswoman when he wrote in *Thinking, Fast
and Slow*, "The CEO has had several successes in a row, so failure doesn't
come easily to her mind."[7] But he might have been thinking of Thatcher
at this late stage of her career.

Activist ministers can certainly congratulate themselves in one regard.
They have made a substantial contribution in recent decades to expanding the sheer physical volume of the statute book. Although the number
of individual Acts passed by parliament has not increased significantly
in recent decades, the total number of pages of new legislation certainly
has – from an average of 1645 pages a year during the 1980s, to 1803 pages
during the 1990s to 2804 pages during the 2000s, an increase of 70 per cent
over the three decades. The number of pages of new secondary legislation,
in the form of statutory instruments, has also ballooned – from an average of 6644 pages during the 1980s, to 8705 during the 1990s to 10,421
during the 2000s, an increase of 36 per cent.[8] Home secretaries and their
ministerial colleagues have been especially assiduous in legislating on the
country's behalf. During the most recent whole decade, 2000–09, no fewer
than thirty-eight separate Acts of Parliament emanated from the precincts
of the Home Office. Whether such a large volume of legislation is desirable or not is arguable, but it certainly testifies to ministers' reluctance to
sit on their hands – and it does increase the sheer arithmetical probability
of blunders being committed.

Ministerial activism by no means necessarily results in blunders. Neither
does speed necessarily lead to fatal accidents. Ministers are sometimes
right to insist on cracking on. They are also sometimes right, perhaps often
right, to override the advice of their officials. But perhaps ministers need
to be more wary of hyperactivism on their own part – and on the prime

minister's part – and need positively to encourage, even if they cannot bring themselves sincerely to welcome, expressions of scepticism on the part of their more experienced officials (if they are fortunate enough to have any). Except in times of national crisis, "Make haste slowly" is not a bad maxim. Another good one is "Don't attempt to do too many things all at once". Aneurin Bevan, the architect of the NHS, used to say that the religion of socialism was the language of priorities. It should be – but patently is not – the language of modern British governments.

24

Accountability, lack of

The folklore of the British constitution demands that government ministers, especially cabinet ministers, are responsible for whatever goes on in their department, that they are accountable to parliament both for their own actions and for the actions of their officials and that, if either they or their officials have been seriously at fault they should resign. Sir Ivor Jennings, a constitutional lawyer of the old school, was adamant on the point: "Each Minister is responsible to Parliament for the conduct of his Department. The act of every Civil Servant is by convention regarded as the act of his Minister."[1] It followed that any minister who could not justify his or his officials' conduct to parliament should step down at once or else be forced to.

All that was – and still is – almost pure fantasy. Most ministers who make mistakes, however egregious, do not resign and are most unlikely to be sacked. If they do leave the government, it is seldom voluntarily, never at the behest of parliament. It is either because they have lost the backing of the prime minister, or the backing of their own backbenchers, or both. More often than not, they go simply because they have, for whatever reason, become a source of embarrassment to the government – or seem to be about to become one. As a driver of a minister's sudden departure from any administration, scandal trumps policy or administrative failure every time. The doctrine known solemnly as the convention of "individual ministerial responsibility" has been largely a myth for well over a hundred years. Lord Carrington's resignation as foreign secretary for his part in failing to forestall Argentina's invasion of the Falkland Islands in 1982 is remembered only bei use it was so unusual, all but unique. Ministers do sometimes resign on a point of principle, as Robin Cook did over Britain's involvement in the invasion of Iraq in 2003. But resignations of that kind are a different matter. They seldom relate to the resigning minister's performance of his or her ministerial duties.

Yet the idea that individual ministers should be held accountable still has a hold on the British psyche. People want to believe it. They half do believe it. They imagine that from time to time, even if not often, ministers who make serious mistakes *are* held accountable and *are* punished accordingly. Whenever a cabinet minister is in trouble, the House of Commons resounds with opposition cries of "Resign!", and editorials in newspapers often call for resignations. Whenever an individual minister has signally failed in either policy or administrative terms, it is somehow felt that he or she *ought* to resign, that he or she might possibly do the honourable thing and actually choose to resign. It is also felt that, if the individual in question does not resign voluntarily, then the prime minister should step in and sack him or her. Sadly, our study of blunders points in the opposite direction. It suggests that the doctrine of individual ministerial responsibility is even more mythical than most people realise. It suggests that ministers guilty of even the grossest blunders are almost never held to account or punished in any way. On the contrary, most minister-blunderers, even if they can be clearly identified, survive politically and prosper.

The language here is important. "Culpability" implies that someone, or some group of people, has committed a crime or sinned in some other way and should be punished for it. "Responsibility" is more neutral. Someone or some group may be responsible either for killing someone or for saving someone's life. To say that they were responsible for whatever happened is to say nothing more than that they themselves did it; the issue of punishment or reward does not arise. "Accountability" is more ambiguous. To say that someone is accountable need not imply that they did whatever it was that happened and that therefore they are personally responsible for it; it may merely mean that they are required by law, custom or convention to give some account of whatever happened to some other person or group. More commonly, however, to say that someone "should be held to account" implies that they themselves *were* personally responsible for whatever happened, that they actually did it, that whatever it was that they did was in some way reprehensible and that therefore they should be reprimanded or punished in some manner. When most people in Britain say that someone should be held to account, they almost certainly mean to use the phrase in this latter, stronger sense. The lack of accountability to which we refer in the title of this chapter implies that someone has done something that they ought not to have done but has not paid any price (or, alternatively, has not done something that he or she should certainly have done and has similarly not paid any price).

Tracking through our list of blunders and asking who, if anyone, was held to account in that latter, stronger sense is a salutary experience.

A considerable number of individuals were responsible, in a perfectly neutral sense, for the introduction of the poll tax. Had it been a success, they would have deserved praise. As it was not, they deserved blame or at least some share of the blame. The list of those culpable on that occasion would have to include, in no particular order, Margaret Thatcher, Patrick Jenkin, Kenneth Baker, William Waldegrave, Nicholas Ridley and possibly Sir Terry Heiser, the then permanent secretary in the Department of the Environment. Thatcher was not held to account in any formal sense; she was never hauled before a parliamentary committee or subjected to censure by either House. However, she did pay a price for her championing of the tax, almost the heaviest imaginable price for a politician; it was largely as a result of her championing of the tax that in 1990 she was forced from office by a combination of discontented cabinet ministers and fearful Tory backbenchers.

But she alone was sacrificed. Hers was the only blood on the carpet. Patrick Jenkin, the godfather, if not the actual father, of the tax, left the government before it was introduced for unconnected reasons. Kenneth Baker, whom Thatcher described in her memoirs as "the foster-father of the community charge", was first promoted to the cabinet as Jenkin's successor and then went on to become secretary of state for education and science, chancellor of the Duchy of Lancaster, chairman of the Conservative party and home secretary.[2] In 1992 he left the government, also for reasons unconnected with the poll tax. William Waldegrave also prospered, winning promotion within the Environment Department and then at the Foreign Office before joining the cabinet as, successively, health secretary, chancellor of the Duchy of Lancaster, minister of agriculture, fisheries and food and chief secretary to the Treasury. Nicholas Ridley resigned from the government in 1990, not because of the poll tax or because Thatcher had sacked him (she was very reluctant to see him go), but because of rude remarks he had made about Germany's role in Europe. Sir Terry Heiser, in the best British tradition of civil-service neutrality, remained head of the Environment Department to oversee the poll tax's replacement by the council tax.

In a similar way, no one seems to have been held to account for the massive mis-selling of personal pensions; the only people who paid any price were the millions who were either mis-sold them or bought them when they should not have done – and should have been positively discouraged from doing so. The two cabinet ministers who were probably most responsible, Norman Fowler and David Young, remained safely ensconced in the government, departing at a time of their own choosing. In the case of Britain's exit from the ERM, it is almost impossible to point the finger of blame. The one thing that is clear is that Norman Lamont, the incumbent chancellor, was far from being exclusively at fault, and may well have been less at fault than others; but he was the only one who paid a price, and he paid a heavy one. The prime minister, John Major, sacked him as chancellor seven months after the event. The justice, if it was justice at all, was exceedingly rough. If there was a case for holding Lamont to account at all – which, apart from his occasional public-relations gaffes, was at least doubtful – he should presumably have been sacked on 17 September 1992, the day after Black Wednesday, not on 23 May 1993. The electorate did hold the whole Major government to account at the time of the 1997 general election; but that justice, too, was rough, ending as it did the political careers of ministers who, apart from simply being members of the government, had had nothing whatsoever to do with the Black Wednesday debacle.

On several occasions, individuals who were caught up in the commission of blunders were held to account, in the sense of having to resign or being dismissed, but they were far from being the ministers, or even the permanent secretaries, responsible for taking the initial decisions. Ros Hepplewhite, the Child Support Agency's first head, resigned at an early stage of the agency's history, and, although there were widespread doubts about her administrative capacity, the consensus of opinion was that the agency in its original incarnation had been given impossible tasks to perform. Several of her successors were sacked outright, but no ministerial heads rolled. Jennie Page lost her job as chief executive of the New Millennium Exhibition Company Ltd shortly after the opening of the ill-fated Dome even though almost no one blamed her personally for most of what had gone wrong. Again, no ministerial heads rolled. Jane Earl turned out to be the last as well as the first head of the Assets Recovery Agency, which was closed down; but few believed that anyone could have achieved what the Treasury insisted that the agency try to achieve. Certainly no one else has succeeded. Yet again, no ministerial head has ever rolled.

In the case of the Rural Payments Agency, it may be that Johnston McNeill, its executive head when Defra opted for the most complicated method of making single EU payments to English farmers, was more culpable than the people just mentioned. He, more than anyone else, persuaded his superiors that the agency could deliver the proposed scheme, and he apparently went on insisting that it could deliver it even when it patently could not. As we saw in Chapter 12, he was sacked, but the responsible minister who took the crucial decision, Margaret Beckett, far from being sacked, was rewarded with promotion to the Foreign Office. Unusually, Defra's permanent secretary, Sir Brian Bender, was both named and ticked off by the Public Accounts Committee for his part in the single-payments affair; but he, too, was rewarded with promotion, in his case to the larger and more prestigious Department of Trade and Industry.[3]

No blame seems to have attached to either Gordon Brown or his principal aide, Ed Balls, for their leading role in introducing tax credits before ascertaining whether or not they could be properly administered. Likewise, no one – except Britain's taxpayers – paid any kind of price for the Metronet fiasco. As in the case of the poll tax, it is possible in the Metronet case to identify the principal culprits, if not to allocate blame entirely fairly among them. They were Gordon Brown, John Prescott, Geoffrey Robinson and to a lesser extent Shriti Vadera, with Tony Blair, as we saw in Chapter 14, only in the background. None of those listed suffered politically or in any other way for initiating what proved to be – and was widely predicted to be – an incredibly costly shambles. Apart from transport experts and a handful of political columnists, few seemed to notice that Brown and Prescott had, between them, cost taxpayers billions, and Brown went on to become prime minister, while Prescott remained firmly established as deputy prime minister until Tony Blair stood down in 2007. Robinson did resign as a minister but, as usual, for reasons having nothing to do with Metronet. Vadera became a life peer and a government minister as soon as Brown became prime minister.

The almost total lack of ministerial accountability in the strong sense – of ministers being held to account for their actions and being penalised for their more egregious misjudgements and errors – is one of the most striking features of the British system of government. Or, rather, it would be striking if only more people were aware of it. The ancient doctrine of individual ministerial responsibility is breached far more often than it is honoured. The notion of a strong chain of responsibility linking officials via ministers to parliament, with ministers being held personally responsible for their blunders and suffering in consequence, bears no resemblance to reality.

To be sure, politics is, by universal consent, a rough old trade, and ministers of all governments constantly find themselves subjected to harassment and abuse in the House of Commons – as well as in the press and on *Newsnight* – for their real and imagined failings. Ministers who cannot give a good account of themselves and who cannot hold their own in parliament and on television are unlikely to be promoted or remain in office for long. But the harassment and abuse are almost always prompted, not by the commission of gross blunders of the kind described here, but by specific incidents and episodes: alleged improprieties, excessively long queues at airports, spectacular prison escapes and the loss by government departments of computer disks containing personal information. Britain's exit from the ERM was one such episode. It caused mayhem in the media, but parliament was in recess and the authors of the blunder – which they insisted, of course, was not a blunder – remained in place, at least until the sacking of Lamont the following year.

Gross blunders can on occasion, of course, cost their authors dear. Margaret Thatcher lost her job largely as a result of the poll tax. John Major eventually lost his job largely as a consequence of Black Wednesday. Tony Blair's reputation suffered lasting damage as a result of his deep involvement (which he, along with others, still insists was not a blunder) in the 2003 invasion of Iraq. Kenneth Baker's chances of ever becoming

Conservative leader were probably not much improved by his handling of the Dangerous Dogs Act. But parliament as an institution played little part in any of these developments; and, more important, as we have just seen in this chapter, most of the authors of the blunders we have detailed emerged totally unscathed. In a number of cases, they went on to greater things. Of accountability, in any sense of the term, there was none or precious little.

There are various explanations for this lack. One of them is obvious – and also important. To pillory an individual minister is to pillory the whole government. The instincts of ministerial and party solidarity almost always kick in. The prime minister will defend the actions of the minister under threat; after all, he appointed him or her in the first place. Similarly, backbench MPs on the government side almost invariably rally to the side of the besieged minister, especially if the assaults on his or her competence emanate, as they usually do, from the opposition or, worse, the hated media. Normally, if a minister is in trouble, backbench MPs from the governing party make the rounds of the radio and television studios robustly (if not always persuasively) defending the minister's conduct. Only if members of the offending minister's own party turn against him or her is the minister in question liable to get into real trouble. That does happen; ministers do have to watch their backs. It happened spectacularly in the case of Margaret Thatcher. But it does not happen very often.

Another obvious explanation of the lack of accountability in the British system is that it is often hard to know who, in particular, should be held to account. Bills introduced into parliament almost always have the names of a number of ministers on their backs, and blunders usually have multiple authors, with the result that a large number of ministers, not only one or two individuals, risk being drawn into the firing line. The prime minister is unlikely to be able to escape responsibility altogether. The effect is the same as before. Once again, the wagons circle: the government and the governing party as a whole gather round to protect the individuals under threat. In a curious way, the more authors a blunder has, the more likely it is that all the blunderers will escape censure. Of all the blunders described in Part II, only one of them can be said indubitably to have had only one ministerial author. That was Margaret Beckett in the case of the muddled payments and non-payments to English farmers. And even that isolated individual largely escaped censure.[4]

But there are other, less obvious explanations of the lack of account-ability. One is simply that, occasionally, few people notice that a blunder has actually been committed. The crime, so to speak, goes undetected. That was certainly the case with the Metronet fiasco, which was highly com-plicated and technical in character and incomprehensible to most people (including, apparently, the prime minister). The media took scarcely any notice of it. The media would undoubtedly have taken notice of a major incident, such as a crash on the London underground resulting in many fatalities, but Metronet's and British taxpayers' financial crash was largely ignored. The sheer passage of time may also result in non-accountability. By the time the Thatcher government's exciting new personal pensions had been mis-sold on a vast scale, the relevant ministers and probably most of their senior officials had long since passed on. It would have been almost impossible to hold any of them to account. The same was broadly true of the Child Support Agency, which enjoyed a period of calm before the storm broke, by which time all the ministers originally involved had either left the government or were already serving in other departments. By the same token, the consequences of successive governments' innumerable IT cock-ups did not in most cases become apparent until years after those who had initiated the projects and negotiated the unsatisfactory contracts had departed the scene. When, to put it crudely, the shit hits the fan, most of those in government who deserve to be splattered are almost invariably in another room – or have left the building altogether.

The chances of anyone being held to account are also likely to be reduced if the blunder, however large, manifests itself in practice, not as one enormous blunder, but as a sequence of lesser blunders. The poll tax was a huge blunder, one that affected millions of people simultaneously. It could not begin to go unnoticed. Britain's exit from the ERM also had a Big Bang quality, if of a different sort. But the mis-selling of pensions, the farce of trying to collect maintenance payments from absent parents, the tax-credits debacle and the bungled payment of single credits to English farmers all had in common that they adversely affected, over a consider-able period of time, disparate groups of people in different walks of life and over widely dispersed parts of the country. Individual bad-luck stories easily made the local news, but no one in a position of power and author-ity – and no reporters for national TV channels and newspapers – had ever heard of most of the people affected. As a result, there was no national hue and cry of the kind that might conceivably have focused attention on the misdeeds of particular Westminster politicians.

Another explanation for the lack of accountability in the British system is more institutional in character. Since they were established in their present form in 1980, the House of Commons' departmental select committees have had wide-ranging remits to enquire into almost any aspect of the making and implementation of government policy within their own specialist sphere. The select committee that shadowed the Department for the Environment, Food and Rural Affairs during the 2000s published scathing reports about Defra's handling of single EU payments to farmers, and the select committee that dealt with transport during the same decade was, if anything, even more scathing about the government's PPP for the London underground. However, the Commons' single most formidable committee, the Public Accounts Committee, is specifically precluded by its remit from enquiring into either the formulation or the substance of government policy; and most of the departmental select committees, seeking to operate on an all-party basis, seldom seek to delve deeply into the origins of policies as distinct from their merits and generally fight shy of addressing issues that already are, or might become, issues of partisan controversy. They thus engage in a form of collective self-censorship. The National Audit Office, like the Public Accounts Committee, concerns itself with how efficiently and effectively government money is spent, not with how policy is formulated or with the wisdom or otherwise of the policy itself. Ministers often appear as witnesses before House of Commons committees, and on those occasions they have to give an account of themselves, but they are never held to account in the strong sense referred to above. Civil servants are sometimes given a rougher ride and their careers may suffer in consequence, but they too are seldom held to account in the strong sense.

In short, despite the traditional doctrine of individual ministerial responsibility and the lip service still paid to it, a deficit of accountability exists in the British system. Ministers are under constant pressure. They are shot at all the time. They spend a lot of their time dodging bullets, from the media as well as from opposition MPs and sometimes their own backbenchers. But they are seldom seriously wounded and almost never killed by the bullets; and, if they are killed politically, it is almost always as a result of gaffes and personal failures, not as a result of policy failures. Ministers' mistakes, however serious, almost never catch up with them. Harold Wilson said, "A week is a long time in politics". But the most important policy decisions made by governments and ministers typically take years, sometimes even decades, not days or weeks, to play themselves out. By the time they do, the ministers responsible are seldom still in place.

This deficit of accountability has serious consequences. It impacts directly on the structure of ministers' incentives. Ministers – especially activist ministers, the great majority – live in the here and now. They have every incentive to press ahead with their preferred policy initiatives as quickly as they can, to deal efficiently with the contents of their red boxes, to promote their own and their department's interests, to attract the attention of the media, to attract the prime minister's attention, to perform well at the despatch box, to respond to questions in parliament and on television with confidence and aplomb, to appeal to members of their own party and of course to rubbish the opposition parties and their spokesmen. They also have a strong incentive to avoid looking foolish or being made to look foolish. It goes without saying that few ministers are utterly self-serving. Most take seriously the substantive issues they have to deal with, and many of them have strong views about what they think should be the overall thrust of government policy. Most ministers are undoubtedly serious.

However, there is one incentive that they lack: to think a long way ahead, to contemplate seriously the probable consequences for future generations of whatever it is that they do today. They may choose to think ahead. They may worry about future generations. They may even worry about their place in history, if they think they may have one. But beyond their own consciences they have no positive incentive, in the here and now, to do any of those things. The chances of their being held accountable in the future for their actions in the immediate present approach zero. Fear of being held accountable at some time in the future has little power to act as a deterrent in the present. In the case of one former cabinet minister whom we interviewed and one of whose most cherished policies had gone badly awry, it was clear that he had not given the matter a moment's thought since. He was conscientious, he had mastered the details of his policy, and he sincerely believed in it; but once he had left office he had forgotten all about it. It no longer had anything to do with him. Civil servants can occasionally be heard saying, with evident surprise as well as pleasure, that they are currently working for a minister who does think years ahead. But that does not happen often.

Economists use the phrase "moral hazard" to describe situations in which one party to a transaction is prepared to take dangerous risks because the individual or firm in question knows that, if the worst happens, the other parties to the transaction will be the ones that suffer. Banks take dangerous risks knowing that, if they fail, the government and taxpayers will bail them out; holders of insurance policies are liable to take risks that they would not take if they were not insured. Moral hazard is evidently a feature of policymaking in government as well as in economic life. In the absence of mechanisms for ensuring accountability, today's government ministers can take risks, including dangerous ones, conscious or at least vaguely aware that, if the worst does happen, they are almost certain to have moved on long since and that others, not they, will suffer. Even if they mean well, and most ministers do, there is nothing in their working environment to remind them constantly of their duty today to take tomorrow – that is, the future – into account.

There are, alas, no foolproof mechanisms for increasing the chances that blundering ministers will be held to account. There never have been: the old doctrine was always a myth. But there are a number of possibilities.

It would probably help if ministerial turnover were reduced and ministers remained in the same office for longer. At best, they might come to feel a greater sense of ownership of the policies they were advocating and of commitment to their long-term success. At worst, it might be easier to identify them as culprits if things went badly wrong, even at some time in the distant future. It might also help if a larger proportion of ministers were drawn from, or introduced into, the as yet unelected House of Lords. In the modern era, most ministers, currently drawn from the House of Commons, are inevitably career politicians, eager to use their ministerial posts as staging posts in the advancement of their political careers. Lords ministers, whatever their limitations, have the advantage of not being under pressure to act quickly and therefore of being able more easily than Commons ministers to take a long view.

More ambitious, but also less probable, would be the idea of extending the timescale of audit. Audit at the moment takes place mostly on a strictly annual basis. Company accounts are audited annually, and so are the accounts of government departments and agencies. But the test of almost all major government policies, including most of those discussed in Part II, is whether they remain in place and also prove to be effective and efficient over a considerable period of years, say a decade or even longer. There would be a lot to be said for encouraging – and, if necessary, permitting – both the National Audit Office and the select committees of the House of Commons to assess how well government initiatives were continuing to achieve their declared objectives after, say, five, ten or twenty years. Partisan passions would probably have cooled by that time, and it should be possible for the NAO and even for select committees to conduct their enquiries in a reasonably dispassionate way. Those bodies might even be encouraged to identify and then either to applaud or to chastise those ministers who had been principally responsible for launching the initiatives in the first place. The thought of possibly being publicly chastised several years later, but still well within their own lifetime, might – who knows? – give over-hasty and overambitious ministers pause. It might even cause them to ask, before or at the moment of decision, "How will that look in ten years' time?" Those who had been elevated to the House of Lords, assuming that that body remained largely appointive, might even be stripped of their peerages if their blunders were shown to have been peculiarly negligent or crass.

We live in the age of medals, prizes and awards, and another possible way of creating some element of accountability in the British system would be to award a prize every few years to a former minister – it would usually be a former minister – whose policy initiative was still in place, was all but universally accepted, which appeared to be irreversible and which had achieved all or most of its intended outcomes. As in the case of some learned-society awards, the prize could be awarded only after the policy innovation in question had proved its worth over a period of, say, a decade. The awarding body could be the National Audit Office, the Public Accounts Committee, the whole House of Commons or, perhaps more realistically, a non-party or cross-party body specially created for the purpose. It could even be a non-governmental organisation dedicated to better government such as the Institute for Government. The prize itself could be more than honorific. It could include a cash component. A cash award of, say, £50,000 might come cheap at the price if the individual or individuals in question had saved the taxpayer billions of pounds. Had such a prize existed during the 1990s, the winner might well have been Norman Tebbit for his reform of trade-union law. Had it existed during the 2000s, it might have been awarded to Tony Blair and possibly Margaret Beckett for introducing the statutory minimum wage. Of course, consideration would also have to be given, in the interests of increasing accountability, to awarding some kind of negative or wooden-spoon prize to the individual or individuals who had blundered on the largest scale in recent years. It would be tempting in that case to want to impose a pecuniary fine analogous to any cash prize that was currently on offer, but that would probably be impracticable.

Pending the implementation of such outlandish suggestions, all we can say is that the relationship in British politics between, on the one hand, long-term success and failure and, on the other, personal triumph and disgrace is all but non-existent. Most blunderers, however gross their blunders, go unpunished. Ministers know it, a fact that cannot do much to discourage blundering.

25

A peripheral parliament

As is well known, Sherlock Holmes during one of his investigations asked about "the curious incident of the dog in the night-time". "The dog did nothing in the night-time", came the reply. "That was the curious incident", retorted Holmes. Anyone who investigates government blunders is bound to be made aware of another curious incident or, rather, of a large number of curious incidents: namely, that parliament as an institution occasionally barks, frequently nips at its master's heels but very seldom actually bites. By failing to do what might be thought to be its duty, parliament as a whole – and the House of Commons in particular – contrives to be complicit in a large proportion of the blunders that are committed. Government ministers are not the only ones to blame. As a legislative assembly, the parliament of the United Kingdom is, much of the time, either peripheral or totally irrelevant. It might as well not exist.

One small indicator of its peripheral status is how seldom it cropped up spontaneously in the course of our many interviews. Asked about specific blunders, our interviewees almost never volunteered any mention of either parliament or parliamentary proceedings. When asked directly about parliament's role in the commission of any particular blunder, they responded more often than not by shrugging and saying that parliament had been "lax" or even "useless". In connection with the creation of the Child Support Agency, one minister observed that the House of Commons had contributed nothing. Both main parliamentary parties, he said, had been in favour of the bill setting up the agency; indeed, he wished in retrospect that the whole parliamentary process had been more adversarial. He acknowledged that individual MPs had made good points, but they were mostly minor points of detail. Similarly, in connection with Metronet, one interviewee remarked that "nothing anyone said in parliament had any effect". None of the people we spoke to, although many of them were MPs or ex-MPs, spontaneously attributed any significant influence to either the House of Commons or the House of Lords.

As no legislation was required, parliament was scarcely involved in several of our blunders. Parliament was in recess when the Treasury issued a statement on 5 October 1990 announcing that Britain would shortly join the European Exchange Rate Mechanism, and the House of Commons did not debate the matter until more than a fortnight later, by which time British entry was a fait accompli. The same sequence was repeated two years later on 16 September 1992 when Britain abruptly left the ERM. Parliament was in recess that day. The chancellor of the exchequer accordingly announced that Britain was leaving the mechanism, not to MPs but to television cameras outside the Treasury building; and a debate on the affair in the House of Commons – which in the meantime had been recalled from its summer recess – did not take place until a week later. That debate in no way influenced the decision to leave (though it certainly unsettled backbench Conservative MPs and gave a further battering to John Major's already battered reputation).

The decision about how EU payments should be made to English farmers was also a purely executive decision, as were all the IT-related decisions described in Chapter 13. Margaret Beckett's statement to the House of Commons on the single-payments scheme was simply a spelling out and justification of a decision that had already been made, and during the questions and answers that followed only one MP wondered aloud whether the scheme could be introduced successfully on "the somewhat heroic timetable" ministers had adopted.[1] A government minister – a peer serving as parliamentary undersecretary at the Health Department – "launched" the fabulously expensive and ultimately failed NHS National Programme for IT in June 2002, but he launched it at a professional organisation's annual conference, not in parliament, and MPs did not get round to debating the ill-fated programme until the following year.

Parliament's contribution to the great millennium disappointment was also nil. It neither impeded matters nor progressed them. The organisation chart for the exhibition featured ministers prominently on it – but as ministers, not as parliamentarians. Members of the Culture, Media and Sport Select Committee asked questions and expressed doubts, and a scattering of MPs did take part in a short adjournment debate – an occasion for airing views, not for influencing policy – one Wednesday morning two years prior to the event. The two politicians most closely associated with the Dome, Michael Heseltine and Peter Mandelson, both spoke in defence of the project, both adopting a strictly non-partisan tone. Otherwise the tone throughout was partisan and fractious. More than a decade later, most of the criticisms levelled at how the project was developing still resonate. One Conservative MP pointed out that, although the millennium organisers said they were "playing catch-up", they had actually had nearly two thousand years' advance warning. The same MP also pointed out, correctly, that the celebrations shortly to come still lacked "an overriding theme"; the organisers, he said, had a logo and slogans, "a marketing campaign in embryo", but no product.[2] Other MPs wondered whether the event would turn out to be a festival of Christianity or a Disneyland replica. But no one in government was listening. No one in government felt obliged – or was obliged – to listen.

Parliament and parliamentarians had equally little influence on most of the actual pieces of primary legislation that led to the commission of blunders. Members of parliament other than ministers played no part in the development of the poll-tax idea, and few MPs, even on the Labour side, appreciated the importance of the issue until the Thatcher government brought forward its Local Government Finance Bill. At that point, the prospect of being hanged electorally did concentrate wonderfully the minds of several dozen Tory MPs; but, as we saw in Chapter 4, the government made only token concessions to the rebels, the committee stage on the bill was "a futile marathon" and the Conservative whips got their way in the end without much trouble.[3] Parliament, collectively, failed. The same was true, as we have also seen in previous chapters, in the cases of both the Social Security Act 1986, which led to the mis-selling of personal pensions, and the Child Support Act 1992, which outraged millions of absent parents and proved impossible to administer. In the former case, opposition MPs did predict what would happen, but the government of the day, backed by its comfortable parliamentary majority, carried on regardless. In the latter case, most MPs – though not quite all – never seem to have imagined that a measure that looked so amazingly attractive on the face of it could have such dire consequences.

Parliament also failed in connection with individual learning accounts. The Learning and Skills Act 2000 passed through parliament unscathed; and, more to the point, since the Act itself simply enabled the relevant secretary of state to give effect to the legislation, no doubts were raised in parliament at any later stage about the wisdom of running the risk of making payments to people who did not exist as well as training organisations that might, or might not, actually provide training. Ministers, their special advisers and civil servants failed to spot the risks; members of parliament similarly failed to spot them. A few Conservative and Liberal Democrat MPs did notice that Gordon Brown's expanded and ambitious tax-credits scheme might be hard to administer and open to fraud; but, as we saw in Chapter 10, their warnings were ignored. With regard to the setting up of the Assets Recovery Agency, a few MPs were concerned about the human-rights aspects of the legislation, but few, if any, seem to have noticed that the agency stood little chance of achieving its object-ives, and the amendments to the Proceeds of Crime Bill accepted by the government on human-rights grounds merely had the effect of turning the resulting Act into a multi-headed monster.

The complex legislation that established the Greater London Authority – and, with it, the London underground PPP – ground its way slowly through parliament; but the clauses setting up the PPP formed only a small part of the bill, and, as they had been pretty much tacked onto it, they attracted relatively little attention. Labour MPs welcomed the non-privatisation of the underground; Conservative MPs welcomed its part-privatisation. Few MPs expressed doubts about the scheme's practical aspects. Sir Norman Fowler, the opposition's transport spokesman, responding to John Prescott's initial statement announcing the scheme, wanted to know whether there was "not a danger that the system announced today will prove to be the most expensive means of attracting private investment into the scheme?"[4] During the bill's committee stage, another Conservative, John Wilkinson, warned ministers that the kind of contracts they had in mind were "the most difficult form of contract to negotiate and the most fraught with risk".[5] But that was about it. Labour members remained mostly mute. As we saw in Chapter 14, those who doubted the PPP's wisdom were right on almost every count, but most of the doubters were not MPs and, even if they were, ministers took no notice of them.

The only one of our dozen blunders in which parliament and parliamentarians played a more significant and less passive role was in connection with the issue of ID cards. Initially promoted by backbench Conservative MPs, ID cards came under increasing crossfire from both Conservative and Labour backbenchers during the 1990s and 2000s, and, although the Identity Cards Act 2006 did eventually reach the statute book, it was in a considerably mutilated state. Dozens of Labour backbenchers in the House of Commons refused to vote for their own government's bill, and the opposition in the House of Commons undoubtedly encouraged peers in the House of Lords to pass amendments that the government then felt constrained to agree to. The forces that ultimately led to the non-introduction of ID cards included doubts among ministers, growing doubts among Conservatives and sustained public hostility towards the idea of having to pay for the cards; but they also included, beyond doubt, the widespread feeling among MPs on all sides of the House that this particular game was not worth the candle. And the candle was in due course snuffed out.

Unfortunately, the word "parliament" as it is commonly used – and as it has been used so far in this chapter – is ambiguous. It can refer either specifically to government backbenchers or to the institution of parliament as a whole. When historians and journalists refer to a government's having "succumbed to parliamentary pressure", the pressure they are referring to is almost invariably pressure from backbench MPs belonging to the party in power. Backbenchers on the government side often make a fuss, sometimes threaten to vote against the government or abstain and sometimes actually do one or the other. Usually, as in the case of the poll tax, the government of the day stands firm; but sometimes it will yield, reckoning that the political price it would have to pay if it defied its own backbenchers would not be worth paying. Frequently, governments yield quietly in private – before anyone outside notices – rather than risk being humiliated in public. If parliament is construed to mean only backbenchers on the government side, then "parliament" in that restricted sense is often influential – and its influence seems gradually to have been increasing over the past half-century.[6] The government backbencher is now, undoubtedly,

a more formidable figure than he or she once was. Walter Bagehot in
the nineteenth century famously described Conservative backbenchers,
especially those representing shire counties, as "the finest brute votes
in Europe". A latter-day Bagehot would hardly use such a phrase today:
backbenchers can no longer be treated as brutes. The dismissive phrase
"lobby fodder" with reference to government backbenchers has also fallen,
rightly, into disuse.

But the word "parliament" can mean something quite different. It
can mean, not a couple of hundred (or thereabouts) backbenchers on
the government side, but the institutions, practices and mindsets of the
House of Commons and the House of Lords, especially the former, as a
whole; and it is defects in parliament's institutions, practices and mindsets that have led government in Britain to be more blunder-prone than
it needs to be or should be. The parliament of the United Kingdom at the
moment is an essentially passive institution, almost invariably responding to government initiatives, rarely taking initiatives of its own. It could
usefully, in the manner of legislative assemblies in many other countries,
become less boisterous but also less passive and more active, including
more proactive. More MPs could usefully see themselves as real legislators and not just as social workers, cheerleaders, askers of questions and
occasionally – once blunders have already been committed – conductors
of belated post-mortem inquests.

To begin with, it is not immediately obvious why the government of
the day should be the fount of almost all UK legislation, implying that it
is also the fount of almost all wisdom. Whatever else it is, it is not that.
Suppose that during the early and mid-1980s Margaret Thatcher and
her ministers had decided that there were undoubtedly problems about
the rates and that the existing rating system needed to be reformed in
some way. Although Labour MPs were primarily concerned to protect
the poor, and although the Conservatives were more exercised about the
plight of cash-strapped old ladies living all alone in big houses, the rates
had never been a serious bone of contention between the parties. The
bone of contention during the 1980s was between the government in
Whitehall and obstreperous left-wing Labour local authorities. It would
have been open to the government of the day to say that it wanted the
rates problem sorted out and to have assigned the task to a parliamentary

select committee – possibly the existing select committee covering the Department of the Environment – assisted by officials from that department, other departments and possibly external assessors. Such a committee, well chaired, could have consulted widely and held public hearings, and it might well – who knows? – have come up with something like a banded property tax. It would certainly not have come up with a poll tax, let alone a poll tax that was, as Kenneth Baker put it, "to be taken down in one gulp". Had a parliamentary committee come up with such a solution, quite possibly on a cross-party basis, the country would have been spared riotous assemblies, the Conservative party would have been spared ignominy and Margaret Thatcher might well have been allowed by her party – who knows? – to go on and on just as she wished.

Not every policy problem could be tackled in this way, of course; some issues are too contentious between the parties, some are highly technical, and a considerable number involve the government of the day in its relations with foreign governments, the EU and companies and organisations with which it has contractual relationships. But, for example, a House of Commons committee – or a joint committee of the two houses – could have been invited to go away and devise a scheme for putting pressure on absent parents to help pay for their children's upkeep, and both individual learning accounts and ID cards might well have been treated in the same way. The government, in the form of its Commons majority, would have had the final say in each case, and the government might well have needed to put detailed administrative flesh on the bare bones of whatever scheme the select committee in question came up with, but at least the chances of the government as a whole committing a serious blunder might have been reduced. There was no real hurry in any of these instances, and the differences between the parties were minimal. Why should the reputation of the government of the day, and that of the governing party, be engaged in almost everything that happens? Thatcher probably wished she had never invested her reputation in the poll tax.

Any suggestion that the government of the day should hand over that amount of influence to mere backbenchers is bound to be greeted with incredulity, and even the most ardent reformers of parliament have been reticent about going that far; but they have not been reticent in backing the idea that governments ought more frequently to publish their own bills in draft, without committing themselves to them, and that parliamentarians should, as a matter of routine, examine and publish reports on them. A procedure, introduced in the late 1990s and known to connoisseurs of these matters (somewhat clumsily) as "pre-legislative scrutiny", encourages governments to publish bills in draft form before they become irrevocably committed to them and enables parliamentary committees to discuss them and even to hold public hearings on them in advance of publishing their own reports. At least one significant piece of legislation, the Communications Act 2003, which gave the independent media and communications regulator Ofcom the powers it now has, is widely believed to have benefited substantially from being examined in this way. The Blair government in 2003 went so far as to say that governments "should proceed on the assumption that bills will be published in draft for pre-legislative scrutiny unless there is good reason otherwise".[7]

Unfortunately, it turns out that there is nearly always a "good reason otherwise". Governments almost invariably insist on proceeding with their major pieces of legislation come what may, they are typically in a tearing hurry and it is entirely up to them to decide whether to publish their bills in draft form or not. Also, there is no obligation on any parliamentary body – whether or not specially established for the purpose – to examine the draft bills that the government of the day in its wisdom does decide to publish. In other words, the procedure is entirely voluntary on both sides – and one or both sides typically neglects to volunteer. In most years, only about half a dozen government bills, at most, are published in draft; and most of the bills that are published are not remotely flagship bills, more like rowing boats or skiffs. That being so, parliamentary committees, MPs and peers ignore a large proportion of them. In a typical recent year, 2008–09, the government introduced twenty-six bills, of which it published only seven in draft, of which a parliamentary body of any kind took an interest in only three.

A considerable proportion of our blunders – those resulting from primary legislation as distinct from ministerial action – might have been avoided if pre-legislative scrutiny had been a matter of routine instead of a special event; and almost every committee and commission that has ever looked into the matter has called for it to be made a matter of routine except of course in cases of extreme urgency. The Hansard Society for

Parliamentary Government has published a series of reports over many years – two of them based on the work of all-party commissions chaired by former cabinet ministers – stating flatly that "pre-legislative scrutiny by parliamentary committee ought to be the norm for most bills".[8] But nothing happens. Governments seemingly cannot let go. Members of parliament cannot bring themselves to insist on their letting go.

Pre-legislative scrutiny, at least on the scale recommended, would be something of a novelty, one that has not been tried in most other parliamentary democracies; but detailed examination by a parliamentary committee of proposed legislation once it has been approved in principle by a vote of the whole chamber is commonplace. It happens everywhere. What distinguishes the parliament of the United Kingdom is how badly it is done. The present arrangements have countless detractors and few known admirers, but they remain firmly in place because they suit all governments' purposes. British governments want their legislation to pass with as few amendments as possible (except, of course, those proposed by themselves) – and the present arrangements, at least those in the House of Commons, are ideal from governments' point of view. But they are not ideal from any other point of view. They almost guarantee the passage of bad legislation.

At present, once the House of Commons as a whole has voted to approve a bill, it is referred for detailed line-by-line examination to what used to be called a standing committee and is now called, since 2007, a public bill committee. Public bill committees have a dozen salient characteristics, almost all of which work against serious parliamentary consideration of the government's proposed piece of legislation.

First, the committees' partisan composition reflects as accurately as possible the partisan composition of the House of Commons as a whole. Second, the person in the chair of a committee functions as a stand-in for the speaker of the whole House; he or she does not seek to assist the committee in reconciling differences among its members or in reaching decisions. Third, the government minister in charge of the bill plays the same role in the committee as he or she would in the chamber, principally batting away opposition amendments – and after a day or two the cabinet minister responsible for the bill often departs, leaving junior ministers to take the bill the rest of the way through. Fourth, the whips do their best to ensure that their party's MPs on the committee vote in strict accordance with the party's wishes. Fifth, the job of MPs on the government side is to help the government get its legislation, and the job of MPs on the opposition side is to give the government a hard time; neither side's job is mainly to improve the legislation's quality. Sixth, by the same token, MPs on public bill committees almost always see themselves as partisan advocates, not as dispassionate law-makers. Seventh, members of committees need not be, and usually are not, specialists in the subject matter of the bill under consideration; they may not know anything at all about it. Eighth, a given public bill committee is unlikely to have a membership that in any way resembles, let alone coincides with, the membership of the relevant Commons select committee (so that, for example, a bill emanating from the Home Office is never dealt with by either the Home Affairs Select Committee or by the members of that committee functioning as a public bill committee). Ninth, the committee has no professional staff. Tenth, the departmental civil servants responsible for the bill are not allowed to play any part in the committee's proceedings. Eleventh, the committee will almost never collect evidence, summon witnesses or hold hearings (any more than the whole House of Commons does). Twelfth, public bill committees typically debate the policies underlying bills – which, of course, have already been debated in the whole House – instead of concentrating on the practical issues surrounding the bill's implementation – which, of course, have usually not been debated. The result is that government bills usually emerge from public bill committees in little or no better shape than they went in, save possibly as the result of the government's introducing its own amendments. The party-political battle almost invariably trumps careful consideration.

Not surprisingly, standing committees, now public bill committees, have a terrible reputation. According to one reform-minded Conservative MP, "It is unlikely that much would be lost if Standing Committees were abolished."[9] Public bill committees and their proceedings are variously described as "sterile", "dire", "inane", "inadequate", "pointless" and "a complete waste of time".[10] A generation ago, one mordant commentator, Ferdinand Mount, was scathing about their proceedings: "the Ministers wearily reading out their briefs, the opposition spokesmen trotting out the same old amendments purely for the purposes of party rhetoric and without any serious hope of improving the bill, the government back-benchers – pressed men present merely to make up the government's majority – reading the newspapers or answering their letters".[11] A more recent commentator, Peter Riddell, is even more brutal:

> The system has been geared entirely to getting Bills through, regard-less of whether they are properly scrutinized. During the standing committee stage of line-by-line scrutiny, government backbenchers are actively discouraged from participating lest their speeches delay progress on a bill, so they can be seen doing their constituency correspondence and, depending on the season, their Christmas cards ... The more important, and controversial, the bill, the less likely is Parliament to play a creative part in its scrutiny. The result is a mass of hastily considered and badly drafted Bills, which often later have to be revised.[12]

Although no United Kingdom government is likely to adopt it except under extreme duress, another country does have an alternative model of how legislative committees can function usefully and effectively in a parliamentary system. That other country is not the United States, whose political system differs far too radically from that of the UK to make any comparison worthwhile. Rather, it is Germany, which has a parliamentary system not unlike the UK's and a parliament, the Bundestag, that is almost as government- and party-dominated as the parliament at Westminster. Despite the similarities, the experience of the Bundestag shows clearly that a parliament in which almost all bills are introduced by the government and in which the political parties and their whips are at least as power-ful as those in the UK can nevertheless enact legislation that is far from being "hastily considered and badly drafted". Perhaps it is no accident that governments in Germany since the Federal Republic's inception in 1949 have almost certainly committed fewer egregious blunders than govern-ments in the UK.

In Germany, as in the UK, almost all important bills are government bills. The Bundestag is not an initiating body, and bills in Germany are not subject, any more than most government bills in the UK are, to pre-legislative scrutiny. Moreover, in Germany, as in the UK, the committees

371

that subject government bills to detailed examination are multi-party committees, with members of the governing parties in the majority. But at that point resemblance between the two countries' systems ceases. Unlike the UK's public bill committees, the legislative committees in Germany resemble in composition, and function in the style of, Britain's select committees. They are, in effect, "specialized parliaments within parliament", and their members typically know a good deal about the subject matter of the bills that come before them.[13] The committee chairs, who may be members of the opposition, seek to promote agreement and facilitate progress rather than being studiously neutral. Government ministers and whips are not present, but civil servants and members of the committees' staff are. The committees themselves collect evidence and, if they want to, hold hearings. They usually confer in private, and their style of discourse is deliberately conversational rather than confrontational. Perhaps most important of all, the members of the Bundestag's committees see themselves as legislators, as actual law-makers. Their job as they see it is to improve legislation, not either to rubber-stamp it or obstruct it. Government-sponsored bills are, of course, almost always passed by parliament in the end, but only after they have been subjected to rigorous and normally quite non-partisan and dispassionate scrutiny. Moreover, in this regard Germany is far from being an outlier. The parliaments of the Netherlands and the Nordic countries function in much the same way.

What may come as a surprise to many people in England is to learn that the legislatures of Scotland and Wales also function in much the same way. As readers may have noticed already, most of the references in this chapter have been to the UK or the Westminster parliament, not to the British parliament. That is because the UK parliament is no longer the only British parliament. If the English are in search of wisdom – or at least of alternative ways of legislating – they no longer have to travel abroad. They can conduct their enquiries closer to home.

The Scottish parliament at Holyrood differs as much from the Westminster parliament in its methods of working as it does in its physical appearance. As at Westminster, most legislation in Scotland is initiated by the Scottish government; but the committees of the Scottish parliament are far more influential than their (very rough) equivalents at Westminster. Like committees in the German Bundestag, Scottish parliamentary committees are all-purpose bodies. They perform the functions of both the Westminster select committees and Westminster's public bill committees. For example, the Scottish Health and Community Care Committee, unlike its Westminster counterpart, shadows the Scottish Health Department and conducts enquiries into health-related matters in Scotland. It also examines in detail all proposed legislation relating to health in Scotland, whatever its origins. Members of Scottish parliamentary committees are thus considerably more likely than members of public bill committees at Westminster to have acquired at least a modicum of knowledge and expertise relevant to the matter in hand.

The influence of Scottish parliamentary committees also extends across a broader range. Unlike their Westminster counterparts (and, for that matter, their counterparts in Germany), they can actually initiate legislation. The Scots introduced a ban on smoking in public places a year before the introduction of a similar ban in England; and, although the relevant Scottish legislation was eventually adopted as a Scottish government measure, it started its life in the parliament's health committee. Also unlike their Westminster and German counterparts, the specialist committees of the Scottish parliament routinely engage in pre-legislative scrutiny, examining proposed legislation well before it is formally introduced into the parliament as a bill. Both at the pre-legislative stage and during the passage of legislation, Scottish committees are empowered to – indeed required to – consult widely with the public and outside interested bodies, collecting evidence and, if need be, holding hearings (or, as Scots are disposed to call them, "interviews"). Civil servants also take part in their proceedings. Political parties undoubtedly count for as much in Scotland as in most parliamentary democracies; Scottish politics, like UK politics, is predominantly party politics. Even so, members of the Scottish parliament when dealing with legislation appear to resemble members of the Bundestag more than members of the UK parliament in the way they approach their work. They think of themselves as law-makers and display "a commitment to seeking pragmatic rather than dogmatic solutions".[14] The convenors of Scottish parliamentary committees, like the chairs of Westminster select committees, are often opposition members.

The bottom line is obvious. It is hard to imagine many of the blunders described in this book – the poll tax, the original Child Support Act, individual learning accounts, tax credits, the setting up of the agency for recovering criminals' assets – having been perpetrated with the backing of statutes if those statutes had been subjected to the kind of detailed and relatively non-partisan parliamentary scrutiny that is normal in Germany, the Netherlands, Scandinavia, Scotland and many other parliamentary democracies. Furthermore, parliamentary scrutiny as practised in Germany, Scotland and elsewhere is not narrowly or exclusively parliamentary but instead extends outwards to involve members of the public, professional bodies, academic experts, lawyers and so forth as well as the usual lobby groups. In the United Kingdom, unlike anywhere else, an unelected House of Lords currently acts as a kind of legislative backstop; but it lacks the House of Commons' power and authority and most of the time functions only as a backstop.

Until now, most members of parliament, as one prominent reformer, Tony Wright, has put it, "have been willing accomplices in their own subjection".[15] It is ultimately up to MPs to decide whether or not they want to improve the legislative process in the interests of making government less blunder-prone. Change is in their hands. Sadly, although a majority of them seem to be willing to countenance relatively minor reforms, such as allowing MPs to elect the chairs of select committees, they seem quite unwilling to contemplate more radical changes, ones that would give rank-and-file MPs a significantly greater say in the final form that legislation takes. Undoubtedly, the present flawed arrangements suit the convenience of government ministers. They are manifestly less satisfactory from the point of view of citizens, taxpayers and the country as a whole.

26

Asymmetries of expertise

Asymmetries of knowledge and expertise are everywhere. The householder who calls in an electrician typically knows little or nothing about amperes and circuit breakers. Someone who goes to the doctor with chest pains probably has no idea how to distinguish between angina and precordial catch syndrome. The directors of a firm that manufactures plastic mouldings may know that it desperately needs a new IT system but is most unlikely to know which system would suit it best, or even what its precise IT requirements are. In all these cases, and countless others like them, the purchaser, who knows little, is heavily dependent on the electrician, doctor or IT supplier, who knows (or is supposed to know) far more. Purchasers are dependent on suppliers' honesty and integrity, on their technical competence and on their capacity to deliver.

Partly to ensure that suppliers are at once honest, competent and able to deliver, organisations making purchases need to be able to manage projects, especially ones that are ambitious and complicated. A "project", according to the *Concise Oxford English Dictionary*, is an "enterprise carefully planned to achieve a particular aim". If a project thus defined is indeed both ambitious and complicated, then a number of requirements need to be met. Some individual or team of individuals needs to be in charge of ensuring that it *is* carefully planned and that appropriate contracts are negotiated with suppliers. The individual or team also needs to ensure that costs are monitored closely, that progress towards the project's ultimate goal or goals is closely monitored, that quality is assured and that the various elements that constitute the project – financial, legal, technical and so forth – are well integrated. In the private sector, large projects are typically managed by professionally trained project managers, whose job it is to increase the chances of projects being completed on time and to budget.

To put it politely, the performance of successive British governments in negotiating contracts and managing projects has not been entirely satisfactory. Ministers and officials have occasionally been ripped off; they have sometimes been gulled into thinking that suppliers possessed knowledge and expertise that they did not possess; and, most commonly, they have been misled into believing that their suppliers could deliver by a specified date products and services that they could not possibly deliver then or possibly ever. United Kingdom governments are far from being unique in this regard. Foreign governments have suffered similarly, and so have innumerable private-sector companies and not-for-profit bodies. But in recent decades some of UK governments' contractual and project-management errors, resulting in soaring costs, long delays, administrative chaos, human misery and sometimes total failure to deliver, have been quite spectacular.

One strange feature of several of the blunders we have studied is that, although they had all of the characteristics of ambitious and complex projects, they appear never to have been thought of in those terms – as "projects". The ministers and officials involved treated them as though they were somehow a normal part of the ongoing business of government; and, even when individual projects were thought of as projects, they were not professionally managed as such. For example, the enormously complicated task of establishing the Child Support Agency – that is, of giving practical effect to the Major government's highly innovative child-maintenance policies – was initially put in the hands of someone recruited from the voluntary sector who lacked any high-level management experience. Similarly, having devised individual learning accounts without involving knowledgeable outsiders in their design, ministers and officials simply handed over the task of administering them to a private IT firm. It did not occur to them that the creation of independent learning accounts was a major project, one that needed to be carefully managed in close co-operation with the IT firm. In the case of delivering single

EU payments to English farmers, someone with management experience was in charge – the chief executive of the Rural Payments Agency – but no one seemed to notice that he was not up to the job until much of the damage had been done.

Nearly a generation on, the Millennium Dome still provides vivid illustrations of how not to manage a large project. The organisers of the London 2012 Olympic and Paralympic Games clearly learned from that experience. In the case of the Dome, a named individual was put in charge of the New Millennium Exhibition Company – or at least was held responsible for it – and she was a highly competent administrator. But neither she nor anyone else was ever in charge of the whole project, which, going back to the dictionary definition, was neither "carefully planned" nor designed "to achieve a particular aim". On the contrary, everyone within earshot had a share of the action: Peter Mandelson as the single shareholder, Michael Heseltine, who was still personally engaged, the Millennium Commission, the New Millennium Exhibition Company, the Department for Culture, Media and Sport, the Department for the Environment, London Transport and a large number of private companies that had either agreed to exhibit or else were in the course of being approached in the hope that they might exhibit. Of project management in any realistic sense, there was none at all. "Ministers", as one senior official put it to us, "were all over the project like a rash." As for the Dome's particular aim, the same senior official asked rhetorically: "What was it supposed to be? Education? Entertainment? Britishness? Cool Britannia? Inclusiveness? What?" No one knew; or, rather, everyone thought they knew, but everyone seemed to know something different.

The upgrading of the London underground was a "project" if ever there was one; but in this case there was not even a nominal project manager. It is clear from the evidence that neither Gordon Brown nor John Prescott conceived of the enterprise as a project, one which, precisely because it was a project and a very large one at that, would need to be continuously and aggressively managed. They saw their public-private partnership solely as a highly desirable financial and accounting instrument. Their focus was on money and the accounts, notably the government's balance sheet, not on outcomes. Management, they seemed to think, could be left to look after itself. But, while some of the day-to-day and month-to-month management was in the hands of London Underground, some was in the hands of Metronet (which was notoriously badly managed), some was in the hands of Tube Lines (which was better managed), and much of it was in the hands of the many, many firms to which Metronet and Tube Lines chose to let contracts. Because so many organisations were in charge, none of them was.

Governments not only launch projects (whether or not they think of them as projects): they also commission all manner of services and purchase all manner of supplies. Most of the time, they do so routinely and economically, and no one notices. But sometimes they signally fail. They buy the wrong or low-quality products, or they pay too much for them, and the National Audit Office and the House of Commons Public Accounts Committee come along later and voice their complaints. Like all purchasers of goods and services, ministers and officials are often at a disadvantage. They do not know as much about the goods and services they are minded to buy as the persons or companies selling them.

Economists have long recognised the existence of flourishing markets for "lemons". Markets for lemons are the kind of markets created by, for example, the ability of car-dealers to sell to unwitting buyers cars that the dealers, but not the buyers, know to be lemons – cars that are by no means the best available at the price and may even not be roadworthy.[1] Often dealers may also be able to take advantage of the fact that they are much less keen to sell than the buyers are to buy. Under those circumstances, dealers can jack up their prices and cause the buyers to pay far more for the goods or services than they intended.

The case that we call Metronet is an extreme, but not unique, example of ministers and officials purchasing lemons in quantity. Ministers and officials knew little or nothing about how to negotiate the kinds of complicated contracts that the proposed PPP required (partly because no such weirdly convoluted contracts had ever been written before). Many of them also knew little or nothing about the detailed workings of the transport indus-try or its suppliers. They were therefore forced to outsource many of the negotiations and most of the drafting of the contracts to firms of lawyers, consultants and accountants. The lawyers, consultants and accountants had a vested interest in making the whole enterprise as time-consuming and therefore income-generating as possible, and most of them also

378

knew little or nothing about the transport industry and therefore of the substantive issues that they were dealing with. Some of them seemed not to know much about elementary economics, so that the financial details of some contracts were – amazingly – denominated in pounds without its being specified whether the pounds in question were nominal or inflation-proofed pounds. Our interviewees condemned the contracts variously as being "structurally flawed", "poor technically", "badly cross-referenced", "excessively rigid" and "insanely complicated". When tested in the courts, they frequently failed.

The government's heavy dependence on outside lawyers and consultants also meant that conflicts of interest were bound to arise. The firms of lawyers and consultants – sellers of lemons in this context – had every incentive to charge exorbitant prices, knowing that ministers were irrevocably committed to the PPP and were in no position to undertake the necessary work in-house. The number of hours billed by lawyers mounted and went on mounting. Why should they not? There was no one there to stop them. Bob Kiley, the transport commissioner for London imported from the US, was excoriating about the role in the whole enterprise of the consultancy firm PricewaterhouseCoopers, which had originally championed the idea of a PPP, which continued to champion the idea and which Kiley claimed in an interview at the time

> wears enough hats to support a lifetime of visits to the Ascot royal enclosure. Most notably, it is adviser to the London Transport board, and therefore to London Underground. But it was also commissioned by the Department of Transport to look at the financing of London Underground. Meanwhile, PwC also promotes itself as the leading adviser to the PPP community [employing 500 people across the world in that role], a role it could hardly maintain were it to conclude that the largest such transaction did not provide value for money.[2]

The writer who conducted that interview with Kiley adds: "You do not need to be a Leftist conspiracy theorist to see that consultants tend to come up with schemes that require more consultants and which err on the side of complexity."[3]

Ministers and officials also bungled the process of tendering for the contracts in such a way that the bidders gained the upper hand in all the PPP-related negotiations. The bidders effectively became the bidden, the main reason being that there were considerably fewer bidders for the contracts than ministers and officials had imagined there would be. Consolidation in the railway-supply industry had brought about a substantial reduction in the number of firms in the industry; the well-publicised mutual antagonism between Gordon Brown and Ken Livingstone created the risk that the whole enterprise might be aborted; and the PPP's sheer novelty and scale put off several potential bidders ("The City doesn't, in fact, like risk", as one of our interviewees put it). In the event, the number of bidders, initially small in any case, was narrowed down to only two – Metronet and Tube Lines – at which point the government, given its absolute determination to go ahead with the PPP, was absolutely stuck. The two firms had the government's negotiators over a barrel – and both sides knew it. That was the background against which a reluctant Treasury agreed to guarantee 95 per cent of the two consortia's loans. The City, it appeared, need not have worried. From the point of view of the private-sector firms involved, the PPP was now virtually risk-free. It was taxpayers who bore the risk.

The Metronet case was admittedly extreme, but there were others like it. Ministers and officials in the Department for Education and Skills compounded their blunder in the way they introduced individual learning accounts by failing to appreciate the significance of the fact that all the other bidders for the relevant IT contract in due course withdrew, leaving only Capita in the field. In addition, the department almost certainly erred in not involving Capita in the design as well as the implementation of the new scheme. For its part, Capita seems to have felt sufficiently detached from the whole enterprise to feel that it did not owe it to the department to alert it to the strange fact that the number of self-proclaimed training providers was turning out to be far larger than expected. Officials grumbled, but they were probably partly responsible for Capita's seemingly "nowt to do with us, guv" attitude. Capita was merely doing the job it had been asked to do.

The gap between the knowledge and expertise of ministers and officials on the one hand and that of suppliers of goods and services on the other is likely, of course, to be at its widest when new technologies are involved. Caveat emptor (buyer beware) is a hard doctrine. With new technologies, it can be hard or impossible for buyers to know what they should beware of. The most common new technology in civilian society is information technology; and, despite the ubiquity of home computers, laptops and iPads, it is ambitious new IT that is most likely to cause trouble to government departments and agencies (as well as to stock exchanges and banks).

Most of the IT hardware and software bought by British government departments and agencies – and, by the same token, supplied to them – works well, apart from the occasional glitch, and saves many thousands of hours and billions of pounds; but, as we have seen repeatedly in this book, some failures on the part of ministers and officials in the mysterious world of IT have been gross.

The sources of most of the blunders are well known. If suppliers are not always conscientious and competent suppliers, ministers and officials are at least as often not conscientious and competent purchasers. They fail to consult end-users. They fail to draw up contingency plans. They fail to specify clearly and exactly what it is that they want. They constantly change their specifications. They fail to allow for the possibility that relevant circumstances, including the government's own policies, may change. They insist on commissioning bespoke software when software bought off the peg would perform perfectly well and often, in practice, much better. They opt for entirely new systems instead of adapting and upgrading existing ones. As in the case of the misbegotten NHS National Programme for IT, the goals they set for new IT schemes can be wildly overambitious.

Of course, it is also the case that IT suppliers are frequently themselves at fault. They deliberately underbid, hoping (often with good reason) that, if they secure the contract and start work, they can negotiate a better financial deal later. Very occasionally, they engage in outright fraud, as in the case of one of the subcontractors to the NHS programme. And IT suppliers themselves, like those who buy their wares, can be overconfident and overambitious. Hubris is not unknown in the IT industry. One UK civil servant who visited a US firm's Texas headquarters came away both amused and appalled by the firm's macho culture and its "phallic" (his word) building.

But at bottom a large part of the difficulty is, as so often, an asymmetry of knowledge and expertise between purchasers and providers. Several of our interviewees drew attention to the asymmetry. One career civil servant, whose department reckoned he "had earned his spurs" as a negotiator with IT suppliers, complained that his superiors had, in effect, given up on their own ability to negotiate and manage IT contracts and had concluded that the only way forward was to outsource. Before that, the department's systems had been developed mostly "in-house, with some external consultancy support" – and they had usually worked. The effect of relying wholly on outside lawyers and consultants, in his view, was that officials within the department ceased to be able to act as "intelligent customers". In turn, that meant that officials were not able to brief and, if need be, to warn their ministers. Outsourcing so comprehensively had, he believed, "added an extra layer of complexity" to the whole contracting and management process. The department had been "left vulnerable" and had "lost its ability to scrutinise". Another interviewee, in a different context, referred to what he called "the de-professionalisation of the civil service". Either because not enough civil servants were up to the job of supervising contract negotiations and drafting contracts, or because ministers believed they were not up to it, huge amounts of work were being subcontracted to exceedingly expensive law practices and consultancy firms.

The National Audit Office has hammered away at these issues for many years, but continues to be dismayed by the persistence of serious problems. In a 2009 report, the NAO estimated that the total value of the government's Major Projects Portfolio (forty-three of the government's most complex projects) amounted to approximately £200 billion and declared that "To achieve value for money, the Government needs to ensure that these and other complex projects are being delivered by project teams with the required commercial skills ... and [are] approved, led and governed by commercially aware senior civil servants and departmental boards". It defined "commercial skills as the ability to interact on equal and professional terms with the private sector".[4] Against that backdrop, the report's findings were gloomy. Only eight out of sixteen government departments could boast of effective commercial leadership from their commercial director; only ten out of eighteen so-called Senior Responsible Owners of complex projects had previously acquired substantial commercial experience; and, out of a dozen complex projects that had recently been assessed, eight suffered from gaps among their staff in commercial skills and experience. As a result, large volumes of essential work were being done by temporary staff ("interims") and bought-in advisers. "The biggest gaps", the report noted, "are in contract management, the commissioning and management of advisers [a.k.a. consultants], risk identification and management, and business acumen."[5] The report attributed some of the shortfalls, though not all, to the rapid rate at which those members of staff who were commercially aware turned over.

Two years later the NAO, still dissatisfied, returned to the attack. It highlighted the fact that 78 per cent of the civil servants questioned in a recent survey had claimed that there were serious skills gaps in their organisations. "Our recent work", the report went on, "has shown that skills gaps can have a significant impact on government's ability to meet its objectives and provide good value for money."[6] At one point, it identified 246 posts that, if they were to be filled properly, required knowledge and expertise either in programme and project management or in procurement and contract management; but only 197 of the 246 posts identified were filled by people with the requisite expertise – a shortfall of one position in five. As in the earlier report, the NAO highlighted not only the civil service's difficulty in recruiting people with relevant expertise but the poor use that it made of many of them when it had succeeded in taking them on. Departments often failed to keep people in post for any substantial period, thus limiting their "ability to embed skills and experience": "One of our case study departments found examples of staff moving after only nine months."[7] Reviewing the reports of 184 studies conducted by the NAO over the previous three years, the 2011 report observed that around one-third of them made reference to skills gaps in government, resulting in risks to financial management, risks to the achievement of objectives, risks to the quality of services provided and risks to departments' future ability to deliver value-for-money services.[8] The authors of the report did not give the impression that they expected to see significant improvements in the near future.

The blunders of our governments are not, of course, caused solely by skills shortages among officials. They have multiple causes. But skills shortages increase markedly the chances that gross blunders of the kind committed so frequently in the past will continue to be committed well into the future. In recent years, ministers and officials have begun belatedly to address the issue of skills shortages, but for the time being UK governments appear destined to go on buying lemons by the basketful, always at others' expense.

27

A deficit of deliberation

One of the most frequently lauded features of the British political system is the freedom that it gives British governments to take decisive action. Britons have no need to endure the gridlock and paralysis that so often afflict the governments of other countries. If a British government wants to act, it can. UK governments are very rarely dependent on the votes of minor parties in the House of Commons; they can almost always count on the support of a majority in parliament. The House of Lords lacks the power and authority of, say, the US Senate; it can certainly be an irritant from time to time but is seldom more than that. Even after the passage of the Human Rights Act, the Supreme Court of the United Kingdom lacks the power and authority of, say, Germany's Constitutional Court or the US Supreme Court. The British system lacks – and is widely thought to benefit from lacking – a significant number of what are sometimes called "veto-players": individuals and institutions whose backing is needed for the taking of any major initiative and who are able, precisely because their backing is essential, to veto or block any initiative that they find objectionable or that threatens their interests. One thinks immediately of the small far-right Zionist parties in the Israeli Knesset that can and do block Israeli governments' initiatives that they dislike.

The only trouble with a system in which it is easy to take decisions is that it is every bit as easy to take the wrong decisions as it is to take the right ones. Good decisions are facilitated, but so are bad ones. The very strength and decisiveness of British governments may be a curse as well as a blessing: one of the strengths of the British system may simultaneously be one of its weaknesses. Although ministers would hate it, perhaps it would be a boon if the British system accommodated more veto-players rather than fewer. Our study of blunders certainly points in that direction. All the governments that committed the blunders we investigated were strong and decisive governments, and their very strength and decisiveness made possible – indeed positively encouraged – their blundering. Ministers thought that, if they were taking decisive action, they were succeeding, but their successes in the short term frequently proved to be failures in the long term. Their bold initiatives did not achieve their stated aims and did much harm (although, as we saw earlier, almost never to ministers' careers).

We have already identified a number of features of the British system that appear to make it blunder-prone: the weakness, despite appearances, of Number 10, the speed at which ministers are moved from post to post, the pressure on ministers – and ministers' own desire – to be constantly active, the lack of effective individual accountability in the system, parliament's near irrelevance and the absence in Whitehall of sufficient quantities of relevant and essential skills. But there is another feature of the British system – or rather a non-feature – that is worth noting. There is at the heart of the British system a deficit of deliberation.

"Deliberation" is not a word one hears very often in connection with British politics – for the good reason that very little deliberation actually takes place. British politicians meet, discuss, debate, manoeuvre, read submissions, read the newspapers, make speeches, answer questions, visit their constituencies, chair meetings and frequently give interviews, but they seldom deliberate.

The activity of deliberation has three distinct but interconnected components. The first is one of careful consideration, of weighing up. For example, anyone wanting to buy a car that is fast, comfortable and reliable should proceed with due deliberation in the sense of not buying the first car that he or she sees advertised on television. Instead, he or she should consult motoring magazines such as *Which? Car* and test-drive a variety of models. The second component is that of not being over-hasty, of taking one's time. Unless one's old car has completely broken down and needs to be replaced immediately, there is no hurry; and taking one's time gives one breathing space in which to think, acquire more information and perhaps go for more test drives. The third component is that of conferring and taking counsel, of reaching out. It is sensible to seek the advice of the owners of a wide variety of new cars. In addition, buying a new car is unlikely to be a decision only for the buyer. Others – perhaps a spouse or partner – are likely to have a personal stake in the choice, and simple prudence suggests that they should be consulted. Otherwise important information may be lost and ructions follow. Altogether, a decision emanating from a process of due deliberation seems likely to be a better decision than one taken off the cuff, in haste and in isolation.

In no case were the decision-making processes that led to the committing of the blunders we have investigated processes of due deliberation, involving all of these three elements. The inventors of the poll tax did not test-drive, even in their own minds, a variety of alternatives to the rates (perhaps to conclude that there were no real alternatives to some kind of property-based local tax); they were put under intense time pressure; they conferred with almost no one outside Whitehall (and ignored the views of the two outside assessors whom they did consult). Unsurprisingly, they screwed up. The inventors of personal pensions did consider various options, and they did take their time, but they appear not to have conferred with their neighbours in the Department of Trade and Industry, and the few others whom they did consult appear to have comprised only representatives of the insurance industry, that is, business people, some of whom had a vested interest in selling the new pensions. No one who might have warned of the possibility of large-scale mis-selling was involved in the process. The Labour opposition was allowed its say, but it was not involved in policymaking in any realistic way – and what it did say went unheeded.

The Child Support Agency was the bastard child of Whitehall infighting between the Treasury and the Department of Social Security, not the child of a more public process of deliberation, which would almost certainly have thrown up the obvious facts that some absent fathers would not pay, that many of them could not pay and that some had already made their own arrangements; it would probably also have thrown up the fact that lone mothers might not be keen to co-operate with the agency, especially if they were not going to derive any personal financial benefit from co-operating. In the case of the introduction of individual learning accounts – slow to begin with, then rushed – it is hard to imagine that, if policymakers had had their ears closer to the ground, they would not have picked up the fact that unscrupulous persons might notice that, by making multiple claims for small amounts, they could defraud the government of huge amounts of money; £150 × 100 = £15,000 is tempting, and £150 × 1000 = £150,000 is even more tempting.

The tax-credits debacle would likewise seem to have suffered from a lack of before-the-event deliberation. Tax credits were gestated in the womb of the Labour party and in the minds of Ed Balls and Gordon Brown, and in principle they may well have been a good idea, but no effort was made to find out whether they could be put efficiently and effectively into practice. In this case, too, a decision-making process that had drawn in more participants would almost certainly have picked up the misfit – that is, the cultural disconnect – between what the government was demanding of the recipients of tax credits and what they could reasonably be expected to provide. Disinterested pressure groups did try to tell ministers that something was wrong, or might well go wrong, but such groups were not integrated into the decision-making process, and anyway no one – certainly no one in the Treasury – cared to know. Strangely, organisations of farmers were consulted fully in the lead-up to the making of single EU payments in England – and there was widespread support among farmers for the government's proposals – but the organisations in question seem to have assumed that ministers knew what they were doing and for that reason failed to ask pertinent questions about practicalities. They apparently accepted ministerial assurances that they might not have accepted had they been more closely involved in the whole decision-making process.

It almost goes without saying that the decision-making process that led to the Metronet fiasco broke every rule of deliberation. As in the case of the poll tax, there was no weighing up; no serious consideration was given to alternatives to a public-private partnership. The desperate desire of Gordon Brown and John Prescott to have their own scheme cemented in place before an elected mayor of London arrived on the scene meant that most of the crucial decisions were taken in undue haste (though apparently not repented, at leisure). Brown, Prescott and their allies also made sure that, to the extent that outsiders were consulted at all, the consultations were purely nominal; four businessmen, tasked with exploring the options, duly and predictably reported back in favour of the PPP. In other words, there was no genuine taking of counsel. Had there been, the idea of a private-finance initiative on the magnificent scale proposed would almost certainly have been laughed out of court. The whole idea, as the American transport expert told John Prescott to his face, was insane.

Circumstances may on occasion preclude proper deliberation. Decisions may be needed within hours, and secrecy may be essential. But such circumstances are in fact very rare. Certainly they were not present in connection with the great majority of our blunders. Even in the case of Britain's exit from the ERM, it would have been possible for a small committee of Treasury and Bank of England officials to have met secretly over the summer of 1992 to ponder possible alternative courses of action in case the pound did finally come under intolerable pressure. When the time came, they could have presented a range of pre-considered options to Major, Lamont and other interested parties. After all, they had a model available to them: President Kennedy's top-secret "Executive Committee", which managed to deliberate carefully and calmly under enormous pressure during the Cuban missile crisis. Black Wednesday's absurd blend of panic and farce could have been avoided. British politicians in general have a curious habit of functioning in crisis mode – at high speed and in an agitated state – even when no crisis exists. They seem to enjoy it. It seems to give many of them a high.

Deliberation is not entirely absent from the British policymaking scene – an enormous amount of deliberation went into the introduction of power-sharing in Northern Ireland and a great deal into the final report of Lord Turner's Pensions Commission during the early 2000s – but not much of it goes on. Why should this be so?

The fact that Britain's political system is a power-hoarding system, with governmental power and authority heavily concentrated in Whitehall, is part of the explanation. A power-hoarding regime certainly has the capacity to weigh up options, and it need not operate at high velocity (the wheels of Whitehall can grind wonderfully slowly); but in practice it does mean that ministers and officials, although ready to consult others, are usually reluctant to engage fully with them and to see them as active participants in the policymaking process. The government of the day is in charge. It makes policy. The role of others is merely to respond. The autobiography of a former cabinet minister captures the spirit perfectly. Its title is simply

Ministers Decide.[1] Ministers' reluctance to engage fully with outsiders is reinforced by Whitehall's deeply engrained culture of secrecy. Individual ministers and officials are seldom secretive by nature, but their working presumption is that outsiders should know as little as possible about what ministers are thinking and about what they may be about to announce. Outsiders should know only what ministers and officials want them to know. Leaks are frequent, of course, and have undoubtedly become more frequent in recent decades; but the very concept of a leak implies the existence of a sealed container from which no liquid should be allowed to escape.

The *modus operandi* of the mass media – and, even more, of new media – are of course antithetical to deliberation. If politicians are often on a high, journalists and broadcasters seem permanently to be on one. Excitement is what they crave and what they seek to project. "Breaking news" is the best kind of news – the more of it the better – and breaking news should ideally be put on air "live". Journalists pounce on every ministerial indiscretion and on any statement made by one minister that seems to contradict what some other minister has said. Ministers who take time to make up their minds are said to be dithering, and the same is likely to be said of the few ministers who publicly acknowledge that they are having to weigh up finely balanced arguments. If a minister declines to go into a broadcasting studio, even at short notice, the presenter is apt to say icily, "We asked for an interview, but no one was available" – as though it was ministers' duty, despite all their other duties, to be instantly available to broadcasters. The pressure is incessant, and ministers find it hard not to succumb. The media's hyperactive tempo becomes theirs.

Intense partisanship is also the enemy of deliberation. The government of the day hoards power, and the main opposition party is bent on seizing that government's hoard of power – every last bit of it. Britain's us-versus-them, winner-takes-all style of politics makes it hard for British politicians even to contemplate the possibility of engaging in deliberative policymaking. Deliberation involves taking counsel and reaching out, and a government that sought to operate in that mode would necessarily have to reach out not merely to the general public and to non-governmental organisations of all kinds but also to the opposition parties. Attempts are occasionally made along these lines – for a time, there was cross-party deliberation in connection with social care for the elderly – and the Conservative and Labour parties were able to co-operate effectively for years over the future of Northern Ireland. But such attempts have been infrequent and, except in the case of Northern Ireland, have seldom come to much. Power-sharing in the government of Northern Ireland is all very well, but the idea of power-sharing as a routine in the government of the whole UK has historically been anathema, certainly to the two major parties. Even when a coalition government was in power after May 2010, the parties in the coalition showed no disposition to engage with Labour. The country's governing style remained the same. Ministers still decided, even though the predictable disagreements among ministers were aired in public more often than was once customary.

British governments' persistent reluctance to concede even a tiny part of the action to the opposition parties is odd, on the face of it. Labour ceased decades ago to be a genuinely revolutionary party, if it ever was one, and is no longer a truly socialist party; the Conservative party in Britain bears almost no resemblance to America's Tea Party movement, let alone to France's *Front National* or other far-right parties on the Continent. The divisions within the two major parties are sometimes as conspicuous as the divisions between them, and opinion among the general public is probably less polarised today than at any time during the last 100 years. It is odd that, while the electorate has become less polarised, and while the ideological differences between the major parties are far less pronounced than they were a generation ago, the parties themselves continue to be overwhelmingly adversarial in their political style. In the House of Commons on Wednesdays during Prime Minister's Question Time, MPs often sound like rival bands of warring gorillas. The parties seem determined to create conflict where none exists or needs to exist.

A striking aspect of the blunders we studied was how few of them had, or needed to have, a party-political dimension. A banded local property tax would probably have been acceptable to Labour from the beginning; the fight over the poll tax was quite unnecessary. Neither party actually willed the mis-selling of pensions, and Labour was never adamant in its opposition to the principle of personal pensions. The Child Support Agency was set up, as we saw, with Labour's full support. Both parties welcomed Britain's entry into the ERM enthusiastically, and both broadly supported the principle of holding a great national exhibition at the time of the millennium. The Conservatives did not object to individual learning accounts, and did not object strenuously to the idea of tax credits. The setting up of the Assets Recovery Agency had all-party support, and such debate as occurred over the wisdom of adopting the most ambitious method for making single EU payments to English farmers was never along party lines. No party was ever against IT as such, and members of all parties would probably have been delighted if the NHS National Programme for IT had actually succeeded. Although the little debate that took place over Metronet was conducted almost exclusively along party-political lines, it need not have been, given that both major parties were content to accept some kind of public-sector, private-sector mix. The fact that the debate was, quite unnecessarily, conducted along partisan lines, meant that the serious practical flaws inherent in Gordon Brown's scheme were never properly exposed. In all of these instances, the outcomes would probably have been more satisfactory – or at least less unsatisfactory – if representatives of the opposition party or parties had been invited to participate in policymaking from the outset. The government of the day would still have had the last word, but more minds would have been brought to bear.

The party-political battle is far from being a sham. Over a wide range of issues – taxation, public spending, liberty, equality, green issues and many aspects of education – the parties' disagreements are real, their differences profound. But there are many issues on which their disagreements are more synthetic than real, and on which truces in the partisan battle could easily be called. Just as a decline in tribalism among the electorate has made it harder to predict a person's partisan preferences from his or her social location, so it has become harder to predict someone's policy preferences on a wide range of substantive issues from his or her partisan preferences. Even MPs of the same party differ about such matters as Europe, wind farms, the future of green belts, high-speed rail, the location of airports, the war in Afghanistan and what, if anything, should be done about the banks. Against that background, more in the way of deliberative policymaking ought to be possible. Already a large proportion of House of Commons select committee reports are agreed unanimously.

There is another point to be made about British governments' supposed decisiveness. It is certainly true that the British system of government makes decisive action possible in a way that some others do not. Whereas successive Democratic administrations in the United States failed for decades to introduce universal health insurance, the postwar Labour government in Britain simply went ahead and created the National Health Service. Similarly, whereas the Thatcher government was able to undertake an extensive programme of privatisation during the 1980s, other governments in Europe and elsewhere are still struggling in the 2010s – thirty years later – to privatise inefficient state-owned industries. New Labour came to power in 1997 having pledged to introduce a Human Rights Act and proceeded to do just that. It likewise came to power pledged to devolve substantial governmental powers to Scotland and Wales, and it proceeded to do that. British governments have certainly not been ineffectual in the manner of governments in, say, Greece or Italy.

However, the traditional portrait of British governments as being strong and decisive badly needs to be retouched. British governments have often been remarkably slow off the mark. They have left things undone that sorely needed to be done. Conservative governments during the 1950s were slow to recognise Britain's relative economic decline and even slower to respond to it. Harold Macmillan concluded in 1959 that Britain should join what was then the Common Market, but Britain did not formally apply to join until 1961 and did not actually join until 1973 (and the fault was not entirely on the part of the French). By the mid-1960s virtually the entire British political élite – as well as a large majority of the British people – agreed that the power of the trade unions needed to be curbed; but, as we saw in Chapter 3, both of two major efforts to curb their power were botched and effective reform did not take place until the mid-1980s – two decades later. More recently, successive governments have failed to adopt in good time measures to expand and improve the quality of vocational education, to respond to climate change, to address the multiple problems posed by an ageing population, to ensure that the country does not suffer severe power shortages in the future and to expand the capacity of airports in the South East of England. The list could be extended. The notion that British governments have a special gift for decisiveness and the taking of tough decisions is largely a myth – a myth propagated mainly by governments themselves. In truth, they prevaricate, procrastinate and defer as often as they decide.

One reason is that all British governments are coalitions in reality if not in name, and factions within governing parties are among the few bodies capable of acting as veto-players in the British system. Conservative and Labour Eurosceptics alike delayed Britain's entry into the Common Market. Trade unionists within the Labour party blocked the Wilson government's efforts to reform the unions. Because the Conservative party was so deeply divided during the 1990s between those still rejoicing at Margaret Thatcher's fall and those still mourning it, and because the party's parliamentary majority was so small, the Major government attempted very little. In the face of strong opposition from within the Labour party, the Blair government in 2004 only just managed to enact top-up fees for students attending English universities. Governments are always subject to being constrained by their own parliamentary followings.

But there is an even more powerful constraint on governments in Britain. Precisely because they hoard power, they find themselves entirely out on their own, with prime ministers and their colleagues knowing in advance (or at least believing) that the electorate will hold them collectively responsible for everything they have done and failed to do. In reality, the connection between governments' actions and the electorate's reactions is not that simple; but prime ministers and their colleagues, if they want to be re-elected (and they always do), cannot afford to take chances. If they choose to act decisively, and if their decisive actions turn out to be unacceptable to key sections of the electorate, they and they alone may pay – and know in advance that they may pay – the ultimate price of electoral defeat. Their political careers may be at an end. Understandably, ministers' elemental fear of losing the next election is a great inducer of caution. It tempts them to put off tackling what someone shrewdly dubbed "the wicked issues". Equally understandably, it tempts them to hesitate before taking any action, decisive or otherwise, that is likely at the next election to cost them votes and seats. For good reason, British governments are often more pusillanimous than they appear, or certainly as they like to present themselves. Unlike governments in some other countries, they may not be constrained by powerful courts and parliamentary upper houses, but they are constrained by the electorate. In the British system, the country's voters are the ultimate veto-players – and those in government know it.

There is thus a conundrum. On the one hand, ministers know there are long-term issues that they ought to be tackling. On the other hand, they know that tackling them effectively may damage them electorally. As a possible way out of this conundrum, the practice of deliberation – of weighing up, proceeding without haste and taking counsel together – may be of use. Involving other stakeholders, the opposition parties included, in the tackling of thorny issues holds out some hope of spreading the political risks. If a broad range of stakeholders, including the opposition parties, can agree on a way forward – if their fingerprints are clearly visible on whatever agreement is ultimately negotiated – then it may be possible to take the issue out of politics or, if not out of politics altogether, then at least out of electoral politics. Agreements reached by way of deliberation also stand a good chance of being widely accepted, not least because more individuals and organisations will have had their opinions and interests taken into account. The government of the day will not be the sole initiator. In addition, policies that secure widespread agreement are more likely to "stick", not to be abandoned or reversed when there is next a change of government.

All that is by no means as utopian or Panglossian as it may appear.[2] The best-governed countries in Europe are probably the Nordic countries and the Netherlands, and they all practise deliberation, not across the entire range of political issues, of course, but as a core part of their repertoire for dealing with difficult long-term issues – in the case of the Netherlands, for example, how to keep out the waters of the North Sea. The governments of those countries indulge in deliberation but show no signs of suffering from sclerosis or paralysis. A substantial element of deliberation is also built into the proceedings of the German Bundestag. Even in the UK, on the relatively rare occasions when it has been practised, deliberation has often proved successful. Deliberation of a rather higgledy-piggledy sort led to England's ban on smoking in public places, and deliberation of a much more calculated kind, organised by the Pensions Commission chaired by Lord Turner, led to the passage of the Pensions Act 2007 and to acceptance by politicians and the public alike of the idea that, if the state pension were to survive, the pensionable age for both men and women would have to be raised. The form that devolution to Scotland took at the end of the 1990s owed much to the careful deliberations of the Scottish

Constitutional Convention, a non-governmental body that nevertheless greatly influenced the Labour party's thinking on the issue. In the absence of careful deliberation, the Wilson government's proposals for devolution to Scotland, gestated in Whitehall in the usual way, collapsed in a heap during the 1970s.

Careful deliberation involving outsiders in the course of developing policy is almost certainly a good idea; but not deliberating is beyond any doubt a very bad idea. The risks inherent in functioning in that way are far outweighed by the risks of not doing so. As we have seen, a lack of sensible deliberation contributed to the committing of a large proportion of the blunders we investigated. In most cases, deliberation would have been possible: in most cases, there were no unbridgeable differences either between the parties or within the broader society. But nothing of that kind occurred, and disaster ensued. Unwillingness to deliberate in a measured and grown-up way has almost certainly contributed also to successive governments' reluctance to tackle a range of difficult issues. Deliberation can take place in a variety of settings: in parliamentary committees, in Royal Commissions and committees of inquiry, in the course of public hearings and even, on occasion, in bodies specially created for the purpose. But few such mechanisms are exploited by governments in Britain. We should add that really serious deliberation is often best conducted in private, behind closed doors, in settings where people find it easier to change their minds and work out compromises. One of the greatest deliberative assemblies in the history of the world, the United States constitutional convention of 1787, took place behind closed doors, with the windows closed, guards at the gate and the delegates pledged – a pledge that every one of them honoured – not to report to outsiders anything that went on.

There is always, whenever a blunder has been committed, an irresistible temptation to ask who committed it. Who was the culprit? Who was to blame? And in these pages we confess to having yielded from time to time to that temptation. We have occasionally pointed the finger of blame at named individuals: Margaret Thatcher and various of her colleagues in the case of the poll tax, Gordon Brown and John Prescott in the case of Metronet. But there is another and more important question to ask: what was there about the political institutions and the political culture that made such blunders possible? Perhaps, after all, the fault lies not primarily in individuals but in features of the whole system within which individual political leaders operate.

Readers must have been struck by the fact that the blunders we identified seemed often to emerge from nowhere, with no one in particular to blame, and also that in recent decades blunders seem to have been committed more or less continually: under different prime ministers, during the course of different administrations and with different political parties in power. Some of the blunders have even been perpetuated – much in the manner of batons being handed on in a relay race – from one government to another, including between governments of different parties. During the period we studied, no one party seems to have been especially at fault. Conservative and Labour governments were equally blunder-prone. In other words, what we observed – and still observe today – is not a sequence of unrelated episodes but a pattern. It would seem to follow that, if the incidence of blunders is to be reduced, it is the British governing system, and the ways in which people function within that system, that needs to change. Karl Marx used to insist that his followers direct their political fire not at individual capitalists but at the capitalist system. In the same vein, we take the view that in Britain our attention is too often directed towards the failings and foibles of individual politicians and parties and not nearly often enough towards the flaws in our political system. Our study of blunders has made both of us far more sympathetic towards radical change than we were when we started out.

"First, do no harm" has long been a valuable medical maxim. It is one that men and women in government ought also to heed. And they would find it far easier to do no harm if the system of government itself were adjusted so as to make the committing of blunders less commonplace. No system is perfect. There will always be blunders. It would just be good if there were fewer of them in the UK and they were less serious.

Postscript

(June 2013)

The research we conducted for this book covered only the decades before the coming to power of the present coalition government under David Cameron in May 2010, but of course a great deal has happened since then. We wish we could conclude by reporting that the new government has committed significantly fewer blunders than its predecessors. Sadly, we cannot do that. The opposite seems equally likely. The present government has been at least as blunder-prone as its predecessors, possibly more so. "Omnishambles" – in 2012 dubbed "the word of the year" by Oxford University Press – is scarcely too strong a word to describe some of its performance so far. The present government's performance serves to reinforce what has been our central point all along: that the British system of government itself is blunder-prone and not just particular governments and named individuals.

On one major issue, we believe that, for the reasons given in Chapter 1, we should suspend judgement. Has the Cameron government blundered badly, or at all, in the field of macroeconomic policy? Many people think it has and have good reasons for doing so. We are disposed to hold back. The events of the early and mid-2010s may look very different in 2020 or 2030 from the way they look now. The British economy may remain in the doldrums for years or even decades. On the other hand, the government's insistence on tough measures to reduce the present fiscal deficit and restore growth may succeed. Moreover, even if the government's economic measures do not in the end prove successful, we might still be reluctant to label them a blunder. Whoever had found himself at the Treasury in May 2010 – whether George Osborne, Alistair Darling or someone else – would have had to make extraordinarily difficult decisions, with the world in economic turmoil and with little relevant past experience to draw on. In other words, he would have had to make difficult judgement calls. And, as we remarked in Chapter 1, judgement calls that turn out to have been wrong are not necessarily to be dismissed as blunders. A blunder is a stupid or careless mistake. The present government's macroeconomic policies may be misguided, but they are hardly the product of either stupidity or carelessness.

The same cannot be said, alas, of some of the government's other policy ventures. The Cameron government's radical overhaul of the National Health Service in England may turn out in the fullness of time to have been a success (although the consensus of opinion at the moment is that at best it will prove to have been only a partial success and one bought at too high a price). But the political process that led to the passage of the Health and Social Care Act 2012 was remarkably shambolic. It even involved a "pause" in the passage of the relevant legislation, when Downing Street at last realised just how unpopular and unconvincing the government's proposals were, not least among doctors and NHS professionals. Nicholas Timmins, the widely respected former public policy editor of the *Financial Times*, has already written an interim history of the episode. He is less than impressed.[1]

The coalition government appears to have learned little from the mistakes of its predecessors. Until it was too late, the prime minister was uninvolved. No one at or near Number 10 alerted him to what seemed likely to happen. The cabinet and its committees were useless as a check on what was being proposed. The "right people", as Jonathan Powell calls them, were never in the room.[2] The wrong people – that is, ministers who knew little or nothing about either the NHS or the reform proposals – too often were. They were in no position to challenge Andrew Lansley, the cabinet minister in charge. Lansley himself had been the Conservatives' lead spokesman on health for more than six years, and the proposals were overwhelmingly the product of his imagination. Unlike the inventors of the poll tax, who hid themselves away, Lansley talked extensively to people elsewhere in the field; but he kept his thoughts, as they developed, largely to himself and, like Patrick Jenkin's original review team, he was determined to come up with a "final solution" to all the NHS's organisational problems. The intellectual tidiness of Lansley's scheme was matched only by its political clumsiness. He was a very clever man, and clever people are not always very sensible.[3]

Lansley was not only clever: he was also a man in a hurry. He did care about the health service and its long-term future – he was far from being a crass careerist intent only on making his mark – but he was determined to produce a bill more or less instantly and to get the whole of it onto the statute book as quickly as possible. In attempting to move so fast, he tripped over his own feet. Whether civil servants did as much as they should have done to warn Lansley of the practical and political elephant traps ahead is an open question; but they appear, like their predecessors under previous governments, to have been exceedingly reluctant to do anything that might cross their newly appointed chief, someone who clearly knew his own mind. Because David Cameron had dismantled most of the elaborate Number 10 support structure that Tony Blair had so carefully erected, Health Department officials were also conscious that there was no one in Number 10 they could talk to and, if need be, warn. For all these reasons, operational disconnect seems to have been all but total. The architect, Andrew Lansley, had his grand design. Detailed drawings that the builders on site could actually work from appear to have been virtually non-existent.

The absence of due deliberation was strange under the circumstances. As Nicholas Timmins points out, Lansley's plans built to a large extent on ideas that had already been developed by a number of his predecessors at the Department of Health – Labour health secretaries such as Alan Milburn as well as Conservatives such as Kenneth Clarke. He could have built on them incrementally. There was no need for radical legislation. For their part, the Liberal Democrats were also by nature decentralisers, more than willing to embrace reforms that took power from NHS management in Whitehall and handed it to local bodies. Among both the political parties and health professionals, something like a consensus was gradually emerging about the general direction in which the NHS in England ought to go.

But Lansley insisted on going it alone. His plans, by now much revised, may yet prove to have been the right ones, but there was almost certainly no need to cause such a commotion in attempting to give effect to them. The fact that Lansley's party was in coalition with the Liberal Democrats undoubtedly complicated matters, but most of the problems that arose would have arisen even without them. A more deliberative process might also have kept Lansley himself in post. Unlike so many errant ministers before him, he was held to account. In 2012 the prime minister removed him from the Department of Health. He became instead leader of the House of Commons, the equivalent of Siberia in British politics.

If only time will tell in the case of the English NHS, time has already told in the case of the West Coast Main Line franchise. Privatising the railways in the way that it was handled during the 1990s may possibly have been a blunder, but the handling of the bidding for the West Coast Main Line franchise during the 2010s undoubtedly was. The Department for Transport was in charge of the process. Four firms and consortia competed for the franchise. A company called First West Coast Ltd won. Another company, Virgin Trains Ltd, appealed. Virgin's appeal was successful, and the whole franchise-bidding process was restarted. No one was killed, but the initial cost to taxpayers was £40 million and is bound in time to mount far higher. An independent report into the episode by the Transport Department's lead non-executive director, Sam Laidlaw, was damning.[4] In his report, his media interviews and a subsequent appearance before the Commons transport select committee, Laidlaw attributed the fiasco to the Transport Department's loss of key staff (creating an asymmetry of expertise between the department and the bidding companies), rapid turnover among the department's permanent secretaries (it had no fewer than four between May 2010, when the coalition came to power, and July 2012, when the franchise-bidding process was aborted), and the fact that middle-level officials – who had been working under intense time pressure – felt inhibited about alerting their superiors to the concerns they had. The department's organisational structure was complex and confusing, and both ministers and senior officials apparently had no idea what was going on.[5] The whole affair was eerily redolent of the Rural Payments Agency and Metronet fiascos of a decade before, if on a more modest scale.

One of the first actions of the new coalition government was to light a "bonfire of quangos" – a cull of semi-autonomous, government-sponsored bodies, some of which had executive responsibilities, some of which were purely advisory. Initially, the government's Public Bodies Bill gave ministers the power to axe quangos at will. A schedule attached to the bill would have enabled the government to abolish no fewer than 151 separate organisations, including the Law Commission, the Judicial Appointments Commission, Her Majesty's Inspector of Prisons and regulatory bodies such as Ofcom and the Office of Fair Trading. On this occasion, however, parliament – the House of Commons as well as the Lords – proved anything but peripheral. On the grounds that the proposed bonfire would neither save money nor increase accountability, as the government claimed, and that ministers in any case should under no circumstances be granted such sweeping powers, MPs and peers of all parties rebelled and the government backed off. It wrote the offending schedule out of the bill and under the Public Bodies Act 2011 granted parliament substantial powers over ministers' decisions relating to quangos. In this case, what would probably have turned out to be a major blunder was narrowly averted.

Soon after his election as Conservative leader in 2005, David Cameron floated the idea of people directly electing an individual man or woman to act as their local police commissioner. His government, with Liberal Democrat compliance, duly enacted the Police Reform and Social Responsibility Act 2011. Its aims were to improve police performance and by means of democratic elections to make police forces more locally accountable.[6] The first elections of police and crime commissioners in England and Wales took place in November 2012. Creating the commissioner posts may yet prove a success, but the first elections turned out to be, by almost universal consent, a spectacular flop. Turnout across England and Wales outside London, where there were no elections, averaged 15.1 per cent, by far the lowest in any comparable round of elections since 1832. Turnout on Merseyside was a derisory 12.4 per cent, in Staffordshire an even more derisory 11.6 per cent. Nobody at all bothered to vote at one polling station in Gwent. In what ways, and to whom, the new commissioners will be accountable remains a mystery.

The Cameron government conspicuously bungled its relationship with the Murdoch-controlled media giant News International. Cameron was not only personally close to some News International personnel, notably its chief executive Rebekah Brooks, but he and several of his senior colleagues also favoured the bid by News Corporation – News International's American owner – to purchase all the shares in the satellite British broadcaster BSkyB. But Vince Cable, the Liberal Democrat business secretary, took a different view. He believed the proposed takeover might breach UK competition rules and sought the opinion of Ofcom. However, before he could take the final decision he was lured into revealing to undercover *Daily Telegraph* journalists that he had "declared war" on Rupert Murdoch.[7] Cameron thereupon transferred the decision to Jeremy Hunt, his culture, media and sport secretary. Hunt, unlike Cable, favoured the bid. Ofcom, however, was wary. It argued that it had a duty to be satisfied that the holder of a broadcasting licence was "fit and proper" to hold such a licence.[8] Amid controversy over News Corp's bid and a scandal over widespread phone-hacking at News International's Sunday paper, the *News of the World*, Murdoch and News Corp withdrew their bid. The outcome was not the one that Cameron and Hunt had wanted, both men were accused of impropriety, and, although Hunt kept his job and was later promoted, the controversy rumbled on for months.

Cameron compounded the confusion by appointing an inquiry into press standards by an Appeal Court judge, Lord Leveson, declaring at the same time that, unless Leveson's recommendations were "bonkers", he and his government would accept them.[9] But when Leveson's recommendations were published Cameron rejected out of hand one of the main ones: that there be regulation of the press underpinned by statute. It followed logically that Cameron thought that Leveson, whom he himself had appointed, had done something bonkers. The sequel was chaotic. It was generally agreed that the existing industry-dominated Press Complaints Commission had failed in its duty. The aim now was to replace it by a new form of "independent self-regulation". But what that Delphic phrase meant – or what it could be got to mean in practice – was unclear. Cameron himself, backed by a large section of the Conservative party and a clear majority of newspaper owners and editors, emphasised the *self* in self-regulation. The Liberal Democrat and Labour leaders, backed by their own parties, a smaller section of the Conservative party and a small minority of newspaper owners and editors, emphasised the *independent* in the same phrase. Following several rounds of cross-party talks, the last of which ended in the small hours of a March morning, a large majority of MPs of all parties gave their backing to a Royal Charter system of self-regulation, but one buttressed by "a bit of statute".[10] However, although the House of Commons approved of this new system, the bulk of the newspaper industry did not, and its willingness to co-operate was crucial. If there was to be self-regulation, the self – in the form of the newspaper industry – had to co-operate. No co-operation, no *self*-regulation. Defying the government and the leaders of all three main parties, a consortium of newspaper groups proceeded to write its own version of a Royal Charter system, one that was wholly statute-free. Many months after the publication of Lord Leveson's report, no new arrangements for regulating the press, either voluntary or statutory, were in place.

The coalition government bungled in a big way over increasing university tuition fees – quite apart from Nick Clegg and the Liberal Democrats' going back on their campaign pledge not to raise the fees. No one who was not involved, and probably no one who was, can give a coherent account of the fraught interparty and interdepartmental negotiations that resulted in the new regime for English university fees that was put in place towards the end of 2010. But the two main aims were clear enough. One was to reduce further the burden on taxpayers of funding higher education by forcing students to contribute more towards the cost of their education. The other was to achieve that effect, but in such a way that students from poorer families were not deterred from going to university. A report by Lord Browne, commissioned by the previous government, recommended that the existing £3290 cap on universities' fees should be abolished and that universities should be free to charge whatever they wanted. However, at the same time university students should be provided with substantial upfront loans to cover their fees and living expenses. Students would then repay their loans over an extended period following their graduation and only after they had started to earn a salary of £21,000 or more. Universities would gain financially. Students would benefit from the loans and also the easy repayment terms on offer. Taxpayers and the Treasury would benefit in the end because the loans, or a large proportion of them, would be repaid.

The new government rang the changes on Browne. It did not allow universities to charge whatever fees they wanted. Instead, it imposed on all universities a cap of £9000 – on the clear understanding, however, that most universities would charge nearer £6000. The government would then pay over to universities the whole of these increased fees in order to improve the state of their finances. As Browne had recommended, students would be provided with generous upfront loans. Also as Browne recommended, graduates would not have to begin repaying their loans until their annual salary reached £21,000. Any graduates' debts that had not been repaid after thirty years would be written off. The Treasury would eventually get most of its money back. All sides would benefit. It was a classic win–win solution to a long-standing problem. Both houses of parliament endorsed it.

But the whole thing was flawed from the start. Predictably, most universities raised their fees above £6000, the majority of them to £9000. No university wanted to appear cut-rate. The government initially reckoned that the average fee would be about £7500. It turned out to be nearer £8500. The Treasury had no choice: it had to pay up. Moreover, it had to pay up immediately, whereas the student loans would not begin to be repaid until several years later. The size of the government's debt would increase substantially in the meantime. In any event, will the great majority of the outstanding loans be repaid? Almost certainly not. Many graduates will take some years before their salaries reach £21,000, especially if incomes across the country continue to rise only slowly. Graduate underemployment, already high, seems unlikely to fall substantially in the near term. English universities depend heavily on attracting EU students, who pay the same fees and are entitled to the same loans for their fees as English students; but large numbers of EU graduates are unlikely ever to repay them in full and many will never repay a penny. Especially if they live in Eastern Europe, many of them are unlikely to earn as much as £21,000 a year, and some will just disappear. Many English students who emigrate to other countries following graduation are also unlikely to repay all or part of their loans. In short, a scheme designed, among other things, to reduce the government's fiscal deficit is all but certain to have the opposite effect.

No party or government can avoid the issue of immigration. It ranks high on millions of British voters' personal agendas, and net migration into the UK in recent decades has reached record levels. The Conservative manifesto for the 2010 election promised that a Tory government would "take steps to take net migration back to the levels of the 1990s – tens of thousands a year, not hundreds of thousands" – a pledge echoed somewhat more vaguely in the Conservative–Liberal Democrat *Coalition programme for government*.[11] After the election, the new prime minister announced that the government's target was to reduce net inward migration to below 100,000 a year by 2015. That target was never going to be easy to meet because nearly half of all immigrants are either EU nationals, entitled to live and work in the UK, or else returning British citizens. A smaller but still substantial proportion comprises family members who are entitled to join immigrants already in the UK. That means that considerably less than half of all of inward migration can be tackled by means of tougher restrictions.

The Home Office, responsible for immigration, was thus left with only two real options: to impose strict limitations on the number of people coming from outside the EU to work in Britain and to impose even stricter limitations on the larger number of people wanting to come to the UK to study. It did both. In 2011 ministers imposed a cap of roughly twenty-two thousand on the numbers coming to the UK to work. As was already the case, visas would be granted only to those whose skills or wealth made it likely that they would make a positive contribution to Britain's economy. Ministers also made it much harder for non-EU students to come to Britain (where many of them, even if they actually studied, also found jobs and subsequently stayed on). In future, all overseas would-be students would be subject to far more stringent visa requirements, and universities and colleges would have to monitor their attendance and progress far more closely. The new rules also made it harder for overseas students to work while studying.

So far at least, the changes have not been a success. They have failed to reduce inward migration on anything like the scale promised, and they have caused all manner of collateral damage. Overall immigration, including from EU countries, fell in the early 2010s, but not by nearly enough to enable the government to achieve its 2015 target. The prime minister acknowledged as much in a radio interview, redefining substantial cuts in immigration as more "an ambition" than a policy.[12] As fewer non-EU students applied to study in the UK, many universities and colleges suffered. So did businesses, which complained that harsh visa requirements and bureaucratic delays made it difficult, often impossible, to recruit the

skilled foreign staff they badly needed. Small and medium-sized enterprises, including start-up technology firms, were especially hard hit. *The
Economist* in 2012 condemned the coalition's immigration controls as
"The Tories' barmiest policy" and urged the government to speed up and
simplify the whole visa system and to make it easier for overseas students
to study – and, if they needed to, to work while they studied – at Britain's
leading universities. *The Economist* concluded:

> As emerging countries grow, the enthusiasm of young, talented
> foreigners to get an education at a British university or to sell their
> wares to Britain's relatively prosperous consumers is likely to dimin-
> ish. For now, though, the country's global popularity gives it a huge
> advantage, which the government is squandering. The world is a
> competitive place. Britain is trying to run with its shoelaces tied
> together.[13]

It is hard to believe that future generations will not judge the Cameron
government's immigration policies – indeed its immigration "ambition" –
to have been a significant blunder.

Infinitely less serious as blunders go, but blunders nevertheless, were
a pair of tax changes announced by George Osborne, the chancellor, in
his 2012 budget. Both resulted from a glorious combination of cultural
and operational disconnect. One was immediately dubbed the "pasty
tax". It proposed to increase to 20 per cent the rate of VAT levied on all
hot takeaway snacks, such as sausage rolls and pasties, that were baked
on the premises. The proposal suffered from being wholly logical and,
simultaneously, completely preposterous. Who was to decide, everyone
wondered, and how were they to decide, whether a sausage roll or pasty
was or was not "hot"? The question was unanswerable. People wanted
to know whether all the checkout staff in supermarkets were supposed
to be equipped with thermometers. The *Sun* newspaper ran a "Let them
eat cold pasty" campaign.[14] At the same time, the chancellor drew fire for
proposing to maintain the zero rate of VAT on the purchase of residential
caravans but to impose the top VAT rate of 20 per cent on caravans used
for holidays. That tax was widely derided as a "caravan tax" and would, it
was claimed, lead to more than four thousand redundancies in the caravan

industry. Ministers rapidly rescinded both measures. No harm was done – except to Osborne's and the government's reputations.

The coalition government, like its Labour predecessors, was keen on outsourcing. Like Labour, it was prejudiced in favour of the private sector and against the public. Like Labour, too, it was often ill-informed and gullible in negotiating and managing contracts with private-sector companies. The coalition believed that much of the work currently done by civil servants and others employed directly by the state should be contracted out to private-sector organisations. Unfortunately, the firms to which work was outsourced sometimes proved venal, incompetent or both. It was not clear that they were providing a cheaper service, let alone a better service, than the government or local authorities would have done. The coalition government had particular problems with a firm called A4E. That firm had worked for the previous Labour government under its Pathways to Work programme. It then became one of the biggest contractors under the coalition's welfare-to-work Work Programme. A4E failed by wide margins to meet its targets under both schemes. The chair of the Public Accounts Committee complained that its record under Pathways to Work had been so "abysmal" that it should never have been awarded a Work Programme contract in the first place.[15] In addition, four A4E employees were arrested on suspicion of fraud, and a former A4E auditor told the Public Accounts Committee he had seen evidence at the company of "unethical culture" and "systematic fraud".[16] In the end, Chris Grayling, the then employment minister, terminated one of A4E's contracts, but the company held onto eleven others, all of them worth more than the one it lost.

Another company profiting from outsourcing was a French-owned firm called Atos Healthcare. It came under similar fire. It was contracted by the Department for Work and Pensions to conduct disability assessments. Witnesses claimed that its call centres were often impenetrable, that appointments were systematically overbooked and that Atos's assessment centres were sometimes inaccessible to the very people who were supposed to be assessed.[17] In January 2013 Michael Meacher, the same MP who had predicted the mis-selling of personal pensions during the 1980s, initiated a debate in the House of Commons, referring to what he called "the dysfunctional and malfunctioning of Atos assessments".[18] He cited the case of one man suffering from epilepsy whom Atos assessed as being fit for work and whose benefits, since he had not returned to work, had been reduced. Partly as a consequence, he died three months later, and it was only after his death, too late, that the department wrote to say it had made a mistake and that his benefits would be restored. Allegations of that sort abounded and still do. Improvements to the assessment system, in so far as they have come at all, have been very slow to come.

The Cameron government will almost certainly get its way over same-sex marriages: on 5 February 2013 the House of Commons voted in favour of such marriages by 400 votes to 175, a vote substantially repeated by the Lords in June. Indeed, the introduction of same-sex marriages, whether desirable or undesirable, may eventually be remembered as one of the most significant developments of the Cameron era. But ministers have certainly blundered along the way. In his speech to the 2011 Conservative party conference, David Cameron announced, to the surprise and dismay of many Conservative activists (and his mother), that he was now in favour of same-sex marriage. "I don't support gay marriage despite being a Conservative", he declared. "I support gay marriage because I'm a Conservative."[19] Soon afterwards the government launched a consultation document that elicited the largest number of responses any such document had ever received. A large majority were in favour. However, the Church of England and the Roman Catholic Church continued to make clear their opposition. The government persisted, knowing that it had broad public support while at the same time insisting that no religious organisation would be put under any obligation to conduct same-sex marriages. But then, in a strange twist, Maria Miller, the Conservative culture secretary, announced in the House of Commons not merely that the Church of England and the Church of Wales would not be obliged to conduct gay marriages but that they – and apparently the clergy in both denominations – would be forbidden by law from doing so. In what appeared to be a non sequitur, she told MPs: "Because the Churches of England and Wales have explicitly stated that they do not wish to conduct same-sex marriage, the legislation will explicitly state that it would be illegal for the Churches of England and Wales to marry same-sex couples."[20] Gay men and women who happened to be Anglicans were thus to be discriminated against. However, the government subsequently changed course, including in its proposed legislation provisions allowing the two Churches, if they wished, to opt in to conducting same-sex marriages at some time in the future. Partly as a result, the government's Marriage (Same Sex Couples) Bill evolved into one of hideous complexity.[21]

In June 2013 the government seemed almost certain to get its way over removing from the country the militant Muslim cleric Abu Qatada; but, again, it blundered conspicuously along the way. Under intense media pressure, notably from the *Daily Mail*, Theresa May, the home secretary, repeatedly gave the impression that Qatada's deportation to Jordan was imminent when it was not and on several occasions pursued legal actions that appeared to have – and turned out to have – almost no chance of success. In April 2012 May told the House of Commons that assurances she had received from the Jordanian government meant "that we can soon put Qatada on a plane and get him out of the country for good".[22] But more than a year later Qatada was still in the country (although also in prison). In November 2012 Britain's Special Immigration Appeals Tribunal ruled that Qatada could not be deported legally because there was still a chance that, if the Jordanian authorities tried him on terrorist charges, they might use against him evidence that had been obtained by torture. May at once appealed to the Court of Appeal, but lost, with the court refusing her permission to appeal further to the Supreme Court. No outsider can know how far her repeated legal setbacks were the result of bad advice she was receiving from her advisers and how far she was choosing to ignore their advice.[23] But, although almost everyone in the country, including the Labour opposition, wanted to see Qatada expelled from the UK, a large proportion of May's moves had a distinctly symbolic, public-relations air about them.

Episodes like those just described are not the only blunders that the Cameron government has been guilty of. In some cases, coalition ministers have had the courage – more than ministers in many previous govern-ments – to perform U-turns when they realised they were heading in the wrong direction; but perhaps they should not have been heading in that direction in the first place. In 2010 the Ministry of Defence announced that it would pay to reconfigure one of the two aircraft carriers ordered by the previous government in order to enable it to carry a new type of aircraft;

but then in 2012 it reversed itself, cancelled the reconfiguration and said it would revert to ordering the somewhat older type of aircraft that the previous government had had in mind. Estimates of how much this change of mind cost vary between £100 million and £250 million. The House of Commons Defence Committee applauded the government's U-turn but condemned the original 2010 decision as having been "rushed and based upon incomplete and inaccurate policy development ... without the MoD understanding how the change could be implemented." It described the decision as "one of the ... most spectacular examples of the procurement process getting it wrong".[24]

Also in 2010 – ministers that year were in a tremendous hurry – Caroline Spelman, then the environment secretary, announced government plans to raise £5 billion by selling off the Forestry Commission's substantial assets. She and her colleagues also raised doubts about the future of the Forestry Commission itself. But howls of protest from environmentalists and others induced the government to abandon the project. "I'm sorry", Spelman told the House of Commons in a rare moment of ministerial candour, "we've got this one wrong."[25] The forests are still publicly owned. The Forestry Commission still exists.

On a more recent occasion, Michael Gove – a self-professed "man in a hurry" – was equally candid if less apologetic. In September 2012 Gove as education minister for England announced his intention to replace the existing examinations for sixteen-year-olds with a new set of exams that would lead to the award of an English Baccalaureate Certificate, the EBacc. In addition, the existing examination boards were to be replaced by single boards that would oversee the examinations in each of a range of core subjects. But Gove's project ran into a blizzard of opposition. The teaching unions – the usual suspects – objected, but so did the Liberal Democrats (who appear never to have been consulted), Ofqual, the relevant regulatory agency (whose chief executive wrote to Gove warning him that the EBacc might "exceed what is realistically achievable through a single assessment"), the House of Commons Education Committee (which expressed concern that the government was "trying to do too much, too fast") and civil servants in his own department (who were afraid that the single-examiners aspect of the project might fall foul of European competition policy).[26] Not wanting to be snowed under, Gove slammed on the brakes, acknowledging to MPs in February 2013 that his EBacc scheme was clearly "one reform too many at this time".[27] Were Gove's ministerial colleagues aware in advance – was the prime minister aware in advance – of what Gove was up to? Seemingly not.

Famously, the world's credit-rating agencies from time to time put firms and even whole governments on "negative watch", with the result that their credit worthiness begins to be called into question. It is far too early to condemn as demonstrable blunders a number of the present government's initiatives: some or all of them may turn out to have been a great success. Nevertheless, a range of them deserve to be put on negative watch for now. They bear the hallmarks of blunders-in-waiting.

At present, the most conspicuous example is the business of introducing the Universal Credit, which shows every sign of being as shambolic as the introduction of Gordon Brown's much-vaunted (at least by him) tax credits during the 1990s. The principle underlying the new credit may be sound, but no policy is better than the capacity of the government of the day and its agents to deliver it. As we saw at the end of Chapter 10, Iain Duncan Smith initially moved slowly and circumspectly to introduce the Universal Credit. He took his time and, unlike Brown, made sure that his new credit was piloted. But by the spring of 2013 it was clear that all was not well. Initially, ministers planned to conduct four pilot schemes, all in the North West of England, but after a few months the four were whittled down to one, and even that one covered only a tiny fraction of those who would soon be able to claim the new credit. The others would come later. Managers of Duncan Smith's ambitious project came and went; the rollout of the credit, scheduled to take place in October 2013, was said to be on the Treasury's watchdog list of projects in crisis. Rumours, never convincingly denied, abounded to the effect that work on the project's essential IT underpinning was proceeding haltingly with innumerable glitches. In the summer of 2013 the chances of Iain Duncan Smith's performance improving significantly on that of Gordon Brown a decade earlier did not look good.

Needless to say, there are a number of other initiatives undertaken by the present government that should probably be put on negative watch. We have already referred to the Lansley reforms to the NHS in England, which may in time turn out to have been a major blunder. David Cameron, in a speech in January 2013, undertook to renegotiate the terms of Britain's membership of the European Union by 2017 and then in that year to hold an in-or-out referendum on the issue. Long before 2017, that pledge in itself may – or may not – impact negatively on the level of investment in the British economy and on Britain's influence in Europe and the wider world. Michael Gove's traditionalist reforms to the English schools curriculum have encountered intense opposition and seem unlikely on the face of it to survive his time in office for long. In the aftermath of George Osborne's 2013 budget, the House of Commons Treasury Committee expressed grave doubts about the wisdom of the chancellor's Help to Buy scheme for house-buyers, in particular the guarantees it offered to mortgage lenders. The government, the committee pointed out, was now "an active player in the mortgage market", with "a financial interest in maintaining house prices to limit losses to the taxpayer."[28] But the very existence of the guarantee might make mortgage lenders readier than in the past to foreclose on mortgages, thereby reducing house prices and leading to the Treasury facing large losses. Shades, possibly, of Metronet.

Another item to add to the list is a move lauded by its proponents among ministers as abolishing "the spare bedroom subsidy" and derided by its opponents as "a bedroom tax". Critics claim that forcing tenants in social housing to choose between losing benefits on account of having spare accommodation in their flat or house or else moving to somewhere else will not only cause great personal hardship but, more to the point, will in the end actually cost the government money instead of saving it. The critics claim that the increase in the total amount of state benefits paid out as a result of individuals and families having to move – or else becoming homeless – will actually push up the cost of the change to the exchequer instead of pushing it down. Finally (for now), there is the case of High Speed Rail 2 (HS2), condemned in advance by the National Audit Office as being unlikely to provide good value for taxpayers or even, as promised, to help regenerate the Midlands and the North of England.[29] If, of course, HS2 is ever built in whole or in part, the ministers responsible will long since have moved on. Once it exists, HS2 will simply exist, taken for granted, like France's TGV. No one will therefore bother to assess whether or not it was ever sensible and cost-effective – and whether the ministers responsible a generation earlier did or did not blunder.

The one indubitable domestic success of David Cameron's first three years in office was the 2012 London Olympic and Paralympic Games. That enterprise bore a striking resemblance to the introduction of decimal currency in the UK almost exactly forty years before. The bid to hold the games in London went ahead with the support of both the prime minister and the leader of the opposition. Its champions at the International Olympic Committee meeting in Singapore that finally chose the site were Tony Blair, the Labour prime minister, and Lord Coe, a Conservative peer and aide to the former Conservative leader, Iain Duncan Smith. Planning for the Games began years in advance. At least as much attention was paid to implementation as to policy. Co-operation between the public and private sectors was close. The project was well-managed throughout. Cultural connect actually displaced cultural disconnect. Only one thing went wrong. A private security firm, G4S, failed to fulfil its contract to provide adequate numbers of properly trained security staff. Armed-services personnel had to make do instead. They performed magnificently.

Few, however, would claim that the Cameron government's overall performance has been magnificent so far, save possibly in the field of macroeconomic policy, where history will judge. As we said at the beginning of this Postscript, the Cameron government thus far appears to have been no less blunder-prone than its predecessors and may possibly turn out to be the most blunder-prone government of modern times. It is certainly ragged around the edges; it often appears ragged at the centre. Indeed, its performance so far underlines almost all the weaknesses inherent in the British system of government that we have been describing throughout this book. The fiscal deficit still persists. So does the British system's deficit of deliberation.

Notes

All the reports by House of Commons (HC) select committees listed below were published by the Stationery Office or its predecessor organisation, Her Majesty's Stationery Office, during the period of the parliamentary session indicated (for example, 'HC 2006–07'). House of Commons debates as recorded in Hansard are cited as "HC *Deb*".

Chapter 1: Blunders, judgement calls and institutions

1   Madison's remarks appear in *Federalist 62*. The *Federalist Papers* are currently available in many editions, all with the same essay numbering.
2   During the McCarthy period in the United States, Walter Reuther offered his duck test as a possible way of identifying someone who was a Communist or might have Communist affiliations. Quoted in Antony Jay, ed., *The Oxford Dictionary of Political Quotations* (Oxford: Oxford University Press, 1996), p. 303.

Chapter 2: An array of successes

1   D. R. Thorpe, *Supermac: The Life of Harold Macmillan* (London: Chatto & Windus, 2010), p. 281.
2   Anne Perkins, *Red Queen: The Authorized Biography of Barbara Castle* (London: Macmillan, 2003), p. 216.
3   Barbara Castle, *Fighting All the Way* (London: Macmillan, 1993), p. 376.
4   HC *Deb* 15 January 1980, col. 1443.
5   She was visiting Japan on her way to China. "While in Japan", she writes, "I met the President of Nissan, whose company was considering at that

time whether to go ahead with the construction of the plant it eventually built in Sunderland. We had a useful talk, though I could not at this stage draw from him any explicit commitment." She devotes only three more sentences to the subject, saying nothing about the subsequent negotiations and suggesting that an investment by Nissan in Britain would be as good for Japan as for the UK. See Margaret Thatcher, *The Downing Street Years* (London: HarperCollins, 1993), pp. 496–7.

6   Norman Tebbit, *Upwardly Mobile* (London: Weidenfeld & Nicolson, 1988), p. 188.

7   Ibid., p. 182.

8   John Major, *The Autobiography* (London: HarperCollins, 1999), p. 245.

9   HC *Deb* 22 July 1991, col. 767.

10   Ibid.

11   Public Services Select Committee, *The Citizen's Charter* (HC 1996–97, 78-I), para. 92.

12   HC *Deb* 18 June 1998, col. 507.

13   Quoted in *The Times*, 27 April 2005.

14   Transcript of "Welcome to Smokefree Britain" press conference, Department of Health, 1 July 2007.

15   Deirdre Hine, *The 2009 Influenza Pandemic: An Independent Review of the UK Response to the 2009 Influenza Pandemic*, July 2010, p. 1. The review was jointly commissioned by the health ministers of England, Scotland, Wales and Northern Ireland.

16   Quoted in Andrew Ross Sorkin, *Too Big to Fail: The Inside Story of How Wall Street and Washington Fought to Save the Financial System – and Themselves* (New York: Penguin, 2009), p. 514. Unfortunately, Brown in the House of Commons somewhat marred his otherwise world-class performance when, instead of saying that his government had saved the world's banks, he said in a slip of the tongue, "We have saved the world" (HC *Deb* 10 December 2008, col. 527). See also William Keegan, *"Saving the World"? Gordon Brown Reconsidered* (London: Searching Finance, 2012).

Chapter 3: Blunders past and present

1   Kenneth O. Morgan, *Labour in Power 1945–1951* (Oxford: Clarendon Press, 1984), pp. 332–3.

2   Keith Kyle, *Suez* (London: Weidenfeld & Nicolson, 1991), p. 532.

3   Robert Taylor, "The Heath government and industrial relations: myth and reality", in Stuart Hall and Antony Seldon, eds, *The Heath Government 1970–74: A Reappraisal* (London: Longman, 1996), p. 176.

4   Public Accounts Committee (HC 1975–76, 584), p. 675.

5   Quoted in *Daily Telegraph*, 20 May 1985.

6   HC *Deb* 17 January 1989, col. 150.

7   Lord Justice Taylor, *The Hillsborough Stadium Disaster (15 April 1989): Inquiry by Rt. Hon. Lord Justice Taylor, Final Report*, Cm 962 (London: Her Majesty's Stationery Office, 1990), p. 3.

8   Ibid., p. 75.

9   HC *Deb* 22 May 1991, col. 263.

10 Quoted in Philip Johnston, *Bad Laws* (London: Constable, 2010), p. 64.

11 Johnston, *Bad Laws*, p. 66. Figures published by the House of Commons Library in 2010 showed that during the decade between 1998 and 2008 the number of individuals prosecuted under the terms of the Dangerous Dogs Act 1991 increased by nearly two-thirds, from 764 to 1247, and the number of individuals convicted more than doubled, from 406 to 889. The police attributed the increase to a rise in the number of young men buying dangerous dogs as status symbols and to use as weapons. See Elena Ares, *Dangerous Dogs*, House of Commons Library Standard Note SN/SC/4348, 2 June 2010, p. 5. As recently as February 2013, the Commons Environment, Food and Rural Affairs Committee published a report drawing attention to the costs to the NHS of treating severe dog-attack injuries and asserting flatly that "current dangerous dog laws have comprehensively failed to tackle irresponsible dog ownership". See *Dog Control and Welfare* (HC 2012–13, 575-I), p. 3. Shortly after the report was published, four out-of-control dogs mauled to death a teenage girl, Jade Anderson, in Manchester.

12 Interviewed on BBC Radio 4's *Today* programme, 10 March 1999.

13 HC *Deb* 27 March 2007, col. 1384.

14 HC *Deb* 30 April 2007, col.1280.

Chapter 4: A tax on heads

1   The full story of the poll tax is complicated, but fortunately it has already been well told, by David Butler, Andrew Adonis and Tony Travers in their

aptly titled *Failure in British Government: The Politics of the Poll Tax* (Oxford: Oxford University Press, 1994). Our account supplements and glosses theirs, but in only a few minor respects. Theirs is the definitive history, and we have drawn heavily upon it. See also Michael Crick and Adrian Van Klaveren, "Mrs Thatcher's Greatest Blunder", *Contemporary Record* 5:3 (1991) 397–416 and Christopher Foster, *British Government in Crisis, or, The Third English Revolution* (Oxford: Hart, 2005), ch. 8.

2   F. W. S. Craig, *British General Election Manifestos 1959–1987* (Aldershot, Hants: Dartmouth, 1990), p. 224.

3   Speech in Romford, 3 October 1974 (Conservative Party Archive CCOPR GE149/74).

4   Quoted in Butler *et al.*, *Failure in British Government*, p. 34.

5   Ibid., p. 44.

6   In *Failure in British Government*, Butler *et al.* write (pp. 52–3): "It is hard to exaggerate the political potency of the 'little old ladies' to the poll tax debate. As a beleaguered minority they excited the anguish of everyone involved in the review; and as an image in the minds of Tory politicians, they usurped rational thinking on the subject of the pros and cons of different taxes and the capacity of rebates to iron out flagrant anomalies. Almost every Tory politician – and several officials – we encountered invoked for us the spectre of the widow (always a widow, usually aged) living next door to the family of father and several earning sons (always sons, often strapping)."

7   Quoted in Butler *et al.*, *Failure in British Government*, p. 47.

8   C. D. Foster, R. A. Jackman and M. Perlman, *Local Government Finance in a Unitary State* (London: George Allen & Unwin, 1980), esp. p. 222.

9   At least one person involved in the discussions leading up to the adoption of a flat-rate poll tax hoped – indeed assumed – that the poll tax would eventually, perhaps quite quickly, morph into a local income tax, with most individuals paying something towards the costs of local government but with the actual amounts collected determined in part by people's ability to pay. In retrospect, he wished he had made the case for a local income tax openly instead of trying, in effect, to introduce one by the back door.

10   Butler *et al.*, *Failure in British Government*, p. 73.

11   Quoted in Kenneth Baker, *The Turbulent Years: My Life in Politics* (London: Faber and Faber, 1993), p. 122.

12 Ibid.

13 Quoted in Butler *et al.*, *Failure in British Government*, p. 32.

14 L. H. Hoffmann, *Local Government Finance*, memorandum marked "Confidential", March 1985, para. 2.3.3. We are grateful to Lord Hoffmann for lending us his copy of this document.

15 Nigel Lawson, *The View from No. 11: Memoirs of a Tory Radical* (London: Bantam Press, 1992), pp. 561, 562.

16 Ibid., p. 572.

17 Ibid., p. 574.

18 Butler *et al.*, *Failure in British Government*, p. 85.

19 Steve Norris, then the MP for Oxford East, quoted in Butler *et al.*, *Failure in British Government*, p. 101.

20 Department of the Environment, *Paying for Local Government*, Cmnd 9714 (London: Her Majesty's Stationery Office, 1986), p. 76.

21 Craig, *British General Election Manifestos*, p. 448.

22 Butler *et al.*, *Failure in British Government*, p. 79.

23 *The Times*, etc. quoted in Butler *et al.*, *Failure in British Government*, pp. 93–4.

24 Eric Cockeram, MP for Ludlow, and Keith Hampson, MP for Leeds North West, speaking in the House of Commons on 28 January 1986 and quoted in Butler *et al.*, *Failure in British Government*, pp. 94–5.

25 Margaret Thatcher, *The Downing Street Years* (London: HarperCollins, 1993), p. 652.

26 See the account in Butler *et al.*, *Failure in British Government*, pp. 119–20.

27 Butler *et al.*, *Failure in British Government*, pp. 116–7.

28 Thatcher quoted in Nicholas Ridley, *'My Style of Government': The Thatcher Years* (London: Hutchinson, 1991), p. 129. Ridley adds: "I remember her relief sitting next to me on the bench when the teller announced the result of the Division."

29 Baker describes his efforts to limit the impact of the tax in *The Turbulent Years*, pp. 127–31. The relevant pages are headed "The Fatal Mistakes of 1987 and 1988".

30 HL *Deb* 9 May 1988, col. 840.

31 Baker, *Turbulent Years*, p. 129.

32 HC *Deb* 16 December 1987, col. 1141.

33 Quoted in Butler *et al.*, *Failure in British Government*, p. 87.

34 Tony Benn, *The End of an Era: Diaries 1980–90* (London: Hutchinson, 1992), pp. 585–6.

35 Butler *et al.*, *Failure in British Government*, p. 125.

36 Ibid., p. 265.

37 Quoted in Butler *et al.*, *Failure in British Government*, p. 150.

38 Chris Patten, *Not Quite the Diplomat: Home Truths about Foreign Affairs* (London: Allen Lane, 2005), p. 21.

Chapter 5: Pensions mis-sold

1   SERPS was meant to act as a state-supported top-up to the basic state retirement pension, which for long had generally been regarded as inadequate. It was intended to cover primarily employees who were not enrolled in a satisfactory occupational pension scheme. Employers, employees and the state all contributed to SERPS, with the size of an individual's pension under the scheme related to his or her previous earnings. Employers who operated satisfactory occupational schemes could contract their employees out of SERPS.

2   Nigel Vinson and Philip Chappell, *Personal and Portable Pensions for All* (London: Centre for Policy Studies, 1983), p. 1.

3   HC *Deb* 16 July 1984, cols 25 (Meacher), 27 (Fowler).

4   HC *Deb*, Standing Committee B, 4 February 1986, cols 4–5.

5   HC *Deb*, Standing Committee B, 4 February 1986, col. 23.

6   HC *Deb*, Standing Committee B, 6 February 1986, col. 51.

7   HC *Deb*, Standing Committee B, 13 February 1986, cols 128–9.

8   *Observer*, 16 October 1988. See also Julia Black and Richard Nobles, "Personal Pensions Misselling: The Causes and Lessons of Regulatory Failure", *Modern Law Review* 61 (1998), p. 796.

9   *Social Security Bill 1986: Report by the Government Actuary on the Financial Effects of the Bill on the National Insurance Fund*, Cmnd 9711 (London: Her Majesty's Stationery Office, 1986), para. 22. The Government Actuary at the time was Sir Edward Johnston.

10 Black and Nobles, "Personal Pensions Misselling", p. 793.

11 Andrew Marr, *Ruling Britannia: The Failure and Future of British Democracy* (London: Michael Joseph, 1995), p. 149. See also Marr's savage critique in the *Independent*, 23 June 1994, "Who is to blame for these useless pensions?"

12 *Observer*, 8 May 1994.

13 Department of Health and Social Security, *Reform of Social Security*, Vol. 2, Cmnd 9518 (London: Her Majesty's Stationery Office, 1985), paras 1.58, 1.59.

14 HC *Deb* 28 January 1986, col. 821.

15 HC *Deb*, Standing Committee B, 4 February 1986, col. 27.

16 Black and Nobles, "Personal Pensions Misselling", p. 789.

17 Quoted in Black and Nobles, "Personal Pensions Misselling", p. 809.

18 HL *Deb* 11 July 1986, col. 621.

Chapter 6: Support for children – or taxpayers?

1   HC *Deb* 29 October 1990, col. 729.

2   Ibid.

3   "Absent fathers face higher child payments", *Guardian*, 30 December 1992.

4   House of Commons Library, *Child Support*, Research Paper 94/20, 31 January 1994, pp. 13, 19.

5   Social Security Committee, *The Operation of the Child Support Act: Proposals for Change* (HC 1993–94, 470), p. xi, para. 21.

6   *Observer*, 27 July 1997.

7   Parliamentary Commissioner for Administration, *Investigations of Complaints Against the Child Support Agency* (HC 1994–95, 135). See also "Ombudsman censures CSA failures", *Guardian*, 19 January 1995.

8   Ernie W. Hazlewood, *Annual Report of the Chief Child Support Officer 1994–95* (London: Her Majesty's Stationery Office, 1995).

9   Letter from the chief executive of the Child Support Agency, Ros Hepplewhite, to the chairman of the House of Commons Social Security Committee, published in Social Security Committee, *The Operation of the Child Support Act* (HC 1993–94, 470-IV).

10 Child Support Agency, *The First Two Years*, Annual Report for 1993–94 and Business Plan for 1995–96 (London: Her Majesty's Stationery Office, 1994). See also David Brindle, "Four in ten assessments are wrong", *Guardian*, 27 October 1994.

11 Anthony Bevins, "Child agency hit as savings fall far short of target", *Observer*, 3 April 1994, quoting a Treasury supply estimate presented to the House of Commons.

12 Public Accounts Committee, *Child Support Agency: Client Funds and Accounts 1996–97* (HC 1997 98, 313).

13 Chris Mullin, *A Walk-on Part: Diaries 1994–1999* (London: Profile, 2011), p. 189.

14 Department for Work and Pensions press release quoted in *Guardian*, 27 July 2001.

15 Work and Pensions Select Committee, *The Performance of the Child Support Agency* (HC 2004–05, 44-I), p. 61.

16 HC *Deb* 16 November 2005, col. 964.

17 *Recovering Child Support: Routes to Responsibility*, Sir David Henshaw's Report to the Secretary of State for Work and Pensions, Cm 6894 (London: Stationery Office, 2006), pp. 1, 4.

Chapter 7: Britain exits the ERM

1 Margaret Thatcher, *The Downing Street Years* (London: HarperCollins, 1993), p. 726. Much the best and fullest account of Britain's entry into, and then exit from, the ERM is Philip Stephens, *Politics and the Pound: The Tories, the Economy and Europe* (London: Papermac, 1997). See also Helen Thompson, *The British Conservative Government and the European Exchange Rate Mechanism, 1979–1994* (London: Routledge, 1996).

2 "ERM and the Tarnished Scenario", *Observer*, 14 October 1990. When Britain's entry into the ERM, and the rate at which it entered, was debated in the House of Commons in October 1990, a number of MPs – most of them critics of Britain's European Community membership – voiced doubts about whether the DM2.95 rate was appropriate. Ron Leighton (Labour, Newham North East) was quite clear: "It is always dangerous to prophesy, but I guarantee that the policy will fail. It will not be possible to sustain the exchange rate of the pound at DM2.95." See HC *Deb* 23 October 1990, cols 195–291, esp. col. 261.

3 Stephens, *Politics and the Pound*, pp. 246–7.

4 HM Treasury (anonymous official), *The UK's Membership of the ERM* (21 December 1993), p. B4.

5 John Major, *The Autobiography* (London: HarperCollins, 1999), p. 318. See also the account in Sarah Hogg and Jonathan Hill, *Too Close to Call:*

Power and Politics – John Major in No. 10 (London: Little, Brown, 1995), pp. 187–8.

6 John Williamson, "Planned FEERs and the ERM", *National Institute Economic Review* 137:1 (1991), p. 50.

7 Stephens, *Politics and the Pound*, p. 41; see also p. 26.

8 Kenneth Baker, *The Turbulent Years: My Life in Politics* (London: Faber and Faber, 1993), p. 370.

9 Stephens, *Politics and the Pound*, p. xvi.

10 Sir Samuel Brittan quoted in Alan Budd, *Black Wednesday: A Re-examination of Britain's Experience in the Exchange Rate Mechanism* (London: Institute of Economic Affairs, 2005), p. 60.

11 Stephens, *Politics and the Pound*, p. 222.

12 Major, *Autobiography*, p. 315. See also Anthony Seldon with Lewis Baston, *Major – A Political Life* (London: Weidenfeld & Nicolson, 1997), p. 297.

13 Douglas Hurd, *Memoirs* (London: Little, Brown, 2003), p. 425.

14 Kenneth Clarke quoted in Hurd, *Memoirs*, p. 425.

15 Michael Heseltine, *Life in the Jungle: My Autobiography* (London: Hodder & Stoughton, 2000), p. 431.

16 Norman Lamont, *In Office* (London: Little, Brown, 1999), p. 226. See also Stephens, *Politics and the Pound*, pp. 208–9, and the somewhat different impression left by Major, *Autobiography*, pp. 317–8, where he says, "We had looked over the precipice and decided against jumping."

17 HM Treasury, *UK's Membership of the ERM*, p. B30. See also Stephens, *Politics and the Pound*, pp. 222, 227.

18 Howe quoted in Lombard Street Research, *The Turning Point: Black Wednesday and the Rebirth of the British Economy*, Symposium Transcript, 14 November 2007, pp. 4, 5–6.

19 Brittan quoted in Lombard Street Research, *Turning Point*, p. 28.

20 Stephens, *Politics and the Pound*, p. 214.

21 Ibid., pp. 236–7. Major in his *Autobiography*, p. 326, says that he gave the Scottish CBI speech against the advice of Sarah Hogg ("to Sarah's dismay, I went for broke") and notes wryly: "Events were making a dissembler of me. I had been discussing suspending our membership of the ERM, but to protect against market damage I was nailing my reputation firmly to staying within the mechanism. It was an irony not lost on me as I delivered the speech."

22 Quoted in Stephens, *Politics and the Pound*, p. 236.

23 Lamont, *In Office*, p. 213.

24 Stephens, *Politics and the Pound*, p. 214.

25 Quoted in Stephens, *Politics and the Pound*, p. 244.

26 Major, *Autobiography*, p. 329.

27 Quoted in Stephens, *Politics and the Pound*, p. 254.

Chapter 8: "Cool Britannia"

1   National Audit Office, *The Millennium Dome*, Report of the Comptroller and Auditor General, HC 936 (London: Stationery Office, 2000), p. 39.

2   National Audit Office, *Millennium Dome*, p. 7.

3   "Cool Britannia" was one of those phrases that caught on briefly, but only briefly. It was used by marketing people to market the UK and by the Labour party to market itself. Some of New Labour's spin doctors liked to project the idea that the party under Tony Blair was itself cool. Those who used the phrase exploited its association with the Spice Girls, fashionable Brit Art and popular Brit Pop bands such as Oasis (reputedly one of Blair's favourites).

4   Alastair Campbell, *The Alastair Campbell Diaries*, Vol. 2, *Power and the People 1997–1999* (London: Hutchinson, 2011), p. 63.

5   Memorandum by the Department for Culture, Media and Sport (HC 340-II 1997–98), p. 107.

6   Culture, Media and Sport Select Committee, *The Millennium Dome* (HC 1997–98, 340-I), pp. 8–9.

7   Blair spoke in the course of another visit to the Dome, an indication of how seriously he took the project. The speech was reported under the heading "Dome Will Be Ready – Blair" in BBC News Online, 19 December 1999.

8   According to a MORI survey of visitors to the Dome conducted in April 2000, 84 per cent were "satisfied" with their visit, 77 per cent would recommend a visit to the Dome to their friends and 70 per cent thought their visit had been "good value for money". See the IPSOS/MORI online archive for 28 April 2000.

Chapter 9: The great training robbery

1   *The Times Guide to the House of Commons May 1997* (London: Times Books, 1997), p. 312.

2   Training and Enterprise Councils were local bodies established in the early 1990s to administer publicly funded training programmes and to promote training and business enterprise in association with other local organisations. They were abolished in 2001.

3   Public Accounts Committee, *Individual Learning Accounts*, (HC 2002–03, 544), pp. 6–7.

4   Harry Todd, *The ILA Story: Individual Learning Accounts in England – History and Developments*, Department for Education and Skills, July 2004. *The ILA Story*, which is now available but was not published originally, was a study of the setting up and winding down of the individual learning account programme commissioned by the DfES for internal use.

5   Quoted in *Guardian*, 25 August 2001.

6   *Trading Standards Today*, quoted in *Guardian*, 25 August 2001.

7   HC *Deb* 25 October 2001, Written Answers to Questions, col. 327w.

8   HC *Deb* 25 October 2001, Oral Answers to Questions, col. 398. The opposition backbencher who asked for "frankness and candour" was David Cameron. Morris may also have come under pressure from Gordon Brown to obfuscate the apparent scale of fraud – and its role in her closing down of the scheme – in order to limit the political damage the whole episode was causing. See Tom Bower, *Gordon Brown* (London: Harper Perennial, 2005), p. 365.

9   HC *Deb* 6 November 2001, cols 128–9.

10 Quoted in Todd, *ILA Story*, p. 22.

11 Quoted in Todd, *ILA Story*, p. 23.

12 National Audit Office, *Individual Learning Accounts*, HC 1235 (London: Stationery Office, 2002), p. 14.

13 Quoted in Todd, *ILA Story*, p. 23.

14 Public Accounts Committee, *Individual Learning Accounts* (HC 2002–03, 544), p. 5.

15 Education and Skills Select Committee, *Individual Learning Accounts* (HC 2001–02, 561), pp. 33, 14.

16 National Audit Office, *Individual Learning Accounts*, pp. 11, 13–18.

17 According to the National Audit Office report *Individual Learning Accounts* (p. 15), fewer than one in five of all those who took up individual learning accounts lacked any previous qualifications whereas approximately two in five were already qualified at degree-level or above. See also Peter Kingston, "Learning called to account", *Guardian*, 11 September 2001.

Chapter 10: Tax credits and debits

1   William Keegan, *The Prudence of Mr Gordon Brown* (London: John Wiley, 2003), p. 245.

2   Labour's vague manifesto pledge on tax credits is reprinted in *The Times Guide to the House of Commons May 1997* (London: Times Books, 1997), p. 321. For Gordon Brown's budget statement, see HC *Deb* 9 March 1999, cols. 182–4.

3   Tony Blair, *A Journey: My Political Life* (London: Hutchinson, 2010), p. 587.

4   Alastair Campbell, *The Alastair Campbell Diaries*, Vol. 3, *Power and Responsibility* (London: Hutchinson, 2011), p. 666.

5   Andrew Rawnsley, *The End of the Party: The Rise and Fall of New Labour* (London: Viking, 2010), p. 71.

6   HC *Deb* 7 March 2001, col. 302.

7   Tom Bower, *Gordon Brown* (London: Harper Perennial, 2005), p. 234.

8   The speaker was David Ruffley, MP for Bury St Edmunds. See HC *Deb* 10 December 2001, col. 631.

9   Public Accounts Committee, *Inland Revenue: Tax Credits and Tax Debt Management* (HC 2002–03, 332), Ev 2, Q1.

10 HC *Deb* 22 June 2004, col. 791.

11 Quoted in Parliamentary and Health Service Ombudsman, *Tax Credits: Putting Things Right* (HC 2005–06, 124), p. 32.

12 *Guardian*, 11 October 2005.

13 *Guardian*, 28 April 2003.

14 Parliamentary and Health Service Ombudsman, *Tax Credits: Putting Things Right*, p. 21.

15 David Blunkett, *The Blunkett Tapes: My Life in the Bear Pit* (London: Bloomsbury, 2006), pp. 498, 493.

16 Figures calculated from the report published annually by the Office for National Statistics, "Child and Working Tax Credit Statistics Finalised Annual Award Supplement on Payments".

17 Parliamentary and Health Service Ombudsman, *Tax Credits: Getting it Wrong?* (HC 2006–07, 1010), pp. 33–4.

18 Katie Lane and John Wheatley, *Money with your name on it? CAB clients' experience of tax credits*, Citizens Advice with Citizens Advice Scotland, June 2005, pp. 43–44.

19 Parliamentary and Health Service Ombudsman, *Tax Credits: Putting Things Right*, pp. 3, 5–6, 7, 13, 26, and also *Tax Credits: Getting it Wrong?*, pp. 3, 20.

20 Lane and Wheatley, *Money with your name on it?*, p. 2.

21 Treasury Committee, *The Administration of Tax Credits* (HC 2005–06, 811-II), Ev 77, col. 2, Q467.

22 Public Accounts Committee, *Tax Credits and PAYE* (HC 2006–07, 1060-I), p. 5.

23 HC *Deb* 12 July 2007, cols 1591–2.

24 Polly Toynbee and David Walker, *The Verdict: Did Labour Change Britain?* (London: Granta, 2010), p. 206.

25 HC *Deb* 11 November 2011, cols 438–9.

26 David Lammy, *Out of the Ashes: Britain after the Riots* (London: Guardian Books, 2011), pp. 29–30.

Chapter 11: Assets unrecovered

1 Public Accounts Committee, *Assets Recovery Agency* (HC 2006–07, 391), Ev 14, Q125.

2 Cabinet Office Performance and Innovation Unit, *Recovering the Proceeds of Crime*, June 2000.

3 Home Office press notice, "Taking the Profits out of crime", 23 February 2003.

4 Public Accounts Committee, *Assets Recovery Agency*, p. 10.

5 Public Accounts Committee, *Assets Recovery Agency*, Ev 5, Q39.

6 National Audit Office, *The Assets Recovery Agency*, HC 253 (London: Stationery Office, 2007), p. 5.

7 Grant Shapps, *Report into the Underperformance of the Assets Recovery Agency*, memorandum, House of Commons, 12 June 2006. Shapps was interviewed on the same subject on the *Today* programme on BBC Radio 4 two days later and also reported in the *Guardian* on 14 June.

8 National Audit Office, *Assets Recovery Agency*, p. 5.

9 Vernon Coaker, *Government News*, 31 March 2008.

10 http://www.soca.gov.uk/about-soca/how-we-work/asset-recovery, 5 June 2012.

11 Public Accounts Committee, *Assets Recovery Agency* (2006–07, HC 391), Ev 3, Qq15–21.

Chapter 12: Farmers fleeced

1 National Audit Office, *Department for Environment, Food and Rural Affairs, and Rural Payments Agency: The Delays in Administering the 2005 Single Payment Scheme in England*, HC 1631 (London: Stationery Office, 2006), p. 2. See also Margaret Beckett's statement in the House of Commons, HC *Deb*, 12 February 2004, cols 1585–7.

2 Unsurprisingly, Beckett's "bloody livid" phrase was widely quoted. See, for example, Fiona Harvey, "Beckett 'bloody livid' over late payment of agricultural subsidies", *Financial Times*, 22 February 2005.

3 National Audit Office, *Delays in Administering the 2005 Single Payment Scheme*, p. 5.

4 National Audit Office, *Department for Environment, Food and Rural Affairs, and Rural Payments Agency: A Progress Update in Resolving the Difficulties in Administering the Single Payment Scheme in England*, HC 10 (London: Stationery Office, 2007), p. 5.

5 National Audit Office, *A Second Progress Update on the Administration of the Single Payment Scheme by the Rural Payments Agency*, HC 880 (London: Stationery Office, 2009), p. 1.

6 *Report of the Comptroller and Auditor General on the Rural Payments Agency 2009–2010 financial statements*, 15 August 2011, para. 1.

7 Public Accounts Committee, *The Delays in Administering the 2005 Single Payment Scheme in England* (HC 2006–07, 893), p. 7.

8 National Audit Office, *Delays in Administering the 2005 Single Payment Scheme*, p. 4.

9 Ibid.

10 Quoted in National Audit Office, *A Progress Update*, pp. 32, 33.

11 The chairman of the committee was Edward Leigh, MP for Gainsborough. See Public Accounts Committee, *Delays in Administering the 2005 Single Payment Scheme in England*, Ev 1, Q1.

12 Ibid., Ev 25, Q211 (David Curry, MP for Skipton and Ripon).

13 The relevant parliamentary select committee stated bluntly beforehand: "We are … concerned about the capacity of the Rural Payments Agency to deliver the new Single Payment Scheme." See Environment, Food and Rural Affairs Committee, *Implementation of CAP Reform in the UK* (HC 2003–04, 226-I), p. 3 and also pp. 12–13.

14 Quoted in National Audit Office, *A Progress Update*, p. 34.

15 Public Accounts Committee, *A Progress Update in Resolving the Difficulties in Administering the Single Payment Scheme in England* (HC 2007–08, 285), p. 3.

16 National Audit Office, *A Second Progress Update*, p. 5. The NAO condemned the high cost of the innumerable IT upgrades and adaptations and pointed out (p. 6) that the cost of administering each claim in England was £1743 compared with the equivalent figure in Scotland of £285, with no sign that the English figure was coming down.

17 *Report of the Comptroller and Auditor General on the Rural Payments Agency*, 15 August 2011, para. 17.

18 Johnston McNeill appearing before the Public Accounts Committee on 2 July 2007. See Public Accounts Committee, *A Progress Update*, Ev 23, Q200.

19 Environment, Food and Rural Affairs Committee, *The Rural Payments Agency and the Implementation of the Single Payment Scheme* (HC 2006–07, 107-I), p. 52.

Chapter 13: IT – technology and pathology

1   Richard Overy, *Why the Allies Won*, 2nd edn (London: Pimlico, 2006), p. 247.

2   Public Administration Select Committee, *Government and IT – "a recipe for rip-offs" – time for a new approach* (HC 2010–12, 715-I). See also Justine Stephen, James Page, Jerrett Myers, Adrian Brown, David Watson and Ian Magee, *System Error: Fixing the Flaws in Government IT* (London: Institute for Government, 2011).

3   Public Administration Select Committee, *Government and IT*, pp. 3–4.

4   Ibid., p. 48.

5   Public Accounts Committee, *Crown Prosecution Service* (HC 1997–98, 526), p. 2.

6   Sir Michael Partridge quoted in the *Observer*, 7 May 1995.

7   National Audit Office, *The Cancellation of the Benefits Payment Card Project*, HC 857 (London: Stationery Office, 2000), p. 5.

8   For detailed accounts and analyses of early blunders in both the private and the public sectors, see Tony Collins with David Bicknell, *Crash: Ten Easy*

Ways to Avoid a Computer Disaster (London: Simon & Schuster, 1997). If *Crash* had been more widely read by ministers and civil servants as soon as it was published, there might have been fewer crashes. At the very least, people in government would have been alerted to the risks they were running.

9   Public Accounts Committee, *Home Office: The Immigration and Nationality Directorate Casework Programme* (HC 1999–2000, 130), p. 2.

10 National Audit Office, *The Immigration and Nationality Directorate's Casework Programme*, HC 277 (London: Stationery Office, 1999), p. 5.

11 National Audit Office, *Report of the Comptroller and Auditor General on the National Insurance Fund Account 1998–99*, HC 146 (London: Stationery Office, 2000), p. 9.

12 David Davis quoted in *Guardian*, 26 January 1999.

13 Jeff Rooker quoted in *Daily Telegraph*, 2 December 2000.

14 However, by 2003 – that is, three years later – the Passport Agency's IT problems had largely been solved and almost all, 99.5 per cent, of straightforward passport applications were being turned around, as the agency's target demanded, within ten working days. In later years, customer-satisfaction surveys sometimes found the Passport Agency and its successors rated in the same class as such private-sector firms as Amazon, Tesco and Marks and Spencer. It took time, but the agency's IT initiative proved successful in the end.

15 Public Accounts Committee, *New IT Systems for Magistrates' Courts: The Libra Project* (HC 2002–03, 434), p. 4.

16 Civil servant quoted anonymously in National Audit Office, *The National Offender Management Information System*, HC 292 (London: Stationery Office, 2009), p. 22.

17 Ibid., p. 9.

18 Edward Leigh quoted in *Computer Weekly*, 12 March 2009.

19 National Audit Office, *The Failure of the FiReControl Project*, HC 1272 (London: Stationery Office, 2011), p. 4.

20 Ibid., pp. 7, 5.

21 Public Accounts Committee, *The Failure of the FiReControl Project* (HC 2010–12, 1397), p. 5.

22 HC *Deb* 23 October 2006, col. 74 (James Purnell).

23 Quoted in the Wikipedia entry "NHS Connecting for Health" accessed on 10 April 2012.

24 Michael Cross, "Blair's £40bn gamble on IT", *Guardian*, 25 April 2002.

25 Tony Collins, "Major incidents hit NHS national systems", *Computer Weekly*, 19 September 2006.

26 Richard Brooks, "System Failure: How this government is blowing £12.4bn on useless IT for the NHS", *Private Eye*, 2–15 March 2007, No. 1179. Brooks's detailed report is much the fullest – and therefore the most devastating – account of the origins and early years of the NHS National Programme.

27 The witness, Professor Peter Hutton, had previously resigned as the project's clinical leader. See Public Accounts Committee, *Department of Health: The National Programme for IT in the NHS* (HC 2006–07, 390), Ev 9, Q58.

Chapter 14: Down the tubes

1 *The Times Guide to the House of Commons May 1997* (London: Times Books, 1997), pp. 348, 324.

2 William Keegan characterised Brown's views in *The Prudence of Mr Gordon Brown* (London: John Wiley, 2003), p. 270. See also Steve Richards, *Whatever it Takes: The Real Story of Gordon Brown and New Labour* (London: Fourth Estate, 2010), p. 120.

3 Karen Buck, MP for Regent's Park and Kensington North and chair of the London group of Labour MPs, quoted in Christian Wolmar, *Down the Tube: The Battle for London's Underground* (London: Aurum, 2002), p. 138. Wolmar's book was published before the Metronet drama had been fully played out, but it contains a detailed account of the story to that point and sets out clearly the nature of the issues involved along with an analysis of the opinions and interests of the various protagonists. We quote frequently from *Down the Tube* in what follows. Wolmar takes the story further, but also more briefly, in *The Subterranean Railway: How the London Underground was Built and How it Changed the City Forever* (London: Atlantic, 2012), ch. 15.

4 HC *Deb* 20 March 1998, cols. 1542, 1539.

5 Quoted in Wolmar, *Down the Tube*, p. 168.

6 Quoted in Wolmar, *Down the Tube*, p. 156.

7 That view was Wolmar's own: *Down the Tube*, p. 200.

8 Ibid., p. 117.

9   Ibid., pp. 200–1.

10 Bob Kiley, Transport for London's first commissioner, quoted in Wolmar, *Down the Tube*, p. 211.

11 As the authors of a textbook on PPPs put it drily, "If risks that, in fact, cannot be best managed by the private sector continue to be transferred to public bodies, value for money will decline since the premium demanded by the private sector will outweigh the benefit to the public sector." See Darrin Grimsey and Mervyn K. Lewis, *Public Private Partnerships: The Worldwide Revolution in Infrastructure Provision and Project Finance* (Cheltenham, Glos.: Edward Elgar, 2004), p. 136.

12 One of our interviewees told the story of someone who was trying to raise loan finance in New York for one of the PPP bidders. He found it all but impossible to convince the bankers in New York that the terms on offer from the UK government were really so risk-free from their point of view. They also could not figure out why, if the terms were really so risk-free, the interest rates on offer were so high. In general, the further away anybody was from the PPP, the more peculiar it looked.

13 HC *Deb*, Standing Committee A, 23 February 1999, col. 760 (John Wilkinson, MP for Ruislip Northwood).

14 Wolmar, *Down the Tube*, p. 216.

15 Quoted in Wolmar, *Down the Tube*, p. 223.

16 Stephen Glaister, Rosemary Scanlon and Tony Travers, *The Way Out: An Alternative Approach to the Future of the London Underground*, LSE LONDON Discussion Paper No. 1 (London: London School of Economics, 1999), pp. 18–20.

17 *Guardian*, 9 February 2008.

18 Transport Committee, *The London Underground and the Public-Private Partnership Agreements* (HC 2007–08, 45); National Audit Office, *Department for Transport: The Failure of Metronet*, HC 512 (London: Stationery Office, 2009); Public Accounts Committee, *Department for Transport: The Failure of Metronet* (HC 2009–10, 390).

19 Transport Committee, *London Underground*, pp. 31, 32.

20 Ibid., p. 10.

21 Public Accounts Committee, *Failure of Metronet*, Ev 7.

22 National Audit Office, *Failure of Metronet*, Executive Summary, para. 8.

23 Wolmar, *Down the Tube*, p. 184.

24 Transport Committee, *London Underground*, p. 21.

25 Tim O'Toole, "A well-intentioned mess", *New Statesman*, 17 September 2009. O'Toole knew what he was talking about. He had been managing director of London Underground between 2002 and earlier in 2009. At least one professional observer was not even sure that significant improvements had been achieved. On p. 14 of its report, the House of Commons Transport Committee quoted Tony Travers of the London School of Economics as estimating that by the autumn of 2007 some £5–£7.5 billion had been spent over the previous five years on the tube network. In Travers's view, that was "a huge amount of money to have delivered – at the very best – a train service that's overall no different [from] where we began".

26 O'Toole, "A well-intentioned mess".

Chapter 15: ID cards swiped

1 Quoted in Philip A. Thomas, "Identity Cards", *Modern Law Review* 58 (1995) 702–13, p. 704. Thomas's article traces the history of the debates over identity cards in the UK during and after the Second World War until the mid-1990s.

2 Goddard quoted in Thomas, "Identity Cards", pp. 705–6.

3 Memorandum by the Secretary of State for the Home Department, "I.R.A. Terrorism in Great Britain", 24 November 1974, C(74) 139. The minutes of the cabinet meeting held the next day – CC(74) 49th. Conclusions – suggest that the idea of introducing identity cards found no support among cabinet ministers and was, indeed, scarcely discussed.

4 Tony Favell, MP for Stockport, quoted in House of Commons Library, "Identity Documents Bill", Bill 1 of 2010–11, Research Paper 10/41, 4 June 2010, p. 3.

5 Home Affairs Committee, *Practical Police Co-operation in the European Community* (HC 1989–90, 363-I); and see the Government Reply, Cm 1367, January 1991, p. 10.

6 Quoted in *Guardian*, 4 October 1995.

7 *Times Guide to the House of Commons May 1997* (London: Times Books, 1997), p. 349.

8 Evidence quoted in Home Affairs Committee, *Identity Cards* (HC 1995–96, 172-I), p. xxiii.

9   Ibid.

10 Ibid., p. xxiv.

11 Ibid., p. xxiii. The body referred to in the text as acting on behalf of the West Indian community was called the West Indian Standing Conference. The term Afro-Caribbean was not then in general use.

12 Ibid., p. xxv.

13 HC *Deb* 14 June 1999, cols 2–3.

14 David Blunkett interviewed by John Humphrys on BBC One, *On the Record*, 23 September 2001.

15 Identity Cards Act 2006, 1(7)e.

16 HC *Deb* 28 June 2005, col. 1205. See LSE Department of Information Systems, *The Identity Project: An Assessment of the UK Identity Cards Bill and its Implications*, 27 June 2005.

17 HC *Deb* 28 June 2005, col. 1174. Davis added: "We have seen window taxes and poll taxes, but this is a breathing tax" (col. 1175).

18 HC *Deb* 28 June 2005, col. 1176.

19 Anthony King, "We may not like ID cards but we'll put up with them", *Daily Telegraph*, 27 February 2006. The survey's actual findings somewhat belied the *Telegraph*'s headline.

20 *Sunday Times*, 12 October 2003.

21 Chris Mullin, *Decline and Fall: Diaries 2005–2010* (London: Profile, 2010), p. 352.

22 HC *Deb* 28 June 2005, col. 1212. He added with reference to the past history of the whole identity-cards project: "It was then and is now a solution looking for a problem."

23 Transcript of presentation by David Cameron, then shadow leader of the Commons and a backbench member of the Home Affairs Committee, speaking at an event held at the LSE on identity cards in 2004, p. 2.

24 HC *Deb* 18 January 2006, col. 832.

Chapter 16: Cultural disconnect

1   Quoted in *Daily Telegraph*, 1 July 2000.

2   Quoted in *Daily Telegraph*, 28 March 2012.

3   One of our informants thought that something like a poll tax had once been tried in Mongolia. Another claimed that Norman Tebbit was in favour of

the poll tax precisely because it would lead some Labour voters to disappear from the electoral register: "It's time we did something for *our* people!"

4   Parliamentary and Health Service Ombudsman, *Tax Credits: Getting it Wrong?* (HC 2006–07, 1010), p. 21.

5   David Butler, Andrew Adonis and Tony Travers, *Failure in British Government: The Politics of the Poll Tax* (Oxford: Oxford University Press, 1994), pp. 252–3.

Chapter 17: Group-think

1   Irving L. Janis, *Victims of Groupthink: Psychological Studies of Foreign-Policy Decisions and Fiascoes* (Boston, MA: Houghton Mifflin, 1972); Irving L. Janis, *Groupthink: Psychological Studies of Policy Decisions and Fiascoes*, 2nd edn (Boston, MA: Houghton Mifflin, 1982).

2   Janis, *Groupthink*, 2nd edn, p. 174.

3   Philip Stephens, *Politics and the Pound: The Tories, the Economy and Europe* (London: Papermac, 1997), p. 152.

4   Ibid., p. 214.

5   Janis, *Groupthink*, 2nd edn, pp. 10, 244.

6   Ibid., pp. 270–1.

7   Ibid., p. 271.

Chapter 18: Prejudice and pragmatism

1   William Greider, *The Education of David Stockman and Other Americans* (New York: E. P. Dutton, 1982), p. 64.

2   Quoted in "Prescott to rescue for public servants", *BBC News*, 7 July 1999.

3   See above p. 203; Christian Wolmar, *Down the Tube: The Battle for London's Underground* (London: Aurum, 2002), p. 138.

4   Ken Livingstone, *You Can't Say That: Memoirs* (London: Faber, 2012), p. 488.

5   Steve Richards, *Whatever It Takes: The Real Story of Gordon Brown and New Labour* (London: Fourth Estate, 2010), p. 120.

6   That formulation is a close paraphrase of the definition of pragmatism given in the *Concise Oxford English Dictionary*, 11th edn, revised (Oxford: Oxford University Press, 2006), p. 1127.

Chapter 19: Operational disconnect

1   Tony Blair, *A Journey: My Political Life* (London: Hutchinson, 2010), p. 255.
2   Andrew Dunsire, *Implementation in a Democracy* (Oxford: Martin Robertson, 1978), p. 155.
3   Tony Blair, *A Journey*, p. 364. He was quoting the Gospel according to St Luke, 14:28.
4   Richard E. Neustadt and Harvey V. Fineberg, *The Epidemic that Never Was: Policy-Making and the Swine Flu Affair* (New York: Vintage, 1982), p. 125. President Gerald Ford's administration had feared the outbreak of a terrible swine flu pandemic and had ordered the vaccination of almost the entire American population. It proved impossible to do that, and much harm was caused by the attempt. In the event, no such pandemic occurred.
5   The phrase "Next Steps agencies" is derived from a report published in 1987 by Margaret Thatcher's Efficiency Unit entitled *Improving Management in Government: the Next Steps*. For an account of the introduction of the agencies, see Kate Jenkins, *Politicians and Public Services: Implementing Change in a Clash of Cultures* (Cheltenham, Glos: Edward Elgar, 2008), chs 5–7.
6   Jack Straw, *Last Man Standing: Memoirs of a Political Survivor* (London: Macmillan, 2012), p. 297.
7   Graham T. Allison, *Essence of Decision: Explaining the Cuban Missile Crisis* (Boston, MA : Little, Brown, 1971), p. 267.

Chapter 20: Panic, symbols and spin

1   *Daily Express*, 16 May 1991.
2   Quoted in Philip Johnston, *Bad Laws* (London: Constable, 2010), p. 61.
3   *The Times*, 14 May 1991. In his autobiography, David Lipsey, who was editing *The Times* the day before the paper's leading article appeared, confesses that he was responsible for the hard line that the paper took and, by extension, the offending Act itself: "On Monday morning, or so it was reliably reported to me, Kenneth Baker, the Home Secretary, read [the] persuasive leader. Cautious Home Office advice was swept aside and 'Kill the dangerous dogs' became government policy. By common consent, the resulting Act is one of the worst passed by Parliament in many years. I can

plead nothing in mitigation. I apologise to the unfairly martyred dogs and their owners." See *In the Corridors of Power: An Autobiography* (London: Biteback, 2012), pp. 167–8.

4   *Independent*, 12 May 1991.

5   *Guardian*, 21 May 1991.

6   *Sunday Express*, 19 May 1991.

7   HC *Deb* 10 June 1991, col. 655.

8   HC *Deb* 11 June 1997, col. 1162.

9   *Evening Standard*, 19 December 1997.

10 Quoted in *The Economist*, 18 December 1999.

11 Tony Blair, *A Journey: My Political Life* (London: Hutchinson, 2010), pp. 256–7.

12 HC *Deb* 30 October 2001, col. 762.

13 *Sunday Express*, 23 February 2003.

14 *Observer*, 2 February 2003.

15 Fiscal Responsibility Act 2010, ch. 3.

16 Lembit Opik, HC *Deb* 5 January 2010, col. 64.

17 HC *Deb* 5 January 2010, cols. 72–5.

18 Alistair Darling, *Back from the Brink* (London: Atlantic Books, 2011), pp. 267–8.

Chapter 21: The centre cannot hold

1   Nigel Lawson, *The View from No. 11: Memoirs of a Tory Radical* (London: Bantam, 1992), p. 582.

2   R. A. W. Rhodes, *Everyday Life in British Government* (Oxford: Oxford University Press, 2011), pp. 112, 211.

3   Christian Wolmar, *Down the Tube: The Battle for London's Underground*, (London: Aurum, 2002), p. 184. Kiley somewhat exaggerated the size of Blair's desk, which was big but not quite that big. When Brown later got wind of the private meeting, he suspected, amazingly, that Blair was plotting with Ken Livingstone to undermine him.

4   Richard Brooks, "System Failure: How this government is blowing £12.4bn on useless IT for the NHS", *Private Eye*, 2–15 March 2007, No. 1179, p. 1.

5   Lord Egremont (John Wyndham), *Wyndham and Children First* (London: Macmillan, 1968), pp. 166–7.

6   Edward Heath, *The Course of My Life: The Autobiography of Edward Heath* (London: Hodder & Stoughton, 1998), p. 316. "All in all", Heath writes, "the CPRS provided a valuable reinforcement of the government's capacity for the analysis of government policy at the centre." On Wilson's invention of the Policy Unit, see Harold Wilson, *The Governance of Britain* (London: Weidenfeld and Nicolson, 1976), pp. 98–9.

7   James Callaghan, *Time and Chance* (London: Collins, 1987), p. 404.

8   Margaret Thatcher, *The Downing Street Years* (London: HarperCollins, 1993), p. 277.

9   Jonathan Powell, *The New Machiavelli: How to Wield Power in the Modern World* (London: Bodley Head, 2010), p. 60.

10   Ibid., p. 81. Powell on the same page describes the huge *Bundeskanzleramt* as "ossified, slow and overly bureaucratic".

Chapter 22: Musical chairs

1   See, for example, John D. Huber and Cecilia Martinez-Gallardo, "Cabinet Instability and the Accumulation of Experience: The Fourth and Fifth Republics in Comparative Perspectives", *British Journal of Political Science* 34 (2004), pp. 37–41.

2   Peter Riddell, Zoe Gruhn and Liz Carolan, *The Challenge of Being a Minister: Defining and Developing Ministerial Effectiveness* (London: Institute for Government, 2011), pp. 35–42.

3   R. K. Alderman, "A Defence of Frequent Ministerial Turnover", *Public Administration* 73:4 (1995), p. 499.

4   David Butler, Andrew Adonis and Tony Travers, *Failure in British Government: The Politics of the Poll Tax* (Oxford: Oxford University Press, 1994), p. 200.

5   Simon Jenkins, *Thatcher and Sons: A Revolution in Three Acts* (London: Allen Lane, 2006), p. 141.

6   Quoted in Alderman, "A Defence of Frequent Ministerial Turnover", p. 497. See also Riddell *et al.*, *The Challenge of Being a Minister*, p. 20.

7   Riddell *et al.*, *The Challenge of Being a Minister*, p. 21.

8   Public Administration Select Committee, *Good Government* (HC 2008–09, 97-II), Ev 37, 39.

9   Jack Straw, *Last Man Standing: Memoirs of a Political Survivor* (London: Macmillan, 2012), pp. 549–50. Straw says of the frequent reshuffles that

occurred during the Blair and Brown years: "For most of the individuals involved, the constant churn (especially of junior ministers) led to them, and the government as a whole, functioning far less well than they could have done if they'd had the time and security to learn their jobs and get on with them" (p. 549).

Chapter 23: Ministers as activists

1   Richard E. Neustadt, "White House and Whitehall", in Anthony King, ed., *The British Prime Minister*, 2nd edn (Basingstoke, Hants: Macmillan, 1985), p. 159.

2   Antony Jay, ed., *The Oxford Dictionary of Political Quotations* (Oxford: Oxford University Press, 1996), p. 362.

3   David Butler, Andrew Adonis and Tony Travers, *Failure in British Government: The Politics of the Poll Tax* (Oxford: Oxford University Press, 1994), p. 48.

4   Jonathan Powell, *The New Machiavelli: How to Wield Power in the Modern World* (London: Bodley Head, 2010), p. 72.

5   Ibid.

6   Butler *et al.*, *Failure in British Government*, p. 50.

7   Daniel Kahneman, *Thinking, Fast and Slow* (London: Allen Lane, 2011), p. 136.

8   Figures recalculated from House of Lords Library Note, *Volume of Legislation*, 16 September 2011.

Chapter 24: Accountability, lack of

1   Sir Ivor Jennings, *The Law and the Constitution*, 5th edn (London: University of London Press, 1959), pp. 207–8. The first edition of Jennings's book was published as long ago as 1933.

2   Margaret Thatcher, *The Downing Street Years* (London: HarperCollins, 1993), p. 420.

3   Public Accounts Committee, *The Delays in Administering the 2005 Single Payment Scheme in England* (HC 2006–07, 893), p. 7, para. xi.

4   She did not escape entirely. See Environment, Food and Rural Affairs Committee, *The Rural Payments Agency and the Implementation of the Single Payment Scheme* (HC 2006–07, 107-I), pp. 6, 50–1. The committee was

tough on Beckett, remarking at one point: "It will seem strange to many in the rural community that right at the top of Defra no price for failure has been paid by the now Foreign Secretary. Leaving others to get on with the day to day delivery of services should not remove the obligation from the holders of high office to do more than just apologise and mouth the words 'I am taking responsibility'. It should be the case that when a Department fails to deliver a key programme right at the heart of its fundamental responsibilities the holder of the office of Secretary of State should not be rewarded with promotion but its reverse" (pp. 50–1). Beckett was promoted all the same.

Chapter 25: A peripheral parliament

1   HC *Deb* 12 February 2004, col. 1595. The speaker was Michael Jack, the MP for Fylde.
2   HC *Deb* 28 January 1998, cols 261, 263. The speaker was Christopher Fraser, the MP for Mid Dorset and Poole South.
3   See above p. 55.
4   HC *Deb* 20 March 1998, col. 1542.
5   HC *Deb* Standing Committee A, 23 February 1999, col. 760. Ed Davey, a Liberal Democrat, insisted that means could be found of raising money for the underground within the public sector without the sums raised having to figure in the Public Sector Borrowing Requirements; see HC *Deb* Standing Committee A, 25 February 1999, cols 790–3.
6   See, for example, Philip Cowley, *Revolts and Rebellions: Parliamentary Voting under Blair* (London: Politico's, 2002), pp. 45, 182–3, 231–2, and Philip Cowley, *The Rebels: How Blair Mislaid his Majority* (London: Politico's, 2005), pp. 2–5, 9–11. Conservative backbenchers have been as assertive since May 2010 as Labour MPs were during the Blair and Brown years, probably even more so.
7   Quoted in Ruth Fox and Matt Korris, *Making Better Law: Reform of the Legislative Process from Policy to Act* (London: Hansard Society, 2010), p. 139.
8   Ibid., p. 140.
9   Andrew Tyrie, *Mr Blair's Poodle: An Agenda for Reviving the House of Commons* (London: Centre for Policy Studies, 2000), p. 51.

10   See, for example, Alex Brazier, ed., *Parliament, Politics and Law Making: Issues and Developments in the Legislative Process* (London: Hansard Society, 2004), p. 11 (Lord Norton of Louth) and pp. 15–16 (Alex Brazier).

11   Ferdinand Mount, *The British Constitution Now: Recovery or Decline?* (London: Heinemann, 1992), p. 162.

12   Peter Riddell, *Parliament Under Blair* (London: Politico's, 2000), pp. 11–12. For one backbench MP's reflections on the same matter, see Sarah Wollaston, "Creeping patronage, new politics and the payroll vote", *Guardian*, 10 February 2011.

13   Klaus von Beyme, *The Legislator: German Parliament as a Centre of Political Decision-making* (Aldershot, Hants: Ashgate, 1998), p. 38.

14   Neil McGarvey and Paul Cairney, *Scottish Politics: An Introduction* (Basingstoke, Hants: Palgrave Macmillan, 2008), p. 98.

15   Tony Wright, *Doing Politics* (London: Biteback, 2012), p. 172.

Chapter 26: Asymmetries of expertise

1   George A. Akerlof, "The Market for 'Lemons': Quality Uncertainty and the Market Mechanism", *Quarterly Journal of Economics* 84 (1970), pp. 488–500.

2   Christian Wolmar, *Down the Tube: The Battle for London's Underground* (London: Aurum, 2002), p. 211.

3   Ibid., p. 212.

4   National Audit Office, *Commercial Skills for Complex Government Projects*, HC 962 (London: Stationery Office, 2009), p. 4.

5   Ibid., p. 7.

6   National Audit Office, *Identifying and Meeting Central Government's Skills Requirements*, HC 1276 (London: Stationery Office, 2011), p. 5.

7   Ibid., p. 7.

8   Ibid., p. 13.

Chapter 27: A deficit of deliberation

1   Norman Fowler, *Ministers Decide: A Personal Memoir of the Thatcher Years* (London: Chapmans, 1991).

2   A Panglossian is a person who remains hopeful and optimistic whatever

the circumstances. Pangloss was mentor to the hero of Voltaire's novella *Candide*. In Pangloss's view, "In this best of possible worlds ... all is for the best." Candide in time learned better.

Postscript

1   Nicholas Timmins, *Never Again? The Story of the Health and Social Care Act 2012* (London: Institute for Government and the King's Fund, 2012). Timmins refuses to be drawn on the question of whether he thinks the Act will, or will not, be thought at some time in the future to have achieved its broad aims – "Time alone will tell" (p. 145) – but he is clearly extremely doubtful. See also Jill Rutter, *Learning the Lessons from 'Never Again?'* (London: Institute for Government, 2012).

2   Timmins, *Never Again?*, pp. 318–19.

3   Chris Patten writes regarding the genesis of the poll tax: "Ministers had run through almost every option without picking a winner before a collection of very clever minds hit upon a woefully foolish scheme." See his *Not Quite the Diplomat* (London: Penguin, 2006), p. 20.

4   *Report of the Laidlaw Inquiry into the Lessons Learned for the Department for Transport from the InterCity West Coast Competition*, HC 809 (London: Stationery Office, 2012). Because Laidlaw was on the Transport Department's board and because he exonerated the department's ministers, some critics claimed his report was a whitewash. It does not read like one.

5   See Transport Committee, *Cancellation of the InterCity West Coast Franchise Competition* (HC 2012–13, 537), Ev 10–23, and also Gwyn Topham, "West coast mainline fiasco: ministers and senior civil servants 'not to blame'", *Guardian*, 19 December 2012.

6   Introducing the bill in the House of Commons, Theresa May, the home secretary, repeatedly emphasised the strictly democratic aspects of her proposals, saying at one point, for example: "With a strong democratic mandate from the ballot box, police and crime commissioners will hold their chief constable to account for cutting crime." See HC *Deb* 13 December 2010, col. 708, also cols 709–11.

7   Robert Winnett, "Vince Cable: I have declared war on Rupert Murdoch", *Daily Telegraph*, 21 December 2010.

8   Katherine Rushton, "Phone hacking: News Corp bid for BSkyB may be scuppered by 'fit and proper' test", *Daily Telegraph*, 7 July 2011.

9   The prime minister apparently told Hugh Grant, one of the victims of the phone-hacking scandal, that he would implement Lord Leveson's recommendations provided they were not bonkers. Andrew Marr subsequently – on BBC One's *Andrew Marr Show* on 7 October 2012 – asked Cameron: "Since we've just had Hugh Grant, I should probably start by asking you about that. You told him that if what Leveson suggested was 'not bonkers', you would implement it. Is that still the case?" To which, the prime minister replied: "Absolutely."

10   It is not clear who first introduced the phrase "a bit of statute" into the discussion, but it was quoted in virtually all the press and broadcast reports on 18 March 2013 following the late-night meeting among the party representatives.

11   *Times Guide to the House of Commons 2010* (London: Times Books, 2010), pp. 327, 19. It was suggested at the time that in making their ambitious manifesto pledge the Conservatives had simply forgotten or overlooked the fact that no UK government could curb immigration from most of the EU member states.

12   Interviewed on BBC Radio 4's *Today* programme on 19 April 2011.

13   *The Economist*, 20 October 2012. The cover of *The Economist*'s UK edition was dominated by a big sign reading "IMMIGRANTS KEEP OUT". Other signs read "Short stay only", "No talent beyond this point" and "Young? Gifted? Foreign? Bugger orf!"

14   Tom Newton Dunn and Steve Hawkes, "Pasty la vista, taxman", *Sun*, 29 May 2012. The prime minister claimed to be keen on pasties, especially hot ones. He seemed to remember eating one at the West Cornwall Pasty Company's outlet at Leeds railway station. It turned out that the outlet had closed some years earlier.

15   Margaret Hodge used the word "abysmal". See Public Accounts Committee, *Department for Work and Pensions: The Introduction of the Work Programme* (HC 2010–12, 1814), Ev 17–8, Q146. In the case of Labour's Pathways to Work scheme, A4E had apparently achieved a success rate of only 9 per cent compared with its target rate of 30 per cent.

16   The former auditor was Ernie Hutchison who submitted written evidence to the Public Accounts Committee that was published by the *Daily Telegraph*

on 22 May 2012. In the wake of the fraud allegations against A4E, its founder and principal shareholder, Emma Harrison, resigned as the company's chairman in February 2012.

17 See Work and Pensions Select Committee, *The Role of Incapacity Benefit Reassessment in Helping Claimants into Employment* (HC 2010–12, 1015-I), esp. pp. 19–25.

18 HC *Deb* 17 January 2013, col. 1050.

19 David Cameron, "Leadership for a better Britain", 5 October 2011.

20 HC *Deb* 11 December 2012, col. 156. There were undoubtedly complications relating to canon law and the fact that both the Church of England and the Church of Wales are legally established, but clergy in both Churches were startled to be told that it would actually be illegal for them to do something that they were not legally obliged to do.

21 One Conservative backbencher, Angie Bray (Ealing Central and Acton), complained that she despaired when she heard of government lawyers who were "not even able to deal with the basic detail of the change to marriage under [the] new laws" (HC *Deb* 5 February 2013, col. 174).

22 HC *Deb* 17 April 2012, cols 173, 175.

23 In the course of conversation, we were told by an official who had worked closely with a Conservative home secretary during the 1990s that his boss sometimes flew in the face of the best legal advice and appealed against court judgments that he found unpalatable even though he was told that he stood almost no chance of winning. Our informant took it for granted that he did so for political reasons, hoping to ingratiate himself with the media and the Tory rank and file. The cumulative costs to the taxpayer must have been considerable.

24 Defence Committee, *Defence Acquisition* (HC 2012–13, 9), p. 12.

25 HC *Deb* 17 February 2011, col. 1155.

26 Ofqual's chief executive, Glenys Stacey, was quoted in the *Guardian*, 7 February 2013. For the Education Committee's verdict, see *From GCSEs to EBCs: The Government's Proposals for Reform* (HC 2012–13, 808-I), p. 3.

27 HC *Deb* 7 February 2013, col. 441.

28 Treasury Committee, *Budget 2013* (HC 2012–13), p. 71.

29 National Audit Office, *High Speed Rail 2: A Review of Early Programme Preparation*, HC 124 (London: Stationery Office, 2013). The transport secretary, Patrick McLoughlin, rubbished the NAO report, dismissing it

as the work of bean-counters. But Simon Jenkins, a long-time opponent of HS2, insisted in his *Guardian* column (17 May 2013) that HS2 was wholly PR-driven, unlikely to produce substantial benefits and offering substantial rewards only to the line's backers and the government of the day, which could claim credit for it in the here-and-now – because it was sponsoring a major infrastructure project at a time of recession – without having to worry about its enormous future costs.

Acknowledgements

We are grateful to the Economic and Social Research Council for its substantial and flexible project grant, which provided research assistance and the time to conduct the research and write the book. The Research and Enterprise Office at the University of Essex, and in particular Shereen Anderson and Gary Williams, gave us useful advice and administrative support. The Department of Government at Essex accommodated the project and many of our colleagues listened and responded helpfully to our ideas in the course of the research. University College Oxford was a hospitable venue for the two residential seminars on government blunders that we arranged, with the able assistance of Marion Hawtree.

We also wish to thank the Audit Commission for asking Anthony King to give its sixth Annual Lecture in July 2010, the British Academy for inviting the authors to chair a Forum on "Malfunctioning in British Government: People or Systems?" in April 2010 and the Institute for Government for hosting a seminar on "'Bearing the Scars of Battle': Explorations in Policy Failure" in March 2011. On all three occasions we were given the opportunity to present work in progress to an audience of senior officials, former ministers, academics and policy analysts and we left better informed and educated by the stimulating discussion at each event.

We owe an immense debt of gratitude to Ross Christie, our Research Assistant from September 2009 to December 2011. He laid the groundwork of the book by undertaking a formidable amount of painstaking research of his own for the briefings and document folders which proved invaluable for our interviews and writing. We were also very efficiently aided by Cécile Morales in the final stages of the project.

We asked a large number of ministers, officials and commentators who directly observed or participated in the government blunders described in the book to reflect on how and why they occurred. Some were invited to talk to us about policy failures that we later decided not to include in our case studies. Almost none refused our invitation and all who spoke to us did so generously and frankly. Many went to the trouble of preparing or providing documents for our interviews and some talked to us on two or more occasions. We thank: Steve Allen, Lord (Kenneth) Baker, Sir Brian Bender, Baroness (Tessa) Blackstone, Chris Bolt, Sir John Bourn, Christopher Brearley, Roger Bright, Lord (Robin) Butler, Ann Chant, John Chisholm, David Colin-Thomé, Lord (Nigel) Crisp, Jane Earl, Mike Farrar, Frank Field MP, Marshall Field, Sir Christopher Foster, Lord (Norman) Fowler, Simon Fradd, Vince Gaskell, Stephen Glaister, Paul Gray, Derek Grover, Michael Hallsworth, Peter Hendy, Sir David Henshaw, Nick Holgate, Lord (David) Hunt, Lord (John) Hutton, Lord (Patrick) Jenkin, Kate Jenkins, Philip Johnston, Dame Tessa Jowell MP, Peter Lauener, Sir Leigh Lewis, Peter Lilley MP, Anthony Mayer, Iain McLean, Sir Nicholas Montagu, Michael Moran, Lord (Tony) Newton, Sir David Omand, Ed Page, Sir Michael Partridge, Lord (Chris) Patten, Jonathan Powell, Peter Riddell, Lord (Richard) Ryder, Nick Stuart, Gerry Sutcliffe MP, Tony Travers, Lord (William) Waldegrave, Christian Wolmar, Lord (Stewart) Wood and Sir Robin Young.

We also wish to acknowledge the contribution made to our thinking by those who participated in the discussions at the Audit Commission, British Academy and Institute for Government events described above: Lord (Andrew) Adonis, Margaret Aldred, Nicholas Allen, Lord (Michael) Bichard, Hugh Biddell, Sir Alan Budd, Steve Bundred, Sir Andrew Cahn, Selina Chen, Robert Chote, David Cruikshank, Paula Diggle, Ian Dodge, Dan Drillsma, Alun Evans, Mark Gilmartin, Robert Hazell, Susan Hitch, Alison Inman, Hywel Lloyd, Rachel Lomax, Rose Manise, Andy McKeown, Sir Nicholas Monck, Sir Robin Mountfield, Michael O'Higgins, David Orr, David Peretz, Jonathan Portes, Jill Rutter, Lord (Andrew) Turnbull, Peter Unwin, Simon Virley, David Walker, Peter Watkins, Simon Webb and Lord (Larry) Whitty.

ACKNOWLEDGEMENTS

At short notice Meriel Barclay, Tim Melville-Ross, Chrissie Mines, Paul Mines, Sir Stephen O'Brien and Hazel Woolfson kindly read the entire typescript, and Jonathan Powell and Tony Wright read individual chapters. Their hawk-eyed reading and constructive comments have made the book considerably better than it would otherwise have been and we are indebted to them. The remaining flaws are ours alone.

Index

INDEX